THE COMPUTER
AND
THE DECISION-MAKING
PROCESS

Buros-Nebraska Symposium
on
Measurement & Testing

Series Editor

JANE CLOSE CONOLEY

Buros Institute of Mental Measurements
and
Department of Educational Psychology

University of Nebraska-Lincoln

THE COMPUTER AND THE DECISION-MAKING PROCESS

Edited by
TERRY B. GUTKIN
STEVEN L. WISE
UNIVERSITY OF NEBRASKA-LINCOLN

LEA LAWRENCE ERLBAUM ASSOCIATES, PUBLISHERS
1991   Hillsdale, New Jersey   Hove and London

Lawrence Erlbaum Associates, Inc., Publishers
365 Broadway
Hillsdale, New Jersey 07642

Library of Congress Cataloging-in-Publication Data
The Computer and the decision-making process / edited by Terry B.
Gutkin, Steven Wise.
    p. cm. — (Buros-Nebraska Symposium on Measurement & Testing)
Includes bibliographical references and indexes.
ISBN 0-8058-0610-5
1. Psychological tests—Data processing. 2. Psychodiagnostics—Data
processing. 3. Educational tests and measurements—Data processing. 4. Psychology,
Applied—Data processing. 5. Psychometrics—Data processing. I. Gutkin, Terry B., 1947–
II. Wise, Steven L. III. Series: Buros-Nebraska Symposium on Measurement & Testing
(Series) ; v. 4.
BF176.2.C65   1990
150'.28'7—dc20   90–44639
                                                                         CIP

Printed in the United States of America
10 9 8 7 6 5 4 3 2 1

Contents

Preface

This volume in the Buros-Nebraska Series on Testing and Measurement provides state-of-the-art contributions concerning the interface between computer technology and traditional psychometrics. The volume title, *Computers and the Decision-Making Process,* describes both reality and potential in a field that provides a dizzying array of promises and problems to be pursued and be solved.

This volume like the previous ones in our series reflects papers given at the annual Buros-Nebraska Symposium on Testing and Measurement and those especially commissioned for the book. Each of the contributors has a special expertise to examine the complex issues raised by the addition of the computer to the field of measurement.

The reader will notice the book has chapters concerning guidelines for computer testing, validity issues, personality testing and behavioral assessment, intelligent systems, applications in industrial/organizational psychology, and legal issues. The volume editors have endeavored successfully to provide a review of the many content areas affected by computer technology, new applications of the computer to solve old measurement problems, and new problems created by the use of the computer.

The major sections of the book are as follows: an introduction and overview of the promise of psychodiagnostic systems by Drs. Jackson, Watkins, and McDermott; analysis of validity concerns both in general about computer-based test interpretation and more specifically about programs related to the MMPI by Drs. Moreland, Eyde, Kowal, and Fishburne; applications of computer technology in behavioral assessment and industrial/organizational psychology by Drs. Kratochwill, Doll, Dickson, and Shoenfeldt; an indepth review of expert systems of computer assisted instruction by Drs. Noonan, Sarvela, O'Neil, and Baker; and finally, legal cautions and standard setting by Drs. Bersoff, Hofer, and Green.

An analysis of our list of contributors will indicate the editors have gathered together an impressive group of scholars to create this volume. They represent measurement experts from across the country who have particular strengths in their chosen areas. The Buros Institute of Mental Measurements is very grateful to each of these professionals for contributing their special wisdom in the creation of this book.

Jane Close Conoley
Series Editor

THE COMPUTER
AND
THE DECISION-MAKING
PROCESS

1 Computer-Assisted Personality Test Interpretation: The Dawn of Discovery

Douglas N. Jackson
University of Western Ontario

My aim in this chapter is to outline some of the substantive and psychometric bases on which we can build a science of assessment that takes advantage of the enormous potential inherent in the digital computer and in artificial intelligence. Some of these foundations are within the traditions of classical assessment. But others represent urgently needed areas of explication and research.

It is my view, in the tradition of Cronbach (1954), that developers of computer software for testing should listen to what psychometricians say, and, as well, psychometricians should be sensitive to new research ideas waiting to be solved that arise out of the experience of preparing software for test interpretation. This is particularly true because some of classical test theory based on fixed sets of items is rendered obsolete by the prospect of adaptive testing. The fact that psychometricians and authors of interpretive software are rarely prone to listen to one another brings to mind a quotation from the world-weary French novelist and philosopher, André Gide, cited by Block (1978): "It has all been said before, but you must say it again, since nobody listens."

SOME PRECONDITIONS FOR VALID COMPUTER-ASSISTED TEST INTERPRETATION

Accurate test interpretations depend on valid data. Stated another way, the validity of the score data set an upper bound for the accuracy of test interpretations. This sounds like such a truism as to appear almost trivial. But surprisingly little attention has been directed at this issue by those who write and write about computer software for test interpretation. For example, in a recent book devoted to computer-based test interpretation (Butcher, 1987) there is scant attention directed at fundamental questions about the reliability of scores or indexes forming the bases for interpretations.

I would like to outline five preconditions for valid computer-assisted test interpretations and to discuss each in turn. These preconditions point both to the traditional wisdom of testing that can be incorporated appropriately into thinking about test interpretations, and, as well, to areas of needed research. Let me list the five: (1) Interpretations should, in general, be built around constructs of broad import; (2) Interpretations should bear an explicit substantive relationship to the constructs underlying the measures employed; (3) Where predictions are made about specific behaviors, both the reliability of the assessment data and the reliability of the criterion to be predicted should be taken into account; (4) The implications of evaluative biases both in the assessment situation and in outcomes need to be given explicit attention; and (5) Attention needs to be directed to base rates, both in the assessment situation and in outcome situations. I would like to discuss each of these points in turn.

The Usefulness of Personality Constructs

With regard to the importance of theory-based constructs, I do not know whether I should say a great deal or very little. There is a substantial literature in personality and social judgment bearing on this topic. But there is an unfortunate tendency for psychologists to consider new areas such as computerized test interpretation in isolation as if little were to be gained from treating it as part of a larger assessment endeavor. But there is something to be learned from the knowledge and controversies of personality and assessment. One of the most controversial issues in the personality literature over the past two decades is the question of whether or not there are broad personality traits or dispositions. One of the strongest advocates of the position that there are not is Walter Mischel, who has argued forcefully that what appear to be broad behavioral consistencies are in fact illusory. The evidence proffered in support of this position and its implications for computerized assessment warrant careful examination.

Mischel and Peake (1982) presented evidence that they believed failed to support the existence of broad traits of conscientiousness and friendliness. They intercorrelated behaviors purportedly representing each of these traits and interpreted mean intercorrelations of the order of .13 as evidence indicative of doubt about the existence of broad traits. But their analyses and interpretations are illustrative of the sort of ad hoc theorizing that is tempting when constructing computerized-based test interpretation systems. Mischel and Peake merely assumed that certain behaviors were linked to the traits of conscientiousness and friendliness without providing any explicit bases in the form of definitions or classification rules for their categorization. Nor did they fully consider the importance of aggregating data prior to inferring broadly based personality dispositions. Jackson and Paunonen (1985) undertook a reconceptualization and re-analysis of the Mischel and Peake data on conscientiousness, distinguishing separate dimensions of studiousness, punctuality, and academic diligence by conceptual and empirical means. We estimated reliabilities for 20 behaviors relevant to our reinterpreted dimensions of .93, .95, and .86, respectively. A major import of these findings is that in drawing inferences about behavior from sample observations, the steps in construct validation (Jackson, 1971; Loevinger, 1957; Wiggins, 1973) do not only apply to tests, but apply equally to other formal and informal assessment situations, such as might be involved in combining behavioral "signs" in a computerized interpretation. The whole assessment procedure should be evaluated. A number of our conclusions (Jackson & Paunonen, 1985) have special relevance to automated test interpretations. First, in drawing an inference about a respondent based on the magnitude of a score representing a trait or disposition, a crucial aspect of construct validation is the explicit definition of traits and of situations, including their theoretical and empirical implications, and their differentiation from other related traits. Second, the structure of behavioral representations of traits and of different situations should be evaluated in a multidimensional framework. For example, if the bases for linking predicted behaviors to scores on a test is expert clinical judgment, it would be fitting to provide expert judges with a set of construct-based trait definitions and to instruct them to perform a multidimensional scaling of these traits and a larger set of predicted behavioral exemplars. Third, a crucial step in the appraisal of the predictability of behavior is its evaluation in a multitrait-multimethod context in which situations are also carefully defined and empirically studied. As an initial step in such an undertaking it is appropriate to employ scales or scores that possess appropriate levels of convergent and discriminant validity. If differential predictions are to be made on the basis of scale scores, or if profile shape is the basis for classification, it can be demonstrated that predictions or classifications will be more accurate if the constituent scales are minimally intercorrelated and discriminantly valid. This is often difficult to achieve because many measures of personality, particularly those of psychopathology, share a large common component reflecting general psychopathology or self-evaluation. The presence of such a large elevation component, while perhaps facilitating the classification of the person's results into a global category of psychopathology, militates against accuracy in differential prediction, for example, of specific manifestations of psychopathology. The simple implication of the foregoing is that good automated test interpretation systems depend on good tests, a point to which I shall return.

Linking Interpretations to Constructs

The point that interpretations should bear a substantive link to the constructs underlying the measures employed, like the remaining points, can be considered as special cases of the first point on the importance of broadly based constructs. In the construction of personality tests, at least for those whose scales are designed to represent constructs, items are selected so that they show higher degrees of association with the factor underlying their own scale than with those underlying irrelevant scales or response biases. It is reasonable to require that behavioral exemplars external to the testing situation show a similar pattern of association. I have already suggested that expert judgments might be used to evaluate the substantive links between constructs and external behaviors. Here I am suggesting that interpretations be validated empirically. It might be objected that some types of behavioral predictions, for example, "likely to engage in assaultive behavior when ridiculed," are not easily evaluated empirically. This is true, but if one employs a conceptualization of constructs as encompassing domains containing related behaviors, then it is possible to sample relevant behaviors that are easier to elicit and manage under controlled conditions. Tendencies to engage in monetary risk taking, for example, might be assessed by observing the person gamble large sums of money in the real world, but might equally be represented by a person's indicating a preference for the job of commodity trader, by volunteering for an experiment involving monetary risk, or by evaluating a person's behavior when in the role of an economic decision-maker in an Internation Simulation to make or not to make long-term investments in research and development (Jackson, Hourany, & Vidmar, 1972). Thus, by a process of exemplar sampling, the underlying construct may be validated, and the validation may be generalized to other exemplars not actually observed.

Aggregation, Reliability, and Validity

The effects of aggregation on reliability have been recognized by psychometricians at least since the time of Spearman just after the turn of the century. Much recent literature has reminded us of this important requirement for assessment (Epstein, 1983; Rushton, Jackson, & Paunonen, 1981). But many psychologists—even those who write interpretive software systems—act as if this matter is only the concern of psychometricians. (An exception is Roy Schafer [1954] who cautioned that for Rorschach interpretation an important principle is that there should be "sufficient evidence" for the interpreted tendency, since Rorschach responses, like other responses, are multiply determined.) But aggregation and reliability also have implications for preparing automated test interpretations. For example, basing interpretive statements on responses to single critical items is fraught with error. If a 90-year span of experience with psychological testing has taught us anything, it is that individual episodic events are inherently difficult to predict. As exemplars of an item universe, they suffer from the possibility of being unrepresentative, unstable over time, and subject to error variance from a number of sources. Given the well-known relationship between predictor and criterion reliability and validity, validity inevitably will suffer if measures are not dependable. However, in many areas of psychological prediction we can produce very creditable results if the criterion that is being predicted is aggregated. It follows then that interpretive statements are more likely to be accurate if reference is made to probabilities within a specified domain rather than if predictions of specific events are attempted. An aggression scale will predict aggression as a probabilistic series of events, but will not do well at allowing one to state with accuracy that person X will kick his or her dog on a certain day.

Evaluative Biases and Base Rates

In regard to taking into account base rates and desirability in preparing interpretative reports, I believe the situation is rather poorly understood in spite of the very extensive literature on the subject. But even though the situation is more complex than the first papers in this area in the 1950s and 1960s would have us believe, I do not think that it should be ignored. Psychometrically, there is a very serious problem if all or most scales in the psychopathology area correlate very substantially with a marker scale for undesirable responding. Ideally, personality scales should be developed in such a way as to avoid undue saturation with a general desirability factor. However, some item pools are so saturated with evaluative bias that it is very difficult to construct homogeneous scales that are free from desirability responding. For example, Reddon, Marceau, and Jackson (1982) found that five of six factors identified in an item factor analysis of the MMPI had items showing higher correlations with desirability scales than with their own factors, even on the derivation sample. Many people argue that psychopathology is inherently undesirable and the best way to deal with this problem is to ignore it. But since we now have capabilities for recognizing the multidetermined nature of psychological responses, it is possible to partition variance on scales into variance associated with content unique to the scale and variance associated with general factors such as those attributable to response bias. For example, multivariate regression procedures can be used to identify component scores with sources of response bias statistically removed and treated as a separate component score. Jackson and Reddon (1987) have recently shown that by transforming MMPI scale scores so that they are mutually uncorrelated, a new set of scores can be produced that are relatively free from desirability variance but nevertheless correlate substantially with the original scores. Even though raw scores have confounded content and stylistic variance, computer programs for interpreting scores can first unconfound these distinct sources of variance. Where desirability variance is elevated, for example, under conditions of impression management, appropriate statistical means are available to weigh this elevation in generating interpretations.

But desirability variance and variance associated with what Wiggins terms hypercommunality do not only represent invalid variance. Under certain circumstances knowledge of this from a respondent may increase one's ability to predict accurately the respondent's behavior. Indeed, although the "Barnum effect" of simply making high base rates statements in an interpretative report is to be avoided, knowledge of how a particular respondent conforms with societal norms is useful in enhancing the accuracy of statements made about that person.

THE DAWN OF DISCOVERY

After paying homage to some traditional concerns in assessment as they apply to test interpretation, it is appropriate now to suggest some ways in which we can do better with computer-assisted test administration and interpretation. Again, I will focus my remarks on the personality assessment area, although many of these apply as well to other kinds of assessment.

I would like to review with you a few of the possibilities that are beginning to be realized in computer-aided test administration and interpretation. It is fortunate, I believe, that we are now in a position to go beyond the old traditions of testing. We can now avoid the mold of being constrained to a particular response format and a fixed set of items. I also see much hope in our potential for developing systems that transcend the human frailties of memory in, for example, only being able to distinguish a small number of types of personality or of ability constellations. I see at least five areas that show considerable potential: (1) branching; (2) the evaluation and use of explicit models for the processes underlying responding; (3) the development of more sophisticated methods for detecting invalid or nonpurposeful responding; (4) expansion in the use of different stimulus materials and response formats; and (5) the development and refinement of prototypes to aid in interpretation.

Adaptive Testing by Computer

Much has been written about adapting the difficulty level of items to the respondent's ability level as estimated from previous responses. It has been shown in the ability area that only approximately half the number of items is required to arrive at a level of reliability comparable with that of the longer scale. I am now happy to report that this finding also appears to hold even more strongly for personality scales in the area of psychopathology. Richard MacLennan, working in my laboratory, has been able to demonstrate that he can get 4 items to do the work of 20 if they are appropriately chosen to be consistent with the individual's level of psychopathology as measured by a particular scale. Of course, the method for branching depends on the question that one wishes to address. As long ago as 1969, if you can believe it, I undertook a study to see how few items were required to rule out the possibility that a given scale for psychopathology was elevated beyond two standard deviations. Our conclusion, at that time unpublished (I believed then that no one was interested in the result), was that four items were all that were required. Wayne Velicer (personal communication) has informed me that he came to the same conclusion on mathematical grounds, although I have not seen his reasoning in this regard. This sort of finding raises interesting questions about the nature of the items and in what order they should be presented. Ideally we would like items that are highly differentiating, but, as well, items that have a sufficiently high level of variance that they provide useful information. In 1969 I developed an index to permit an optimal item ordering based on information derived from endorsement proportions and content saturation, but further empirical work is needed to show that this index indeed is optimal.

Whereas in the ability area branching has traditionally served to identify more accurately and more efficiently an individual's location on a single underlying dimension, the problem in the domains of psychopathology and of vocational interests is the question of which dimensions are descriptive of the person. Even for psychiatrically hospitalized individuals, most scales of psychopathology will reveal scores for most patients in the normal ranges. Of course it is inefficient to focus on areas that have little probability of yielding evidence of elevated scores for that person. Thus, branching can also operate hierarchically. I am now in the process of undertaking a large scale study of psychiatric patients, using an item pool of approximately 5,000 items and developing an algorithm to identify the best 300 to 400 items for the purpose of identifying critical dimensions for a particular individual. If the person, for example, responds to a general scale of somatic complaints, then it is appropriate to probe more deeply into areas such as hypochondriasis and imaginary symptoms and to seek to identify the focus of the somatic complaints, as well as to investigate related disorders, such as headaches proneness, dietary habits, health concern, loss of energy, and similar dimensions. For other people for whom there is little evidence of somatic concern, this area will be touched over lightly and the time can be used to probe more extensively in areas that are relevant to the person. This provides a basis for computer interpretative reports that are more relevant to the individual patient or respondent and more reliable. This is possible because items can more optimally be assigned to areas of greater concern.

Process Models and Response Latencies

Psychometricians have been accused, perhaps fairly, of studying response outcomes, namely black marks on answer sheets, to the exclusion of the processes entering into respondents' decisions. Latency data and explicit formulations of the response process provide a framework for investigating other facets of responding than the outcome. For example, Fekken and Holden (1988; Holden & Fekken, 1987) following up earlier work begun at the University of Western Ontario, have reported a series of studies investigating latencies for items with different characteristics. Long response times were associated with items in which responses prove to be unstable. One of the models investigated was the threshold model for responding. This model involves an individual operating characteristic in which items are scaled for a particular characteristic and individuals show different levels of sensitivity to and threshold for responding in the keyed direction. As expected, latencies are greater for items near the individual's threshold. Of special interest are the data related to the validity of latencies. For scales on which respondents receive high scores, they are quicker to endorse relevant items and slower to reject them. This finding holds also when an external criterion instead of the scale score is used. There is even evidence that latencies contribute incrementally to validities based on scale scores. Fekken and Holden are now investigating the use of latencies to items on particular scales to predict psychiatric classification with some very promising results. Another investigator working at the University of Western Ontario, Edward Helmes (1978), pursued this line of work with a multidimensional model employing content scale values and permitting the separation of response determinants due to general desirability and to content. The implications for computer-aided administration and interpretation are that these kinds of data may serve to enhance and corroborate data from traditional sources.

Identifying Nonpurposeful Responding

A number of approaches are possible for identifying records that contain nonpurposeful responses. One approach is to compute a kind of person reliability by summing an individual's responses to odd-numbered items in a set of personality subscales and even-numbered items in the same set. This yields pairs of values consisting of odd and even responses to each of a number of scales. These may be correlated, using as N the number of scales. The resulting correlation coefficient may be interpreted as indicating the consistency to which an individual has responded over several scales. The individual reliabilities so obtained have a central tendency of about .85 for a well-constructed test and show excellent separation from responses that are generated randomly. A number of other techniques are possible for unobtrusive assessment of the consistency of responding, for example, in the correlation of an individual's pattern of responses with frequency of endorsement values for each of a large number of items. Atypical response latencies might also be diagnostic of motivated distortion or random responding.

A Game-like Approach to Assessment

One nice feature of computer presentation is that one is not limited to stationary figures and the true–false response. At the moment we are doing two or three things in this area but perhaps the most interesting is the development of game-like stimuli which capture both the accuracy of judgment, speed of response, and some psychomotor and perceptual skills (Jackson, Vernon, & Jackson, 1988). Our findings indicate that performance levels on such a task correlate as highly with general intelligence as do standard intelligence subtests while capturing new factors not measured by traditional IQ tests, one in which cognitive styles may become apparent.

Prototypes

Finally, there is the possibility of employing prototypes. We have conducted a series of studies using a technique called *modal profile analysis* in which similar profile types have been grouped analytically. Using such a procedure, we discovered that occupational group vocational interest profiles could be classified cogently—all physician groups formed one cluster, as did various types of salespeople, merchandisers, and educators. We extended this approach to alcoholics, psychiatric patients, university students, and military personnel, and found that whereas there was not one, but 16, alcohol personality profiles, many of these same types were also identified among the psychiatric patients and university students (Jackson, 1983). To investigate the degree to which these types were cogent exemplars of a class of people, we conducted a series of studies (e.g., Reed & Jackson, 1975) in which judges were asked to predict a pattern of responses to a particular type, described in a few sentences. Judges showed very high reliability. Then we identified a number of patients who had the characteristics described and asked our judges again to predict their pattern of responses. When components of the judgments were separated, and we took account of desirability and base rate, as well as content, judges proved to be highly accurate in their estimates. The implication is that knowledge of salient characteristics implies membership in a type, which, in turn, permits accurate identification of response probabilities. But not any old type will do. The evidence is that arbitrary types do not yield meaningful results.

Overview

With accelerating advances in computer technology, including the advent of touch screens, voice recognition, rapid access to massive stored data, and the like, we have the capability at hand to do justice to the complexity of personality in computerized interpretation. But to achieve this promise, our conceptualizations of personality, understanding of the process of responding, and implementation of this knowledge in computer software must keep pace. This is a large, labor-intensive undertaking, but if the dawn of discovery is to be realized, such implementation is essential.

REFERENCES

Block, J. (1978). Some enduring and consequential structures of personality. In A. I. Rabin (Ed.), *Further Explorations in Personality* (pp. 27–43). New York: Wiley.

Butcher, J. N. (1987). *Computerized psychological assessment.* New York: Basic Books.

Cronbach, L. J. (1954). Report on a psychometric mission to clinicia. *Psychometrika, 19,* 263–270.

Epstein, S. (1983). Aggregation and beyond: Some basic issues on the prediction of behavior. *Journal of Personality, 51,* 360–392.

Fekken, G. C., & Holden, R. R. (1988, August). *Response latency evidence for viewing personality dimensions as schema.* Paper presented at meeting of the American Psychological Association, Atlanta.

Helmes, E. (1978). *A multidimensional approach to personality inventory responding.* Unpublished doctoral dissertation, University of Western Ontario, London, Canada.

Holden, R. R., & Fekken, G. C. (1987, August). *Reaction time and self-report psychopathological assessment: Evidence for convergent and discriminant validity.* Paper presented at a meeting of the American Psychological Association, New York.

Jackson, D. N. (1971). The dynamics of structured personality tests. *Psychological Review, 78,* 229–248.

Jackson, D. N. (1983). Differential Personality Inventory types among alcoholics. In W. M. Cox (Ed.), Identifying and measuring alcoholic personality characteristics. *New Directions for Methodology of Social and Behavioral Science* (No. 16). San Francisco: Jossey–Bass, pp. 87–100.

Jackson, D. N., Hourany, L., & Vidmar, N. J. (1972). A four-dimensional interpretation of risk taking. *Journal of Personality, 40,* 483–501.

Jackson, D. N., & Paunonen, S. V. (1985). Construct validity and the predictability of behavior. *Journal of Personality and Social Psychology, 49,*554–570.

Jackson, D. N., & Reddon, J. R. (1987). Construct interpretation of Minnesota Multiphasic Personality Inventory (MMPI) Clinical scales: An orthogonal transformation. *Journal of Psychopathology and Behavioral Assessment, 9,* 149–160.

Jackson, D. N., Vernon, P. A., & Jackson, D. N. (1988). *Visual-spatial ability and psychometric test performance.* Unpublished manuscript.

Loevinger, J. (1957). Objective tests as instruments of psychological theory. *Psychological Reports, 3*(Monograph No.9), 635–694.

Mischel, W., & Peake, P. K. (1982). Beyond deja vu in searching for cross-situational consistency. *Psychological Review, 89,* 730–755.

Reddon, J. R., Marceau, R., and Jackson, D. N. (1982). An application of singular value decomposition to the factor analysis of MMPI items. *Applied Psychological Measurement, 6,* 275–283.

Reed, P. L., & Jackson, D. N. (1975). Clinical judgment of psychopathology: A model for inferential accuracy. *Journal of Abnormal Psychology, 84,* 475–482.

Rushton, J. P., Jackson, D. N., & Paunonen, S. V. (1981). Personality: Nomothetic or idiographic? A response to Kenrick and Stringfield. *Psychological Review, 88,* 582–589.

Shafer, R. (1954). *Psychoanalytic interpretations in Rorschach testing.* New York: Grune & Stratton.

Wiggins, J. S. (1973). *Personality and prediction: Principles of personality assessment.* Reading, MA: Addison–Wesley.

2 Psychodiagnostic Computing: From Interpretive Programs to Expert Systems

Marley W. Watkins
SouthWest EdPsych Services, Inc., Phoenix

Paul A. McDermott
University of Pennsylvania

As amply demonstrated by the chapters in this volume, computer applications have pervaded all aspects of psychological practice. Although thought by some to be relatively new (Nolen & Spencer, 1986), semiautomatic scoring of the Strong Vocational Interest Blank was accomplished more than 50 years ago (Campbell, 1968) and systems of computer-based test interpretation have been operational for 25 years (Fowler, 1985).

DEVELOPMENT OF ADMINISTRATION AND INTERPRETATION PROGRAMS

Early automated programs typically focused upon the scoring or interpretation of a single psychological test. Most frequently, that test was the Minnesota Multiphasic Personality Inventory (Fowler, 1985) but the Rorschach was interpreted as well (Piotrowski, 1964). In addition to automated interpretation, there were attempts to administer existing psychological tests directly by computer. The MMPI was again the test of choice (Lushene, O'Neil, & Dunn, 1974) although the Wechsler Adult Intelligence Scale (Elwood, 1972), Slosson Intelligence Test (Hedl, O'Neil, & Hansen, 1973), Peabody Picture Vocabulary Test (Klinge & Rodziewicz, 1976), and the California Psychological Inventory (Scissons, 1976) were also administered by computer.

Computer-administered Tests

Efforts to equate the conventional MMPI with computer-administered versions have continued unabated. White, Clements, and Fowler (1985) administered the full-length MMPI via microcomputer and standard booklet to 150 volunteer undergraduates. The two MMPI versions were generally equivalent in terms of mean scale scores, test–retest correlations, and stability of high-point codes. There was, however, a greater tendency for the computerized version to result in larger numbers of "cannot say" responses. Rozensky, Honor, Rasinski, Tovian, & Herz (1986) investigated the attitudes of psychiatric patients to computerized vs. conventional MMPI administrations. The computer group found the testing experience to be more interesting, more positive, and less anxiety-provoking than did the paper-and-pencil group. The equivalency of other conventional personality (Katz & Dalby, 1981; Lukin, Dowd, Plake, & Kraft, 1985; Skinner & Allen, 1983; Wilson, Genco, & Yager, 1986), neuropsychological (DeMita, Johnson, & Hansen, 1981), cognitive ability (Beaumont, 1981; Eller, Kaufman, & McLean, 1986), and academic (Andolina, 1982; Wise & Wise, 1987) tests to their computerized versions are also being widely explored.

The promise of parallel automated test forms has provoked investigations of the differences between computerized and conventional item presentations and their possible impact upon test reliability and validity (Hofer & Green, 1985). Jackson (1985) reviewed the evidence regarding equivalence of conventional and computerized tests and posited four methodological differences: (1) modifications in the method of presenting stimulus material; (2) differences in the task required of the examinee; (3) differences in the format for recording responses; and (4) differences in the method of interpretation. Despite these threats to equivalence, Moreland (1985) opined that "the bulk of the evidence on computer adaptions of paper-and-pencil questionnaires points to the tentative conclusion that non-equivalence is typically small enough to be of no practical consequence, if present at all" (p. 224). A more cautious note was sounded by Hofer and Green (1985). They suggested that for most computer-presented tests, "practitioners will have to use good judgment in interpreting computer-obtained scores, based on the available but inconclusive evidence" (p. 831). This conservative opinion seems well founded if automated testing is to influence the critical classification, placement, and treatment decisions made by psychologists.

Computer-interpreted Tests

Computerized interpretation of the MMPI has remained a major line of inquiry. Honaker, Hector, and Harrell (1986) asked psychology graduate students and practicing psychologists to rate the accuracy of interpretative reports for the MMPI that wee labeled as generated by either a computer or licensed psychologist. Their results demonstrated similar accuracy ratings for computer-generated and clinician-generated reports and did not support the claim that computer-generated reports are assigned more credibility than is warranted. Butcher (1987) reviewed early MMPI systems, summarized desirable attributes of automated systems, and described the development and use of the *Minnesota Clinical Interpretive Report* (University of Minnesota Press, 1982) computerized MMPI interpretive system. Limited attention has been given to automated interpretations of other personality tests (Exner, 1987; Greene, Martin, Bennett, & Shaw, 1981; Harris, Niedner, Feldman, Fink, & Johnston, 1981; Lachar, 1984), neuropsychological measures (Adams & Heaton, 1985; Adams, Kvale, & Keegan, 1984), and ability and achievement instruments (Brantley, 1986; Hasselbring & Crossland, 1981; Johnson, Willis, & Danley, 1982; Oosterhof & Salisbury, 1985; Webb, Herman, & Cabello, 1986).

As noted by Moreland (1985), investigations of the accuracy of computer-based clinical interpretations of personality tests have been limited almost exclusively to the MMPI. A thorough review of the types of MMPI validity studies, computer interpretation systems, and outcomes are presented by Moreland (1987). He summarized these findings by concluding:

> Things look pretty good for computer-based MMPI interpretations. Consumers give them high marks, and the results of properly controlled studies indicate that this high acceptance rate is not the result of generalized reports that are equally applicable to most clients. (p. 43)

In contrast, Matarazzo (1985) noted that currently available automated interpretation systems are erected upon rather tenuous empirical bases and involve varying degrees of clinical and actuarial data accumulation and interpretation which have considerable potential for harm if used in isolation. These disparate views can be reconciled by Butcher's (1987) assertion that the computerized report should be used "only in conjunction with clinical information obtained from other sources" (p. 167).

Current Status

There has been much controversy surrounding computerized test administration and interpretation. Sampson (1983) enumerated and reviewed the potential benefits of such systems: namely, (a) better client response to the testing situation, (b) cost-effectiveness, (c) ability of the computer to do interactive testing, (d) generation of standardization data, (e) more efficient use of staff time, (f) more efficient scoring, (g) reduced error rates in scoring and administration, (h) validity of interpretation of results, and (i) potential assistance to persons with visual or auditory handicaps. Arguments against the concept of computerized assessment have been compiled by Sampson (1983) and Space (1981). Possible problems include: (a) depersonalization of the client, (b) idiographic information lost in favor of nomothetic information, (c) poor interface between person and machine, (d) loss of efficiency with difficult clients, (e) confidentiality of client information may be at risk, (f) inability to discriminate between normal error and pathological response, and (g) introduction of bias into the testing situation. Matarazzo (1983, 1985, 1986) has been most outspoken about computerized psychological testing, arguing that automated psychological test interpretations offer considerable potential for the future, but currently fail to meet even minimal validation standards.

It is apparent from the foregoing discussion that there is no professional consensus regarding computerized administration and interpretation of psychological tests. However, comprehensive reviews of the literature and thoughtful analyses are presented by Space (1981), Fowler (1985), Hofer and Green (1985), as well as by the authors represented in this volume. Moreover, the American Psychological Association's guidelines (APA, 1986) for computer-based tests and interpretations summarize pertinent ethical, professional, and technical standards relevant to this issue.

NOVEL ADMINISTRATION AND
INTERPRETATION PROGRAMS

As observed by Hofer and Green (1985), early applications of technology in any field tend to be derivative. For example, the first automobiles were simply attempts to duplicate traditional horse-drawn carriages, pioneer television broadcasts mimicked familiar radio formats, and the first computers were used to cross-check mechanically the counts of interview cards collected by U.S. census takers. The application of computer technology to psychology is no exception. At present, computerized assessment is primarily devoted to a literal translation of existing paper-and-pencil tests or interpretive systems to the computer without modifications to take advantage of the computer's unique features. As in other technologies, psychological assessment will make revolutionary advances when novel, creative applications are computerized; not when existing applications are slavishly re-created on the computer.

Computer-administered Tests

Item Types.   New types of test items can capitalize on the strengths of the computer and thereby contribute to novel and informative assessment techniques. The computer can readily capture reaction times of examinees and can present test items that involve movement, color, speech, sound, and interactive graphics. These possibilities are just beginning to be explored. For example, Jones, Dunlap, and Bilodeau (1987) utilized video games to establish dimensions of individual differences in cognitive and perceptual functioning. These computerized video games contained variance not captured by conventional paper-and-pencil cognitive tests. Colby and Parkison (1985) described an innovative program which converts natural language expressions into conceptual patterns and key ideas to produce a taxonomy of neurotic patients.

Technological advances in computer hardware have made possible much more realistic graphics and sound than were exploited by Jones et al. (1987) or by Colby and Parkison (1985). Videodisk and compact digital disk developments offer interactivity with television quality visuals, digital sound, and print quality graphics (Gonsalves, 1987). With such capabilities, it might be possible to tap examinees' reactions to social situations by placing them in a simulated, but realistic, context and monitoring their character's verbalizations and movements. Vocabulary knowledge could be evaluated by providing an interactive dictionary and monitoring examinees' usage. Alternately, free responses by examinees could be compared word by word with massive tables of word frequencies. Parents and teachers could rate child behaviors by creating characters via screen animation rather than relying, as is now necessary, on written item descriptions. The advantages of using computer technology to assess human abilities, attributes, and skills in novel ways are almost unlimited and await only the development of well-researched and imaginatively implemented methods.

Test Types. Irrespective of types of items involved, psychological assessment must move away from the linear, fixed-item presentations necessitated by paper-and-pencil formats. With traditional tests, all examinees typically respond to the same test items. Each examinee receives items that are too easy and items that are too difficult. If test items are too difficult, an examinee might resort to random guessing or omission of responses. Easy items may dampen motivation. Conventional testing technology thereby entails a restricted range of accuracy for nonaverage examinees. Although capable of expediting the test scoring and test interpretation process, a computerized copy of conventional methods provides neither improved efficiency nor advanced psychometric properties (Weiss & Yale, 1987).

What is required is a type of test that capitalizes on the capabilities of the computer to improve test efficiency and accuracy. Such a test methodology was developed independent of computer technology, but its adaptability to computerization was immediately recognized (Weiss, 1985). Labeled *adaptive* testing, the computer presents the items to the examinee, receives and scores the item responses, chooses the next item to administer, based on the examinee's prior performance, and terminates the test when appropriate. Unlike conventional tests, adaptive test items are selected *during* rather than *before* administration. By doing so, each test item can be optimally useful for measuring each individual examinee (McKinley & Reckase, 1980).

Research on computerized adaptive testing has revealed that it is more precise and efficient than conventional testing (Weiss, 1958). As a consequence, average test length can be reduced about 50% without compromising measurement quality (Weiss & Vale, 1987). Computerized adaptive testing has in the past been predominately restricted to academic and ability tests (Sands & Gade, 1983; Watkins & Kush, 1988). Its application to personality testing (Jackson, 1985) and to diagnostic interviews (Stein, 1987) has been described, and its utility in other areas of psychological testing has recently been speculated upon by Krug (1987). Adaptive testing, particularly when combined with novel test items, could result in dramatic improvements in the efficiency, accuracy, and relevance of psychological assessment.

COMPUTERIZED INTERPRETATION SYSTEMS

Expert Systems

Computer software, like hardware, is a rapidly emerging technology. In recent years the development of artificial intelligence (AI) software has received much attention. That is, attempts to make computers exhibit, or at least simulate, different aspects of intelligent behavior. Perhaps the most popular and well-known example of AI is computerized chess. Once thought to be incapable of more than rudimentary play, chess programs have evolved to a point where they can now beat all but the best human players (Krutch, 1986).

Probably the "hottest" topic in AI is expert systems (Chadwick & Hannah, 1987). *Expert systems* are computer programs designed to reason as would most expert humans. Although still uncommon in psychology, expert system applications are relatively well established and highly publicized in medicine, economics, chemistry, geological exploration, aeronautics, and other scientific, human service, and industrial areas (Buchanan, 1985).

There is no single, universally accepted definition of an expert system. Chadwick and Hannah (1987) indicated that an expert system "is a computer program that simulates the reasoning of a human expert in a certain domain. To do this, it uses a knowledge base containing facts and heuristics, and some inference procedure for utilizing its knowledge" (p. 3). Krutch (1986) indicated that "An expert system can be described as an intelligent database that can make decisions, give advice, and come to important conclusions" (p. 3). In addition to definitions, many authors specify a number of attributes which they consider to be essential characteristics of an expert system (Buchanan, 1985).

Computerized psychological assessment systems are in their infancy and whether or not an existing application is an expert system will be widely debated (Roid, 1986). Deupree (1985) reviewed existing software and opined that WISC–R analysis programs are fundamental AI applications. It is doubtful that Waterman (1986) would agree, given that author's extensive definitional criteria and estimate of 6 person-years required to develop even a moderately difficult expert system.

A New Model

It seems pointless to become entangled in a definitional quagmire concerning expert psychological systems. Rather, psychologists must focus their attention on the underlying knowledge base of any computerized system. That is, after all, the area in which psychologists are expert. To this end, a two-dimensional framework is offered as a model for analysis and production of computerized psychological assessment systems. The first dimension, *scope,* refers to the scope or breadth of knowledge covered by the system. A continuous concept, scope may range from narrow to broad. The second dimension, *authority,* represents the consensus of experts regarding the verity of the underlying "knowledge" used by the program. To use a more familiar term, authority could be equated to validity and might span from low to high along its own continuum. It is possible to simplify this two-dimensional continuous model by collapsing it into four cells; that is, narrow scope with low authority, narrow scope with high authority, broad scope with low authority, and broad scope with high authority. This simplification is depicted in Fig. 2.1. Real computer systems would, of course, rarely be so well delineated or easily classified. Nevertheless, it is clear that high authority is a prerequisite to utility, irrespective of the scope of knowledge incorporated in an expert system.

Narrow Scope and Low Authority.   For an example, consider an intelligence test interpretation program which bases its expertise on Glasser and Zimmerman's (1967) *Clinical Interpretations of the Wechsler Intelligence Scale for*

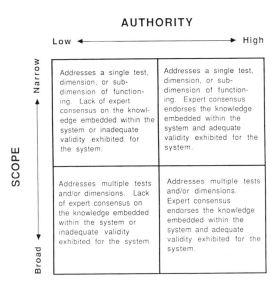

FIG. 2.1.   Framework for analysis of computerized psychological assessment systems.

Children. Such an application necessarily would be considered of narrow scope, given its coverage of only one aspect of human functioning—intelligence. On the authority dimension, such a program's conclusions would be refuted strongly by many experts who demonstrate empirically that profile and scatter analysis of the WISC is not defensible (Kavale & Furness, 1984) and has the potential for doing more harm than good (Kramer, Henning–Stout, Ullman, & Schellenberg, 1987). Alternatively, it is quite possible for a program having very narrow scope to proceed with high authority; as, for instance, the letter capitalization program described by Watkins and Kush (1988).

A review of recent publications dealing with computerized psychological assessment (Butcher, 1987; Fowler, 1985; Jackson, 1985) reveals that most current applications are relatively narrow in scope. Even so, newer computer applications tend to rest on greater authority and should yield improved efficiency and accuracy for psychological assessment.

Broad Scope and High Authority.   It is intuitively apparent that development of computerized psychological assessment systems with broad scope and high authority entails problems of a different nature and magnitude than those encountered during scoring or interpretation of an individual psychological test. Before attacking these problems, it would be instructive to determine if expert system developers in other disciplines have encountered similar difficulties and, if so, consider how they have dealt with them.

Perhaps medicine is the most logical field for comparison because, like professional psychology, it encompasses a vast array of human-care activities, many guided by available empirical knowledge but many more still remnants of traditional thinking and popular convention. Expert medical systems have been in use for years and efforts to develop broadly useful systems have been undertaken by several experimenters (Buchanan, 1985). It was recognized at an early stage that computer programs were more successful in narrow, constrained arenas of medicine where much hard laboratory knowledge existed, largely because expert systems which produced complicated decisions involving multiple diseases were confronted by problems of inadequate consensus concerning the underlying knowledge base (Schoolman & Bernstein, 1978). Similar problems have been noted in psychiatry, where limitations in validity of the diagnostic system itself arose as barriers to computerized expertise (Spitzer & Fleiss, 1974). This problem surfaced in many other expert system applications (Bhatnagar & Kanal, 1986) and may be described formally as *reasoning with uncertainty* or (inasmuch as empirical inquiry in the behavioral sciences never substantiates absolute truth) *reasoning with unknown certainty.*

There are striking similarities across disciplines when solutions to the uncertainty problem are reviewed. Szolovits and Pauker (1978) suggested that an expert medical system would have to use a judicious combination of categorical and probabilistic reasoning. In psychiatry, Erdman, Greist, Klein, Jefferson, and

Getto (1981) recommended a combination of statistical and clinical judgment. Bhatnagar and Kanal (1986) concluded that the management of uncertainty in automated decision making required application of numerical methods, such as probability theory, within the framework of logic.

A PSYCHOEDUCATIONAL DIAGNOSTIC MODEL

The process of identifying, classifying, and programming for childhood developmental, social, and learning difficulties is nontrivial and realistically can be deemed broad in scope. It can be argued further and without contradiction that the existing psychoeducational diagnostic knowledge base is marked by considerable uncertainty. In fact, McDermott (1986) has characterized conventional methods of child diagnosis and classification as woefully inadequate.

On the surface, then, a computerized system for applying psychoeducational diagnostic expertise to childhood disorders seems untenable. The domain is too broad, is marked by a lack of professional consensus, and requires extensive reasoning with uncertainty. Nonetheless, the problems presented by psychoeducational diagnosis closely parallel those encountered during the development of expert systems in other disciplines and may be amenable to similar resolutions.

Diagnostic Reliability

Meehl's (1954) seminal book on clinical and statistical classification was instrumental in sensitizing psychologists to potential reliability and validity limitations in psychodiagnostic practice. Evaluation research over the intervening years has demonstrated repeatedly that psychiatrists and psychologists are unable to render reliable psychological diagnoses (Algozzine & Ysseldyke, 1981; Cantwell, Russell, Mattison, & Will, 1979; Epps, Ysseldyke, & McGue, 1984; Freeman, 1971). Typically, agreement among child specialists has been found to be more commensurate with guesswork or unskilled decision making. For example, McDermott (1980b) observed near-chance levels of agreement among experienced psychologists' diagnoses, while Visonhaler, Weinshank, Wagner, and Polin (1983) found that single clinicians diagnosing the same cases twice achieved only 0.20 mean diagnostic agreement with themselves. The ramifications of such poor diagnostic agreement are profound because unreliable diagnoses must, by definition, be invalid (Spitzer & Fleiss, 1974).

Diagnostic Error

The factors contributing to classificatory incongruity are many, complex, and incompletely understood (McDermott, 1982). Nevertheless, they may be viewed conceptually as falling under two broad categories: inconstancy in human information processing and judgment and faults in diagnostic decision-making rules.

Human Error.   There is often a considerable amount of disagreement among observers and judges even when they observe relatively concrete events. Thus, Koran (1975) revealed that physicians often disagreed, concerning even relatively quantifiable tasks, in one out of five instances. And so it would follow that judgments rendered under more nebulous and less-quantifiable circumstances (as so often "psychological" contexts would seem to appear) are likely to be very unreliable.

One limiting factor which may contribute to classificatory unreliability is the tendency for diagnoses to be negatively biased by client characteristics. Social class (DiNardo, 1975), gender (Broverman, Broverman, Clarkson, Rosenkrantz, & Vogel, 1970), and race (Franks, 1971) have, among other client attributes, been found to influence classification decisions. Diagnostic constancy also has been found inversely related to the information-processing load (Lueger & Petzel, 1979) and to the amount of direct probabilistic analysis required (Eddy & Clanton, 1982; Kahneman & Tversky, 1982). Sources of human error in judgment and diagnosis have been analyzed by Arkes (1981) and McDermott (1981). Judgmental impediments summarized by these authors include: (a) inconsistent theoretical orientation, (b) inability to assess covariation accurately, (c) influence of preconceived notions or expectancies, (d) minimal awareness of one's own judgment process, (e) overconfidence, (f) hindsight bias, (g) preference for unverifiable or inexclusive diagnoses, (h) inconstancy of diagnostic style, and (i) preference for a determinative diagnostic posture (i.e., the practice of responding to uncertainty by rendering rather than deferring decisions).

Decision Rule Error.   Historically, there have been two general approaches to classification of psychoeducational disorders: clinical and actuarial. Both strategies afford important advantages as well as specific weaknesses. Quay (1986) comprehensively reviewed the foundation, development, and application of clinical diagnostic strategies. In brief, clinical methods evolved from observations by clinicians working with patients. Typically, clinicians noted the covariance of certain characteristics and determined through consensual validation that such constellations of phenomena should constitute unique diagnostic categories. Thereafter, groups of such categories were interrelated to comprise a complete clinical classification system. Examples of existing clinical systems include the American Psychiatric Association's revised *Diagnostic and Statistical Manual of Mental Disorders* (DSM–III–R; 1987) and the World Health Organization's ninth edition of the *International Classification of Diseases* (ICD-9; 1978).

Clinical decision rules are based largely on popular theory and accepted practice and are dependent on the individual psychologist for interpretation. They offer a wealth of useful constructs and recorded case experience but are heavily reliant upon competent human judgment in weighing the elements of any specific case. Ironically, reliance on human judgment represents both the major strength and the major weakness of the clinical approach. On the positive side, humans may be more likely to identify isolated and unusual characteristics, behaviors, and patterns of behavior. However, as seemingly unique characteristics compound and become confused with the greater universe of natural human variation, dependence on clinical judgment invariably increases error.

Actuarial strategies, although often grounded in conventional theory, were derived from controlled studies of incidence and prevalence of normality and abnormality in representative general populations (McDermott, 1982). Classifications were developed by defining distinctly similar and reliable patterns of functioning, and assignment criteria were presented in the form of statistical decision rules. Individual psychologists do not interpret the decision rules because it is a straightforward matter of assigning classifications that are statistically probable and discarding those that are improbable.

Given their objective foundations and implementation, actuarial decision rules are quite reliable and control for many of the sources of human decision error that plague clinical diagnosis. Actuarial methods are limited, however, by the necessity for sound and comprehensive data concerning the characteristics of patient populations and by a general lack of the technical resources required for implementation of complex statistical decision rules.

Minimizing Diagnostic Error

Arkes (1981) proffered three major suggestions for improvement of the accuracy and reliability of human judgment: consider alternatives, use statistical principles, and decrease reliance on memory. It is readily apparent that actuarial assessment approaches and empirical decision rules would allow the clinician to utilize statistical principles and thereby decrease diagnostic error. On the other hand, good actuarial information is frequently unavailable. Consequently, it is reasonable to regard clinical and actuarial processes as complementary, each mitigating the other's inherent weaknesses. This combination of statistical and clinical principles to improve reasoning in an uncertain domain emulates resolutions emanating from leading expert systems research (Bhatnagar & Kanal, 1986; Erdman et al., 1981; Szolovits & Pauker, 1978). Effective utilization of actuarial strategies can be facilitated by computers, which can rapidly and accurately calculate and apply a host of complicated statistical decision rules. Consideration of alternatives may be promoted by the adoption of a systematic decision process; that is, a process that capitalizes on modern decision theory (Dailey, 1971) and systems analysis (Nathan, 1967) to ensure logical sequencing and efficiency. Computerization can ensure the prompt and precise application of pertinent systems logic and guide the process so as to reduce substantially the demands made upon the clinician's memory.

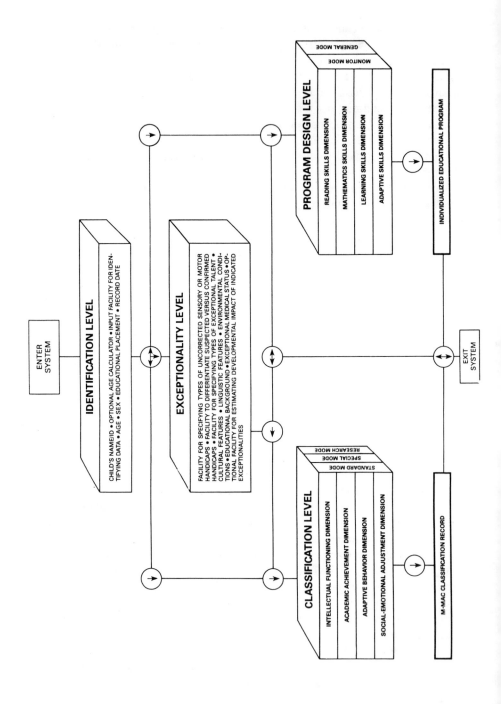

22

A COMPUTERIZED PSYCHOEDUCATIONAL
DIAGNOSTIC SYSTEM

From the foregoing discussion, it is apparent that an efficient computerized diagnostic expert system should embody both clinical and actuarial methods and should implement each when optimally appropriate. Moreover, it should employ a systematic decision process to maximize consistency and reliability and thereby enhance authority. It should address multiple sources of diagnostic data (tests, demography, unusual characteristics, etc.) and dimensions of human functioning (intellectual, social, physical) to gain broad scope. The prototype of such a system was introduced by McDermott (1980a) for the diagnosis of childhood disorders. The system was described in considerable detail (McDermott, 1980c) and validated with a large group of children (Hale & McDermott, 1984; McDermott & Hale, 1982). Subsequently, its capabilities were extended and it was made operational on microcomputers (McDermott & Watkins, 1985, 1987). The remainder of this chapter is devoted to a description of that expert system.

The *McDermott Multidimensional Assessment of Children* (M.MAC) is a comprehensive microcomputer system for use by psychologists and other child specialists in assessing the psychological and educational functioning of children 2 through 18 years old. It produces objective classifications of childhood normality and exceptionality and designs instructional programs based upon actual performance in fundamental educational areas. An overview of the M.MAC system's structure and organization is presented in Fig. 2.2.

Identification

The first component encountered in operation of the M.MAC system is the Identification Level. This preparatory stage entails collection and compilation of basic demographic information about the child, including age, grade, sex, and educational placement. This information allows the program to retrieve appropriate data (i.e., population means, standard deviations, reliability and validity coefficients, prevalence rates, etc.) from its memory for use in later levels of the system. There are almost 10,000 discrete units of statistical data stored within the M.MAC system, which are accessed by age, grade, and gender. Accurate child demographic identification is, therefore, essential for precise application of actuarial rules. Identification information also serves the traditional function of allowing the system to refer to the child by name in reports and to tailor gender references properly.

FIG. 2.2. Structure of the M.MAC system. From the microcomputer systems manual for McDermott Multidimensional Assessment of Children, P. A. McDermott and M. W. Watkins, 1985, 1987. New York: Psychological Corporation. Copyright (1985, 1987) by Psychological Corporation. Reproduced by permission. All rights reserved.

Exceptionality

As denoted by the flow chart in Fig. 2.2, the Exceptionality Level is an optional component of a case study. Its purpose is to allow the classification process to consider unusual personal features of the child or the child's environment that might affect diagnosis. The psychologist informs the M.MAC system about sensory and physical handicaps, special language and cultural features, health problems, environmental stress, and educational disadvantage. The examiner also characterizes, based upon medical records and best clinical judgment, each factor as either confirmed or suspected.

Confirmed or suspected exceptional conditions can produce a variety of consequences in later M.MAC analyses. Each exceptional factor is regarded as a possible threat to the validity of formal assessment and each is systematically analyzed for its potential impact. In cases where exceptionalities are determined to be indirect threats to validity, the M.MAC system produces cautionary notices and may append a "provisional" label to a diagnosis which could be secondary to identified exceptional factors. An exceptionality which constitutes direct interference with a child's performance results in alteration of decision rules in subsequent classificatory analyses. As a simple example, confirmed vision impairment evokes alterations in use of the WISC–R performance IQ score. Furthermore, the exceptionality level permits the psychologist to identify talents and evaluate the extent to which a child has coped with exceptional circumstances.

Classification

Classification is based upon four principal dimensions of child functioning: intellectual functioning, academic achievement, adaptive behavior and social-emotional adjustment. When proceeding through the successive classification dimensions, the psychologist may select from 24 separate assessment instruments and methods. These are listed in Table 2.1. Scores obtained from these devices are entered into the M.MAC system and processed in relation to normative statistics and child population characteristics (major *actuarial* components of the system's knowledge base).

As detailed in Fig. 2.3, a wide variety of analyses are performed within and across dimensions. There are commonalities among all data entry formats and analyses across classification dimensions that contribute to ease of use and functionality. Standardized instruments used for data collection in each dimension supply a bewildering array of scores. Many instruments naturally provide standard scores based upon a mean of 100 and standard deviation of 15, but some scores are based upon a mean of 100 and standard deviation of 16. Other instruments use standard scores with a mean of 50 and standard deviation of 10, whereas many scales provide only raw scores. To reduce confusion, M.MAC automatically calculates standard scores for instruments that report only raw scores and then applies the mixed categorical-dimensional approach to classifica-

TABLE 2.1
Assessment Scales and Methods Supported by the Four M.MAC Classification
Dimensions

INTELLECTUAL FUNCTIONING
  Wechsler Intelligence Scale for Children-Revised
  Wechsler Preschool and Primary Scale of Intelligence
  Wechsler Adult Intelligence Scale-Revised
  Stanford-Binet Intelligence Scale
  McCarthy Scales of Children's Abilities
  Peabody Picture Vocabulary Test-Revised

ACADEMIC ACHIEVEMENT
  Basic Achievement Skills Individual Screener
  Peabody Individual Achievement Test
  Woodcock-Johnson Tests of Achievement
  Woodcock Reading Mastery Test
  KeyMath Diagnostic Arithmetic Test
  Wide Range Achievement Test-Revised

ADAPTIVE BEHAVIOR
  Adaptive Behavior Inventory for Children
  AAMD Adaptive Behavior Scale-School Edition
  Vineland Adaptive Behavior Scales
  Vineland Social Maturity Scale-Revised
  Professional judgment/Other indices (AAMD guidelines)

SOCIAL-EMOTIONAL ADJUSTMENT
  Bristol Social Adjustment Guides
  Conners Teacher Rating Scale
  Kohn Problem Checklist and Social Competence Scale
  Louisville Behavior Checklist
  Revised Behavior Problem Checklist
  Professional judgment/Other indices (DSM-III criteria)

tion advocated by Cromwell, Blashfield, and Strauss (1975), whereby underlying standard score ranges are associated with terminology that describes comparable levels of functioning.

Another common classification feature is application of only those test scales and subscales for which construct validity has been demonstrated through factor- or cluster-analytical research. The only exception to this general rule is within the academic achievement dimension, where reliance on factoral constructs not recognized by school and society would create unnecessary confusion. The Peabody Individual Achievement Test (PIAT) provides a good example of this exception to the general rule. The PIAT measures and reports scores for five widely accepted academic areas (Mathematics, Reading Recognition, Reading Comprehension, Spelling, and General Information) but has been found by Wikoff (1978) to contain only two factors. Utilizing empirically derived factor scores in such a case would not foster clear communication with teachers, parents, or students.

Derived standard scores are reported across all dimensions, along with upper and lower score limits based upon confidence in reliability. Within an area of functioning, the deviation of each subarea from a child's own average level is analyzed (Davis, 1959) and the increased risk of error associated with multiple statistical comparisons is automatically controlled through Bonferroni correc-

CLASSIFICATION LEVEL

ALTERNATE ANALYSIS OF DATA FROM A SINGLE SCALE ONLY

INTELLECTUAL FUNCTIONING DIMENSION

SELECTION OF SCALES • BYPASS FOR UNADMINISTERED SUBSCALES • CORRECTION FOR SIMUL-
TANEOUS STATISTICAL TESTS • CONFIDENCE LIMITS FOR OBTAINED SCORES • SIGNIFICANCE AND
ESTIMATED PREVALENCE OF VERBAL-PERFORMANCE IQ DIFFERENCE • OPTIONAL CALCULATION OF
FACTOR DEVIATION QUOTIENTS • DEVIATIONS FROM CHILD'S AVERAGE FUNCTIONING LEVEL • RE-
LATIONSHIP TO SUSPECTED AND CONFIRMED SENSORY-MOTOR OR LANGUAGE IMPAIRMENTS •
QUALITATIVE LEVEL OF INTELLECTUAL FUNCTIONING • SUMMARY TABLES, INTERPRETATION, AND
VERBAL REPORT OF RESULTS • NOTICE OF DIRECT VALIDITY THREATS BY SITUATIONAL OR CHILD
EXCEPTIONALITY • DIMENSION SUMMARY

ACADEMIC ACHIEVEMENT DIMENSION

SELECTION OF SCALES • ADJUSTMENT FOR UNADMINISTERED SUBSCALES • AUTOMATIC BYPASS
FOR PRESCHOOL LEVEL CHILDREN • CORRECTION FOR SIMULTANEOUS STATISTICAL TESTS • CON-
FIDENCE LIMITS FOR OBTAINED SCORES • DEVIATIONS FROM CHILD'S AVERAGE ACHIEVEMENT LEVEL
• ALTERNATE REGRESSION OR ESTIMATED TRUE DIFFERENCE ANALYSES TO DETERMINE ACHIEVE-
MENT PROBLEMS • SIGNIFICANCE AND ESTIMATED PREVALENCE FOR DETECTED UNDER- AND
OVERACHIEVEMENT • POSTING OF COEFFICIENTS USED TO CALCULATE EXPECTED ACHIEVEMENT
• QUALITATIVE STATUS OF ACHIEVEMENT RELATIVE TO EXPECTANCY IN EACH SUBJECT AREA •
QUALITATIVE LEVELS OF ACHIEVEMENT RELATIVE TO AGE OR GRADE PLACEMENT • SUMMARY TA-
BLES AND VERBAL REPORT FOR EACH SUBJECT AREA • NOTICE OF DIRECT VALIDITY THREATS BY
SITUATIONAL OR CHILD EXCEPTIONALITY • DIMENSION SUMMARY

ADAPTIVE BEHAVIOR DIMENSION

SELECTION OF SCALES • ALTERNATE FACILITY FOR EVALUATION BASED ON PROFESSIONAL JUDG-
MENT AND/OR UNSPECIFIED INDICES • CORRECTION FOR SIMULTANEOUS STATISTICAL TESTS •
CONFIDENCE LIMITS FOR OBTAINED SCORES • DEVIATIONS FROM CHILD'S AVERAGE ADAPTATION
LEVEL • ALTERNATE ANALYSIS BY CUTTING-SCORE, DISCRIMINANT FUNCTION, OR GENERALIZED
DISTANCE TECHNIQUE FOR CERTAIN SCALES • INDEX OF PROFILE SIMILARITY TO EXISTING MR POP-
ULATIONS • AUTOMATIC CROSS-VALIDATION OF MULTIVARIATE GROUPING ANALYSES AGAINST
CONVENTIONAL CUTTING-SCORE ANALYSIS • QUALITATIVE LEVEL OF ADAPTATION RELATIVE TO
AGE FOR EACH SUBSKILL AREA • ALTERNATE FACILITY FOR CLINICAL DIAGNOSIS OF DEFICIENCY
AREAS UNDER AAMD GUIDELINES • SUMMARY TABLES AND VERBAL REPORT OF RESULTS • NO-
TICE OF INDIRECT VALIDITY THREATS BY SITUATIONAL OR CHILD EXCEPTIONALITY • DIMENSION
SUMMARY

SOCIAL-EMOTIONAL ADJUSTMENT DIMENSION

SELECTION OF SCALES • ALTERNATE FACILITY FOR EVALUATION BASED ON PROFESSIONAL JUDG-
MENT AND/OR UNSPECIFIED MEASURES • CALCULATION OF STANDARD SCORES • CONFIDENCE
LIMITS FOR STANDARD SCORES • ALTERNATE ANALYSIS BY CUTTING-SCORE OR SYNDROMIC PRO-
FILE TECHNIQUE FOR CERTAIN SCALES • INDEX OF PROFILE SIMILARITY TO EXISTING ADJUSTED
AND MALADJUSTED SUBPOPULATIONS • QUALITATIVE ADJUSTMENT LEVEL OR MALADJUSTMENT
SEVERITY LEVEL • ALTERNATE FACILITY FOR CLINICAL DIAGNOSIS OF PRIMARY AND SECONDARY
CHILDHOOD DISORDERS BY TYPE AND SUBTYPE UNDER DSM-III CRITERIA • SUMMARY TABLES AND
VERBAL REPORT OF RESULTS • NOTICE OF INDIRECT VALIDITY THREATS BY SITUATIONAL OR CHILD
EXCEPTIONALITY • DIMENSION SUMMARY

M·MAC CLASSIFICATION RECORD

CHILD'S NAME/ID • AGE • SEX • EDUCATIONAL PLACEMENT • RECORD DATE • ASSESSMENT METH-
ODS (SCALES, PROFESSIONAL JUDGMENT, ETC.) • OPERATIONS MODE • STATISTICAL CRITERIA •
ALTERED CUTTING-SCORES • NOTICE OF PARAMETER ALTERATIONS • NOTICE OF COMBINATIONS
OF DATA FROM TWO INFORMANTS OR OBSERVERS • TYPES OF SITUATIONAL AND CHILD EXCEP-
TIONALITY AND ESTIMATED DEVELOPMENTAL IMPACT • MULTIDIMENSIONAL CLASSIFICATION
SUMMARY • TYPES OF EXCEPTIONAL TALENT • INTELLECTUAL GIFTEDNESS • INTELLECTUAL
FUNCTIONING LEVEL • MENTAL RETARDATION LEVEL • EDUCATIONAL RETARDATION LEVEL • TYPES
OF COMMENSURATE ACHIEVEMENT • TYPES OF SPECIFIC LEARNING DISABILITIES • TYPES OF DE-
VELOPMENTAL LEARNING DISORDERS • TYPES OF PROVISIONAL LEARNING DISABILITIES OR DE-
VELOPMENTAL LEARNING DISORDERS • TYPES OF ACADEMIC OVERCOMPENSATION • POSSIBLE
VISUAL-MOTOR OR COMMUNICATION DISORDERS • SOCIAL-EMOTIONAL ADJUSTMENT LEVEL •
SEVERITY LEVEL OF SOCIAL-EMOTIONAL MALADJUSTMENT • MALADJUSTMENT TYPE BASED ON
EMPIRICAL CLASSIFICATION OR PRIMARY AND SECONDARY TYPES AND SUBTYPES BASED ON CLIN-
ICAL CLASSIFICATION • M·MAC REFERENCE CODE FOR EACH CLASSIFICATION • OPTIONAL RELATED
REFERENCE CODES FOR DSM-III AND WORLD HEALTH ORGANIZATION CLASSIFICATION SYSTEMS

tions (Silverstein, 1982). Additionally, reports of statistical significance are supplemented, whenever possible, by actuarial knowledge of prevalence; that is, the percentage of children in the general population showing deviations as serious as currently being manifested (Silverstein, 1981a, 1981b).

Beyond these commonalities, the classification level can be operated in one of three separate modes: Standard, Special, or Research. The mode chosen is dependent on the flexibility required by the psychologist. Each mode enables the examiner to select appropriate actuarial information, adjust classificatory criteria for special circumstances, or alter data bases of actuarial information. Functions and features of these operational modes are summarized in Fig. 2.4.

The Standard mode is automatically chosen by the M.MAC system unless the examiner specifies otherwise. This mode applies general population norms, conventional cutting-scores, standard prevalence levels, and conventional probability test levels. Operation under the Standard mode is recommended by the authors (McDermott & Watkins, 1985, 1987), unless exceptional circumstances intervene, because it guarantees a *reference standard* for assessment, thereby lending comparability to decisions across psychologists, agencies, and regions. The Special mode is intended for special needs arising in regular practice while the Research mode is reserved for applied research and needs not arising in everyday practice. Further detailed descriptions and applications of M.MAC's operational modes are provided by Glutting (1986a), McDermott (1990), and McDermott and Watkins (1985, 1987).

The M.MAC system produces 113 empirical and 35 clinical classifications. For a given child, at least one or as many as four classifications are rendered for each dimension. Each classification may be accompanied by values specifying qualitative level of functioning (e.g., mild, adequate, etc.) and by specific subtype designations (e.g., attention deficit disorder with hyperactivity, without hyperactivity, etc.). In addition, psychologists may elect to have DSM–III and ICD–9 codes accompany each M.MAC classification.

Although a complete discussion of all M.MAC classification features and logic is beyond the scope of this chapter, several examples are provided to demonstrate the multidimensional nature of diagnoses and complex interplay of clinical and actuarial methods. Fig. 2.5 illustrates the basic logic for differential classification of cognitive functioning. Review of this figure reveals that the M.MAC system first examines the child's intellectual functioning in relation to the prespecified *mild mental retardation cutting-score* value. In Standard Mode, this value is set at two standard deviations below the mean, in congruence with accepted diagnostic standards (Grossman, 1977). Based upon this rule, an obtained IQ equal to or greater than the rutting-score value precludes the classifica-

---

CLASSIFICATION LEVEL

STANDARD MODE

SYSTEM SECURITY ON DECISION RULES TO ENSURE INTER-AGENCY AND INTERNATIONAL CLASSIFICATION CONSISTENCY • PARAMETERS (M, SD, r) BASED ON GENERAL POPULATION NORMS • 95% CONFIDENCE LIMITS FOR OBTAINED SCORES • MAXIMUM .05 PROBABILITY LEVEL FOR ACCEPTING STATISTICAL SIGNIFICANCE • MAXIMUM 6% OVERALL ESTIMATED PREVALENCE LEVEL FOR ACCEPTING ABNORMALITY OF SCALE DISCREPANCIES • AAMD CUTTING-SCORE CRITERIA FOR MENTAL RETARDATION LEVELS • POSITIVE 2 STANDARD DEVIATION CUTTING-SCORE FOR INTELLECTUAL GIFTEDNESS • MAXIMUM 3% ESTIMATED POPULATION PREVALENCE LEVEL FOR ACCEPTING ABNORMALITY OF EACH TYPE OF ACHIEVEMENT PROBLEM • USE OF READING AND/OR MATHEMATICS PERFORMANCE FOR DETECTING SPECIFIC LEARNING DISABILITIES AND DEVELOPMENTAL LEARNING DISORDERS • 70 T-SCORE CUTTING-SCORE FOR SOCIAL-EMOTIONAL MALADJUSTMENT

SPECIAL MODE

ALL STANDARD MODE OPTIONS AVAILABLE • ALTER CUTTING-SCORES FOR INTELLECTUAL GIFTEDNESS AND ANY LEVELS OF MENTAL RETARDATION • SET MAXIMUM ESTIMATED PREVALENCE LEVEL FOR ACCEPTING ABNORMALITY OF ACHIEVEMENT PROBLEMS • SET MAXIMUM PROBABILITY LEVEL FOR ACCEPTING SIGNIFICANCE OF ESTIMATED TRUE DIFFERENCES BETWEEN EXPECTED AND OBSERVED ACHIEVEMENT • SELECT SUBJECT AREAS USED FOR DETECTING SPECIFIC LEARNING DISABILITIES AND DEVELOPMENTAL LEARNING DISORDERS • ENTER AND STATISTICALLY COMPARE ADAPTIVE BEHAVIOR DATA FROM TWO INFORMANTS • SELECT OR COMBINE INFORMANTS' DATA • ENTER AND STATISTICALLY COMPARE SOCIAL-EMOTIONAL ADJUSTMENT DATA FROM TWO OBSERVERS • SELECT OR COMBINE OBSERVERS' DATA • ALTER CUTTING-SCORE FOR SOCIAL-EMOTIONAL MALADJUSTMENT • AUTOMATIC RETRIEVAL OF STANDARD MODE CUTTING-SCORES AND STATISTICAL CRITERIA

RESEARCH MODE

ALL STANDARD AND SPECIAL MODE OPTIONS AVAILABLE • CALCULATE ESTIMATED TRUE SCORES AND CONFIDENCE LIMITS • SET CONFIDENCE LEVEL FOR OBTAINED AND ESTIMATED TRUE SCORES • SET MAXIMUM PROBABILITY LEVEL FOR ACCEPTING ABNORMALITY OF DEVIATIONS FROM AVERAGE PERFORMANCE • SET MAXIMUM ESTIMATED PREVALENCE LEVEL FOR ACCEPTING ABNORMALITY OF VERBAL-PERFORMANCE IQ DIFFERENCE • MEMORY STORAGE AND APPLICATION OF NONSTANDARD REGRESSION COEFFICIENTS FOR DETERMINING EXPECTED ACHIEVEMENT • MEMORY STORAGE AND APPLICATION OF ADAPTIVE BEHAVIOR PARAMETERS (M, SD, r) FOR SPECIAL POPULATIONS BY AGE LEVEL • MEMORY STORAGE AND APPLICATION OF SOCIAL-EMOTIONAL ADJUSTMENT PARAMETERS (M, SD, r) FOR SPECIAL POPULATIONS BY AGE LEVEL AND SEX • AUTOMATIC RETRIEVAL OF STANDARD MODE PARAMETERS AND STATISTICAL CRITERIA

FIG. 2.4. Operation modes of the classification level. From the microcomputer systems manual for McDermott Multidimensional Assessment of Children, P. A. McDermott and M. W. Watkins, 1985, 1987. New York: Psychological Corporation. Copyright (1985, 1987) by Psychological Corporation. Reproduced by permission. All rights reserved.

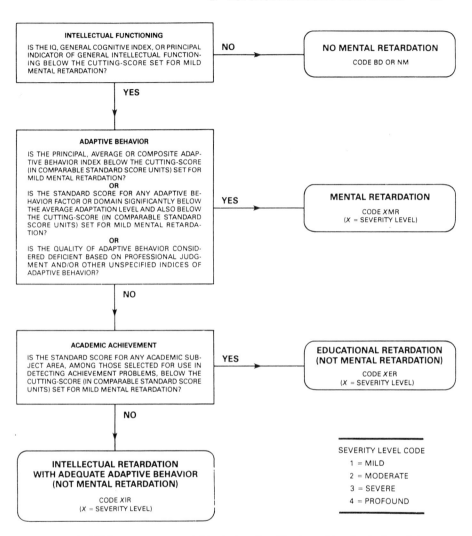

FIG. 2.5. M.MAC systems-actuarial logic for classification of intellectual proficiency and retardation. From the microcomputer systems manual for McDermott Multidimensional Assessment of Children, P. A. McDermott and M. W. Watkins, 1985, 1987. New York: Psychological Corporation. Copyright (1985, 1987) by Psychological Corporation. Reproduced by permission. All rights reserved.

tion of mental retardation. An obtained IQ lower than the rutting-score value invites consideration, sequentially, of adaptive behavior and academic achievement. Adaptive behavior may be determined empirically or clinically, but must be considered deficient by one of these two methods to result in a mental retardation diagnosis (Grossman, 1983; APA, 1987).

Differential classification of academic functioning is modeled in Fig. 2.6. For

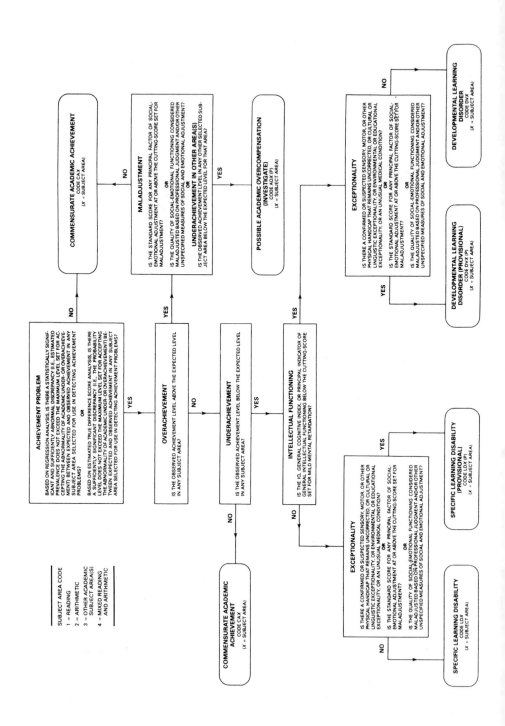

SUBJECT AREA CODE

1 = READING

2 = ARITHMETIC

3 = OTHER ACADEMIC SUBJECT AREA(S)

4 = MIXED READING AND ARITHMETIC

ACHIEVEMENT PROBLEM

BASED ON REGRESSION ANALYSIS, IS THERE A STATISTICALLY SIGNIFICANT AND SUFFICIENTLY ABNORMAL DISCREPANCY (I.E., ESTIMATED PREVALENCE DOES NOT EXCEED THE MAXIMUM LEVEL SET FOR ACCEPTING THE ABNORMALITY OF ACADEMIC UNDER- OR OVERACHIEVEMENT) BETWEEN EXPECTED AND OBSERVED ACHIEVEMENT IN ANY SUBJECT AREA SELECTED FOR USE IN DETECTING ACHIEVEMENT PROBLEMS?

OR

BASED ON ESTIMATED TRUE DIFFERENCE SCORE ANALYSIS, IS THERE A SUFFICIENTLY SIGNIFICANT DISCREPANCY (I.E., THE PROBABILITY LEVEL DOES NOT EXCEED THE MAXIMUM LEVEL SET FOR ACCEPTING THE ABNORMALITY OF ACADEMIC UNDER- OR OVERACHIEVEMENT) BETWEEN EXPECTED AND OBSERVED ACHIEVEMENT IN ANY SUBJECT AREA SELECTED FOR USE IN DETECTING ACHIEVEMENT PROBLEMS?

COMMENSURATE ACADEMIC ACHIEVEMENT
CODE CAX
(X = SUBJECT AREA)

COMMENSURATE ACADEMIC ACHIEVEMENT
CODE CAX
(X = SUBJECT AREA)

OVERACHIEVEMENT

IS THE OBSERVED ACHIEVEMENT LEVEL ABOVE THE EXPECTED LEVEL IN ANY SUBJECT AREA?

UNDERACHIEVEMENT

IS THE OBSERVED ACHIEVEMENT LEVEL BELOW THE EXPECTED LEVEL IN ANY SUBJECT AREA?

MALADJUSTMENT

IS THE STANDARD SCORE FOR ANY PRINCIPAL FACTOR OF SOCIAL-EMOTIONAL ADJUSTMENT AT OR ABOVE THE CUTTING-SCORE SET FOR MALADJUSTMENT?

OR

IS THE QUALITY OF SOCIAL-EMOTIONAL FUNCTIONING CONSIDERED MALADJUSTED BASED ON PROFESSIONAL JUDGMENT AND/OR OTHER UNSPECIFIED MEASURES OF SOCIAL AND EMOTIONAL ADJUSTMENT?

OR

UNDERACHIEVEMENT IN OTHER AREA(S)

IS THE OBSERVED ACHIEVEMENT LEVEL IN ANY OTHER SELECTED SUBJECT AREA BELOW THE EXPECTED LEVEL FOR THAT AREA?

POSSIBLE ACADEMIC OVERCOMPENSATION (INVESTIGATE)
CODE AOX (P)
(X = SUBJECT AREA)

INTELLECTUAL FUNCTIONING

IS THE IQ, GENERAL COGNITIVE INDEX, OR PRINCIPAL INDICATOR OF GENERAL INTELLECTUAL FUNCTIONING BELOW THE CUTTING-SCORE SET FOR MILD MENTAL RETARDATION?

EXCEPTIONALITY

IS THERE A CONFIRMED OR SUSPECTED SENSORY, MOTOR, OR OTHER PHYSICAL HANDICAP THAT REMAINS UNCORRECTED, OR CULTURAL OR LINGUISTIC EXCEPTIONALITY, OR ENVIRONMENTAL OR EDUCATIONAL EXCEPTIONALITY, OR AN UNUSUAL MEDICAL CONDITION?

OR

IS THE STANDARD SCORE FOR ANY PRINCIPAL FACTOR OF SOCIAL-EMOTIONAL ADJUSTMENT AT OR ABOVE THE CUTTING-SCORE SET FOR MALADJUSTMENT?

OR

IS THE QUALITY OF SOCIAL-EMOTIONAL FUNCTIONING CONSIDERED MALADJUSTED BASED ON PROFESSIONAL JUDGMENT AND/OR OTHER UNSPECIFIED MEASURES OF SOCIAL AND EMOTIONAL ADJUSTMENT?

EXCEPTIONALITY

IS THERE A CONFIRMED OR SUSPECTED SENSORY, MOTOR, OR OTHER PHYSICAL HANDICAP THAT REMAINS UNCORRECTED, OR CULTURAL OR LINGUISTIC EXCEPTIONALITY, OR ENVIRONMENTAL OR EDUCATIONAL EXCEPTIONALITY, OR AN UNUSUAL MEDICAL CONDITION?

OR

IS THE STANDARD SCORE FOR ANY PRINCIPAL FACTOR OF SOCIAL-EMOTIONAL ADJUSTMENT AT OR ABOVE THE CUTTING-SCORE SET FOR MALADJUSTMENT?

OR

IS THE QUALITY OF SOCIAL-EMOTIONAL FUNCTIONING CONSIDERED MALADJUSTED BASED ON PROFESSIONAL JUDGMENT AND/OR OTHER UNSPECIFIED MEASURES OF SOCIAL AND EMOTIONAL ADJUSTMENT?

SPECIFIC LEARNING DISABILITY
CODE LDX
(X = SUBJECT AREA)

SPECIFIC LEARNING DISABILITY (PROVISIONAL)
CODE LDX (P)
(X = SUBJECT AREA)

DEVELOPMENTAL LEARNING DISORDER (PROVISIONAL)
CODE DVX (P)
(X = SUBJECT AREA)

DEVELOPMENTAL LEARNING DISORDER
CODE DVX
(X = SUBJECT AREA)

YES   NO

30

each subject area considered, achievement is approached from three perspectives: qualitatively compared with other children of like age or grade, deviation of subareas from the child's average level of academic performance, and discrepancy between levels of expected and observed academic performance. The first two perspectives allow the psychologist to understand better the child's academic performance in relation to other children's skills and in relation to the child's own skills. That is, nomothetic and idiographic analysis, respectively.

Discrepancy between expected and observed academic performance forms the foundation for classification of academic functioning. Expected achievement is the level of academic performance that would be manifested if essential elements in a child's life were to remain relatively constant and if no extraordinary assistance or interference with the child's learning were to occur. When observed achievement is markedly discrepant from expectancy, it suggests that something unusual may be influencing, either positively or negatively, academic performance.

Discrepancies between expected and observed achievement have been operationalized through a variety of methods, most of which have been demonstrated to be fatally flawed (Reynolds, 1985). Consistent with accepted theory, the M.MAC system utilizes level of general intellectual functioning to estimate academic expectancy (Kirk & Bateman, 1962). Discrepancy is calculated through regression analysis, employing the standard error of discrepancy from prediction (Thorndike, 1963) or, when certain actuarial data are unavailable, through estimated true difference analysis, using the standard error of measurement of estimated true difference (Stanley, 1971). These methods have been determined to be statistically and professionally sound (Glutting, McDermott, & Stanley, 1987; Reynolds, 1985).

Achievement in any given subject area may be found to be higher, lower, or reasonably consistent with expected levels. Underachievement is, of course, indicative of a learning problem and the M.MAC system logic displayed in Fig. 2.6 outlines the reasoning process which would result in diagnosis of a learning disability or developmental learning disorder. Overachievement suggests that learning has been inordinately induced, rather than inhibited. Such inducement may be correlated with maladaptive social-emotional functioning. McDermott (1990) has noted that educators rarely assess for overachievement or consider the possibility of attendant social-emotional maladaption. M.MAC systematizes the analysis of achievement to assess *both* possibilities and thereby ensure that all possible diagnostic alternatives are considered.

FIG. 2.6.   M.MAC systems-actuarial logic for classification of academic functioning. From the microcomputer systems manual for McDermott Multidimensional Assessment of Children, P. A. McDermott and M. W. Watkins, 1985, 1987. New York: Psychological Corporation. Copyright (1985, 1987) by Psychological Corporation. Reproduced by permission. All rights reserved.

PROGRAM DESIGN LEVEL

SELECT SINGLE OR COMBINATION OF SKILLS DIMENSIONS

READING SKILLS DIMENSION

SELECTION OF CRITERION-REFERENCED SCREENING OR DIAGNOSTIC SCALES • BEHAVIORAL OBJECTIVES KEYED TO CRITERION- AND/OR LEVEL-BASED PERFORMANCE • AUTOMATIC INTEGRATION OF CRITERION PERFORMANCE LEVELS ACROSS SUBSKILL AREAS • 6 SUBSKILL AREAS • LETTER IDENTIFICATION • WORD RECOGNITION • PHONETICS: CONSONANT SOUNDS • PHONETICS: VOWEL SOUNDS • WORD COMPREHENSION • PASSAGE COMPREHENSION

MATHEMATICS SKILLS DIMENSION

SELECTION OF CRITERION-REFERENCED SCREENING OR DIAGNOSTIC SCALES • BEHAVIORAL OBJECTIVES KEYED TO CRITERION-BASED PERFORMANCE • AUTOMATIC INTEGRATION OF CRITERION PERFORMANCE ACROSS SUBSKILL AREAS • 11 SUBSKILL AREAS • NUMERATION: WHOLE NUMBERS AND DECIMALS • NUMERATION: GEOMETRY, SYMBOLS AND SCALES • NUMERATION: RATIONAL NUMBERS • ADDITION OPERATIONS • ADDITION APPLICATIONS • SUBTRACTION OPERATIONS • SUBTRACTION APPLICATIONS • MULTIPLICATION OPERATIONS • MULTIPLICATION APPLICATIONS • DIVISION OPERATIONS • DIVISION APPLICATIONS

LEARNING SKILLS DIMENSION

SELECTION OF CRITERION- AND NORM-REFERENCED SCALES • BEHAVIORAL OBJECTIVES KEYED TO CRITERION- AND NORM-BASED PERFORMANCE LEVELS • 19 SUBSKILL AREAS • TASK INITIATIVE • SELF-DIRECTION • ASSERTIVENESS • ACCEPTANCE OF ASSISTANCE • GROUP LEARNING • CONCENTRATION • ATTENTION • TASK RELEVANCE • TASK PLANNING • PROBLEM SOLVING • CONSEQUENTIAL THINKING • LEARNING FROM ERROR • FLEXIBILITY • TASK COMPLETION • TASK COMPLIANCE • RESPONSE DELAY • WORK HABITS AND ORGANIZATION • RECOGNITION OF THE TEACHER • RECOGNITION OF OTHER LEARNERS

ADAPTIVE SKILLS DIMENSION

SKILL AREAS KEYED TO AAMD BEHAVIORAL CLASSIFICATION SYSTEM • SELECTION OF PERFORMANCE OBJECTIVES BASED ON PARENT INTERVIEW AND/OR CHILD OBSERVATION • 17 SUBSKILL AREAS • SELF-HELP: EATING • SELF HELP: DRESSING • SELF HELP: TOILETING • SELF-HELP: HYGIENE AND GROOMING • SELF HELP: TRAVELING • SELF-HELP: MONEY MANAGING • COMMUNICATION: PREVERBAL • COMMUNICATION: VERBAL • COMMUNICATION: SYMBOL USE • SOCIALIZATION: PREGROUP ACTIVITY • SOCIALIZATION: GROUP ACTIVITY • SENSORY-MOTOR: PREWALKING • SENSORY-MOTOR: GROSS CO-ORDINATION • SENSORY-MOTOR: FINE COORDINATION • OCCUPATION: SIMPLE TASKS • OCCUPATION: COMPLEX TASKS • OCCUPATION: FORMAL WORK

INDIVIDUALIZED EDUCATIONAL PROGRAM

CHILD'S NAME/ID • AGE • SEX • EDUCATIONAL PLACEMENT • RECORD DATE • ASSESSMENT METHODS (SCALES, PARENT INTERVIEW, ETC.) • OPERATIONS MODE • LIST OF BEHAVIORAL PERFORMANCE OBJECTIVES FOR EACH SUBSKILL AREA • OPTIONAL REFERENCE CODES FOR COMPUTER-ASSISTED INSTRUCTION AND COMPUTER-MANAGED INSTRUCTION PROGRAMS KEYED TO SPECIFIC PERFORMANCE OBJECTIVES IN READING AND MATHEMATICS

TABLE 2.2
ASSESSMENT SCALES AND METHODS SUPPORTED BY THE MMAC
PROGRAM DESIGN DIMENSION

READING SKILLS
  Basic Achievement Skills Individual Screener-Reading
  Woodcock Reading Mastery Test
  Stanford Diagnostic Reading Test-Red Level
  Stanford Diagnostic Reading Test-Green Level
  Stanford Diagnostic Reading Test-Brown Level

MATHEMATICS SKILLS
  Basic Achievement Skills Individual Screener Math
  KeyMath Diagnostic Arithmetic Test
  Stanford Diagnostic Mathematics Test-Red Level
  Stanford Diagnostic Mathematics Test-Green Level
  Stanford Diagnostic Mathematics Test-Brown Level

LEARNING SKILLS
  Study of Children's Learning Styles
  Guide to the Child's Learning Style

ADAPTIVE SKILLS
  Parent Interview /.Observation of Child

Program Design

The classification of childhood normality and exceptionality is only one facet of the M.MAC system. Once exceptionality is evident, it is vital to focus upon what a child knows, through more specific second-stage assessments, and to determine what steps may be necessary to promote learning and development. The Program Design level serves this function.

As seen in Fig. 2.7, there are four major dimensions of educational assessment and programming: reading, mathematics, learning, and adaptive skills. Although educational treatment plans for a child are unlikely to involve all four dimensions, the psychologist may elect to utilize as many as deemed necessary. For each selected dimension, the data collection method is specified (i.e., tests, teacher observations, clinical observations, or parent interview) and obtained data are entered into the system for analysis and design of remedial programs. Available instruments and methods are displayed in Table 2.2.

As in classification, there are several overarching concepts which apply to all program design dimensions. Namely, the system embodies a basic skills orientation, is objective, utilizes performance-based objectives, sequences objectives hierarchically, designs individualized programs, and is versatile. It is impossible within the limitations of this chapter to describe all aspects of the program design dimension. However, detailed descriptions and applications are provided by Glutting (1986b), McDermott (1990), and McDermott and Watkins (1985, 1987).

FIG. 2.7. Program design-level organization and features. From the microcomputer systems manual for McDermott Multidimensional Assessment of Children, P. A. McDermott and M. W. Watkins, 1985, 1987. New York: Psychological Corporation. Copyright (1985, 1987) by Psychological Corporation. Reproduced by permission. All rights reserved.

Basic Skills Orientation.   Preference for a basic skills orientation reflects the logic that proficiency in certain basic skills, irrespective of exceptionality, is a fundamental prerequisite to successful school and social adjustment. Primary skills covered by the M.MAC system include: reading and using written language; understanding and applying mathematics concepts; using effective learning strategies; and being reasonably self-sufficient in such adaptive behaviors as personal care, communication, socialization, sensory-motor, and vocational functions.

Objectivity.   Educational programs covering vital basic skills must be objectively developed and based upon well-validated instruments intended for diagnostic educational programming. They must dispense with subjective opinions and unspecified criteria which have, unfortunately, been the norm (McDermott, 1990). The M.MAC system analyzes item responses, observed mastery levels, and other criterion-referenced performances of children and converts those observed performances into content-congruent basic skills objectives.

Performance-based Objectives.   Assessment should lead to objectives which are stated in behavioral or verifiable terms. This does not imply a "behavioral" theoretical orientation, but simply reflects the reality that behavioral objectives are universally understood, provide criteria for judging attainment, and are easy to explain to parents and students. Specialists will, of course, apply the system's behavioral objectives in accordance with their theoretical orientation and within the context of each child's unique needs.

Hierarchical Sequence of Objectives.   A comprehensive compilation of behavioral objectives which encompasses each primary basic skill area would be voluminous. Unstructured educational application of objectives is likely to be inefficient, if not ineffectual. When structured and aligned along educationally and psychologically meaningful dimensions, they can contribute to an orderly and effective educational program.

The M.MAC system contains 1,111 objectives distributed across 4 basic skill areas and 53 subskill areas. Within each subskill area, objectives are ordered hierarchically so that foundation skills precede other skills which are dependent or more difficult. Fig. 2.8 illustrates a representative selection by the M.MAC system from a hierarchical sequence of objectives within subskill areas in the mathematics domain. In areas where subskills are interdependent (e.g., paragraph comprehension skills rest upon word comprehension skills which, in turn, require certain letter identification and phonics skills, etc.), M.MAC objectives are integrated so that performance objectives selected in one subskill hierarchy do not outpace those in other hierarchies. This approach is compatible with conventional curricula and is particularly useful for building skills through step-by-step approximations.

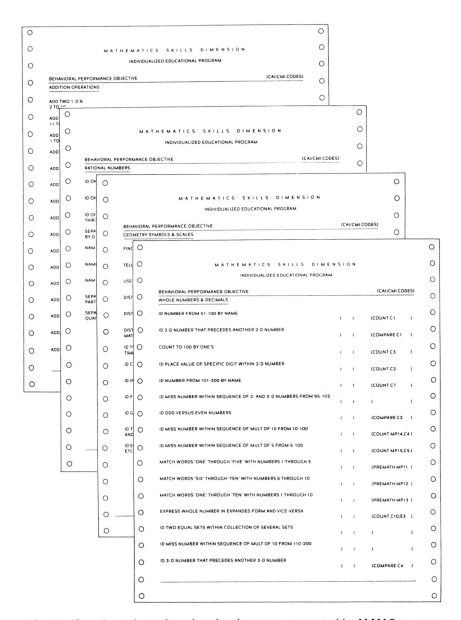

FIG. 2.8. Sample mathematics educational program generated by M.MAC program design level. From the microcomputer systems manual for McDermott Multidimensional Assessment of Children, P. A. McDermott and M. W. Watkins, 1985, 1987. New York: Psychological Corporation. Copyright (1985, 1987) by Psychological Corporation. Reproduced by permission. All rights reserved.

Individualization.   Individualized education programs are far too often oriented to the resources and needs of the school, teacher, or placement rather than to the needs of the child. As noted by McDermott (1990), this is not necessarily the fault of educators, but simply reflects the lack of resources necessary for production of truly individualized programs. M.MAC helps resolve this problem by applying systems-actuarial logic to educational program design; that is, by objectively analyzing a child's actual academic performance to guide a systematic selection of comprehensive skills hierarchies and thereby identify performance objectives directly related to the child's demonstrated educational needs.

Versatility.   As previously noted, current expert systems must utilize both actuarial and clinical methodologies to enhance their authority. The program design component also embodies such a felicitous combinatory approach. Even automated program development may, however, benefit from the interactive guidance of specialists with expertise and personal knowledge of a child's functioning. This added versatility is provided by two operational modes: Monitor and General.

The Monitor mode permits educational programs to be previewed and modified. It allows programs based upon measured criterion-referenced performance to be subsequently refined through professional judgment so as to best meet the unique needs of each child. Under the General mode, assessment moves directly from data input to data analysis to production of an educational program without preview or alteration of system-selected objectives.

Another aspect of versatility is represented in Fig. 2.8 under the "CAI/CMI CODES" heading. This column refers to computer-assisted instruction (CAI) and computer-managed instruction (CMI) resources which might assist children in achieving mastery of selected performance objectives (Kulik & Kulik, 1987; Kulik, Kulik, & Bangert–Drowns, 1985). CAI/CMI Codes are cross-referenced in the M.MAC manual to identify the title and publisher of specific software packages referenced by M.MAC. Thus, the computer can be used by the psychologist as an assessment tool and by the child as an instructional aid.

SUMMARY

Computerized psychological systems must be viewed in light of their scope and authority; that is, the breadth and verity of their underlying knowledge base. Most current psychological applications are relatively narrow in scope and derivative in application. Even so, some do promise improved efficiency, economy, and reliability. Automated psychological systems of broad scope continue to be rare. The M.MAC system is an exception. It applies a judicious combination of the salient aspects of actuarial and clinical reasoning, decision theory, and systems analysis to the psychoeducational assessment of children. The system contains almost 10,000 discrete units of actuarial data and its reasoning is guided by thousands of decision rules. Its authority is established through adherence to standards formulated by appropriate national professional organizations, and through reliance upon some 250 empirical investigations. The M.MAC is a comprehensive, objective, reliable, and versatile system which enhances the validity of psychoeducational diagnosis. As such, it may serve as a model for future developments in computerized psychological expert systems.

REFERENCES

Adams, K. M., & Heaton, R. K. (1985). Automated interpretation of neuropsychological test data. *Journal of Consulting and Clinical Psychology, 53*, 790–802.

Adams, K. M., Kvale, V. I., & Keegan, J. F. (1984). Performance of three automated systems for neuropsychological interpretation based on two representational tasks. *Journal of Clinical Neuropsychology, 6*, 413–431.

Algozzine, B., & Ysseldyke, J. E. (1981). Special education services for normal children: Better safe than sorry? *Exceptional Children, 48*, 238–243.

American Psychological Association. (1986). *Guidelines for computer-based tests and interpretations*. Washington, DC: Author.

American Psychiatric Association. (1987). *Diagnostic and statistical manual of mental disorders* (3rd Ed. revised). Washington, DC: Author.

Andolina, M. (1982). Reading tests: Traditional vs. computerized. *Classroom Computer News, 2*, 39–40.

Arkes, H. R. (1981). Impediments to accurate clinical judgment and possible ways to minimize their impact. *Journal of Consulting and Clinical Psychology, 3*, 323–330.

Beaumont, J. G. (1981). Microcomputer-aided assessment using standard psychometric procedures. *Behavior Research Methods & Instrumentation, 13*, 430–433.

Bhatnagar, R. K., & Kanal, L. N. (1986, October). *Mechanizing decision making with uncertain information*. Paper presented at the Expert Systems in Government Symposium, McLean, VA.

Brantley, J. C. (1986, April). *Decision rule comparisons among eight computer programs for WISC-R profile analysis*. Paper presented at a meeting of the National Association of School Psychologists, Hollywood, FL.

Broverman, L. K., Broverman, D. M., Clarkson, F. E., Rosenkrantz, P. S., & Vogel, S. R. (1970). Sex-role stereotypes and clinical judgments of mental health. *Journal of Consulting and Clinical Psychology, 34*, 1–7.

Buchanan, B. G. (1985). *Expert systems: Working systems and the research literature* (Report No. KSL–85–37). Stanford, CA: Department of Computer Science, Stanford University.

Butcher, J. N. (1987). Computerized clinical and personality assessment using the MMPI. In J. N. Butcher (Ed.), *Computerized psychological assessment* (pp. 161–197). New York: Basic Books.

Campbell, D. P. (1968). The Strong Vocational Interest Blank: 1927–1967. In P. McReynolds (Ed.), *Advances in psychological assessment*. Palo Alto, CA: Science and Behavior Books.

Cantwell, D. P., Russell, A. T., Mattison, R., & Will, L. (1979). A comparison of DSM–II and DSM–III in the diagnosis of childhood psychiatric disorders. *Archives of General Psychiatry, 36*, 1208–1213.

Chadwick, M., & Hannah, J. (1987). *Expert systems for microcomputers*. Blue Ridge Summit, PA: Tab Books.

Colby, K. M., & Parkison, R. (1985). Linguistic conceptual-patterns and key-idea profiles as a new kind of property for a taxonomy of neurotic patients. *Computers in Human Behavior, 1,* 181–194.

Cromwell, R. L., Blashfield, R. K., & Strauss, J. S. (1975). Criteria for classification systems. In N. Hobbs (Ed.), *Issues in the classification of children* (Vol. 1, pp. 4–25). San Francisco: Jossey–Bass.

Dailey, C. (1971). *Assessment of lives.* San Francisco: Jossey–Bass.

Davis, F. B. (1959). Interpretation of differences among average and individual test scores. *Journal of Educational Psychology, 50,* 162–170.

DeMita, M. A., Johnson, J. H., & Hansen, K. E. (1981). The validity of a computerized visual searching task as an indicator of brain damage. *Behavior Research Methods & Instrumentation, 13,* 592–594.

Deupree, C. (1985, Summer). Artificial intelligence and the expert system. *CTASP Newsletter,* pp. 3–5.

DiNardo, P. A. (1975). Social class and diagnostic suggestion as variables in clinical judgment. *Journal of Consulting and Clinical Psychology, 43,* 363–368.

Eddy, D. M., & Clanton, C. H. (1982). The art of diagnosis: Solving the clinicopathological exercise. *New England Journal of Medicine, 306,* 1263–1267.

Eller, B. F., Kaufman, A. S., & McLean, J. E. (1986). Computer-based assessment of cognitive abilities: Current status/future directions. *Journal of Educational Technology Systems, 15,* 137–147.

Elwood, D. J. (1972). Validity of an automated measure of intelligence in borderline retarded subjects. *American Journal of Mental Deficiency, 7,* 90–94.

Epps, S., Ysseldyke, J. E., & McGue, M. (1984). "I know one when I see one"—Differentiating LD and non-LD students. *Learning Disability Quarterly, 7,* 89–101.

Erdman, H. P., Greist, J. H., Klein, M. H., Jefferson, J. W., & Getto, C. (1981). The computer psychiatrist: How far have we come? Where are we heading? How far dare we go? *Behavior Research Methods & Instrumentation, 13,* 393–398.

Exner, J. E. (1987). Computer assistance in Rorschach interpretation. In J. N. Butcher (Ed.), *Computerized psychological assessment* (pp. 218–235). New York: Basic Books.

Fowler, R. D. (1985). Landmarks in computer-assisted psychological assessment. *Journal of Consulting and Clinical Psychology, 53,* 748–759.

Franks, D. J. (1971). Ethnic and social status characteristics of children in E.M.R. and L.D. classes. *Exceptional Children, 34,* 327–338.

Freeman, M. (1971). A reliability study of psychiatric diagnosis in childhood and adolescence. *Journal of Child Psychology and Psychiatry, 12,* 43–54.

Glasser, A. J., & Zimmerman, I. (1967). *Clinical interpretation of the Wechsler Intelligence Scale for Children.* New York: Grune & Stratton.

Glutting, J. J. (1986a). The McDermott Multidimensional Assessment of Children: Applications to the classification of childhood exceptionality. *Journal of Learning Disabilities, 19,* 331–335.

Glutting, J. J. (1986b). The McDermott Multidimensional Assessment of Children: Contribution to the development of individualized education programs. *Journal of Special Education, 20,* 431–445.

Glutting, J. J., McDermott, P. A., & Stanley, J. C. (1987). Resolving differences among methods of establishing confidence limits for test scores. *Educational and Psychological Measurement, 47,* 607–614.

Gonsalves, P. (1987). Interview: Trip Hawkins, President, Electronic Arts. *CD-I News, 1,* 6–8.

Greene, R. L., Martin, P. W., Bennett, S. R., & Shaw, J. A. (1981). A computerized scoring system for the Personality Inventory for Children. *Educational and Psychological Measurement, 41,* 233–235.

Grossman, H. J. (1977). *Manual on terminology and classification in mental retardation* (rev. ed.). Washington, DC: American Association on Mental Deficiency.

Grossman, H. J. (1983). *Classification in mental retardation.* Washington, DC: American Association on Mental Deficiency.

Hale, R. L., & McDermott, P. A. (1984). Pattern analysis of an actuarial strategy for computerized diagnosis of childhood exceptionality. *Journal of Learning Disabilities, 17,* 30–37.

Harris, W. G., Niedner, D., Feldman, C., Fink, A., & Johnston, J. (1981). An on-line interpretive Rorschach approach: Using Exner's comprehensive system. *Behavior Research Methods and Instrumentation, 13,* 588–591.

Hasselbring, T. S., & Crossland, C. L. (1981). Using microcomputers for diagnosing spelling problems in learning-handicapped children. *Educational Technology, 21,* 37–39.

Hedl, J. J., O'Neil, H. F., & Hansen, D. N. (1973). Affective reactions toward computer-based intelligence testing. *Journal of Consulting and Clinical Psychology, 40,* 217–222.

Hofer, P. J., & Green, B. F. (1985). The challenge of competence and creativity in computerized psychological testing. *Journal of Counseling and Clinical Psychology, 53,* 826–838.

Honaker, L. M., Hector, V. S., & Harrell, T. H. (1986). Perceived validity of computer- versus clinician-generated MMPI reports. *Computers in Human Behavior, 2,* 77–83.

Jackson, D. N. (1985). Computer-based personality testing. *Computers in Human Behavior, 1,* 255–264.

Johnson, D. L., Willis, J., & Danley, W. (1982). A comparison of traditional and computer-based methods of teaching students to administer individual intelligence tests. *AEDS Journal, 16,* 56–64.

Jones, M. B., Dunlop, W. P., & Bilodeau, I. M. (1987). Comparison of video game and conventional test performance. *Simulation & Games, 17,* 435–446.

Kahneman, D., & Tversky, A. (1982). The psychology of preferences. *Scientific American, 246,* 160–173.

Katz, L., & Dalby, S. (1981). Computer and manual administration of the Eysenck Personality Inventory. *Journal of Clinical Psychology, 37,* 586–588.

Kavale, K. A., & Furness, S. R. (1984). A meta-analysis of the validity of Wechsler scale profiles and recategorizations: Patterns or parodies? *Learning Disability Quarterly, 2,* 136–156.

Kirk, S. A., & Bateman, B. (1962). Diagnosis and remediation of learning disabilities. *Exceptional Children, 29,* 73–76.

Klinge, V., & Rodziewicz, T. (1976). Automated and manual intelligence testing of the Peabody Picture Vocabulary Test on a psychiatric adolescent population. *International Journal of Man-Machine Studies, 8,* 243–246.

Koran, L. M. (1975). The reliability of clinical methods, data and judgments. *New England Journal of Medicine, 293,* 695–701.

Kramer, J. J., Henning–Stout, M., Ullman, D. P., & Schellenberg, R. P. (1987). The viability of scatter analysis on the WISC–R and the SBIS: Examining a vestige. *Journal of Psychoeducational Assessment, 5,* 37–47.

Krug, S. E. (1987). Microtrends: An orientation to computerized assessment. In J. N. Butcher (Ed.), *Computerized psychological assessment* (pp. 15–25). New York: Basic Books.

Krutch, J. (1986). *Experiments in artificial intelligence for microcomputers.* Indianapolis: Howard W. Sams.

Kulik, J. A., & Kulik, C. C. (1987). Review of recent literature on computer-based instruction. *Contemporary Educational Psychology, 12,* 222–230.

Kulik, J. A., Kulik, C. C., & Bangert–Drowns, R. L. (1985). Effectiveness of computer-based education in elementary schools. *Computers in Human Behavior, 1,* 59–74.

Lachar, D. (1984). *Multidimensional description of child personality: A manual for the Personality Inventory for Children.* Los Angeles: Western Psychological Services.

Lueger, R. J., & Petzel, T. P. (1979). Illusory correlation in clinical judgment: Effects of amount of information to be processed. *Journal of Consulting and Clinical Psychology, 47,* 1120–1121.

Lukin, M. E., Dowd, E. T., Plake, B. S., & Kraft, R. G. (1985). Comparing computerized versus traditional psychological assessment. *Computers in Human Behavior, 1,* 49–58.

Lushene, R. E., O'Neil, H. F., & Dunn, T. (1974). Equivalent validity of a completely computerized MMPI. *Journal of Personality Assessment, 38*, 353–361.

Matarazzo, J. D. (1983). Computerized psychological testing. *Science, 221*, 323.

Matarazzo, J. D. (1985). Clinical psychological test interpretations by computer: Hardware outpaces software. *Computers in Human Behavior, 1*, 235–253.

Matarazzo, J. D. (1986). Computerized clinical psychological test interpretations: Unvalidated plus all mean and no sigma. *American Psychologist, 41*, 14–24.

McDermott, P. A. (1980a). A computerized system for the classification of developmental, learning, and adjustment disorders in school children. *Educational and Psychological Measurement, 40*, 761–768.

McDermott, P. A. (1980b). Congruence and typology of diagnoses in school psychology: An empirical study. *Psychology in the Schools, 17*, 12–24.

McDermott, P. A. (1980c). A systems-actuarial method for the differential diagnosis of handicapped children. *Journal of Special Education, 14*, 7–22.

McDermott, P. A. (1981). Sources of error in the psychoeducational diagnosis of children. *Journal of School Psychology, 19*, 31–44.

McDermott, P. A. (1982). Actuarial assessment systems for the grouping and classification of schoolchildren. In C. R. Reynolds & T. B. Gutkin (Eds.), *The handbook of school psychology* (pp. 243–272). New York: Wiley.

McDermott, P. A. (1986). The observation and classification of exceptional child behavior. In R. T. Brown & C. R. Reynolds (Eds.), *Psychological perspectives on childhood exceptionality: A handbook* (pp. 136–180). New York: Wiley–Interscience.

McDermott, P. A. (1990). Applied systems-actuarial assessment. In T. B. Gutkin & C. R. Reynolds (Eds.), *The handbook of school psychology* (2nd ed.). New York: Wiley.

McDermott, P. A., & Hale, R. L. (1982). Validation of a systems-actuarial computer process for multidimensional classification of child psychopathology. *Journal of Clinical Psychology, 38*, 477–486.

McDermott, P. A., & Watkins, M. W. (1985). *McDermott Multidimensional Assessment of Children: 1985 Apple II version* [Computer program]. New York: Psychological Corporation.

McDermott, P. A., & Watkins, M. W. (1987). *McDermott Multidimensional Assessment of Children: 1987 IBM version* [Computer program]. New York: Psychological Corporation.

McKinley, R. L., & Reckase, M. D. (1980). Computer applications to ability testing. *AEDS Journal, 13*, 193–203.

Meehl, P. E. (1954). *Clinical versus statistical prediction*. Minneapolis: University of Minnesota Press.

Moreland, K. L. (1985). Computer-assisted psychological assessment in 1986: A practical guide. *Computers in Human Behavior, 1*, 221–233.

Moreland, K. L. (1987). Computerized psychological assessment: What's available. In J. N. Butcher (Ed.), *Computerized psychological assessment* (pp. 26–49). New York: Basic Books.

Nathan, P. E. (1967). *Cues, decisions, and diagnoses: A systems-analytic approach to the diagnosis of psychopathology*. New York: Academic Press.

Nolen, P., & Spencer, M. (1986). School psychology and computerized data handling systems: A confrontation. *Computers in the Schools, 2*, 137–143.

Oosterhof, A. C., & Salisbury, D. F. (1985). Some measurement and instruction related considerations regarding computer-assisted testing. *Educational Measurement: Issues and Practice, 4*, 19–23.

Piotrowski, Z. A. (1964). Digital-computer interpretation of ink-blot test data. *Psychiatric Quarterly, 38*, 1–26.

Quay, H. C. (1986). Classification. In H. C. Quay & J. S. Werry (Eds.), *Psychopathological disorders of childhood* (3rd ed., pp. 1–34). New York: Wiley.

Reynolds, C. R. (1985). Critical measurement issues in learning disabilities. *Journal of Special education, 18,* 451–475.

Roid, G. H. (1986). Computer-based test interpretation: The potential of quantitative methods of test interpretation. *Computers in Human Behavior, 1,* 207–219.

Rozensky, R. H., Honor, L. F., Rasinski, K., Tovian, S. M., & Herz, G. I. (1986). Paper-and-pencil versus computer-administered MMPIs: A comparison of patients' attitudes. *Computers in Human Behavior, 2,* 111–116.

Sampson, J. P. (1983). Computer-assisted testing and assessment: Current status and implications for the future. *Management and Evaluation in Guidance, 15,* 293–298.

Sands, W. A., & Gade, P. A. (1983). An application of computerized adaptive testing in U. S. Army recruiting. *Journal of Computer-Based Instruction, 10,* 87–89.

Schoolman, H. M., & Bernstein, L. M. (1978). Computer use in diagnosis, prognosis, and therapy. *Science, 200,* 926–931.

Scissons, E. H. (1976). Computer administration of the California Psychological Inventory. *Measurement and Evaluation in Guidance, 9,* 22–25.

Silverstein, A. B. (1981a). Reliability and abnormality of test score differences. *Journal of Clinical Psychology, 37,* 392–394.

Silverstein, A. B. (1981b). Verbal-Performance IQ discrepancies on the WISC–R: One more time. *Journal of Consulting and Clinical Psychology, 49,* 465–466.

Silverstein, A. B. (1982). Pattern analysis as simultaneous statistical inference. *Journal of Consulting and Clinical Psychology, 50,* 234–240.

Skinner, H. A., & Allen, B. A. (1983). Does the computer make a difference? Computerized versus face-to-face versus self-report assessment of alcohol, drug, and tobacco use. *Journal of Consulting and Clinical Psychology, 51,* 267–275.

Space, L. G. (1981). The computer as psychometrician. *Behavior Research Methods & Instrumentation, 13,* 595–606.

Spitzer, R. L., Endicott, J., Cohen, J., & Fleiss, J. L. (1974). Constraints on the validity of computer diagnosis. *Archives of General Psychiatry, 31,* 197–203.

Spitzer, R. L., & Fleiss, J. L. (1974). A re-analysis of the reliability of psychiatric diagnosis. *British Journal of Psychiatry, 125,* 341–347.

Stanley, J. C. (1971). Reliability. In R. L. Thorndike (Ed.), *Educational measurement* (2nd ed., pp. 356–442). Washington, DC: American Council on Education.

Stein, S. J. (1987). Computer-assisted diagnosis for children and adolescents. In J. N. Butcher (Ed.), *Computerized psychological assessment* (pp. 145–160). New York: Basic Books.

Szolovits, P., & Pauker, S. G. (1978). Categorical and probabilistic reasoning in medical diagnosis. *Artificial Intelligence, 11,* 115–144.

Thorndike, R. L. (1963). *The concepts of over- and under-achievement.* New York: Teachers College Press.

University of Minnesota Press. (1982). *User's guide for the Minnesota Report.* Minneapolis: National Computer Systems.

Visonhaler, J. F., Weinshank, A. B., Wagner, C. C., & Polin, R. M. (1983). Diagnosing children with educational problems; Characteristics of reading and learning disabilities specialists, and classroom teachers. *Reading Research Quarterly, 18,* 134–164.

Waterman, D. A. (1986). *A guide to expert systems.* Reading, MA: Addison–Wesley.

Watkins, M. W., & Kush, J. (1988). Assessment of academic skills of learning disabled students with classroom microcomputers. *School Psychology Review, 17,* 79–86.

Webb, N. M., Herman, J. L., & Cabello, B. (1986). Diagnosing students' errors from their response selections in language arts. *Journal of Educational Measurement, 23,* 163–170.

Weiss, D. J. (1985). Adaptive testing by computer. *Journal of Consulting and Clinical Psychology, 53,* 774–789.

Weiss, D. J., & Vale, C. D. (1987). Computerized adaptive testing for measuring abilities and other psychological variables. In J. N. Butcher (Ed.), *Computerized psychological assessment* (pp. 325–343). New York: Basic Books.

White, D. M., Clements, C. B., & Fowler, R. D. (1985). A comparison of computer administration with standard administration of the MMPI. *Computers in Human Behavior, 1,* 153–162.

Wikoff, R. L. (1978). Correlational and factor analysis of the Peabody Individual Achievement Test and WISC–R. *Journal of Consulting and Clinical Psychology, 46,* 322–325.

Wilson, F. R., Genco, K. T., & Yager, G. G. (1986). Assessing the equivalence of paper-and-pencil vs. computerized tests: Demonstration of a promising methodology. *Computers in Human Behavior, 1,* 265–275.

Wise, S. L., & Wise, L. A. (1987). Comparison of computer-administered and paper-administered achievement tests with elementary school children. *Computers in Human Behavior, 3,* 15–20.

World Health Organization. (1978). *Ninth revision of the International Classification of Diseases.* Geneva: Author.

3 Assessment of Validity in Computer-Based Test Interpretations

Kevin L. Moreland
NCS Professional Assessment Services, Minneapolis

The use of computers to interpret psychological tests is a "hot" topic, both within psychology and without. It is hot in the sense of giving rise to an increasing number of books and articles (e.g., Butcher, 1985, 1987; Eyde, 1987; Krug, 1987). It is hot in the sense of giving rise to an ever-increasing number of business enterprises (compare any recent *APA Monitor* with an issue from 1981). It is hot in the sense of capturing the attention of the news media (e.g., Petterson, 1983). And it is hot in the sense of giving rise to increasing controversy within psychology itself. In a *Science* editorial Matarazzo (1983) expressed concern lest computer-based test interpretations (CBTIs) fall into the hands of unqualified users, his bottom line being: "Until more research establishes that the validity of application of these computer products by a health practitioner is not dependent on the practitioner's experience and training in psychometric science, such automated consultations should be restricted to . . . qualified user groups." Matarazzo (1985, 1986) has continued to write in that same vein, causing others to take up the cudgels to defend CBTI (Ben–Porath & Butcher, 1986; Fowler & Butcher, 1986; Murphy, 1987). Lanyon (1984) in his chapter on personality assessment in the *Annual Review of Psychology,* indicated that he was concerned by the proliferation of CBTI systems: "There is a real danger that the few satisfactory services will be squeezed out by the many unsatisfactory ones, since the consumer professionals are generally unable to discriminate among them. . . ." and ". . . lack of demonstrated program validity has now become the norm" (p. 690). Finally the Subcommittee on Tests and Assessment of the American Psychological Association (APA) Committee on Professional Standards and the APA Committee on Psychological Tests and Assessment have developed standards for the area (American Psychological Association, 1986). I published an article describing attempts to establish the validity of CBTIs and made some suggestions regarding the shape future attempts might take (Moreland, 1985). The heat generated by the debate over CBTI seems not to have dissipated; however, some light seems to have been shed on the field since I was writing in 1984. In view of all this, a revision and expansion of my earlier efforts seems timely.

SOME HISTORY

The use of machines to process psychological test data is not a recent innovation (Fowler, 1985). A progression from hand scoring materials through a variety of mechanical and electronic "scoring machines" to the digital computer, has freed successive generations of beleaguered secretaries and graduate students from laborious hand scoring of objective tests. The first information concerning scoring machines for the Strong Vocational Interest Blank (SVIB) appeared in 1930 (Campbell, 1971). These initial machines were very cumbersome, involving the use of 1,260 Hollerith cards to score each protocol. In 1946, Elmer Hankes, a Minneapolis engineer, built the analogue computer that was the first automatic scoring and profiling machine for the SVIB (Campbell, 1971). A year later, he adapted the same technology to the scoring of the Minnesota Multiphasic Personality Inventory (MMPI) (Dahlstrom, Welsh, & Dahlstrom, 1972). In the mid 1950s, E. F. Lindquist's Measurement Research Center in Iowa City began to use optical (answer sheet) scanning devices instead of card-based scoring equipment. In 1962, National Computer Systems linked an optical scanner with a digital computer and began scoring both the SVIB and the MMPI (Campbell, 1971; Dahlstrom et al., 1972). Most automated test scoring still employs optical scanning/digital computer technology and the number and types of tests scored by this method have grown exponentially during the last three decades. Though automated scoring is most easily accomplished for objective tests with a limited number of response alternatives, sophisticated computer programs have also been developed to score the narrative responses elicited by projective techniques (e.g., Gorham, 1967). Prior to the advent of these programs, extensive training, if not professional expertise, was required to score projective tests. Similar programs have also been developed to evaluate other types of complex verbal productions (e.g., Tucker & Rosenberg, 1980).

In addition to keeping nerves from becoming frayed, automated scoring frees psychologists to spend more time in other functions, such as psychotherapy, where computer technology is not so advanced (see, however, Colby, 1980). It also enables more individuals to undergo psychological assessment. Finally, though not completely immune from the slings and arrows of human imperfections (e.g., Fowler & Coyle, 1968; Grayson & Backer, 1972; Weigel & Phillips, 1967), computer scoring appears to be more reliable than that done solely by humans (Greene, 1980, pp. 25–26; Klett, Schaefer, & Plemel, 1985). A computer, once correctly programmed, will apply scoring rules with slavish consistency, whereas fatigue and other human frailties may render the psychologist, graduate student, or secretary inconsistent in the application of even the most objective scoring rules (Kleinmuntz, 1969).

In the late 1950s, a group of psychologists and psychiatrists decided that similar advantages might accrue if tests were interpreted by computer. Thus the first CBTI system was developed at the Mayo Clinic in Rochester, Minnesota (Rome, Mataya, Pearson, Swenson, & Brannick, 1965; Pearson, Swenson, Rome, Mataya, & Brannick, 1965). The MMPI was administered on special IBM cards that could be marked by the patient and read into the computer by a scanner. The computer then scored the MMPI and printed a series of descriptive statements from among a library of 62 statements, most of which were associated with elevations on single MMPI scales. Soon after the Mayo system was reported in the literature the first CBTI system to receive widespread professional use was developed by Fowler (1966) at the University of Alabama. In 1965, the Roche Psychiatric Service Institute (RPSI), established by Roche Laboratories to make the Fowler system commercially available to psychologists and psychiatrists, initiated the first national mail-in MMPI CBTI service. During the 17 years RPSI operated, approximately one-fourth of the eligible psychiatrists and psychologists in the United States used the service.

The Behaviordyne system (Finney, 1966) and Caldwell Report (Caldwell, 1970) have received wide use in the United States, and are still available. Later MMPI interpretation systems were developed by Lachar (1974b) and Butcher (University of Minnesota, 1982, 1984). Other prominent CBTI systems which have been marketed commercially in the United States interpret the 16 Personality Factor Questionnaire (Karson & O'Dell, 1975, 1987); the Rorschach (Exner, 1987); the Personality Inventory for Children (Lachar, 1987); and the Millon instruments: the Millon Multiaxial Clinical Inventory, Millon Behavioral Health Inventory, and Millon Adolescent Personality Inventory (National Computer Systems, 1989), among others.

TYPES OF CBTI SYSTEMS

CBTI systems can be usefully characterized along two dimensions, the amount of information they provide and the method used to develop them.

Information Provided by CBTIs

Descriptive reports may be distinguished from other types of CBTIs by two factors: Each scale on the instrument is interpreted without reference to the other, scale by scale, and comments on any one scale are usually quite cryptic. These interpretations often involve no more than an adverb modifying the adjectival form of the scale name. Such an interpretation of a high score on an anxiety scale might, for example, read: "Mr. Jones reports that he is very anxious." Thus the interpretive comments directly reflect empirical data. The interpretive statements are as valid as the scales themselves. At first blush, this kind of report may seem so simple minded as to be unhelpful. Not so. This type of report can be especially helpful when a test has a large number of scales or when a large number of tests need to be interpreted in a short period of time. They allow the practitioner to identify quickly and easily the most deviant scales. This kind of report is most helpful if an instrument contains scales that are reported in terms of different types of standard scores (e.g., Ripley & Ripley, 1979) or different normative samples (e.g., Hansen, 1987). The MMPI report developed at the Mayo Clinic was the first report of this type.

Screening reports, like descriptive reports, are cryptic. They are distinguished from descriptive reports in that relationships among scales are usually considered in the interpretation and the interpretive comments are not usually couched in terms of a single scale name. The Minnesota Personnel Screening Report for the MMPI (University of Minnesota, 1984) is a screening report in this sense. The main body of that report is very cryptic—five 6-point rating scales. None of the rating scales corresponds directly to an MMPI scale, however. In fact, the rating on each of the five scales is determined by the configuration of a number of MMPI scales. The rules governing the "Content Themes" presented in that report are also complex. The comment that the client "may keep problems to himself too much" results from consideration of the following set of rules:

L and K are greater than F and
F is less than $55T$ and
D, Pa, Pt, and Sc are less than $65T$ and
    Hy is greater than $69T$ or
    $Hy2$ is greater than $63T$ or
    Hy is greater than $64T$, and $Hy1$ or $Hy5$ is greater than $59T$ or
    R is greater than $59T$ or
    $D5$ is greater than $59T$

Screening reports are most helpful in situations where the same decision can be reached by multiple paths. Take the example of screening commercial pilots for emotional fitness. A screening report such as the Minnesota Report may deem a candidate's emotional fitness "suspect" if he or she: (1) seems to be a thrill-seeking individual; (2) is so obsessive that he or she is unlikely to respond promptly to in-flight emergencies; or (3) may have a drinking problem. Because of this multifaceted approach to the assessment problem, such reports are also likely to be most helpful when they are truly used for screening rather than for making final decisions. They are too deliberately cryptic to be used for the latter purpose. Further investigation, triggered by a screening report, may lead one to discover that a suspect candidate is a recovered alcoholic who has been dry for 10 years.

Like descriptive reports, the output of screening reports is limited. However, the validation of screening reports is not simple and straightforward. As has been illustrated, the simple output may be generated by extensive, complex sets of rules, each of which must be validated.

Dahlstrom et al. (1972) contrasted *consultative reports* for the MMPI to screening reports in the following fashion: "The intent [of consultative reports] is to provide a more detailed analysis of the test data in professional language appropriate to communication between colleagues" (p. 313). In other words, consultative reports are designed to mimic as closely as possible the reports generated every day by human test interpreters. Well-developed reports of this type are characterized by the smoothly flowing prose and detailed exploitation of the data that would be expected from an expert human consultant. Indeed, the chief advantage of these reports is that they can provide busy practitioners with a consultation from someone who has spent years studying and using the instrument in question—an expert to whom the average practitioner would not ordinarily have access. Fowler's system for the MMPI produced the first CBTIs of this type. It is these types of reports that come to most minds upon hearing the phrase "computer-based test interpretations." It is these types of reports that will be the subject of most of this chapter.

How CBTIs Are Developed

In 1956, Paul Meehl called for a good "cookbook" for test interpretation. He was advocating the actuarial approach to prediction and description defined by Sines (1966) as "the empirical determination of the regularities that may exist between specified psychological test data and equally clearly specified socially, clinically, or theoretically significant non-test characteristics of the persons tested" (p. 135). This approach to CBTI development can best be illustrated through the example of one such system.

Unlike the MMPI and most other popular psychological tests, which were developed prior to the computer age, Lachar's CBTI system for the Personality Inventory for Children (PIC) was developed without a considerable "clinical lore" concerning the performance of the PIC scales (Lachar, 1987). (Fowler [1986] considers the concurrent development of test and interpretive system an "ideal" strategy, test development efforts enriching the evolving interpretation system.)

Efforts to compile a data base that would allow the development of empirically supported interpretive guidelines were initiated before the PIC was published. Criterion data collection forms (see Lachar & Gdowski, 1979, Appendix A) were accepted by the staff of an active teaching service as performing clinically meaningful functions. An application form gathered presenting complaints, developmental history, and facts concerning pregnancy and birth. A form mailed to the child's school recorded teacher observations, estimates of achievement, and judgments as to the etiology of observed problems as well as suggested solutions. A final form was completed by the psychiatry resident or psychology intern who conducted the initial evaluation of the child or adolescent and parents. The latter form allowed the collection of dichotomous ratings (present/absent) of descriptors most of which could be arrayed under the following headings: affect, cognitive functioning, interpersonal relations, physical development and health, family relations, and parent description. Psychiatric diagnoses and ideal treatment recommendations were also recorded. Collection of data using these three forms resulted in an actuarial analysis of the PIC scores of 431 children and adolescents (Lachar & Gdowski, 1979).

Development of Lachar's CBTI system for the PIC first focused on the correlates of each scale on the basic PIC profile (Lachar, 1982; Lachar & Gdowski, 1979). The initial goal was to construct an interpretive system similar to the Mayo Clinic MMPI system (see Marks & Seeman, 1963, Appendixes E & F), in which each scale is individually interpreted. The individual scale approach resulted in an interpretation for every PIC profile, while actuarial interpretive systems based on the total profile configuration have proven, in the case of the MMPI, to be of limited value because a significant number of profiles usually remain unclassified.

The actuarial data base that provided the interpretive paragraphs and paragraph assignment to scores was generated in two phases. In the first phase, the 322 descriptive variables from the parent, teacher, and clinician forms were correlated with each of 20 profile scales to develop scale correlates. In the second phase, each identified correlate was studied to determine the relationship between the correlate and PIC scale T-score ranges. That is, correlate frequency was tabulated within a number of contiguous T-score ranges, usually 10 points in width. The goal of this process was to identify appropriate T-score ranges to which a given correlate could be applied, as well as to obtain an estimate of the frequency of each correlate within the T-score ranges. Rules were established to lead to correlate classification rates similar to their base rates within the study sample. A similar analysis determined frequent patterns of elevated T-score ranges and allowed the development of narrative paragraphs that reflected the elevation of two or more profile scales. Those efforts produced interpretive correlates like those in Table 3.1. Those correlates form the basis of the CBTI system for the PIC sold by Western Psychological Services (Western Psychological Services, 1984). It is easy to see that this system conforms with Sines's (1966) definition of an actuarial system. It is also easy to understand Meehl's

TABLE 3.1
Actuarial Correlates of the Personality Inventory for Children Delinquency Rate

Descriptor [1]	Correlations [2]	Base Rate	T-Score Ranges								Decision Rule	Classification Rate
			30-59	60-69	70-79	80-89	90-99	100-109	110-119	>120		
Impulsive Behavior	.25, 39	68[3]	40	57	61	72	76	72	84	100	>79T	79%
Temper Tantrums	.27, .25	43	18	42	40	38	44	63	64	69	> 99T	66%
Involved with Police	.44, .49	17	0	4	6	10	21	19	58	63	(< 60T) > 109T	(47%) 15%
Dislikes School	.18, .38	39	28	28	28	30	48	55	63	70	> 89T	57%
Mother Inconsistent in Setting Limits	.26, .3	59	27	45	61	59	64	82	89	67	(> 99T) < 60T	(79%) 63%

Adapted from Lachar and Gdowski (179).
[1] Clinician ratings.
[2] Ns = 215 and 216, respectively.
[3] Percentage of clients rated as displaying the characteristics.

(1956) enthusiasm for the actuarial approach to test interpretation: the interpretations are, ipso facto, valid within known limits.[1]

Combination of automated scoring and automated, actuarial interpretation would seem to be a marriage made in Assessment Heaven. Unfortunately, this relationship remains in the courtship stage. In spite of the fact that this is the way CBTI systems *should* be developed, only two such CBTI systems are commercially available, that for the PIC and one for the Marital Satisfaction Inventory (Western Psychological Services, 1984). After Meehl published his want ad there were several major attempts to produce actuarial cookbooks for the MMPI (Drake & Oetting, 1959; Gilberstadt & Duker, 1965; Gynther, Altman, & Sletten, 1973; Marks & Seeman, 1963; Marks, Seeman, & Haller, 1974). These herculean efforts have fared poorly outside the settings in which they were developed. Application of the complex profile classification rules necessary for actuarial interpretation causes the bulk of the tests to go unclassified (e.g., Briggs, Taylor, & Tellegen, 1966; Cone, 1966). Even when the cookbooks published by Marks and Seeman, and by Gilberstadt and Duker have been

---

[1]Generalizability is the most pressing question to be answered about actuarial CBTI systems. That is, are there extraneous factors that were not considered in the development of the actuarial CBTI system (e.g., setting) that affect its validity.

combined, the majority of tests have failed to find an interpretive niche (e.g., Payne & Wiggins, 1968). Although ignoring some of the classification rules allowed a greater number of tests to be classified, Payne and Wiggins still could not classify all of their sample. That is to say nothing of the decrement in validity that has been shown to occur when the actuarial correlates are generalized to populations differing in base rates of psychopathology, demographic characteristics, and other important factors (cf. Fowler & Athey, 1971; Gynther & Brilliant, 1968; Palmer, 1971). This state of affairs led some psychologists who were determined to exploit the advantages of automated test interpretation, such as Fowler, to advocate the "automated clinician . . . until the actuary comes" (1969, pp. 109–110).

The essential difference between the automated actuarial and automated clinical approaches is that the former method assigns interpretive statements on the basis of their statistical association with test data, while statements chosen by the latter approach are a function of human decision making. The psychologist who devises the statements and assignment rules in the automated clinical approach typically makes use of available actuarial data but, as suggested by the fate of the actuarial cookbooks discussed herein, is sometimes forced to rely on his or her practical experience in order to ensure that all tests are interpreted (Fowler, 1969). Fowler assumed that even though practical experience must sometimes be resorted to, the psychologist developing the interpretive statements usually possesses greater experience and, presumably, expertise than the average psychologist. (Unfortunately, the advent of microcomputers has made that assumption less tenable than it was when Fowler was writing; cf. Moreland, 1987.) Although undoubtedly not as good as actuarial interpretation, automated clinical interpretation possesses several advantages over human interpretation. In addition to those advantages that have been noted in the context of automated scoring of test data, automated interpretation has an advantage over human interpretation when large and varied populations are involved. Fowler (1969) noted that computers can store tremendous volumes of material and can retrieve them more rapidly and reliably than humans. Thus, while the average psychologist is typically limited in the research literature and population samples to which he or she is exposed and the information about them he or she can retain, the expert human interpreter can see to it that the computer adjusts for relevant demographic and other nontest variables.

The promise of the "automated clinician" has been realized in a number of studies, some employing the MMPI (e.g., Goldberg, 1965, 1970; Kleinmuntz, 1963) and many involving other types of clinical judgments (e.g., Bleich, 1973; DeDombal, 1979; Greist et al., 1973, 1974; McDonald, 1976; but see Blois, 1980; Kleinmuntz, 1968; Weizenbaum, 1976 for counterexamples). It comes as no surprise then, that automated clinicians to interpret psychological tests have proliferated. Several CBTI systems have been developed that interpret, but do not score, the Rorschach (Century Diagnostics, 1980; Exner, 1987; Harris,

Niedner, Feldman, Fink, & Johnson, 1981; Piotrowski, 1964). There has also been work on an interpretive program for the Holtzman Inkblot Technique (Holtzman, 1975), a projective technique that can also be computer-scored (Gorham, 1967). Automated clinical prediction systems have also been developed for the Halstead–Reitan Neuropsychological Battery (Adams, 1975; Finkelstein, 1977). By far the majority of automated interpretive systems have, however, been developed for objective tests. Fowler (1969) has suggested that this is because the administration, scoring, and interpretation of projective techniques is often highly individualistic and based heavily on intuition and clinical experience (cf. Exner & Exner, 1972). Scoring of ability tests such as the Halstead–Reitan often requires professional judgment. By contrast, objective tests have traditionally emphasized standardized administration and scoring, and have emphasized an objective, empirical approach to interpretation.

Of the objective tests, personality inventories have most often been the subjects of automated interpretation. The reasons for this are unclear, but I would speculate that it is due to the fact that data from many scales and indexes, as well as nontest data (e.g., demographic characteristics), are often combined to arrive at complex and lengthy interpretations (cf. Kleinmuntz, 1975). The complexity of this task allows for the fullest use of the advantages conferred by automation noted previously. Of these tests, computer interpretation of the MMPI has been most frequently attempted (Fowler, 1985).

It should come as no surprise then, that MMPI systems have been the subject of most investigations of the validity of CBTIs. These investigations appear to be representative of the few attempts to study the validity of clinical CBTIs and they will provide the focus for most of the remainder of this chapter (but see Adams, Kvale, & Keegan, 1984; Anthony, Heaton, & Lehman, 1980; Goldstein & Shelly, 1982; Green, 1982; Harris et al., 1981; Heaton, Grant, Anthony, & Lehman, 1981; Katz & Dalby, 1981; Klingler, Johnson, & Williams, 1976; Klingler, Miller, Johnson, & Williams, 1977; Moreland & Onstad, 1987a; Mules, 1972; O'Dell, 1972).

VALIDITY STUDIES TO DATE

To date the accuracy of clinical CBTIs has been evaluated in several ways. Some writers have compared CBTIs with test interpretations generated by human interpreters. Most of these comparisons have been anecdotal, often involving several automated interpretations but usually based on only a single case (Adair, 1978; Butcher, 1978; Dahlstrom et al., 1972; Eichman, 1972; Eyde, 1985; Goldstein & Reznikoff, 1971; Graham, 1977; Greene, 1980; Kleinmuntz, 1972; Labeck, Johnson, & Harris, 1983; Manning, 1971; Nichols, 1985; Sundberg, 1985a, 1985b). These comparisons are informative because of the extensive analysis they permit and the fact that the analysis is usually provided by a recognized expert in MMPI interpretation. Obviously, however, this work lacks scientific rigor and, therefore, will not be considered further in this chapter. A few studies have compared CBTIs with human interpretations using more rigorous standards (Bringmann, Balance, & Giesbrecht, 1972; Glueck & Reznikoff, 1965; Johnson, Giannetti, & Williams, 1978). Reports prepared by human interpreters provide a poor criterion against which to judge the validity of CBTIs. The validity of clinicians' interpretations is low enough that a CBTI could be at serious variance with a clinician's interpretation and still be quite valid (cf. Golden, 1964; Graham, 1967; Kostlan, 1954; Little & Shneidman, 1959; Sines, 1959). There is also abundant evidence that clinicians may agree on the meaning of test scores although the presumed relationship between the test sores and the criterion does not, in fact, exist (e.g., Chapman & Chapman, 1967, 1969; Dowling & Graham, 1976; Golding & Rorer, 1972; Kurtz & Garfield, 1978). Hence, this approach will also not be discussed further here. A handful of writers have asked report consumers to fill out symptom checklists or complete Q-sorts based on CBTIs, subsequently comparing those ratings with analogous ratings made by clinicians familiar with each patient. Those studies will be considered subsequently. Most of the more rigorous studies that have employed nontest criteria have involved asking the recipients of CBTIs to rate the accuracy of various elements of the reports. Though disparaged by some writers (Lanyon, 1984; Matarazzo, 1983), these studies are considered promising by other experts (cf. Adair, 1978), especially if slightly modified (cf. Butcher, 1978; Moreland, 1985; O'Dell, 1972; Webb, Miller, & Fowler, 1970), and so merit further consideration.

External Criterion Studies

Several studies have compared rating scale or Q-sort data based on patient contact with the same data generated from computer-based MMPI interpretations. The first such study employed the Roche system (Anderson, 1969). In this study, 24 MMPI experts were asked to rate 12 psychological variables such as ego strength, impulsivity, and motivation for psychotherapy. The 12 variables were culled from a previously studied 27-item list on the basis of criterion rater's perceptions of their importance for treatment. The MMPI experts independently rated the patients' basic MMPI profiles and CBTIs. The patients' psychotherapists provided criterion ratings after 10 hours of individual psychotherapy or 30 days of inpatient treatment or both.

In several respects, this study was one of the best of its kind. A large sample of raters was employed (11 criterion raters, in addition to the 24 MMPI raters), and a comparatively large sample of MMPI respondents ($N = 28$) was studied. Moreover, each patient's basic MMPI profile and CBTI were rated by 6 individuals. Thus, although Anderson chose not to, assessment of interrater reliability of the report- and profile-based ratings was possible. In addition, the assessment of individual differences in rater accuracy was possible. Anderson also took the unusual step of assessing the reliability, over 30 days, of the criterion ratings. The data were analyzed both within individuals, across variables and across individuals, within variables. The former analysis facilitated the detection of inaccurate reports, whereas the latter allowed Anderson to pinpoint variables that could not be accurately rated from the MMPI. If such had been the case, he also could have detected individuals or variables more accurately characterized by the human interpreters than by the CBTIs and vice versa. Anderson also collected average patient ratings from the MMPI raters in an attempt to deal with the problem of discriminant validity. He chose not to analyze those ratings, however, because the genuine ones were so poorly correlated with the criteria (mean $r = .22$).

Anderson did not fully use the multitude of MMPI-based ratings available to him. Knowing how well the average of the MMPI-based ratings or, alternatively, the most reliable ones, correlated with the therapists' ratings would have been useful, particularly because inspection of both the variables and some of Anderson's analyses suggest that some of the variables (e.g., ability to "stay with" feelings) were difficult to rate from the MMPI. The generalizability of the study was limited by the use of MMPI experts to render judgments, rather than using typical MMPI interpreters and CBTI consumers.

Hedlund, Morgan, and Master (1972) attempted to cross-validate the MMPI interpretive system developed at the Mayo Clinic and subsequently modified at the Institute of Living (Glueck, 1966). Two criterion raters completed a 33-item symptom checklist for each case by consulting the final summaries of 100 psychiatric inpatients at a military hospital. Disagreements were resolved by obtaining a consensus among the two raters and a third clinician. Checklist ratings were then compared with the 38 different statements (out of a possible 59) available from the patients' MMPI reports. Three interpretations were prepared for each patient, each based on a different set of MMPI norms.

A number of factors make this study a well-crafted attempt to validate a CBTI system. The sample of patients ($N = 100$) was the largest yet studied in this kind of research. Items were selected that could be rated with high reliability and that appeared especially relevant to the MMPI interpretations under evaluation. Expected relations of criteria to MMPI-based statements were established by consensus of the authors. A number of cases were rated prior to beginning the study to ensure adequate interrater reliability. Some of the cases chosen for the study were discarded before the data were analyzed because the raters believed that they had insufficient information on which to base their judgments or because the cases yielded low interrater agreement. The development of three different reports for each patient also allowed some estimation of the discriminant validity of the system.

The study of Hedlund et al. was not without some shortcomings, most notably the "file drawer" nature of the criterion data. Gdowski, Lachar, and Butkus

(1980) noted that data collected systematically at the time of evaluation often dramatically differs from the same ratings made from records. Moreover, when these differences occur, symptoms and behaviors usually are noted less frequently in records. Thus, the 62% false positive rate of Hedlund et al. might have been due to underrecording of the relevant data in the patients' records. Also important to keep in mind is that the MMPI data were obtained on admission, whereas the final summaries covered the patients' entire hospitalization. As a result, some report-based ratings (e.g., ratings of acute symptoms) might have been deemed inaccurate because they were compared with criterion ratings based on data collected long after the MMPI data. Although this criticism is highlighted in regard to the study by Hedlund et al., it also is applicable to some extent to many of the studies reviewed in this chapter.

The authors of the CBTI system examined by Hedlund and his colleagues could justifiably complain that a significant part of their system (36%) was ignored in the study. Although this shortcoming is common to all of the studies reviewed in this chapter, it is especially serious in regard to this study because of the small size of the interpretive statement library under consideration. Caldwell Report, by way of contrast, contains more than 30,000 sentences (A. B. Caldwell, personal communication, March 8, 1984), and other commercial services also claim large statement libraries.

Chase (1974) compared MMPI data with clinicians' ratings using a 59-item subset of the Minnesota–Ford phenotypic item pool (Meehl et al., 1962). Each patient's MMPI was interpreted in six different ways. MMPI experts wrote interpretive reports and, several weeks later, characterized the patients' MMPIs using the Minnesota–Ford items. Reports were prepared, using the actuarial atlas developed by Marks and Seeman (1963) and CBTIs were supplied by three commercial services: Roche, Behaviordyne (formerly called OPTIMUM), and Caldwell Report. All the reports were then characterized via ratings on the Minnesota–Ford items by 3 of 21 raters from four professions: clinical psychology, psychiatry, social work, and psychiatric nursing. Criterion ratings were supplied by two psychologists who either had worked with the patients or had studied their histories.

Chase's study is notable in that it involved more methods of interpreting the MMPI than any other study to date. Although Chase's method might be faulted because it was MMPI-based, her pool of rating items was selected carefully. She asked three MMPI experts to use the Minnesota–Ford items to rate the modal MMPI profiles for the three Marks and Seeman profile types under study. The items judged most and least characteristic of individuals producing the modal profiles were retained for the study. Consequently, unlike the other investigations discussed in this section, Chase can plausibly argue that her criterion items adequately covered at least the phenotypical behavioral domain germane to the reports studied. Her use of three raters for each report and two criterion raters also is noteworthy. The fact that she averaged the ratings across all raters before intercorrelating them considerably enhances confidence in the reliability of her findings. Her data also allowed for assessment of interrater agreement, individual differences in rater accuracy, and differential accuracy among professions, although she chose not to explore those areas. Chase did present her data in the form of a multiinterpretation–multirating intercorrelation matrix, thus allowing an evaluation of both convergent and discriminant validity.

Another interesting facet of Chase's study is that she found a comparatively large difference between the accuracy of the ratings made from the psychologists' narrative interpretations (.32) and those same psychologists' rating-scale characterizations (.45). This shrinkage suggests that CBTIs are most fairly compared with interpretations generated in the traditional manner, not ratings made directly from test results.

A study similar to Chase's was performed by Crumptom (1974). She submitted the MMPIs of nine randomly selected patients being seen privately for psychotherapy to Caldwell Report, Roche, and the Institute for Clinical Analysis (Butcher, 1978). After four therapy sessions, each therapist characterized his or her patients via the Marks Q-Sort (cf. Marks & Seeman, 1963, Appendix C). Two recently graduated clinical psychologists and a clinical psychology graduate student who had completed all course work used the Q-sort to summarize each of the computer-based MMPI interpretations.

Crumpton's study is most noteworthy for her assessment of interrater reliability of the report ratings (as opposed to the criterion ratings). Her mean reliability coefficient of .62 suggests that this kind of reliability is indeed a factor to be considered in these studies. Validity coefficients in the .50s can hardly be faulted in the face of that kind of reliability! Like Chase, Crumpton averaged the report ratings across all raters before intercorrelating them; however, the criterion ratings were made by only one individual. Crumpton addressed the issue of discriminant validity by assessing the effects of shared patient stereotypes on the report raters' Q-sorts. The low mean interrater correlation of .22 suggests that commonly held stereotypes did not greatly influence Crumpton's results. Two further analyses also would have been of interest: (a) Would there have been as much disagreement about the typical patient among the therapists and between the therapists and the report raters? (b) How did the Q-correlations between the report-rater and therapist sorts compare with the correlations between the stereotype and therapist sorts? Crumpton's design also permitted her to assess therapist and patient-within-therapist effects in addition to the accuracy of the reports.

Crumpton's study, like Chase's, is subject to criticism on the ground of small sample size. This problem is compounded by the fact that the profiles of five of the nine MMPIs were very similar, and Crumpton's data indicate that they yielded very similar interpretations. Her study also can be faulted for using report raters familiar with the MMPI but with little clinical experience. Crumpton analyzed her data across subjects, within the nine conceptual categories of Q-sort items (cf. Marks & Seeman, 1963, Appendix C), but she used the categories as independent variables in an analysis of variance rather than as dependent variables in a multivariate analysis of variance.

Detailed next is a study conducted with the intention of capitalizing on the positive aspects of all foregoing work and improving upon it in several ways (Moreland, 1983). A large ($N = 1186$) initial sample was culled in an effort to gather a representative sample of interpretations. The final sample comprised 70 profiles, divided evenly among the five categories in Lachar's (1974b) MMPI profile typology: within normal limits, psychotic, neurotic, characterological, and indeterminate. Seasoned clinicians who were not familiar with the MMPI were solicited as report raters. Assurance was obtained that none of the raters had used either of the computer services under investigation—Roche and Lachar's CBTI system, which was first sold by Automated Psychological Assessment and is now sold by Western Psychological Services (Lachar, 1974b)—because such prior experience could bias the ratings made in the study. Moreover, no report rater received two reports on the same patient to avoid a recognition problem that could contaminate the report ratings. Criterion ratings were made at the time the patient took the MMPI. Discriminant validity was assessed by comparing report-based ratings with "stereotypical patient" ratings. Both interrater and intrarater (report) reliability data were collected. Profile type was employed as an independent variable in the data analyses.

Needless to say, this study did not avoid all of the shortcomings of its predecessors. To obtain a relatively large and diverse sample, data previously collected for other purposes had to be used. As a result, reliability data were not available for the criterion ratings. The criterion instruments themselves also were less than optimal for a study of computer-based MMPI interpretations. As in Anderson's study, both inspection of the variables and some of the analyses suggest that some of the variables were very difficult to rate from the MMPI.

Another factor noted in this study that may contribute to the low validity coefficients commonly found in studies of this type was the poor metric qualities of the criterion instruments. None of the distributions of criterion ratings approximated normality—a finding typical of psychiatric rating scales (Maxwell, 1971)—whereas the CBTI-based ratings did. If the report raters had received information about the score distributions characteristic of the criterion instruments or, better yet, if they had received actual base rate data, the validity coefficients might have averaged higher than .36. The report raters complained of another metric problem. They pointed out the difficulty of converting terms such as "mild" and "often" into metric ratings. The low interrater reliabilities obtained in this study (generally in the .50s) also attest to this problem. The problem could have been alleviated in two ways. First, pilot cases could have been employed in the manner of Hedlund et al. to ensure that all raters meant the same thing when they checked a statement (e.g., "mild X"). Second, contrary to the assumption made when this study was designed, report raters should have received as much experience as possible with the two CBTI systems prior to beginning the study. In that way, some assurance would have been gained that the raters knew what "severe Y" in a test interpretation looked like in a patient.

A manipulation check suggested that some raters may not have been weighing the various parts of the reports in the same manner as typical consumers. For example, one rater reported that she ignored the entire narrative, considering only the listing of critical items endorsed by the MMPI respondent. This finding calls into question the external validity of the study.

In closing, the most serious shortcoming of the foregoing study and, in fact, of all of the external criterion studies is that none actually evaluated an entire interpretive system, although the investigator's conclusions often suggest they did so. Not only did these studies evaluate only small proportions of the statements available in the interpretive systems but they usually did so using criterion instruments that did not adequately map the behavioral domain covered by the systems.

Having personally attempted an external criterion study, I now believe many of the problems that have been noted are, as a practical matter, insurmountable. Future attempts to validate clinical (as opposed to actuarial) CBTIs are likely to produce more useful data if the external criterion method is abandoned in favor of the "customer satisfaction" method described below.

Customer Satisfaction Studies

The early work in this area was conducted to assess the CBTI system for the MMPI that was developed by Fowler and later sold by the Roche Psychiatric Service Institute and, in a slightly embellished version, by Psychological Assessment Services (Adair, 1978; Butcher, 1978).[2] Webb and his colleagues (Webb, 1970; Webb, Miller, & Fowler, 1969, 1970) asked consumers to use a 5-point rating scale to indicate each report's clarity, accuracy, and usefulness and to note how the CBTIs compared with reports prepared in the usual manner. The specific areas explored in one of these studies can be found in Table 3.2. Bachrach (cited in Fowler, 1966) also studied Fowler's MMPI reports; however, Bachrach asked raters only for a single set of ratings for a group of reports. The foregoing studies, as an aggregate, involved a large, diverse array of clinical raters and patients. Webb and colleagues' use of numerous queries about each CBTI improved upon Bachrach's request for a single set of ratings for a group of reports.

Although useful, these studies were not without major faults. Lachar (1974a) noted that because the reports were rated according to content areas (e.g., psychosomatic symptoms) rather than statement by statement or paragraph-by-paragraph, systematic isolation of weaknesses in the CBTI system was difficult. Some of the studies were large enough to permit breakdown of the ratings according to test or patient characteristics (e.g., MMPI profile type or clinical

---

[2]Similar studies have been conducted to evaluate European adaptations of both Fowler's system (Fowler & Blaser, 1972) and Lachar's system (Engel, 1977).

TABLE 3.2
Questions Used in Some of the Validation Studies of Fowler's MMPI
Interpretation System

The report is well organized and its descriptions are clear.
The report gives a valid overall description of this patient.
The behaviors described are characteristic of this person.
The report is helpful in planning this patient's treatment.
The symptoms reported are accurate.
I could find little good in this report.
Major symptoms of this person are omitted.
The report is in error regarding this person's physical complaints (if described in the report).
This person's mood and feelings are accurrately described.
The report misrepresents this person's relations with family members (if described in the report).
Useless information was included.
The severity of personality desorder was accurately described.
Parts of the report contradicted each other.
The report's prediction of response to therapy was accurate (if described in the report).
The report pointed out things about the patient I had not noticed previously.
I know this patient: very well, well, moderately, somewhat, scarcely at all.
This report, compared with most noncomputerized psychological reports I have seen is: much worse,
    worse, equal, better, much better.

Note. Adapted from Table 1, Webb, Miller, and Fowler (1970). Unless otherwise noted, raters indicated:
strongly disagree, mildly disagree, neutral, mildly agree, strongly agree.

diagnosis). If this had been done, the detection of inaccurate report types or types of patients for whom the reports were inaccurate would have been possible.

Three studies have been conducted to assess the adequacy of the CBTI system for the MMPI developed by Gilberstadt (1970) for the Veterans Administration. Klett (1971) conducted a study virtually identical in approach to that of Bachrach. Thus, the same comments apply to both. The other two studies were conducted by Lushene and Gilberstadt (1972). In their initial study, they collected accuracy ratings on each interpretive statement. They also collected overall report-accuracy ratings on a 6-point scale. They then revised those statements that were rated as accurate less than 60% of the time. The revised system was then studied in the same manner.

The outstanding feature of the work by Lushene and Gilberstadt is that they conducted a second study to assess the adequacy of the revisions prompted by the first. Lushene and Gilberstadt's studies were similar in method to those conducted by Webb et al. Therefore, the same criticisms apply with the exception of one. Because Lushene and Gilberstadt asked raters to judge each statement in each report, they were able to pinpoint weaknesses in Gilberstadt's system. A criticism unique to Lushene and Gilberstadt's studies involves their rating procedure. They asked raters to check one of eight adjectival phrases to describe each interpretive statement: correct, incorrect, irrelevant, redundant, contradictory, base rate, unclear, and don't know. The raters, perhaps believing the accuracy or inaccuracy of the statements to be the crucial consideration, selected the correct and incorrect categories an average of 91% of the time. Unfortunately, the eight categories were not mutually exclusive. For example, correct and incorrect overlapped with redundant and contradictory. The studies would have been more informative had raters been requested to make all applicable ratings (e.g., indicate that statements were both correct and redundant).

Lachar (1974a, 1974b) was able to overcome some of the shortcomings of the studies of the systems developed by Fowler and Gilberstadt in his initial attempt to demonstrate the validity of his CBTI system. Drawing a lesson from the work of Lushene and Gilberstadt, Lachar asked his raters to indicate whether each paragraph of each report was accurate or inaccurate. He also asked that the overall accuracy of each report be rated on a 6-point scale. Moreover, Lachar used a factorial design that included both MMPI and patient characteristics as independent variables. This approach allowed him to determine that some paragraphs in his system were relatively inaccurate, compared with other elements of the system, particularly for certain types of MMPI profiles and certain types of patients.

An outstanding feature of Lachar's study (1974a) is that the accuracy of each interpretive paragraph (the unit of selection is his system) was independently assessed. His conclusions receive added force by the large sample ($N = 1410$) used in the study, which included subsamples from several populations. These positive aspects of the study are tempered somewhat by the fact that 75% of the patients were men and 85%, patients in military medical facilities. Hence, Lachar's sample was not representative of medical and psychiatric patients in the United States, the population with which his reports currently are used.

Two studies of Lachar's system used slight twists on his original methodology. Adams and Shore (1976) completed a partial replication of Lachar's initial study. Their small sample ($N = 100$) did not permit a factorial design, but they asked more of their raters than did Lachar. Each paragraph was rated on a 6-point scale. This innovation allowed Adams and Shore to note that paragraphs containing specific predictions or treatment recommendations usually were given extreme ratings, whereas the ratings of general statements were more evenly distributed. Lachar, Klinge, and Grisell (1976) had clinicians rate the overall accuracy of two types of reports for each of their adolescent patients. One report was based on standard MMPI norms and the other on adolescent norms. This approach permitted the researchers to conclude that Lachar's system was most useful with adolescents when age-appropriate norms were employed.

Although the studies of Lachar's system improved on the investigations of Fowler and Gilberstadt systems, they also contained some weaknesses not apparent in the latter studies. Most important, Lachar (1974b, p. 159) instructed his raters to consider his paragraphs accurate when no criterion information was available. This raises the possibility that some elements of Lachar's system received spuriously high ratings due to a frequent absence of relevant criterion information. Two factors heighten this concern. First, Lachar's article indicates that some ratings were made after as little as 1 hour of contact with the patient. (Limited patient contact is a problem in most of the studies reviewed in this chapter.) Second, some of Lachar's interpretations appear to be impossible to judge without a great deal of information, sometimes longitudinal in nature (see Table 3.3). By contrast, Webb et. al offered, and their raters frequently used, a neutral category that "may [have] represent[ed] a rater's unfamiliarity with the patient" (1970, p. 212). Though seldom used, a don't-know category also was available to those rating Gilberstadt's interpretations.

Less important criticisms of the work of Lachar and his colleagues involved the assessment of report usefulness instead of report validity per se. Asking raters to indicate simply the accuracy or inaccuracy of each paragraph and each report, rather than using multifaceted ratings such as those employed by Webb and his colleagues, involved a tradeoff. It allowed inaccurate paragraphs to be pinpointed but did not permit the identification of those reports that omitted important information. (This same criticism also may apply to the work of Lushene and Gilberstadt, although it cannot be established on the basis of their report.) Lachar's raters also could not point out useless information.

In her doctoral dissertation, Chase (1974) employed the customer satisfaction approach to CBTI validity as an adjunct to the external criterion work described earlier. Clinicians familiar with the patients rated the accuracy of the interpretations globally on a 5-point scale. The Roche and Caldwell reports were judged superior, whereas those from Behaviordyne, poor. The evaluation of the same reports using external criterion ratings reversed this trend, however (see External Criterion Studies section). Although the scope of Chase's study was limited, her findings indicate that the results of most customer satisfaction studies are best viewed skeptically.

Chase's study is unique in gathering both global report ratings and using external criterion ratings. The fact that Chase studied three different CBTIs is also a plus. The selection of cases that cover a broad range of psychopathology is another positive feature of her study, although the examination of only three MMPIs severely restricts the generality of any conclusions drawn from the study.

TABLE 3.3
Excerpts from Lachar's CBTI System for the MMPI in Which Accuracy Appears Difficult to Rate

Response to chemotherapy, psychotherapy, and environmental manipulation is often good.
Rationalization and Intellecutalization are common defense mechanisms.
Chronic adjustment utilizing repression, denial, somatization, and a passive-dependent orientation make any psychological intervention, except temporary supportive measures extremely difficult.
Inconsistency and unpredictability are characteristic. These individuals appear demanding and resistant in therapy.
While the insight these persons show may be good and their protestation of resolve to do better seem genuine, long-range prognosis for behavior change is poor.
These individuals are attempting to deny lowered abilities through overactivity and over-production.
Hostility is likely to be expressed in an indirect manner.
Excessive fantasy is often used as an escape from the direct expression of unacceptable impulses.

Adapted from Lachar (1974b).

TABLE 3.4
Areas Explored in Green's Study of CBTI Validity

Information Adequacy[1]
   1. Confirmation of knowledge
   2. Addition of relevant information
   3. Clarification of case
   4. Exclusion of important information
   5. Inclusion of trivial information
   6. Inclusion of misleading information

Descriptive Accuracy[2]
   1. Interpersonal attitudes and relationships
   2. Affective tone and moods
   3. Personality traits and behaviors
   4. Self-image
   5. Primary symptoms and complaints
   6. Styles of coping
   7. Stress or areas of conflict
   8. Throght processes
   9. Severity of disturbances

Report Format and Utility[2]
   1. Internal Consistency
   2. Organization
   3. Intelligibility and clarity
   4. Helpful in treatment

Adapted from Green (1982).
[1] Raters indicated: substantial, moderate, minimal, none.
[2] Raters indicated: excellent, good, adequate, poor.

Green (1982) compared the accuracy and usefulness of MMPI CBTIs with reports from Millon's CBTI system for the Millon Clinical Multiaxial Inventory (MCMI; Millon, 1982). Her 23 raters rated 100 Roche reports, 100 MCMI reports, and 50 Mayo Clinic reports, using a set of 19 thoughtful queries about information adequacy, descriptive accuracy, and report format and utility (see Table 3.4).

Green's study was unique and pioneering in two respects. First, she compared CBTIs based on two different tests. Her study is useful in pointing up the dangers of doing so. The MCMI was designed to assess the personality styles hypothesized by Millon (cf. Millon, 1981). Thus, it should come as no surprise that the MCMI CBTIs were superior when it came to describing personality traits and coping styles. On the other hand the CBTIs based on the MMPI, which was built primarily to assess major mental illness, provided the most accurate descriptions of primary symptoms and though processes. It should also come as no surprise that the two consultative CBTIs (Roche and MCMI) outstripped the screening CBTI (Mayo) virtually across the board. When setting up a horse race of this sort it is important to make sure that none of the horses are hobbled. Another pioneering feature of Green's study was her effort to rule out base-rate accuracy as an important influence on her results. Of that, more to come. A further positive aspect of Green's study was her effort to make sure her raters were knowledgeable about the clients whose reports they rated. She required that the raters have at least 4 hours of client contact prior to rating the reports. Meehl (1960) has demonstrated that clinicians' views of clients stabilize after 4 hours.

Vincent and Castillo (1984) asked 13 nurses and 1 social worker to indicate their preference for Lachar's CBTI or one developed by the first author (Vincent, Wilson, & Wilson, 1983). Specifically, the raters were asked to "rate [the CBTIs] as to whether you prefer A or B, or A and B are equal, taking into account the report's overall consistency, organization, clarity, readability, and . . . overall usefulness" (p. 30). They were asked to rate reports only for those patients with whom they had "significant personal contact." These instructions led to ratings of pairs of reports on 32 patients out of 50 that were originally eligible for the study.

This study is most noteworthy for its explicitly ipsative, "horse race" character. The results indicated that the raters felt Vincent's CBTI to be superior to Lachar's in most instances but we have no way of knowing, in any absolute sense, how satisfactory they felt either report to be. On the other hand, confidence in the ratings that were made is increased by the fact that the raters were asked to, and did, decline to rate reports on patients with whom they were unfamiliar.

Widespread Problems

Reviewers appear to agree that the major shortcoming of the customer satisfaction studies is what Webb et al. (1970) characterized as the lack of information on base-rate accuracy of the reports (cf. Butcher 1978; Eichman, 1972). Webb and his colleagues were concerned that raters would characterize reports as accurate not because the reports were pointed descriptions of the individuals at issue, but rather because they contained glittering generalities (cf. Baillargeon & Danis, 1984). Butcher (1978) offered the following colorful description of this problem:

> The problem here is very similar to the situation presented by the overzealous, rookie policeman who blows a case by prejudicing the witness as follows: The policeman takes a photograph (and only one photograph) of the suspect to the prime witness and asks if this is the person who committed the crime. Even the police, whose methods and intent are frequently questioned, do not try to get away with this type of validation. Most often they are required to utilize more rigorous methods of gathering evidence that will hold up in court, such as "having the witness pick the guilty person from a lineup." (pp. 617–618)

I referred to this same issue, in the context of the external criterion studies, as the problem of discriminant validity.

This concern is lent credibility by Chase's finding that global accuracy ratings sometimes disagree sharply with the results of external criterion ratings. Thus, the customer satisfaction studies reviewed so far provide only half of the picture. They may correctly indicate that CBTIs have high convergent validity, but they afford little or no information concerning the reports' discriminant validity. The focused questions employed in the evaluations of Fowler's system—especially the one dealing with the inclusion of useless information—might have reduced this problem (see also Green, 1982); it is doubtful that they completely eliminated the problem. Lushene and Gilberstadt's provision of irrelevant and base-rate categories might have ameliorated this problem had raters used these categories more often. Lachar and his colleagues (1976) were afforded some protection from this problem by their request that clinicians rate two reports on each patient. Although the clinicians's ratings of the two types of reports differed only slightly, the reports themselves frequently differed radically (Lachar et al., 1976, Table 2, p. 22). It may be argued that Chase's use of three different CBTI systems allowed some appraisal of base-rate accuracy; however, this argument ignores the fact that differential ratings may result from differences among the reports irrelevant to the question of their validity. Indeed, the comments of Chase's raters provide support of this hypothesis. They complained about the infelicitous use of the English language in the low-rated Behaviordyne reports and praised Caldwell's use of the same. When, on the other hand, the reports were subjected to scrutiny via external criteria, Behaviordyne was found superior.

Green (1982) made the first self-conscious effort to deal with the problem of base-rate accuracy. She had 32 clinical psychology graduate students simulate the responses of two different types of patients on the MCMI. The students then rated the accuracy of two CBTIs, one generated from one of the tests completed by the student and one, with the student unaware, selected at random. Green reported that the students rated the genuine reports excellent or good more than three times more often than the random reports. Notwithstanding the work involved, this approach to the problem of base-rate accuracy is flawed in several ways.

First, the subjects were not clinical clients. They were graduate students with considerable exposure to Millon's personality theory. Their MCMI responses could be expected to reflect those of prototypical patients of the sort they were simulating. Such prototypical cases seem to be the exception rather than the rule in clinical practice, as demonstrated by the poor classification rates usually obtained using the MMPI cookbook prototypes discussed earlier. It is also important to note that the students were rating reports ostensibly based on their own responses to the test. Thus, they were a giant step closer to the raw test responses that led to the CBTIs than are clinicians evaluating clients' test responses. This problem seems especially salient when one recalls that Chase (1974) experienced a 50% decrease in percentage of variance accounted for when taking the step from Q-sorts based on MMPI profiles to Q-sorts by other raters based on narrative reports. Finally, the graduate students were not clinical clients, nor were they the full-fledged practitioners who served as raters in the main part of the study. Because of these problems, Green's efforts can probably best be thought of as yielding a lower-bound estimate of the influence of base rate accuracy in studies of this type. She found that the genuine CBTIs were rated good or excellent more than three times as frequently as the randomly chosen reports.

A recent study of mine provides direct evidence of the importance of assessing the degree to which high base rates contribute to high accuracy ratings (Moreland & Onstad, 1985, 1987b). Seven psychologists and one psychiatrist rated the accuracy of each section of 86 pairs of reports generated by the Minnesota Report: Adult Clinical System developed by Butcher (University of Minnesota, 1982). One report was based on the patient's MMPI profile while the other was based on a test profile similar to, but not the same as, the patient's. Raters believed they were rating one CBTI prepared in the usual manner and one "experimental" CBTI. They did not know which was which. The results of that study are presented in Table 3.5. Those results clearly indicate the importance of having a means of assessing CBTIs' discriminant validity. A recent study by Wimbish (1985) supports this point.

A second serious question about the studies under discussion involves reliability: None of the foregoing customer satisfaction studies assessed the reliability of the ratings across either raters or time. The work of Eyde, Kowal, and Fishburne, detailed elsewhere in this volume, makes it clear that this is an important consideration. The average reliability of pairs of raters for their four cases ranged from .16 to .49. On the other hand, their ratings reached acceptable levels of reliability

TABLE 3.5
Comparative Validity of Genuine and "Experimental" Minnesota Report CBTIs by Section

Report Section	Percentage "Accurate"[1]		G-"E"	z^2	p^3
	Genuine Report	"Experimental" Report			
Profile validity	90% (70/78)	79% (60/76)	11%	1.90	.0300
Symptomatic pattern	74% (62/84)	43% (35/81)	31%	4.08	.0001
Interpersonal relations	80% (61/76)	61% (50/82)	19%	2.60	.0050
Behavioral Stability	90% (65/72)	75% (59/79)	15%	2.38	.0090
Diagnostic Considerations	82% (56/68)	48% (33/69)	34%	4.15	.0001
Treatment Considerations	76% (56/74)	53% (40/75)	23%	2.91	.0020

Adapted from Moreland and Onstad (1985, 1987b).
[1] Accurate/Accurate + Inaccurate.
[2] Test of the difference between correlated proportions.
[3] One-tailed.

TABLE 3.6
High- and Two-Point Code Paragraphs Rated Fewer than Ten Times in Lachar's
CBTI System for the MMPI

Scale	Rule	Number of Ratings
1	>69T	5
7	>69T	6
8	>69T	5
1/6	both >69T	0
1/7	both >69T	6
1/9	both >69T	7
4/3	both >69T. and 4 > 3 by at least 6T	6
3/6	both >69T	4
3/7	both >69T	6
3/8	both >69T	8
3/9	both >69T	7
6/7	both >69T	2
6/9	both >69T	9
7/8	both >69T and 7 > 8 by at least 6T	6
7/9	both >69T	4

Adapted from Lachar (1974b). Patient sample size = 1410; High- and 2-point code paragraph sample size = 51. For high-point codes other clinical scales must be < 70 T; for 2-point codes other clinical scales must be less than or equal to those in the code, ties broken as in the Welsh Code.

when aggregated across raters (range = .70–.92). Taken as aggregates, the studies of the systems developed by Fowler, Gilberstadt, and Lachar involved relatively large, diverse groups of raters. A fair speculation is that such groups might have reduced the problem presented by the lack of data on reliability across raters; however, a large number of raters does not render interrater reliability data completely unnecessary. Consider that even in Lachar's (1974a, 1974b) large study, 15 of the 40 paragraphs composing the heart of his system were rated less than 10 times (see Table 3.6). To be sure, most of these paragraphs pertain to rare configurations of scores, but several pertain to configurations that are quite common in some settings. This problem can only have been much worse in the other, smaller studies reviewed in this section.

The reliability of the reports themselves, both across time and internally, also merits consideration (cf. Hofer & Bersoff, 1983). Because test scores and configurations of test scores are unreliable over time (e.g., Graham, Smith, & Schwartz, 1986), CBTIs are likely to be unreliable, too. The unfailing accuracy with which computers apply rules makes reliability of reports across time a significant consideration because even a 1-point difference on a single scale can cause a radical change in a CBTI (see Table 3.7). Through provision of a contradictory category, Lushene and Gilberstadt did attempt to investigate the internal consistency of Gilberstadt's interpretations. Given the apparent frequency with which CBTI consumers comment on internal inconsistencies, that other researchers have not investigated this problem is surprising.

Problems with the report raters also made the studies reviewed in this section less useful than they might have been. A number of the raters were not usually

TABLE 3.7
Interpretations of Two Very Similar Profiles by Lachar's CBTI System for the
MMPI

Clinical Profile 1: 2, 3 > 69 T; 1, 4, 8, 9 < 65T; 5, 6, 7 0 < 60T:

Individuals who obtain similar profiles are characterized by the ineffective use of repressive defenses and hysteroid mechanisms. Such individuals may show symptoms of apathy, dizziness, and lowered efficiency as well as symptomatic depression. Chronic tension, feelings of inadequacy and self-doubt, bottled-up emotion and general over control are frequently characteristic. He or she may have a hysterical quality. Sexual maladjustment, immaturity and dependency are often characteristic. In general these individuals have little insight, are resistant to psychodynamic formulations of their problems and have little genuine motivation to seek help.

Neuroses are common and characterological impressions are rare. Prognosis is poor.

Clinical Profile 2: 2 > 69 T; 3 = 69 T; 1, 4, 8, 9 < 65T; 5, 6, 7, 0 < 60 T

Individuals who obtain similar profiles are often significantly depressed, worried and pessimistic. Feelings of inadequacy and self-depreciation are likely present. These people internalize stress and usually withdraw when put under pressure. An acute reactive depression is suggested. If depression is denied by this patient, its effects should still be carefully evaluated. Response to chemotherapy, psychotherapy and environmental manipulation is often good.

Reactive depression is suggested.

Note. Adapted from Lachar (1974b).

direct consumers of computer-based MMPI interpretations (e.g., nurses). In addition, a number of raters were students (e.g., psychiatry residents) who probably did not possess an expertise in evaluating the reports that would be commensurate with that of fully qualified clinicians. Finally, none of the studies examined other potential rater effects. For example, biologically oriented psychiatrists could be envisioned as giving high marks to those statements suggesting chemotherapy and low ratings to those with psychodynamic inferences. The converse may hold true for psychoanalytically oriented clinicians, regardless of the accuracy of the statements.

HOW TO VALIDATE "AUTOMATED CLINICAL" CBTIS

Consideration of the pros and cons of the customer satisfaction validation studies completed to date precipitated the formulation of this list of desirable characteristics of future such studies, some of which also can be found elsewhere (e.g., Harris, 1984; Hofer & Bersoff, 1983; Moreland, 1985, 1987):

1. Raters should have prior experience with the interpretive systems under study.

2. Raters should have prior experience with the ratings they are to make.

3. The sample of raters should be representative of those using the report in applied contexts. The sample can be random or stratified, depending on the inferences one wishes to draw.

The relaxation of Guidelines 1–3 may be useful in some cases. For example, attempts to validate jargon-free CBTIs based on normal personality tests may make advantageous the use of ratings completed by individuals who know the test respondent well or the test respondent.

4. The sample of test respondents (or interpretations) should be representative of those found in applied settings. The sample can be random or stratified, depending on the inferences one wishes to draw.

5. Ratings should be completed keeping the appropriate time frame in mind. For example, care should be taken to ensure that ratings of acute symptoms are made, considering only that phase of a patient's illness.

6. Discriminant validity of the interpretations should be assessed. This guideline can be fulfilled by having each rater judge two reports (per test respondent) from the same interpretive system, one of the reports being genuine and the other, bogus. Of course, raters should not know which report is which until after competing the ratings.

7. Interrater reliability should be assessed. Raters should be given access to the same criterion information (e.g., case records).

8. Intrarater reliability should be assessed. Some of the inferences made in CBTIs may remain valid for only a short period of time due to actual changes in the test respondent. Hence, intrarater reliability should be assessed over a short period of time. Raters also should be asked to keep in mind when the test was administered when they are making reliability ratings.

9. Reliability, across time, of the CBTIs themselves should be assessed.

10. Studies should make provisions for indicating contradictory elements of interpretations.

11. Studies should make provisions for indicating useless elements of interpretations.

12. Studies should make provisions for indicating when interpretations omit significant information as well as the nature of that information. Studies with this aim should employ expert test interpreters either to rate the CBTIs or to decide, post hoc, whether the interpretations could have been expected to include such information.

13. Each element of an interpretive statement that is produced by different decision rules should be assessed independently.

EPILOGUE

The attentive reader will have noticed that I have not critiqued the three most recent customer satisfaction studies (Eyde, Kowal, & Fishburne, this volume; Moreland & Onstad, 1985, 1987b; Wimbish, 1985) in detail, as I did the earlier studies. The three most recent studies were designed with the advice offered in my 1985 article in mind. I invite the reader to evaluate for oneself the degree to which those three studies improved upon their predecessors.

ACKNOWLEDGMENT

This chapter represents the views of the author and not necessarily those of National Computer Systems.

REFERENCES

Adair, F. L. (1978). Computerized scoring and interpreting services [Re: Minnesota Multiphasic Personality Inventory]. In O. K. Buros (Ed.), *Eighth mental measurements yearbook* (Vol. 1, pp. 940–942, 945–949, 952–953, 957–960). Highland Park, NJ: Gryphon Press.

Adams, K. M. (1975). Automated clinical interpretation of the neuropsychological test battery: An ability based approach. *Dissertation Abstracts International, 35,* 6085B. (University Microfilms No. 75–13, 289).

Adams, K. M., Kvale, V. I., & Keegan, J. R. (1984). Relative accuracy of three automated systems for neuropsychological interpretation based on two representative tasks. *Journal of Clinical Neuropsychology, 6,* 413–431.

Adams, K. M., & Shore, D. L. (1976). The accuracy of an automated MMPI interpretation system in a psychiatric setting. *Journal of Clinical Psychology, 32,* 80–82.

American Psychological Association. (1986). *Guidelines for computer-based tests and interpretations.* Washington, DC: Author.

Anderson, B. N. (1969). *The utility of the Minnesota Multiphasic Personality Inventory in a private psychiatric hospital setting.* Unpublished master's thesis, Ohio State University.

Anthony, W. Z., Heaton, R. K., & Lehman, R. A. W. (1980). An attempt to cross-validate two actuarial systems for neuropsychological test interpretation, *Journal of Consulting and Clinical Psychology, 48,* 317–326.

Baillargeon, J., & Danis, C. (1984). Barnum meets the computer: A critical test. *Journal of Personality Assessment, 48,* 415–419.

Ben-Porath, Y. S., & Butcher, J. N. (1986). Computers in personality assessment: A brief past, an ebullient present, and an expanding future. *Computers in Human Behavior, 2,* 167–182.

Bleich, H. L. (1973). The computer as consultant. *New England Journal of Medicine, 223,* 308–312.

Blois, M. S. (1980). Clinical judgment and computers. *New England Journal of Medicine, 303,* 192–197.

Briggs, P. F., Taylor, M., & Tellegen, A. (1966). *A study of the Marks and Seeman MMPI profile types as applied to a sample of 2,875 psychiatric patients* (Research Laboratories Report No. PR–66–5). University of Minnesota, Department of Psychiatry.

Bringmann, W. G., Balance, W. D. G., & Giesbrecht, C. A. (1972). The computer vs. the technologist: Comparison of psychological reports on normal and elevated MMPI profiles. *Psychological Reports, 31,* 211–217.

Butcher, J. N. (1978). Computerized scoring and interpreting services [Re: Minnesota Multiphasic Personality Inventory]. In O. K. Buros (Ed.), *Eighth mental measurements yearbook* (Vol. 1, pp. 942–945, 947–956, 958, 960–962). Highland Park, NJ: Gryphon Press.

Butcher, J. N. (Ed.). (1985). Perspectives on computerized psychological assessment (special series). *Journal of Consulting and Clinical Psychology, 53,* 746–848.

Butcher, J. N. (Ed.). (1987). *Computerized psychological assessment: A practitioner's guide.* New York: Basic Books.

Caldwell, A. B. (1970). *Recent advances in automated interpretation of the MMPI.* Paper presented at the fifth annual Symposium on Recent Developments in the Use of the MMPI, Mexico City.

Campbell, D. P. (1971). *Handbook for the Strong Vocational Interest Blank.* Stanford, CA: Stanford University Press.

Century Diagnostics. (1980). *Computer interpreted Rorschach.* Tempe, AZ: Author.

Chapman, L. J., & Chapman, J. P. (1967). Genesis of popular but erroneous psychodiagnostic observations. *Journal of Abnormal Psychology, 72,* 193–204.

Chapman, L. J., & Chapman, J. P. (1969). Illusory correlation as an obstacle to the use of valid psychodiagnostic signs. *Journal of Abnormal Psychology, 74,* 271–280.

Chase, L. L. S. (1974). An evaluation of MMPI interpretation systems. *Dissertation Abstracts International, 35,* 3009B. (University Microfilms No. 74–26, 172).

Colby, K. M. (1980). Computer psychotherapists. In J. B. Sidowski, J. H. Johnson, & T. A. Williams (Eds.), *Technology in mental health care delivery systems.* Norwood, NJ: Ablex.

Cone, J. D. (1966). A note on Marks' and Seeman's rules for actuarially classifying psychiatric patients. *Journal of Clinical Psychology, 22,* 270.

Crumpton, C. A. (1974). An evaluation and comparison of three automated MMPI interpretive reports. *Dissertation Abstracts International, 35,* 6090B. (University Microfilms No. 75–11, 982).

Dahlstrom, W. G., Welsh, G. S., & Dahlstrom, L. E. (1972). *An MMPI handbook. Vol. 1: Clinical applications.* Minneapolis: University of Minnesota Press.

DeDombal, F. T. (1979). Computers and the surgeon: A matter of decision. *The Surgeon, 33,* 57.

Dowling, J. F., & Graham, J. R. (1976). Illusory correlation and the MMPI. *Journal of Personality Assessment, 40,* 531–538.

Drake, L. E., & Oetting, E. R. (1959). *An MMPI codebook for counselors.* Minneapolis: University of Minnesota Press.

Eichman, W. J. (1972). Computerized scoring and interpreting services [Re: Minnesota Multiphasic Personality Inventory]. In O. K. Buros (Ed.), *Seventh mental measurements yearbook* (Vol. 1, pp. 105–110). Highland Park, NJ: Gryphon Press.

Engel, R. R. (1977, August). *Cross-national accuracy of automated MMPI reports.* Paper presented at the sixth World Congress of Psychiatry, Honolulu.

Exner, J. E., Jr. (1987). Computer assistance in Rorschach interpretation. In J. N. Butcher (Ed.), *Computerized psychological assessment: A practitioner's guide* (pp. 218–235). New York: Basic Books.

Exner, J. E., & Exner, D. E. (1972). How clinicians use the Rorschach. *Journal of Personality Assessment, 36,* 403–408.

Eyde, L. D. (1985). Review of the Minnesota Report: Personnel Selection systems for the MMPI. In J. V. Mitchell, Jr. (Ed.), *Ninth mental measurements yearbook* (Vol. 2, pp. 1003–1005). Lincoln, NE: Buros Institute of Mental Measurements.

Eyde, L. D. (Ed.). (1987). *Computerised psychological testing.* London: Lawrence Erlbaum Associates.

Finkelstein, J. N. (1977). BRAIN: A computer program for interpretation of the Halstead–Reitan Neuropsychological Test Battery. *Dissertation Abstracts International, 37,* 5349B. (University Microfilms No. 77–88, 8864).

Finney, J. C. (1966). Programmed interpretation of MMPI and CPI. *Archives of General Psychiatry, 15,* 75–81.

Fowler, R. D. (1966). *The MMPI notebook: A guide to the clinical use of the automated MMPI.* Nutley, NJ: Roche Psychiatric Service Institute.

Fowler, R. D. (1969). Automated interpretation of personality test data. In J. N. Butcher (Ed.), *MMPI: Research developments and clinical applications* (pp. 105–126). New York: McGraw–Hill.

Fowler, R. D. (1985). Landmarks in computer-assisted psychological assessment. *Journal of Consulting and Clinical Psychology, 53*, 748–759.

Fowler, R. D. (1987). Developing a computer-based test interpretation system. In J. N. Butcher (Ed.), *Computerized psychological assessment: A practitioner's guide* (pp. 50–63). New York: Basic Books.

Fowler, R. D., & Athey, E. B. (1971). A cross-validation of Gilberstadt and Duker's 1–2–3–4 profile type. *Journal of Clinical Psychology, 27*, 238–240.

Fowler, R. D., & Blaser, P. (1972). *Around the world in 566 items.* Paper presented at the seventh annual Symposium on Recent Developments in the Use of the MMPI, Mexico City. Cited in J. N. Butcher & P. Pancheri (1976), *A handbook of cross-national MMPI research* (pp. 194–196). Minneapolis: University of Minnesota Press.

Fowler, R. D., & Butcher, J. N. (1986). Critique of Matarazzo's views on computerized testing: All sigma and no meaning. *American Psychologist, 41*, 94–96.

Fowler, R. D., & Coyle, F. A. (1968). Scoring error on the MMPI. *Journal of Clinical Psychology, 24*, 68–69.

Gdowski, C. L., Lachar, D., & Butkus, M. (1980). A methodological consideration in the construction of actuarial interpretation systems. *Journal of Personality Assessment, 44*, 427–432.

Gilberstadt, H. (1970). *Comprehensive MMPI code book for males* (MMPI Research Laboratory Rep. No. 1B 11–5). Minneapolis: Veterans Administration Hospital.

Gilberstadt, H., & Duker, J. (1965). *A handbook for clinical and actuarial MMPI interpretation.* Philadelphia: W. B. Saunders.

Glueck, B. C., Jr. (1966). Current personality assessment research. *International Psychiatric Clinic, 3*, 205–222.

Glueck, B. C., Jr., & Reznikoff, M. (1965). Comparison of computer-derived personality profile and projective psychological test findings. *American Journal of Psychiatry, 121*, 1156–1161.

Goldberg, L. R. (1965). Diagnosticians vs. diagnostic signs: The diagnosis of psychosis vs. neurosis from the MMPI. *Psychological Monographs, 79*(9, Whole No. 602).

Goldberg, L. R. (1970). Man vs. model of man: A rationale, plus some evidence, for a method of improving on clinical inferences. *Psychological Bulletin, 73*, 422–432.

Golden, M. (1964). Some effects of combining psychological tests on clinical inferences. *Journal of Consulting Psychology, 28*, 440–446.

Golding, S. G., & Rorer, L. (1972). Illusory correlation and subjective judgment. *Journal of Abnormal Psychology, 80*, 249–260.

Goldstein, A. M., & Reznikoff, M. (1972). MMPI performance in chronic medical illness: the use of computer-derived interpretations. *British Journal of Psychiatry 120*, 157–158.

Goldstein, G., & Shelly, C. (1982). A further attempt to cross-validate the Russell, Neuringer, and Goldstein neuropsychological keys. *Journal of Consulting and Clinical Psychology, 50*, 721–726.

Gorham, D. R. (1967). Validity and reliability studies of a computer-based scoring system for ink-blot responses. *Journal of Consulting Psychology, 31*, 65–70.

Graham, J. R. (1967). A Q-sort study of the accuracy of clinical descriptions based on the MMPI. *Journal of Psychiatric Research, 5*, 297–305.

Graham, J. R. (1977). *The MMPI: A practical guide.* New York: Oxford University Press.

Graham, J. R., Smith, R. L., & Schwartz, G. F. (1986). Stability of MMPI configurations for psychiatric inpatients, *Journal of Consulting and Clinical Psychology, 54*, 375–380.

Grayson, H. M., & Backer, T. E. (1972). Scoring accuracy of four automated MMPI interpretation report agencies. *Journal of Clinical Psychology, 28*, 366–370.

Green, C. J. (1982). The diagnostic accuracy and utility of MMPI and MCMI computer interpretive reports. *Journal of Personality Assessment, 46*, 359–365.

Greene, R. L. (1980). *The MMPI: An interpretive manual.* New York: Grune & Stratton.

Greist, J. H., Gustafson, D. H., Stauss, F. F., Rowse, G. L., Laughren, T. P., & Chiles, J.

A. (1973). A computer interview for suicide risk prediction. *American Journal of Psychiatry, 130*, 1327–1332.

Greist, J. H., Gustafson, D. H., Stauss, F. F., Rowse, G. L., Laughren, T. P., & Chiles, J. A. (1974). Suicide risk prediction: A new approach. *Life Threatening Behavior, 4*, 212–223.

Gynther, M. D., Altman, H., & Sletten, I. W. (1973). Replicated correlates of MMPI two-point code types: The Missouri actuarial system. *Journal of Clinical Psychology, 28*, 263–286.

Gynther, M. D., & Brilliant, P. J. (1968). The MMPI K+ profile: A reexamination. *Journal of Consulting and Clinical Psychology, 32*, 616–617.

Hansen, J. C. (1987). Computer-assisted interpretation of the Strong Interest Inventory. In J. N. Butcher (Ed.), *Computerized psychological assessment: A practitioner's guide* (pp. 292–321). New York: Basic Books.

Harris, W. G. (1984, August). Use of computer-based test interpretation: Some possible guidelines. In J. D. Matarazzo (chair), *Computer-based test interpretation: Prospects and problems.* Symposium conducted at the annual convention of the American Psychological Association, Toronto.

Harris, W. G. (1987). Computer-based test interpretations: Some development and application issues. In L. D. Eyde (Ed.), *Computerised psychological testing.* London: Lawrence Erlbaum Associates.

Harris, W. G., Niedner, D., Feldman, C., Fink, A., & Johnson, J. H. (1981). An on-line interpretive Rorschach approach: Using Exner's Comprehensive System. *Behavior Research Methods and Instrumentation, 13*, 588–591.

Heaton, R. K., Grant, I., Anthony, W. Z., and Lehman, R. A. W. (1981). A comparison of clinical and automated interpretation of the Halstead–Reitan Battery. *Journal of Clinical Neuropsychology, 3*, 121–141.

Hedlund, J. L., Morgan, D. W., & Master, F. D. (1972). The Mayo Clinic automated MMPI program: Cross-validation with psychiatric patients in an army hospital. *Journal of Clinical Psychology, 28*, 505–510.

Hofer, P. J., & Bersoff, D. N. (1983). *Standards for the administration and interpretation of automated psychological testing.* Unpublished manuscript. (Available from P. J. Hofer or D. N. Bersoff, Suite 511, 17th St. N.W., Washington, DC 20036)

Holtzman, W. H. (1975). New developments in the Holtzman Inkblot Technique. In P. McReynolds (Ed.), *Advances in psychological assessment,* (Vol. 3, pp. 243–274). San Francisco: Jossey–Bass.

Johnson, J. H., Giannetti, R. A., & Williams, T. A. (1978). A self-contained microcomputer system for psychological testing. *Behavior Research Methods and Instrumentation, 10*, 579–581.

Karson, S., & O'Dell, J. W. (1975). A new automated interpretation system for the 16PF. *Journal of Personality Assessment, 39*, 256–260.

Karson, S., & O'Dell, J. W. (1987). Computer-based interpretation of the 16PF: The Karson Clinical Report in contemporary practice. In J. N. Butcher (Ed.), *Computerized psychological assessment: A practitioner's guide* (pp. 198–217). New York: Basic Books.

Katz, L., & Dalby, J. T. (1981). Computer assisted and traditional assessment of elementary-school-aged children. *Contemporary Educational Psychology, 6*, 314–322.

Kleinmuntz, B. (1963). MMPI decision rules for the identification of college maladjustment. *Psychological Monographs, 77*(14 Whole No. 577).

Kleinmuntz, B. (Ed.). (1968). *Formal representation of human judgment.* New York: Wiley.

Kleinmuntz, B. (1969). Personality test interpretation by computer and clinician. In J. N. Butcher (Ed.), *MMPI: Research developments and clinical applications* (pp. 97–104). New York: McGraw–Hill.

Kleinmuntz, B. (1972). *Computers in personality assessment.* New York: General Learning Press.

Kleinmuntz, B. (1975). The computer as clinician. *American Psychologist, 30*, 379–387.

Klett, W. (1971, May). The utility of computer interpreted MMPIs at St. Cloud VA Hospital. *Newsletter of Research in Psychology, 13,* pp. 45–47.

Klett, B., Schaefer, A., & Plemel, D. (1985, May). Just how accurate are computer-scored tests? *VA Chief Psychologist, 8,* p. 7.

Klingler, D. E., Johnson, J. H., & Williams, T. A. (1976). Strategies in the evaluation of an on-line computer-assisted unit for intake assessment of mental health patients. *Behavior Research Methods and Instrumentation, 8,* 95–100.

Klingler, D. E., Miller, D. A., Johnson, J. H., & Williams, T. A. (1977). Process evaluation of an on-line computer-assisted unit for intake assessment of mental health patients. *Behavior Research Methods and Instrumentation, 9,* 110–116.

Kostlan, A. (1954). A method for the empirical study of psychodiagnosis. *Journal of Consulting Psychology, 18,* 83–88.

Krug, S. E. (Ed.). (1987). *Psychware Sourcebook* (2nd ed). Kansas City, MO: Test Corporation of America.

Kurtz, R. M., & Garfield, S. L. (1978). Illusory correlation: A further exploration of Chapman's paradigm. *Journal of Consulting and Clinical Psychology, 46,* 1009–1015.

Labeck, L. J., Johnson, J. H., & Harris, W. G. (1983). Validity of an automated on-line MMPI interpretive system. *Journal of Clinical Psychology, 39,* 412–416.

Lachar, D. (1974a). Accuracy and generalization of an automated MMPI interpretation system. *Journal of Consulting and Clinical Psychology, 42,* 267–273.

Lachar, D. (1974b). *The MMPI: Clinical assessment and automated interpretation.*Los Angeles: Western Psychological Services.

Lachar, D. (1982). *Personality Inventory for Children (PIC) revised format manual supplement.* Los Angeles: Western Psychological Services.

Lachar, D. (1987). Automated assessment of child and adolescent personality: The Personality Inventory for Children (PIC). In J. N. Butcher (Ed.), *Computerized psychological assessment: A practitioner's guide* (pp. 261–291). New York: Basic Books.

Lachar, D., & Gdowski, C. G. (1979). *Actuarial assessment of child and adolescent personality: An interpretive guide for the Personality Inventory for Children profile.* Los Angeles: Western Psychological Services.

Lachar D., Klinge, V., & Grisell, J. L. (1976). Relative accuracy of automated MMPI narratives generated from adult norm and adolescent norm profiles. *Journal of Consulting and Clinical Psychology, 44,* 20–24.

Lanyon, R. I. (1984). Personality assessment. In M. R. Rosenzweig & L. W. Porter (Eds.), *Annual review of psychology* (Vol. 35, pp. 667–701). Palo Alto, CA: Annual Reviews.

Little, K. B., & Shneidman, E. S. (1959). Congruencies among interpretation of psychological test and anamnestic data. *Psychological Monographs, 73*(6, Whole No. 476).

Lushene, R. E., & Gilberstadt, H. (1972, March). *Validation of VA MMPI computer-generated reports.* Paper presented at the Veterans Administration Cooperative Studies Conference, St. Louis.

Manning, H. M. (1971). Programmed interpretation of the MMPI. *Journal of Personality Assessment, 35,* 162–176.

Marks, P. A., & Seeman, W. (1963). *The actuarial description of personality: An atlas for use with the MMPI.* Baltimore: Williams & Wilkins.

Marks, P. A., Seeman, W., & Haller, D. L. (1974). *The actuarial use of the MMPI with adolescents and adults.* Baltimore: Williams & Wilkins.

Matarazzo, J. M. (1983, July 22). Computerized psychological testing. *Science, 221,* 323.

Matarazzo, J. M. (1985). Clinical psychological test interpretations by computer: Hardware outpaces software. *Computers in Human Behavior, 1,* 235–253.

Matarazzo, J. M. (1986). Computerized clinical psychological test interpretation: Unvalidated plus all mean and no sigma. *American Psychologist, 44,* 14–24.

McDonald, C. J. (1976). Protocol-based computer reminders, the quality of care and the non-perfectibility of man. *New England Journal of Medicine, 295,* 1351–1355.

Maxwell, A. E. (1971). Multivariate statistical methods and classification problems. *British Journal of Psychiatry. 119,* 121–127.

Meehl, P. E. (1956). Wanted – a good cookbook. *American Psychologist, 11,* 263–272.

Meehl, P. E. (1960). The cognitive activity of the clinician. *American Psychologist, 15,* 19–27.

Meehl, P. E., Schofield, W., Glueck, B. C., Studdiford, W. B., Hastings, D. W., Hathaway, S. R., & Clyde, D. J. (1962). *Minnesota-Ford pool of phenotypic personality items* (August 1962 ed.). Unpublished materials. (Available from P. E. Meehl or W. Schofield, Department of Psychiatry, 393 Mayo Memorial Building, University of Minnesota, Minneapolis, MN 55455.)

Millon, T. (1981). *Disorders of Personality: DSM–III, Axis II.* New York: Wiley.

Millon, T. (1982). *Millon clinical multiaxial inventory manual* (3rd ed.). Minneapolis: National Computer Systems.

Moreland, K. L. (1983, April). *A comparison of the validity of two MMPI interpretation systems: A preliminary report.* Paper presented at the 18th annual Symposium on Recent Developments in the Use of the MMPI, Minneapolis.

Moreland, K. L. (1985). Validation of computer-based test interpretations: Problems and prospects. *Journal of Consulting and Clinical Psychology, 53,* 816–825.

Moreland, K. L. (1987). Computer-based test interpretations: Advice to the consumer. In L. D. Eyde (Ed.), *Computerised testing.* London: Lawrence Erlbaum Associates.

Moreland, K. L., & Onstad, J. A. (1985, March). *Validity of the Minnesota Report, 1: Mental health outpatients.* Paper presented at the 20th annual Symposium on Recent Developments in the Use of the MMPI, Honolulu.

Moreland, K. L., & Onstad, J. A. (1987a). Validity of Millon's computerized interpretation system for the MCMI: A controlled study. *Journal of Consulting and Clinical Psychology, 55,* 113–114.

Moreland, K. L. & Onstad, J. A. (1987b, summer). A controlled study of the Minnesota Report: Adult Clinical System. *Network News, 1,* 1, 6, 11. (Available from National Computer Systems, P. O. Box 1416, Minneapolis, MN 55440.)

Mules, W. C. (1972). A comparison of conventional modes of interpreting Strong Vocational Interest Blank results to modes which employ a computer generated, prose interpretation. *Dissertation Abstracts International, 33,* 1445a.

Murphy, K. R. (1987). The accuracy of clinical versus computerized test interpretations. *American Psychologist, 42,* 192–193.

National Computer Systems (1989). *Professional Assessment Services 1989 Catalog.* Minneapolis: Author.

Nichols, D. (1985). Review of the Minnesota Report: Personnel Selection System. In J. V. Mitchell, Jr. (Ed.), *Ninth mental measurements yearbook* (Vol. 2, pp. 1008–1009). Lincoln, NE: Buros Institute of Mental measurements.

O'Dell, J. W. (1972). P. T. Barnum explores the computer. *Journal of Consulting and Clinical Psychology, 38,* 270–273.

Palmer, W. H. (1971). Actuarial MMPI interpretation: A replication and extension. *Dissertation Abstracts International, 31,* 3265B.

Payne, F. D., & Wiggins, J. S. (1968). Effects of rule relaxation and system combination on classification rates in two MMPI "cookbook" systems. *Journal of Consulting and Clinical Psychology, 32,* 734–736.

Pearson, J. S., Rome, H. P., Swenson, W. M., Mataya, P., & Brannick, T. L. (1965). Development of a computer system for scoring and interpretation of MMPI in a medical clinic. *Annals of the New York Academy of Sciences, 126,* 684–692.

Petterson, J. (1983, November 9). Computer testing spurs writing of ethics codes. *Kansas City Times,* pp. A1, A11.

Piotrowski, Z. A. (1964). A digital computer administration of inkblot test data. *Psychiatric Quarterly, 38,* 1–26.

Ripley, R. E., & Ripley, M. J. (1979). *Career families: Interpretation manual for the World of Work Inventory* (rev. ed.). Scottsdale, AZ: World of Work.

Rome, H. P., Mataya, P., Pearson, J. S., Swenson, W., & Brannick, T. L. (1965). Automatic personality assessment. In R. W. Stacy & B. Waxman (Eds.), *Computers in biomedical research* (Vol 1., pp. 505–524). New York: Academic Press.

Sines, L. K. (1959). The relative contribution of four kinds of data to accuracy in personality assessment. *Journal of Consulting Psychology, 1959, 23,* 483–492.

Sines, J. O. (1966). Actuarial methods in personality assessment. In B. Maher (Ed.), *Progress in experimental personality research* (Vol. 3, pp. 133–193). New York: Academic Press.

Sundberg, N. D. (1985a). Review of Behaviordyne Psychodiagnostic Laboratory Service. In J. V. Mitchell, Jr. (Ed.), *Ninth Mental Measurements Yearbook* (pp. 1003–1005). Lincoln, NE: Buros Institute of Mental Measurements.

Sundberg, N. D. (1985b). Review of WPS Test Report. In J. V. Mitchell, Jr. (Ed.) *Ninth Mental Measurements Yearbook* (pp. 1009–1011). Lincoln, NE: Buros Institute of Mental Measurements.

Tucker, G. J., & Rosenberg, S. D. (1980). Computer analysis of schizophrenic speech: An example of computer usage in the study of psychopathologic processes. In J. B. Sidowski, J. H. Johnson, & T. A. Williams (Eds.). *Technology in mental health care delivery systems,* Norwood, NJ: Ablex.

University of Minnesota. (1982). *User's guide for the Minnesota Report.* Minneapolis: National Computer Systems.

University of Minnesota. (1984). *User's guide for the Minnesota Report: Personnel Selection System.* Minneapolis: National Computer Systems.

Vincent, K. R., & Castillo, I. M. (1984). A comparison of two MMPI narratives. *Computers in Psychiatry/Psychology, 6*(4), 30–32.

Vincent, K. R., Wilson, A. L., & Wilson, J. L. (1983). *Automated interpretation program for the MMPI.* Houston: Psychometric Services.

Webb, J. T. (1970). Validity and utility of computer-produced MMPI reports with Veterans Administration psychiatric populations (Summary). *Proceedings of the 78th annual convention of the American Psychological Association, 5,* 541–542.

Webb, J. T., Miller, M. L., & Fowler, R. D. (1969). Validation of a computerized MMPI interpretation system (Summary). *Proceedings of the 77th annual convention of the American Psychological Association, 4,* 523–524.

Webb, J. T., Miller, M. L., & Fowler, R. D. (1970). Extending professional time: A computerized MMPI interpretation service. *Journal of Clinical Psychology, 26,* 210–214.

Weigel, R. G., & Phillips, M. (1967). An evaluation of MMPI scoring accuracy by two national scoring agencies. *Journal of Clinical Psychology, 23,* 101–103.

Weizenbaum, J. (1976). *Computer power and human reason: From judgment to calculation.* San Francisco: Freeman.

Western Psychological Services. (1984). *1985–1986 catalog.* Los Angeles: Author.

Wimbish, L. G. (1984). The importance of appropriate norms for the computerized interpretation of adolescent MMPI profiles. *Dissertation Abstracts International, 46,* 3234B. (University Microfilms No. 85-26, 277).

4
The Validity of Computer-Based Test Interpretations of the MMPI

Lorraine D. Eyde
U.S. Office of Personnel Management

Dennis M. Kowal
U.S. Army

Francis J. Fishburne, Jr.
U.S. Army, Retired

With advances in computer technology, computer-based test interpretations (CBTI), first developed in the early 1960s (Fowler, 1985), have proliferated (Eyde & Kowal, 1987). CBTIs have been developed and marketed for a variety of tests used in clinical, counseling, educational, and employment settings. The largest number of commercial CBTI systems are available for the Minnesota Multiphasic Personality Inventory (MMPI; Krug, 1987), the most widely used inventory of its kind in the world, which has a continuously growing literature of more than 8,000 books and articles (Holden, 1986; Lanyon, 1984).

According to Harris

> CBTI refers to the automation of a set of pre-specified rules for use in analyzing, interpreting and assigning certain qualities to a response or response pattern (e.g., test score, profile pattern). The discrete rules are used to form an algorithm that guides the activity of the computer to interpret specific input data. (1987, p. 239)

Consumers of CBTIs have very little information available on the development of the algorithm or the validity of the CBTI systems. Companies selling CBTIs often do not provide a user's guide. The algorithms used in generating the computer interpretations are not available to CBTI users nor are they provided for scholarly review purposes. Notable exceptions to these business practices include Lachar's (1974) presentation of all the rules and interpretive statements for the WPS Test Report, the MMPI CBTI sold by Western Psychological Services. National Computer Systems provided the algorithms for the Minnesota Report:

Personnel Selection System, for scholarly review purposes, and gave an independent evaluation of the extent to which the interpretive statements were based on the MMPI's research literature or on the clinical judgment of the CBTI's author (Eyde, 1985).

Numerous critics have pointed out serious problems arising from the growth of CBTIs. Mitchell (1984) observed that the advent of CBTIs "presents the field of psychology with its most serious and consequential challenge of the next decade." Lanyon (1984) called attention to the exponential growth of available CBTI systems, noting that Meehl's cookbook approach to MMPI interpretation (however carefully designed) has been used to justify and market many inadequate systems. Eyde and Kowal (1987) commented that "the scientific basis for the C.B.T.I., namely the decision rules which codify the rationale and the evidence used to produce the computer interpretations, may wind up locked in a black box, inaccessible to test users" (p. 402). Also, Matarazzo (1986) decried the lack of validity evidence for CBTIs.

The problems associated with CBTIs have to do not only with the lack of validity data, but also with the problem of how to *establish* the validity of a computer interpretive report (Mitchell, 1984; Moreland, 1985, 1987; O'Dell, 1972). Mitchell (1984) notes that purists who want to do the job properly, "are faced with the task of a conducting a statement-by-statement validation involving statements generated by decision rules and decision trees of almost incomprehensible complexity."

Critics of prevailing practices in developing, marketing, and validating computerized applications of knowledge-based systems, may choose, as Eyde and Kowal (1985) have, to do some of the developmental work that should have been done before a computerized test product is sold.

The intent of this chapter is to describe a methodology for studying the validity of the output of CBTI systems. The research focuses on a variety of CBTI systems developed as tools for interpreting the MMPI. The MMPI is the most widely used psychodiagnostic instrument with active-duty military populations (Parkison & Fishburne, 1984). Our methodology is designed so that it may be adapted to CBTIs for other tests or self-report inventories. The study involves a comparative analysis of the accuracy, relevancy, and usefulness of the output of seven CBTI systems for patients in a military hospital which draws its patients from a wide geographical area. The research design allows us to make some inferences about the relative accuracy of CBTI systems for different profile types. A secondary objective of the research was to identify racial differences, if any, in the accuracy of the CBTIs.

This chapter will describe the study, provide basic data, and describe the results. Other chapters will cover (a) the Black/white differences in the accuracy of the CBTIs, which are minimal (Eyde, Kowal, & Fishburne, 1987); and (b) neuropsychological cases vs. nonneuropsychological cases (Fishburne, Eyde, & Kowal, 1988).

MMPI ELEMENTS FOR CBTI USE

Since a major objective of this research was to establish and apply a methodology for validating CBTIs, we will summarize some elements to aid in understanding computer interpretations of the MMPI, the inventory used in this study. Readers are referred to Anastasi (1988) and Graham and Lilly (1984) for a general introduction to MMPI use, and to Dahlstrom, Welsh, and Dahlstrom (1972), Graham (1987), Greene (1980), or Lachar (1974) for more detailed presentations.

The MMPI, a self-report inventory with 566 true–false or cannot-say (omitted) items, has an extensive history dating back to the 1930s. Its derivational groups, which consisted of both normal and clinical groups, were used in developing empirically based scoring keys, to aid in assigning psychiatric diagnostic labels to patients.

The MMPIs content includes items dealing with

> Health, psychosomatic symptoms, neurological disorders, and motor disturbances; sexual, religious, political, and social attitudes; educational, occupational, family, and marital questions; and many well-known neurotic or psychotic behavior manifestations, such as obsessive and compulsive states, delusions, hallucinations, ideas of reference, phobias, and sadistic and masochistic trends. (Anastasi, 1988, p. 526)

The basic MMPI profile provides 10 "clinical" scales and 3 validity scales as described in Table 4.1. An additional validity scale, Cannot Say, which consists of the items omitted by the test taker, is usually reported. Furthermore, several hundred research scales are available.

Scale numbers are used in preference to scale names because diagnostic labels have changed since the inception of MMPI research. The scales have correlates that range far beyond those implied by the labels. Furthermore, with the increased use of the MMPI with nonhospitalized groups it is necessary to avoid the use of stigmatizing labels. From the large empirical research base and clinical lore on these scale scores it is possible to draw inferences about the test taker's personality organization or structure, psychopathology, and other characteristics.

The validity indicators (Cannot Say, L [lie] scale, F scale [items infrequently endorsed by normal test takers] and K scale [to assess clinical defensiveness]) deal with test-taking attitudes. Greene (1980, p. 117) observes that "validity scales serve primarily to establish whether a *specific* clinical scale profile can be safely interpreted" (emphasis added). Dahlstrom et al. (1972, p. 100) differentiate the psychometric term "validity" (that is, the extent to which inferences about the test are meaningful) from its usage with the MMPI *validity indicators* in which the validity "pertains to the appropriateness or acceptability of any *one* administration of the test" (emphasis added).

TABLE 4.1
Sample Interpretive Inferences for Standard Minnesota Multiphasic Personality Inventory Scales

Scale Name	Scale Abbrev.	Scale Number	Interpretation of High Scores	Interpretation of Low Scores
—	L	—	Trying to create favorable impression by not being honest in responding to items; conventional; rigid; moralistic; lacks insight	Responded frankly to items; confident; perceptive; self-reliant; cynical
—	F	—	May indicate invalid profile; severe pathology; moody; restless; dissatisfied	Socially conforming; free of disabling psychopathology; may be "faking good"
—	K	—	May indicate invalid profile; defensive; inhibited; intolerant; lacks insight	May indicate invalid profile; exaggerates problems; self-critical; dissatisfied; conforming; lacks insight; cynical
Hypochondriasis	Hs	1	Excessive bodily concern; somatic symptoms, narcissistic; pessimistic; demanding; critical; long-standing problems	Free of somatic preoccupation; optimistic; sensitive; insightful
Depression	D	2	Depressed; pessimistic; irritable; dissatisfied; lacks self-confidence; introverted; overcontrolled	Free of psychological turmoil; optimistic; energetic; competitive; impulsive; undercontrolled; exhibitionistic
Hysteria	Hy	3	Physical symptoms of functional origin; lacks insight; self-centered; socially involved; demands attention and affection	Constricted; conventional; narrow interests; limited social participation; untrusting; hard to get to know; realistic
Psychopathic Deviate	Pd	4	Asocial or antisocial; rebellious; impulsive; poor judgment; immature; creates good first impression; superficial relationships; aggressive; free of psychological turmoil	Conventional; conforming; accepts authority; low drive level; concerned about status and security; persistent; moralistic
Masculinity/ Femininity	Mf	5	Male: aesthetic interests; insecure in masculine role; creative, good judgment; sensitive; passive; dependent; good self-control Female: rejects traditional female role; masculine interests; assertive; competitive; self-confident; logical; unemotional	Male: overemphasizes strength and physical prowess; adventurous; narrow interests; inflexible; contented; lacks insight Female: accepts traditional female role; passive; yielding to males; complaining; critical; constricted
Paranoia	Pa	6	May exhibit frankly psychotic behavior; suspicious; sensitive; resentful; projects; rationalizes; moralistic; rigid	May have frankly psychotic symptoms; evasive; defensive; guarded; secretive; withdrawn
Psychasthenia	Pt	7	Anxious; worried; difficulties in concentrating; ruminative; obsessive; compulsive; insecure; lacks self-confidence; organized; persistent; problems in decision making	Free of disabling fears and anxieties; self-confident; responsible; adaptable; values success and status
Schizophrenia	Sc	8	May have thinking disturbance; withdrawn; self-doubts; feels alienated and unaccepted; vague goals	Friendly, sensitive, trustful; avoids deep emotional involvement; conventional; unimaginative

78

Scale Name	Scale Abbrev.	Scale Number	Interpretation of High Scores	Interpretation of Low Scores
Hypomania	Ma	9	Excessive activity; impulsive; lacks direction; unrealistic self-appraisal; low frustration tolerance; friendly; manipulative; episodes of depression	Low energy level; apathetic; responsible; conventional; lacks self-confidence;overcontrolled
Social Introversion	Si	0	Socially introverted; shy; sensitive; overcontrolled; conforming; problems in decision making	Socially extroverted; friendly; active; competitive; impulsive; self-indulgent

From J. R. Graham (1978), The Minnesota Multiphasic Personality Inventory (MMPI). In B. B. Wolman (Ed.), Clinical diagnosis of mental disorders: A handbook. New York: Plenum Press. Copyright 1978 by Plenum Press. Reproduced by permission.

The test taker's raw scores on the scales are usually transformed to linear T-scores with a mean of 50 and a standard deviation of 10 (Dahlstrom et al., 1972). In other words, the T- or standard scores are not transformed to approximate the normal distribution. There are two exceptions to this practice relevant to this chapter. Colligan, Osborne, Swenson, and Offord (1983) reported their normative data in terms of T-scores that were transformed to approximate the normal distribution. The Morris–Tomlinson Report is based on these data. Finney, whose normative data form the basis of the current Behaviordyne MMPI CBTIs, also uses normalized T-scores and, in addition, reports the Minnesota standard scores. T-scores aid in making direct comparisons among scales for test takers. Scores of 70 on the clinical scales are commonly used as cutoffs to identify potential deviancy or psychopathology.

The T-score tables are generally based on the normative data collected on Midwestern white adults before World War II (Dahlstrom et al., 1972). A major restandardization effort, using a nationwide sample, sponsored by the University of Minnesota Press, the test publisher, is under way (Holden, 1986). A modern restandardization employing Midwestern whites was reported by Colligan et al. (1983). Finney (1968) developed his norms in Kentucky. Graham and Lilly (1984, p. 238) point out that "the standardization samples used for the T-score conversions are the same normal subjects used in constructing the scales. . . . Thus, the theoretically normal or average person would have T-scores of approximately fifty on all of the scales."

Interpretation of the MMPI generally begins with a review of test taker's scores on the validity indicators, namely, the validity profile. If the test taker appears to have responded to the inventory in a reasonably straightforward manner (e.g., has not attempted to dissimulate), then elevated scores on individual clinical scales or combinations of scales (most often the two that are most elevated) are evaluated in terms of the accumulated evidence about their meaning. Dahlstrom et al. observed that

Groups formed on the basis of the evaluation of a single scale may still be quite heterogeneous and the stable correlates may be rather different in this kind of analysis from those resulting when the groups are formed on the basis of common test *patterns* (i.e., combinations of scales). (1972, p. 178)

Since its inception, the MMPI test authors, Hathaway and McKinley, recognized the diagnostic richness of using configural analysis, for example, basing interpretations on elevations on two scales, that is, two-point codes. In general, the two-point codes are used interchangeably; that is, a 7/2 code and a 2/7 are treated the same.

With these essentials of MMPI interpretation in mind, readers may find it useful to review the general approach to MMPI interpretation used by a scientist-practitioner in his clinical work (Graham, 1977, pp. 150–151).

1. What was the test-taking attitude of the examinee, and how should this attitude be taken into account in interpreting the protocol?
2. What is the general level of adjustment of the person who produced the protocol?
3. What kinds of behaviors (symptoms, attitudes, defenses, etc.) can be inferred about or expected from the person who produced the protocol?
4. What etiology or set of psychological dynamics underlie the behaviors described?
5. What are the most appropriate diagnostic labels for the person who produced the protocol?
6. What are the implications for the treatment of the person who produced the protocol?

These six areas for which inferences may be drawn in interpreting the MMPI appear to have been used, to varying degrees, in the preparation of narrative statements for the libraries of CBTI systems for the MMPI.

CRITICISMS OF RESEARCH ON CBTI SYSTEMS

This chapter reports on a large-scale research project on the validity of the output of CBTI systems for the MMPI, based on a modification of Moreland's 1980 research plan (W. G. Dahlstrom, personal communication, November 20, 1985; Moreland, 1985, 1987). Our research plan took into consideration Moreland's criticism of research on the validity of CBTI systems, his recommendations for future research, and advice to consumers evaluating CBTI systems.

Moreland's (1985, 1987) criteria for evaluating CBTI research served as a model for developing our design. The dependent variable was ratings, by experienced clinical psychologists, of the accuracy of all individual narrative statements or sentences from each CBTI system. Existing (file drawer) case histories or self-report questionnaires (for subclinical normal cases) were used as the criteria against which raters made their evaluations. The independent variables were seven CBTI systems, the nature of the MMPI profiles evaluated (e.g., profile types), and the race of the subjects.

Moreland's (1985, 1987) literature review brings out factors that should be considered in efforts to determine the accuracy of CBTI interpretations. In particular, the design should require raters to evaluate specific interpretive statements; limiting them to global accuracy ratings will limit the usefulness of the ratings for improving the CBTI system. He stressed the need for maximizing the number and variety of cases and the need for developing procedures for selecting an unbiased sample and he noted the importance of assessing rater reliability. He points out the merits of basing ratings on external criteria such as records or special research instruments, which provide raters with a standard criterion, in preference to studies in which clinicians evaluate the accuracy of CBTI's by using their own unsystematic observations on patients.

Moreland's (1987) review indicates that few existing commercial CBTI systems have been so evaluated and they are often evaluated for only a limited number of types of profiles. Moreland reviewed comparative studies of clinicians' ratings of the global accuracy of five CBTI systems. Only two of these (the Minnesota Report and the WPS Test Report) are currently marketed. He also examined four studies which evaluated five CBTI systems against external criteria; three of these (Behaviordyne, the Caldwell Report, and the WPS Test Report) continue to be commercially available. He found that the number of cases and the profile types evaluated tended to be limited in number in these latter four studies. Raters were sometimes students, such as psychiatric residents, rather than fully qualified clinicians and the evaluation of interrater reliability was infrequent.

Moreland (1985) recommended that raters focus on identifying irrelevant (e.g., redundant) statements and separate these statements from those whose accuracy should be rated. He also recommended identifying significant omissions in the CBTI's content (1987). The present study endeavors to incorporate these recommendations in its design.

WRAMC RESEARCH DESIGN AND SETTING

Overview of Research Methodology

The general methodology for this study is outlined in Fig. 4.1. Hospital patients, whose records met specific test and demographic criteria, were selected to form a research sample, stratified by profile type, and within these constraints selected

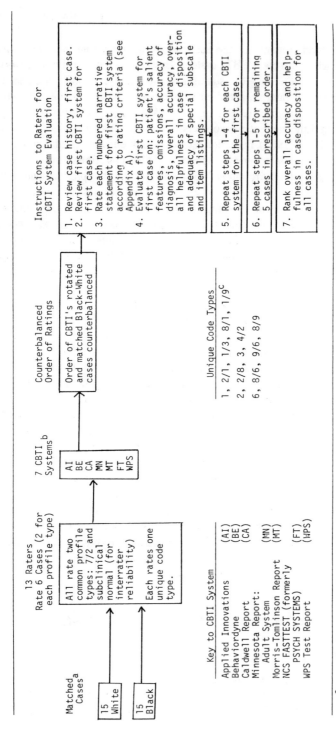

Instructions to Raters for
CBTI System Evaluation

1. Review case history, first case.
2. Review first CBTI system for first case.
3. Rate each numbered narrative statement for first CBTI system according to rating criteria (see Appendix A).
4. Evaluate first CBTI system for first case on: patient's salient features, omissions, accuracy of diagnosis, overall accuracy, over-all helpfulness in case disposition and adequacy of special subscale and item listings.
5. Repeat steps 1-4 for each CBTI system for the first case.
6. Repeat steps 1-5 for remaining 5 cases in prescribed order.
7. Rank overall accuracy and help-fulness in case disposition for all cases.

Counterbalanced
Order of Ratings

Order of CBTI's rotated and matched Black-White cases counterbalanced

7 CBTI Systems[b]

AI
BE
CA
MN
MT
FT
WPS

Unique Code Types

1, 2/1, 1/3, 8/1, 1/9[c]
2, 2/8, 3, 4/2
6, 8/6, 9/6, 8/9

13 Raters
Rate 6 Cases (2 for each profile type)

All rate two common profile types: 7/2 and subclinical normal (for interrater reliability)

Each rates one unique code type.

Matched Cases[a]

15 White

15 Black

Key to CBTI System

Applied Innovations	(AI)
Behaviordyne	(BE)
Caldwell Report	(CA)
Minnesota Report: Adult System	(MN)
Morris-Tomlinson Report	(MT)
NCS FASTTEST (formerly PSYCH SYSTEMS)	(FT)
WPS Test Report	(WPS)

[a]See selection criteria in Table 4.2 for matching according to MMPI profile types.
[b]See Table 6 for selection of CBTI companies.
[c]This code type was rated but was lost in the mail.

FIG. 4.1.   Methodology for the WRAMC study of the validity of CBTI systems for the MMPI.

randomly. Experienced Army clinical psychologists rated the accuracy of MMPI CBTIs generated by several CBTI systems, using case history materials as the criterion. They all rated two pairs of Black/white cases matched on the basis of profile type, making it possible to obtain data on interrater reliability. Each rater also rated one unique code type for a matched pair of Black/white cases. Thus each clinician rated six subjects: (a) a pair of 7/2 code type cases, (b) a pair of cases without significant elevations on MMPI scales, and (c) a pair representing some different (i.e., not 7/2) code type. Each rater rated each numbered sentence of a CBTI for a subject within the context of each paragraph.

Nature of Hospital Population

Our clinical subjects were drawn from inpatient and out-patient files at Walter Reed Army Medical Center (WRAMC), covering a period of 3 years (1983–1985) during which at least 1,500 MMPIs were administered and interpreted. WRAMC draws its inpatient population from active-duty military personnel or their dependents from the east coast of the United States, Europe, and from a large group of retired military families in metropolitan Washington, D.C., area. Patients referred to WRAMC are evaluated for complex diagnostic or treatment problems (including neurological cases) or for determinations of fitness to continue to serve on active duty.

Inpatients at the hospital may be admitted from the local area or from one of the feeder hospitals within the military system. Requests for psychological evaluation may occur at any point in the course of the patient's stay in the hospital; the majority of the requests for psychological evaluations are made within the first 2 weeks of the patient's admission. At the point of the patient's discharge from the hospital, a narrative summary of the patient's hospitalization is prepared by the treating physician. This summary will include all of the pertinent information gathered on the patient over the course of his stay in the hospital and provides the most comprehensive overview of the patient's status at the time of discharge. Although the time between admission and discharge may vary, depending on the nature of the patient's case, it is not unusual for a 6-month period to exist between admission of the patient and dictation of the narrative summary. Thus, the psychological evaluation may have occurred some months prior to the final narrative summary with intervening events accounting for changes in the patient's status.

Psychological reports are also provided for out-patients who are generally referred to the hospital from nearby military installations. Reports include an evaluation of the patient's salient personality and a diagnostic evaluation of possible psychopathology. Treatment recommendations often are not made.

Neuropsychological evaluations are provided by psychologists, largely for inpatients who have experienced a neurological event. The patient's brain-based functioning is evaluated, salient personality characteristics described, and treatment recommendations made.

Selection of Subjects

The criteria for selecting the Black and white subjects, matched by profile type, for our study of the accuracy of CBTIs, are given in Table 4.2. The subjects were restricted to active-duty males, from 20 to 29 years old, who were inpatients or out-patients in WRAMC from 1983 through 1985 or soldiers who were in the Army's normative study of the MMPI (Fishburne & Parkison, 1984).

Each clinical case selected had (a) a case history, (b) an MMPI answer sheet, and (c) met the raw score criteria, set for the basic validity scales in consultation with W. Grant Dahlstrom. These were: Cannot say $\leq$ 49, Lie $\leq$ 10, F $\leq$ 21. The case history may be an inpatient report, an outpatient report, or a neuropsychological evaluation. The subclinical subjects met criteria (b) and (c) and had completed an anonymous self-report questionnaire covering, for example, military disciplinary actions and treatment for emotional problems.

Subjects were not screened on the basis of their K scores, a measure of clinical defensiveness, because it is not appropriate to use this score for rejecting a total profile. Furthermore, only the scales which deal with clinical syndromes were used to select code types; hence, scores on scales 5 (Masculinity–femininity) and 0 (Social Introversion) were not considered.

The matched pairs of subjects were chosen to maximize the number and nature of MMPI code types in the study. Inpatients and outpatients were included as were psychiatric, medical, and neuropsychological cases. Thirty-three spike and two-point code types involving elevations of $T \geq 70$ were sought, representing a range of frequently occurring code types (see Table 4.3). Black-white cases were matched for four spike profiles and 9 two-point code types.

We began searching for the code types as listed in Table 4.3 by searching the 1983 WRAMC files for the first white case for the first code type, a spike 1 profile. All other code types were ignored until the 1′ profile was found. Then we searched until we found the next code type, a 1/2 case. If the code type we were seeking could not be found by going through the 1983 files, we followed

TABLE 4.2
Case Selection Criteria for Black/White Pairs Matched on MMPI Code
Type in WRAMC Validity Study

Inpatient or outpatient, Walter Reed Army Medical Center, 1983-1985
Active duty uniformed personnel
Male
Age 20-29
Documented case history/background information
Race: White (Caucasian) or Black non-Hispanic
MMPI Answer Sheet Available
    Validity Profile Scores
    Cannot say $\leq$ 49 raw score
    Lie $\leq$ 10 raw score
    F $\leq$ 21 raw score
Among 33 spike profile and two-point code types ($T \leq 70$), using stratified sample or in Army normative study and net above criteria with $T \leq 70$ on clinical scales and had no record of disciplinary actions or inpatient or outpatient treatment for emotional problems.

TABLE 4.3
Spike Profile and Two-Point MMPI Code Types of Matched Black/White Cases
Sought for WRAMC CBTI System Validity Study

1[a]	12/21[a]	13/31 [a]	14/41	18/81[a]	19/91[b]		
2[a]	23/32	24/4 [a]	26/62	27/72 [a]	28/8[a]	29/92
3[a]	34/43	36/63	38/83	39/93		
4	46/64	47/74	48/84	49/94		
6[a]	67/76	68/8[a]	69/96[a]			
7	78/87	79/97				
8	89/98[a]					
9						

Note. Systematic search was made for code types listed in Graham (1977), Greene (1980), Lachar (1974), or were present in 1% or greater of two-point code types in Appendix M, Tables 9, 11, 13, and 15 in Dahlstrom, Welsh, and Dahlstrom (1972). Also, two subclinical normal profiles were included in the study.
[a] Spike and two-point code types included in the study.
[b] Ratings were completed, but the data were lost in the mail.

the same procedures for the 1984 and 1985 files. That cycle continued for the remaining white code types, in the order given in Table 4.3. The same steps were taken in the search for the Black cases, beginning with the 1983 files. Cases that could not be matched by race were discarded.

We followed the same procedures for selecting white and Black subclinical normal cases from the U. S. Army's normative study of the MMPI (Fishburne & Parkison, 1984; Parkison & Fishburne, 1984), which covered active-duty males from age 18 to 33, who were stationed throughout the United States and Europe. All the subjects in the normative study, on the average, had 12 years of education, and were, on the average, 25. The two subclinical normal cases were drawn from the sample of 1,032 subjects who met the MMPI validity criteria, scored $\leq$ 5 on the Carelessness Scale (Greene, 1980) and had IQ scores of at least 75 on the Shipley Institute of Living Scale. The subjects met these MMPI validity criteria: Cannot say $\leq$ 29; and $F \leq$ 24. The 1,930 subjects in the normative study were also screened on a 43-item background information questionnaire, which may be obtained from the authors. Soldiers who reported any of the following background factors were excluded: felony convictions, court-martials, a psychiatric hospitalization, a suicide attempt, psychiatric treatment, or treatment for a drug or alcohol problem. A total of 898 subjects from the normative study were excluded on the basis of test scores or legal, behavioral, or treatment criteria. Most of these subjects were excluded because of invalid test scores.

Background of the Subjects

The background of the 28 subjects reported here is given in Tables 4.4 and 4.5.

The common cases, assigned to all raters, consisted of a pair of Black and white cases from WRAMC matched for the 7/2 code type and a pair of Black and white soldiers from the Army normative study with subclinical, that is, all clinical scales < 70 T MMPI profiles. The common cases had the equivalent of

TABLE 4.4
Background Characteristics of Common Cases Evaluated by All Raters

Code Type	Race	Age	Marital Status	Years of Education	Nature of Subject
72/27	White	20	Single	12	Outpatient psychiatric[a]
72/27	Black	21	Married	12	Inpatient psychiatric
Subclinical normal	White	24	Married	12	Normative study
Subclinical normal	Black	22	Married	12 (GED)	Normative study

[a] Involved neuropsychological evaluation.

TABLE 4.5
Background Characteristics of Unique Cases Evaluated by Only One Rater

Background Characteristics

Rater	Code Type	Age	Race	Marital Status	Years of Education	Nature of Subject	
1	1	29	White	–	–	inpatient	medical
1	1	24	Black	single	12	inpatient	medical
2	2/1	22	White	married	13	outpatient	medical[a]
2	2/1	20	Black	–	–	outpatient	medical
3	1/3	23	White	married	12	inpatient	psychiatric
3	1/3	21	Black	single	13	inpatient	psychiatric
4	8/1	24	White	single	16	inpatient	medical[a]
4	1/8	27	Black	single	12	inpatient	medical[a]
6	2	26	White	married	12	inpatient	psychiatric
6	2	25	Black	single	12	inpatient	medical[a]
7	2/8	23	White	divorced	14	inpatient	psychiatric
7	2/8	27	Black	–	–	inpatient	psychiatric
8	3	26	White	married	–	inpatient	medical
8	3	24	Black	married	12	inpatient	medical[a]
9	4/2	29	White	divorced	–	inpatient	psychiatric
9	4/2	20	Black	single	–	inpatient	psychiatric
10	6	22	White	married	16	inpatient	medical[a]
10	6	27	Black	married	–	inpatient	psychiatric
11	8/6	20	White	married	12	inpatient	psychiatric
11	8/6	21	Black	single	12	inpatient	psychiatric
12	9/6	21	White	–	13	inpatient	medical[a]
12	9/6	24	Black	single	12(GED)	inpatient	psychiatric
13[b]	8/9	20	White	single	11	inpatient	psychiatric
13	8/9	27	Black	single	–	inpatient	psychiatric

[a] Involved neuropsychological evaluation.
[b] Materials provided to the rater for this code type included a psychological report written in response to a referral on the patient, which was not congruent with an 8/9 code type.

12 years of education (including G.E.D.), three out of four were married, and they were between 20 and 24. The 7/2 white case was a psychiatric out-patient involved in a neuropsychological evaluation, and the 7/2 Black case was a psychiatric inpatient.

The unique cases consisted of 12 pairs matched for race and MMPI spike or two-point code type. Twelve different MMPI spike or two-point codes were included. Each pair was evaluated by only one rater. The age of the subjects ranged from 20 to 29 years. Ten were single, eight married, two divorced, and data were not available for four subjects. Nine of them had 12 years or its equivalent of education, six had completed 13 to 16 years, one had 11 years education, and data were not available for eight subjects. Of the six subjects with more than 12 years of education, four involved neuropsychological examinations. Seven of the 24 cases involved a neuropsychological evaluation. Twenty-two subjects were inpatients, two out-patients. There were 13 psychiatric cases and 11 medical cases. Included were: (a) 5 code-type pairs which were psychiatric, (b) 4 pairs which were medical cases, and (c) 3 pairs which included a psychiatric and a medical case.

Selection and Nature of CBTI Systems

As of December, 1985, the authors were aware of 14 commercially available CBTI systems for the MMPI (see Table 4.6).

Nine of these systems were invited to participate in the project. The selection of the companies was made *largely* on the basis of the company's expression of interest in attending the 1984 APA-sponsored test publishers' meeting which the first author helped to organize. One company did not reply; eight of these companies agreed to participate. However, one company (Prime Focus' Weathers MMPI Report) later withdrew its software from the project. Thus, seven companies, namely half of the companies, participated. All of the older CBTI systems (Behaviordyne: Report No. 7, Detailed Clinical Report; the Caldwell Report; NCS Minnesota Report: Adult System; and the WPS Test Report) were included. In addition, 3 of the 10 new CBTI Systems (Applied Innovations: MMPI Interpretation, NCS FASTTEST, formerly PSYCH SYSTEMS, MMPI, and Psych Lab: The Morris–Tomlinson Report) participated.

Fowler (1985) has described six CBTI systems for the MMPI, including two earlier systems (Behaviordyne and Caldwell) and two later systems (WPS Test Report and Minnesota Report) covered in this study. The authors requested that each participating CBTI company provide manuals or documentation materials provided to CBTI users. Materials from the companies are cited in this section.

Finney's Detailed Clinical Report, Report No. 7, marketed by Behaviordyne (BE), does not provide a copyright date. Its history can be traced back to the 1960s (Dahlstrom et al., 1972; Finney, 1968; Graham, 1977; Wiggins, 1973) and this CBTI service was reviewed by Adair (1978b), Butcher (1978b), and Sund-

TABLE 4.6
CBTI Systems for the MMPI: Total N, Invitees, and Participants in the WRAMC
Validity Study

Total N. CBTI Systems		CBTI System Invitees	CBTI Systems Participants in Study
1	Applied Innovations: MMIP Interpretation	Y	Y
2	Behaviordyne: Report No. 7 (Detailed Clinical Report)	Y	Y
3	Caldwell Report	Y	Y
4	Integrated Professional System: MMPI Software	Y	N
5	International Information Systems: The MMPI Test	N	N
6	NCS Minnesota Report: Adult System	Y	Y
7	Morris-Tomlinson Report (PSYCH LAB)	Y	Y
8	NCS FASTTEST (formerly PSYCH SYSTEMS) MMPI	Y	Y
9	Precision People: MMPI Computer Report	N	N
10	Psychological Assessment Resources: The MMPI Interpretive System	N	N
11	Psychometric Software: MMPI Report Computer Program	N	N
12	Sienna Software: PSYCHSTAR	N	N
13	Prime Focus: Weathers MMPI Report	Y	Y[a]
14	WPS Test Report	Y	Y

Note. Y = yes; N = no.
[a] CBTI system software was withdrawn by CBTI company.

berg (1985a). The Behaviordyne Reports are based on Finney's norms, using normalized T distributions. Fowler (1985) notes Finney's reports, which are somewhat psychoanalytically oriented, are based on interpretations of the basic clinical scales, configurations and scores from his special scales. Behaviordyne incorporates Finney's idiosyncratic approach to MMPI interpretation. Behaviordyne uses the DSM–III classification system (American Psychiatric Association, 1980). Diagnostic impressions are listed according to the label most likely to fit the subject.

The Caldwell system, marketed as the Caldwell Report, also does not contain a copyright date. According to Fowler (1985, p. 750), this early developed system "is a highly configural simulation of Caldwell's own interpretive style." It is based on a large number of code types (A. B. Caldwell, personal communication, April 4, 1986). A single narrative statement "describing someone with a '49-94' code as 'manipulative, dramatizing, and acting out' might well have five to ten different validation sources for each of the three terms, and those sets of sources would be partially overlapping." Caldwell refers CBTI users to studies such as Chase's (1974) dissertation, which has been reviewed by Moreland (1985). Caldwell's system has been described and reviewed by Dahlstrom et al. (1972), Graham (1977), Adair (1978c), Butcher (1978c), and Greene (1980). The Caldwell Report features sections on treatment planning, early-childhood correlates of profile types, and alternative diagnoses (which are listed in rank order "in terms of probability of fit") (A. B. Caldwell, personal communication, April 4, 1986). Caldwell reported that he was converting the Caldwell Report to the American Psychiatric Association's (1980) *Diagnostic and Statistical Manual* (DSM–III) from its second edition.

The Lachar system, marketed as the WPS Test Report (WPS), is described in great detail in Lachar's (1974) manual. Its report has a 1979 copyright date. The manual reports on the research samples on which the CBTI descriptions for many code types are based. One section of the manual gives the algorithms used in the CBTI. Lachar reports, for example, on the subroutines used to generate 14 possible narrative statements to interpret the validity of the profiles. Adair (1978a), Butcher (1978a), and Sundberg (1985b) have reviewed the WPS Test Report.

The Minnesota Report (MN), authored by Butcher, was developed in the late 1970s and has a 1982 copyright date (Fowler, 1985). National Computer Systems (1982) has issued a user's guide which includes descriptions of the scales used and gives some cutoff scores. Butcher bases his interpretations on code types, individual scales, and on special scales. Butcher and Keller (1984, p. 317) describe this system as one which

Tailors interpretive statements according to the subject's population (mental health outpatient or inpatient, medical, adult, correctional, personnel, or college counseling) and according to demographic data such as education, marital status, and ethnicity, which research has shown to be modifiers of interpretive rules.

The Morris–Tomlinson Report (MT) is a CBTI system with a 1983 copyright date which was prepared by Leon M. Morris and Jack R. Tomlinson and is marketed by Psych Lab. Psych Lab provides CBTI users with a form letter which points out that the CBTI system makes use of the normalized T-scores reported by Colligan et al. (1983). The Morris–Tomlinson Report is based on the DSM–III terminology and the reports "Frequently include statements regarding the patient's social, vocational, and academic functioning as well as statements related to assertiveness and the forensic implications of test findings."

The NCS FASTTEST (FT) interpretation for the MMPI, copyrighted 1984, is one of 30 assessment tools that Psych Systems originally marketed as part of a system combining hardware and software for interpreting psychological instruments. The assets of Psych Systems, including the FASTTEST, were purchased by National Computer Systems (Fowler, 1985). The users of the NCS FAST-TEST (National Computer Systems, undated) received brief documentation materials and reprints such as Miller, Johnson, Klingler, Williams, and Giannetti (1977). The system continues to be available to the original users, but is no longer sold to new users. The FT promotional materials provide the following information:

> Psych Systems uses five different interpretive schemes: it first checks to see if the profile generated is a well known code type. If so, it prints an interpretation based on the profile configuration. If a well known code type is not found and the patient is a male, the program checks to see if there are any elevated scale scores. If there are, it uses linear combinations of scale scores to arrive at both predictive and descriptive statements about the patient. . . . If the profile falls within normal limits, regardless of sex, then a series of special scale interpretations are used to generate an interpretive statement. The emphasis with normal profiles is to interpret results in terms of social relationships, vocational issues, and problems of health behavior.

FT makes use of interpretations based on Gilberstadt and Duker (1965), Stelmacher's interpretations of code types (cf. Lachar, 1974), and "linear regression equations developed by Bloch (1983) relating to Johnson, Butcher, Null and Johnson's (1984) MMPI factor scales."

Applied Innovations (AI) has in the past marketed an MMPI CBTI system, developed by Bruce Duthie, copyright 1984. It is still available to interested purchasers. Recently, AI has also marketed the Marks Adult MMPI Report. This company provided CBTI users with a manual (Duthie, 1985) which addresses the operation of the system. Duthie (1985) reported that Applied Innovations:

> Consider the MMPI Computerized Interpretation Manual to be an application of artificial intelligence. Specifically it is designed to be an expert system for interpreting the MMPI. One of the major criteria of an expert system is that the decision theory be open to scrutiny. This manual explains the decision theory by which individual statements within the software are included in the report. The clinician can establish the clinical validity of any statement as it relates to a particular patient. See the appendices for a list of all possible statements and trigger codes generated by this software. . . . Our philosophy in the MMPI Computerized

Interpretation Manual is to totally illuminate the contents of the black box. (p. 5, subsection 3.22)

AI based its diagnostic suggestions on the DSM–III.

Selection and Background of Raters

The raters were nominated by the third author, who is familiar with the training and experience of the approximately 130 psychologists engaged in clinical assessment in Army facilities throughout the United States and Europe. Thirteen raters were chosen to participate in the project. All raters completed the ratings. However, rating data completed by Rater 5, who was assigned to rate the 1/9 code type, were lost in the mail (Table 4.3).

The 12 raters from whom rating data were received were generally representative of Army clinicians who use the MMPI. They were stationed throughout the United States and Germany. These clinicians, who were employed in an Army mental health function, were white, non-Hispanic men, who had completed clinical internships approved by the American Psychological Association, and were licensed to practice psychology. They had 7.5 median years of postdoctoral experience in clinical psychology. Half of them had worked at WRAMC. Three-fourths had completed a doctorate in clinical psychology and one held a Diplomate in Clinical Psychology awarded by the American Board of Professional Psychology.

Eleven of the 12 raters listed the MMPI reference sources they used. All of them listed Lachar's 1974 manual, which includes the algorithms for the WPS Test Report, and which is regularly used in the Army's clinical training programs. Seven raters reported using Greene's (1980) book, 4 used the Dahlstrom et al. (1972) text, and three listed Graham's (1977) book.

Eleven of the 12 raters listed their experience in using the seven CBTI systems. Five of 11 had no experience with any of the CBTI systems for the MMPI. Of the 6 raters with CBTI experience, 3 had some experience and 2 had extensive experience in using the Minnesota Report; 3 had some experience in using the NCS FASTTEST (formerly PSYCH SYSTEMS), two listed some experience with Applied Innovations, and one reported some experience in using the WPS Test Report.

Rater Materials and Instructions

Input of Answer Sheet Data. The CBTIs were generated from MMPI hand scored and National Computer Systems (NCS) scannable (mark sense) answer sheets from the subjects' files. In order to minimize scoring errors stemming from erasures and variations in the neatness and darkness of marked answer sheets (see, e.g., Grayson & Backer, 1972), we developed a list of potentially problematically marked answers and standardized their interpretation.

Our procedures for handling the data input depended on the preferences and procedures employed by the CBTI service companies. We provided an interpretation of ambiguous answers to those handling the input of the data. For the AI, MT, and FT data, the authors themselves keyed the item data into the computer, using the software provided by the company. The item data for the CA system were keyed in by the staff of the Caldwell Report. For the BE and WPS systems, the authors transcribed the data onto the answer sheets used by each CBTI company. Where possible, NCS answer sheets were scanned by optical mark reader by NCS. For the remaining subjects, who had used hand-scored answer sheets, we transcribed their answers onto NCS scannable forms. NCS provided a check on the accuracy of the transcribed data by keying in the item data themselves. (The authors received these backup data after they mailed the CBTIs to the raters.)

The authors checked the accuracy of the raw scores for the subjects' MMPI by comparing them as they appeared in the printouts for all the CBTI systems, except those from the BE and MT systems. Behaviordyne does not provide raw scores, but does include the publisher's T-scores based on the Minnesota normals. The Morris–Tomlinson Report reports raw scores and normalized T-scores based on the normative group reported by Colligan et al. (1983). In spite of efforts to minimize raw score variations, minor discrepancies did occur. Small raw score differences have been routinely reported in the research literature on the accuracy of computer scoring of the MMPI (cf. Fowler & Coyle, 1968; Grayson & Backer, 1972; Klett, Schaefer, & Plemel, 1985; Weigel & Phillips, 1967).

Rater Instructions.   The raters completed research forms given in Appendix A. The entire narrative, with attachments, was used exactly as it was sold to CBTI users with the company's name identified. The format and editorial style of each CBTI was distinctive. The authors numbered every sentence for each CBTI system, with the exception of those in footnotes. Raters were instructed to rate each numbered narrative statement for the cases in a prescribed order. They began by rating the two common-matched 7/2 code type cases. The 7/2 code type was chosen because it is a two-point code type which appears frequently (Greene, 1980); it is considered to be among the most accurate code types for making diagnoses (see, for example, Hathaway & Meehl, 1951, Tables XVI–XIX). This code type has generated numerous external correlates (Greene, 1980).

All cases were presented to the raters in counterbalanced order by race. The raters received the instructions given in Appendix A and their material was arranged in the prescribed order. The data for each subject included his specially developed identification number, age, race, marital status, educational level, and a description of the source of the subject (inpatient, out-patient, or normative study), as listed in Tables 4.4 and 4.5. The raters were not provided with a listing of the medical, psychiatric, or neuropsychological nature of the cases. A subject was classified as medical if the referral came from a nonpsychiatric physician and psychiatric if referred by a psychiatrist. Cases involving a neuropsychological evaluation were identified by the third author; for most of these cases, test score data from a neuropsychological battery of tests were available to raters. The seven CBTI systems included in the study are listed alphabetically in Fig. 4.1 and were described earlier. Each rater received the printouts for all seven CBTI systems for each assigned case. The CBTI system printouts used were identical to the ones offered by CBTI companies, with each narrative statement numbered to facilitate the ratings. Although the order in which the 13 raters evaluated the CBTI systems was constant (alphabetical as in Fig. 4.1), they started at different points in the list.

The instructions to raters are summarized in Fig. 4.1 (see Appendix A). The rater started by rating individual narrative statements for a CBTI for his first case. Then he evaluated specific features of the CBTI system for the case: (a) overall accuracy of the diagnosis, (b) overall accuracy of the CBTI, and (c) helpfulness of the CBTI system in the disposition of the case, that is, in diagnostic evaluation and in disposition planning. He then repeated these steps for each CBTI system for the first case. These steps were repeated for each case. After all six cases were rated, the rater completed the Final Rating Sheet (Appendix A), in which he ranked the CBTI systems according to overall accuracy. Then he ranked them in terms of their overall helpfulness to the clinician in disposition planning.

Raters were provided with a description of the Colligan et al. (1983) normative study on which the Morris–Tomlinson Report is based because it reports on a recent restandardization effort.

RESULTS

The thesis of this study is that CBTI systems vary in overall relevancy and accuracy, when case histories (or self-report questionnaire) are used as a rating criterion. We will begin by presenting the overall judgments of accuracy although the raters made these judgments after having evaluated the sentence-by-sentence accuracy of individual narrative statements from the printouts (see Fig. 4.1). Global and specific accuracy ratings and indicators of their reliability are given in Tables 4.7 to 4.10.

The manner of analyzing the relevancy and accuracy of each narrative statement is indicated in Tables 4.11 and 4.12. Descriptions of the pooled data (across CBTI companies and raters) for the common cases are presented in Tables 4.13 and 4.14 and Appendix B. The Ns given in these tables refer to the number of percentages involved in the pooled data. Specific data on each rater's evaluation

TABLE 4.7
Final Rank-Order Ratings and Coefficient of Concordance for Overall Accuracy
of MMPI CBTI System by Raters of All Cases

CBTI System	Rank Order of CBTI System Rater Number												Median Rank for CBTI System
	1	2	3	4	6	7	8	9	10	11	12	13	
AI	2	6	5	6	4	6	5	4	5	2	6	5	(5)
BE	6	7	7	7	6	7	7	7	7	7	7	7	(7)
CA	3	5	2	5	3	4	4	2	3	3	3	1	(3)
MN	1	4	3	1	1	2	1	1	1	1	1	2	(1)
MT	7	1	6	4	7	3	6	6	6	6	2	6	(6)
FT	4	2	4	2	2	1	3	5	4	4	5	3	(4)
WPS	5	3	1	3	5	5	2	3	2	5	4	4	(3.5)

Note. W = .60, Chi square = 43.3,.*** df = 6, *** $p < .001$.

TABLE 4.8
Final Rank Order Ratings and Coefficient of Concordance for all Cases in Overall
Helpfulness of MMPI CBTI System by Raters in Case Disposition

CBTI System	Rank Order of CBTI System Rater Number												Median Rank for CBTI System
	1	2	3	4	6	7	8	9	10	11	12	13	
AI	4	6	6	6	4	6	5	5	5	2	4	5	(5)
BE	5	7	7	7	7	7	6	6	7	7	7	7	(7)
CA	3	5	2	5	3	3	2	2	3	3	2	1	(3)
MN	1	4	3	1	1	2	1	1	1	1	1	2	(1)
MT	6.5	1	5	4	6	4	7	7	6	6	6	6	(6)
FT	2	2	4	2	2	1	3	3	4	4	3	3	(3)
WPS	6.5	3	1	3	5	5	4	4	2	5	5	4	(4)

Note. Case disposition, i.e., diagnostic evaluation and disposition planning.
W = .66, Chi square = 47.5***, df = 6, *** $p .< ..001$.

TABLE 4.9
Intraclass Correlation Among 12 Raters for Accuracy Ratings for Each Common
Case and Across Each CBTI System

Profile Type and Race	Intraclass Correlation Among 12 Raters Across Each CBTI (r_{cc})	Intraclass Correlation of an Average of 12 Ratings for Each CBTI System (r_{kk})
7/2 White	.49	.92
7/2 Black	.44	.90
Subclinical Normal White	.49	.92
Subclinical Normal Black	.16	.70

Note. Based on 3-point overall accuracy ratings: 1 = generally inaccurate; 2 = somewhat accurate, and 3 = generally accurate.

TABLE 4.10

Frequency of Specific Overall Ratings of Accuracy of Diagnostic Statements by Code Type for CBTI Systems Across Raters

CBTI Systems	7/2					Subclinical Normal					Unique				
	0	1	2	3	Omit	0	1	2	3	Omit	0	1	2	3	Omit
AI	2	15	4	1	2	6	1	3	14	0	1	10	7	6	0
BE	0	12	11	1	0	0	16	7	1	0	1	10	12	0	1
CA	1	2	11	10	0	3	12	9	0	0	2	8	5	5	4
MN	0	2	11	9	2	9	1	5	9	0	3	3	9	7	2
MT	6	7	8	3	0	13	0	2	8	1	12	2	7	3	0
FT	8	5	9	2	0	10	2	2	9	1	6	5	8	5	0
WPS	3	4	11	6	0	11	7	4	2	0	8	2	10	3	1

Note. 0 = CBTI system does not provide a diagnostic evaluation. 1 = inaccurate; 2 = somewhat accurate; 3 = accurate; omit = item omitted by rater.

TABLE 4.11

Example of Frequency Distribution and Percentages for One Rater Evaluating One CBTI System Using All Rating Categories for One Subject

N = 41 Narrative Statements

Rating Categories for all Narrative Statements	Frequency	Percentage
1. Data insufficient to make a rating.	1	2
2. Generally applicable or repetitive statement.[a]	5	12
3. Inaccurate narrative statement.	13	32
4. Somewhat accurate narrative statement.	17	41
5. Accurate narrative statement.	5	12
Total	41	99

[a] Statement does not contribute to the understanding of the case.

TABLE 4.12
Example of Frequency Distribution and Percentages for One Rater Evaluating
Relevancy and Accuracy for One CBTI System for One Subject

N = 41 Narrative Statements

Rating Categories for Accuracy of CBTI	Frequency	Percentage
Statements Relevant to Case	32[a]	78
(3) Inaccurate	13	41[b]
(4) Somewhat Accurate	17	53[b]
(5) Accurate	2	6[b]

[a] Data reported for rating categories (3), (4), and (5) as in Table 4.11 with three validity profile (VP) statements eliminated from category (5), according to formula: $(\Sigma N\text{-}(1) \text{-} (2) \text{-} VP)$.
[b] Percentage of relevant statements.

TABLE 4.13
Median Percentage for Common Cases and Ratings of Narrative Statements
Across MMPI CBTI Systems and Raters
(N = 168)

	Common Cases	
Rating Categories	7/2	Subclinical Normal
Unratable (1)	14	50
General Repetitive (2)	10	12
Inaccurate (3)	11	00
Somewhat Accurate (4)	27	12
Accurate (5)	26	14

TABLE 4.14
Median Percentage for Common Cases and Ratings of Relevancy and Accuracy
Across MMPI CBTI Systems and Raters
(N = 168)

	Common Cases	
Rating Categories[a]	7/2	Subclinical Normal
Relevant to Case[b]	67	25
Inaccurate (3)	19	00
Somewhat Accurate (4)	42	43
Accurate (5)	35	33

[a] (3) + (4) + (5) - validity profile sttements/ (1) + (2) + (3) + (4) + (5).
[b] (3) or (4) or (5)/ (3) + (4) + (5); except for validity profile statements.

of each subject's CBTIs for all cases are provided in Tables 4.15, 4.16, and 4.22. We conclude by reviewing the data related to the relevancy and accuracy of the CBTI systems for all cases (Tables 4.17 to 4.19). The ratings of the extent to which the CBTIs for the common cases were evaluated as relevant and accurate by each rater are used to evaluate their ratings of the unique cases (Tables 4.20, 4.22, and 4.23). Table 4.21 reports similar data for the subnormal clinical cases.

Rater Reliability

The raters assigned a final overall rank order score to each CBTI system after evaluating the overall accuracy for six cases, including two matched Black/white pairs (7/2 and subclinical normal profile) and one unique code-type pair (Fig. 4.1, Instruction step 7; Table 4.7). Kendall's Coefficient of Concordance (W = .60, chi square = 43.3, df = 6, $p < .001$), a special analysis-of-variance method revealed the highly significant extent to which the 12 raters agreed (see Guilford & Fruchter, 1973, pp. 264–266). The median ranks (across raters) of the CBTI systems showed that the MN Report was rated the highest in overall accuracy and the BE system was the lowest. The raters agreed the most in ranking BE and MN and agreed the least in ranking AT, FT, and WPS. Similar results were found in the ratings of the overall helpfulness of the CBTI system for case disposition, which includes the diagnostic evaluation and disposition planning (Fig. 4.1, Instruction step 7; Table 4.8); here Kendall's Coefficient of Concordance was W = .66, chi square = 47.5, df = 6, $p < .001$. This again demonstrates that there was significant agreement among raters.

Further evidence of interrater reliability was obtained from specific ratings made for each CBTI system for the common cases, using Specific Answer Sheet item 8 (see Appendix A and Fig. 4.1, Instruction to Raters Step 4). Intraclass correlations for each profile type by race (7/2 white, 7/2 Black, subclinical normal white, and subclinical normal Black) were based on three-point ratings of overall accuracy made by each rater for each CBTI system. The analysis was based on the variance between CBTI systems, using the overall accuracy ratings of 12 raters to compute correlations between raters. Intraclass correlations (Table 4.9) for each profile type, analyzed by race, showed the typical intercorrelation for 12 raters. One can say the typical reliability for a single rater's ratings, for three cases, 7/2 White, 7/2 Black, and subclinical normal White was similar (r_{cc} .44 − .49), but lower ($r_{cc} = .16$) for the subclinical normal Black case (Guilford & Fruchter, 1973, pp. 263–264). If we averaged the evaluations of the raters for each CBTI system and could correlate this set of averages with a set of comparable ratings from a similar set of raters, the range of the intraclass correlations would be $r_{kk} = .70 − .92$.

The data on rater reliability show considerable rater agreement on the final overall rank order for evaluating the accuracy of the output of seven CBTI systems. Furthermore, the raters showed significant agreement in rating the overall accuracy for the CBTI systems for each of the following three cases: 7/2

TABLE 4.15
Summary of Chi-Square Data for Rater Evaluations of Relevancy and Accuracy of Common Cases by CBTI Systems

7/2 White Case

| | Chi Square A | | Chi Square B | |
| | df = 24 N = 541 | | df = 18 N = 541 | |
Rater	Table		Table	
1	1	> 148.5***	2	119.6***
2	3[a]	110.1***	4	68.3***
3	5	75.7***	6	49.7***
4	7	> 227.9***	8	> 164.7***
6	9	> 151.4***	10	97.5***
7	11	> 138.3***	12	129.7***
8	13	71.8***	14	56.1***
9	15	96.8***	16	64.1***
10	17	83.6***	18	51.7***
11	19	> 138.3***	20	107.1***
12	21[a]	95.5***	22	62.4***
13	23	69.7***	24	53.2***

7/2 Black Case

| | Chi Square A df = 24 N = 502 | | Chi Square B df = 18 N = 502 | |
Rater	Table		Table	
1	25[a]	102.3***	26	76.5***
2	27[b]	57.1***	28	41.4***
3	29[b]	104.9***	30	75.2***
4	31[b]	79.3***	32	65.2***
6	33[b]	101.1***	34	71.0***
7	35[b]	133.1***	36	114.2***
8	37[c]	81.3***	38	60.7***
9	39[b]	77.1***	40	61.6***
10	41[b]	67.5***	42	48.8***
11	43[c]	102.4***	44	71.3***
12	45[a]	81.0***	46	59.1***
13	47[b]	108.4***	48	71.1***

(continued)

Subclinical Normal White Case

	Chi Square A df = 24 N = 297		Chi Square B df = 18 N = 297	
Rater	Table		Table	
1	49[a]	48.4**	50	28.5*
2	51	60.0***	52	33.0**
3	53	90.6***	54	52.6***
4	55[a]	85.2***	56	48.9***
6	57[a]	76.5***	58	45.8***
7	59	62.6***	60	40.2**
8	61[a]	55.6***	62	24.3
9	63	48.5**	64	29.4*
10	65	68.4***	66	36.4**
11	67[a]	97.1***	68	74.6***
12	69	Analysis not appropriate due to empty cells	70	Analysis not appropriate due to empty cells
13	71	27.1	72	22.2

Subclinical Normal Black Case

	Chi Square A df = 24 N = 313		Chi Square B df = 18 N = 313	
Rater	Table		Table	
1	73[a]	78.7***	74	55.5***
2	75[b]	39.8*	76	16.9
3	77[a]	94.5***	78	59.4***
4	79	37.2*	80	16.5
6	81	66.1***	82	23.2
7	83	64.7***	84	38.5**
8	85[a]	39.3*	86	22.1
9	87[a]	31.5	88	10.9
10	89[b]	58.1***	90	43.9***
11	91	94.9***	92	68.3***
12	93	Analysis not appropriate due to empty cells	94	Analysis not appropriate due to empty cells
13	95	31.6	96	13.8

Note. The rating categories for chi square A are: unratable (1), general repetitive (2), innacurate (3), somewhat accurate (4), and accurate (5). In Chi Square-B, the three accuracy ratings are: inaccurate (3), somewhat accurate (4), and accurate (5). The irrelevant category includes items evaluated as unratable (1), general/repetitive (2), and validity profile statements.
[a] Rater omitted one statement.
[b] Rater omitted two statements.
[c] Rater omitted three statements.
*** $p < .001$; ** $p < .01$, * $p < .05$.

TABLE 4.16
Summary of Chi-Square Data for Rater Evaluations of Relevancy and Accuracy of
Unique Cases by CBTI Systems

Unique White Cases

	Chi Square A df = 24				Chi Square B df = 18			
Rater	Table	Code	N		Table	Code	N	
1	97	1	400	100.3***	98	1	400	61.2***
2	99ᵃ	1/2	395	36.8*	100	1/2	386	20.6
3	101	1/3	540	95.6***	102	1/3	540	65.5***
4	103	8/1	382	81.0***	104	8/1	382	32.3**
6	105	2	410	139.0***	106	2	410	127.8***
7	107ᶜ	2/8	596	136.9***	108	2/8	599	104.9***
8	109	3	339	66.1***	110	3	339	33.6**
9	111	4/2	628	104.4***	112	4/2	628	75.0***
10	113	6	319	90.3***	114	6	319	44.4***
11	115ᵃ	8/6	487	194.6***	116	8/6	488	150.8***
12	117	9/6	434	93.7***	118	9/6	434	74.5***
13	119	8/9	401	134.5***	120	8/9	401	66.1***

Unique Black Cases

	Chi Square A df = 24				Chi Square B df = 18			
1	121	1	340	73.8***	122	1	340	40.1**
2	123	1/2	628	116.7***	124	1/2	628	92.2***
3	125	1/3	461	119.2***	126	1/3	461	91.4***
4	127	8/1	499	167.7***	128	8/1	499	115.6***
6	129	2	337	58.8***	130	2	337	20.9
7	131	2/8	638	100.2***	132	2/8	638	67.9***
8	133	3	366	50.3**	134	3	367	33.6**
9	135	4/2	468	114.8***	136	4/2	468	71.5***
10	137	6	390	83.6***	138	6	390	23.0
11	139ᵇ	8/6	563	60.2***	140	8/6	565	28.8*
12	141	9/6	653	131.8***	142	9/6	653	91.6***
13	143	8/9	435	83.4***	144	8/9	435	40.8**

Note. The rating categories for Chi Square A are: unratable (1), general/repetitive (2), inaccurate (3),
somewhat accurate (4), and accurate (5). In Chi Square B, the three accuracy ratings are: inaccurate (3),
somewhat accurate (4), and accurate (5). The irrelevant category includes items evaluated as unratable (1),
general/repetitive (2), and validity profile statements.
ᵃ Rater omitted 1 statement.
ᵇ Rater omitted 2 statements.
ᶜ Rater omitted 3 statements.
*** $p < .001$, ** $p < .01$, * $p < .05$.

white, 7/2 Black, and the subclinical white case. An additional group of comparable raters would be likely to show agreement with these raters. Interrater reliability was lower for the subclinical black case.

Overall Accuracy of Diagnostic Statements

In order to interpret these data, it is useful to understand how different CBTI systems present diagnostic statements. We will use the 7/2 white case as an example. Only four CBTI systems had separately identified sections which con-

TABLE 4.17
Median Percentages for 7/2 Code Type for Ratings of Relevancy and Accuracy of MMPI CBTI Systems Across Raters and Subjects (N = 24)

CBTI.Systems	Relevant[a]	Rating Categories Inaccurate (3)[b]	Somewhat Accurate (4)[b]	Accurate (5)[b]
AI	68	38	33	24
BE	55	21	49	26
CA	66	04	50	46
MN	77	06	42	49
MT	60	24	34	40
FT	70	24	42	31
WPS	68	20	46	33

TABLE 4.18
Median Percentages for Subclinical Normal Cases for Ratings of Relevancy and Accuracy of MMPI CBTI Systems Across Raters (N = 24)

CBTI Systems	Relevant[a]	Rating Categories Inaccurate[b] (3)	Somewhat Accurate[b] (4)	Accurate[b] (5)
AI	26	00	33	50
BE	22	24	44	36
CA	26	26	42	18
MN	19	00	54	38
MT	36	00	33	33
FT	32	00	50	38
WPS	20	10	43	08

[a] (3) + (4) +(5) - validity profile statements/ (1) + (2) + (3) + (4) + (5).
[b] (3) or (4) or (5)/ (3) + (4) + (5); except for validity profile statements.

TABLE 4.19
Median Percentages for Unique Cases for Ratings of Relevancy and Accuracy of MMPI CBTI Systems Across Raters (N = 24)

CBTI Systems	Relevant[a]	Rating Categories Inaccurate[b] (3)	Somewhat Accurate[b] (4)	Accurate[b] (5)
AI	60	33	40	22
BE	45	32	48	22
CA	52	12	40	34
MN	64	08	34	40
MT	57	09	50	33
FT	60	17	48	24
WPS	54	13	42	40

Note. Covers following code types: 1, 1/2, 1/3,8/1,2, 2/8, 3, 4/2, 6, 8/6, 9/6, and 8/9.
[a] (3) + (4) + (5) - validty profile statements / (1) + (2) + (3) + (4) + (5).
[b] (3) or (4) or (5) / (3) + (4) + (5); except for validity profile statements.

TABLE 4.20
Median Percentages for 7/2 Code Type for Relevancy and Accuracy by Rater Across MMPI CBTI Systems (N = 14)

		Rating Categories		
Rater	Relevant[a]	Inaccurate[b] (3)	somewhat accurate[b] (4)	accurate[b] (5)
1	66	43	49	08
2	57	20	44	32
3	81	08	36	50
4	61	26	58	13
6	59	28	44	22
7	71	16	32	42
8	36	20	46	28
9	76	08	41	42
10	64	36	31	30
11	76	14	44	40
12	50	07	44	44
13	64	08	32	54

a (3) + (4) + (5) - validity profile statements/ (1) + (2) + (3).+ (4) + (5).
b (3) or (4) or (5) / (3) + (4) + (5); except for validity profile statements.

TABLE 4.21
Median Percentages for Subclinical Normal Cases for Ratings of Relevancy and Accuracy by Rater Across MMPI CBTI Systems (N = 14)

		Rating Categories		
Rater	Relevant[a]	Inaccurate[b] (3)	somewhat accurate[b] (4)	accurate[b] (5)
1	40	26	68	04
2	34	00	83	13
3	53	00	36	52
4	28	00	62	32
6	22	24	34	31
7	56	28	25	47
8	06	00	00	00
9	12	00	50	42
10	09	40	00	31
11	46	00	70	16
12	06	00	14	86
13	16	14	00	68

a (3) + (4) ı (5) - validity profile statements/ (1) + (2) + (3).+ (4) + (5).
b (3) or (4) or (5) / (3) + (4) + (5); except for validity profile statements.

TABLE 4.22
Median Percentages for Unique Cases for Ratings of Relevancy and Accuracy by Rater Across MMPI CBTI Systems
(N = 14)

Rater	Code Type	Relevant[a]	Inaccurate[b] (3)	Somewhat Accurate[b] (4)	Accurate[b] (5)
1	1	54	13	63	10
2	1/2	38	12	72	08
3	1/3	64	20	45	36
4	8/1	56	28	65	14
6	2	58	15	48	37
7	2/8	64	08	24	68
8	3	31	39	37	16
9	4/2	74	18	38	42
10	6	52	40	28	28
11	8/6	55	25	40	22
12	9/6	38	04	49	28
13	8/9	64	12	19	69

[a] (3) + (4) + (5) - validity profile statements/ (1) + (2) + (3) + (4) + (5).

[b] (3) or (4) or (5)/ (3) + (4) + (5); except for validity profile statements.

TABLE 4.23
Rank Order of Median Percentages and Accuracy Ratings for 7/2 and Unique Code Types by Rater Across CBTI Systems

Rater	Relevant 7/2	Relevant Unique	Inaccurate 7/2	Inaccurate Unique	Somewhat Accurate 7/2	Somewhat Accurate Unique	Accurate 7/2	Accurate Unique
1	5	8	1	8	2	3	12	11
2	10	10.5	5.5	9.5	5.5	1	7	12
3	1	3	10	5	9	6	2	5
4	8	6	4	3	1	2	11	10
6	9	5	3	7	5.5	5	10	4
7	4	3	7	11	10.5	11	4.5	2
8	12	12	5,5	2	3	9	9	9
9	2.5	1	10	6	8	8	4.5	3
10	6.5	9	2	1	12	10	8	6.5
11	2.5	7	8	4	5.5	7	6	8
12	11	10.5	12	12	5.5	4	3	6.5
13	6.5	3	10	9.5	10.5	12	1	1

Note. Highest median percentages are assigned rank order of 1. Kendall's tau (Siegel, 1956) for rating categories: Relevant =..60**; Inaccurate = .36*; Somewhat Accurate = .61**; Accurate = .54**.
**p <.01.
*p < .05.

tain diagnostic statements. AI provides a brief section on Alcohol and Drugs; BE has a Diagnostic Impression section which provides alternative DSM–III diagnostic labels; CA provides a Diagnostic Impression section which briefly presents the primary and secondary diagnosis; and MN provides a Diagnostic Considerations section describing possible diagnoses and symptoms. FT has a section on Special Medical Symptoms. MT does not use subheadings and WPS limits its headings to Comments, Critical Items, and Supplemental Scale Interpretation. Thus, raters evaluating diagnostic statements must use considerable judgment in locating these statements and in making overall evaluations of numerous—possibly discrepant—diagnostic statements.

Data from ratings of the overall accuracy of the diagnostic evaluation (see Specific Answer Sheet item 4, Appendix A; Fig. 4.1, Instruction step 4) reveal differences across CBTI systems for the 7/2, subclinical normal, and unique profile types (Table 4.10). With the Black and white cases combined for each profile type, there are altogether 24 evaluations for each type. For CBTI systems which were judged to provide a diagnostic evaluation, accuracy was rated using a three-point scale. The MT system was least likely to provide diagnostic evaluations for all cases.

The accuracy of diagnostic evaluations was determined by analyzing CBTI systems with the highest number of accurate evaluations and the lowest number of inaccurate evaluations. For the 7/2 code type, data for the CA and MN systems show that 9 to 10 evaluations of their diagnostic statements were rated as accurate and only two evaluations for each system were rated as inaccurate. Conversely, the majority of the evaluations of the AI ($N = 15$) and BE ($N = 12$) systems were rated inaccurate for the 7/2 type and only one evaluation for each system was rated as accurate.

For the subclinical normal cases, AI received 14 evaluations rated accurate, and only one was rated as inaccurate; whereas BE received 16 inaccurate evaluations and only one accurate. Three companies (MT, FT, and WPS) received 10 to 13 evaluations that the CBTI system did not provide a diagnostic evaluation.

For the unique code types, MN had the largest number of accurate evaluations ($N = 7$) and relatively few inaccurate ($N = 3$) evaluations. BE received no accurate evaluations and 10 inaccurate evaluations. AI received 6 accurate evaluations; it also received 10 inaccurate evaluations.

These evaluations of diagnostic statements show similarities between the results for the 7/2 and unique cases. MN received the highest number of accuracy ratings and the lowest number of inaccuracy ratings for all of the clinical cases. AI and BE received a low number of accuracy ratings and a high number of inaccuracy ratings for the clinical cases. BE also showed this pattern for the subclinical normal cases. AI, on the other hand, received a large number of accuracy ratings and a low number of inaccuracy ratings for the subclinical normal cases. Three companies (MT, FT, & WPS) were accurate in not providing diagnostic evaluations for the subclinical normal cases.

Fundamental Statistical Units

The fundamental statistical units used are percentages, based on the frequencies with which raters assigned one of five ratings to each narrative statement for each CBTI for each case (see example in Table 4.11). Raters were asked to rate the accuracy of each numbered statement in each CBTI against the data in the subject's file (see General Instructions to Raters). Two types of irrelevancy ratings were available; (1) For data insufficient to make a rating, or (2) Statement generally applicable or repetitive, not contributing to the understanding of the case. Relevant statements were evaluated according to a three-point rating of accuracy. The rating categories for accuracy are labeled throughout the chapter as follows: (3) Inaccurate, (4) Somewhat accurate, and (5) Accurate. Raters were instructed to choose only *one* of the five rating categories for evaluating each narrative statement.

Table 4.11 gives an example of the frequencies and percentages for one subject and Table 4.12 presents the same data, rearranged according to its relevancy and accuracy, with validity profile statements considered irrelevant to the accuracy ratings. (Recall that potential subjects with deviant validity profile scores were omitted from the study.)

Length of CBTI Reports

The data in Appendix B (Tables B–1 and B–2) demonstrate that large differences existed in the number of narrative statements per CBTI system. Therefore, percentages, which use the base of 100, were used for comparison purposes. There are 366 narrative statements for BE's white 4/2 code type, but only 9 narrative statements for the white 2 code type from FT or for the Black 6 code type for the MT system.

The BE printouts were the longest for both common cases (126–225) and for the unique cases (median = 187; range 124–366). The MT Report provided the shortest set of narrative statements for the two common cases (8–21) and unique cases (median = 16, range: 9–34). These data present the range of statements for the particular protocols used in this study and do not necessarily represent all the variations in the computer library of each CBTI system for a wider variety of score combinations.

The length of the CBTI narratives and ratings of their overall accuracy do not show a linear relationship. The median rank in overall accuracy assigned by 12 raters (Table 4.7) was examined in relation to the median number of sentences for each CBTI system for the 24 unique cases (Appendix B–2). The MT system which had the lowest number of sentences (median = 16) was rated sixth in accuracy, whereas BE, the system with the highest number of sentences (median = 187), was rated seventh in overall relative accuracy. MN, CA, and WPS, the three companies with the highest accuracy, had relatively short or middle-range narrative lengths. In other words, narrative length is not directly related to ratings of overall accuracy of CBTI systems.

Examples of Data Format

The data throughout the remainder of the chapter are presented in two formats illustrated in Tables 4.11 and 4.12. Table 4.11 reports the data in the same format used by the raters: five mutually exclusive categories. This format labeled A, which is used in the chi-square summary tables, details the specific data related to rater's assessment of relevancy. The first relevancy category (1) dealt with judgments that the criterion data were insufficient to make ratings. The second rating category pertinent to relevancy (2) was used when the narrative statements were generally applicable or repetitive and did not contribute to the understanding of a case. Categories (3) to (5) represent levels of accuracy: (3) Inaccurate; (4) Somewhat Accurate; and (5) Accurate.

Table 4.12 reports the same data as in Table 4.11, but collapses data from rating categories (1) and (2) and the validity profile (which served to identify test-taking attitudes), as statements irrelevant. The narrative statements referring to the validity profile were eliminated by the authors with guidance from the CBTI companies. The validity profile items were used earlier to ascertain whether the overall profile was valid.

In the examples in Tables 4.11 and 4.12, the CBTI included three validity profile (VP) items, all of which were rated as accurate (5) by the rater. In Table 4.12, the total number of narrative statements presented in rating categories for accuracy (3), (4), and (5) was calculated by the formula: $n - (1) - (2) - VP \div 41 - 1 - 5 - 3 = 32$. Percentages are used in the remainder of the chapter to form a common basis for handling CBTIs which vary in length. In this example the percentage of relevant items thus was 78% (32/41). Of the 32 relevant statements rated, 41% were rated Inaccurate, 53% Somewhat Accurate, and 6% Accurate.

When these data are presented in the chi-square tables labeled B in Tables 4.15 and 4.16, they are reported in terms of irrelevant rather than relevant statements in order to provide nonoverlapping data in the cells of the tables. In this example, there are nine irrelevant statements ($41 - 32 = 9$).

Pooled Data for Common Cases

Tables 4.13 and 4.14 present pooled data across CBTI systems and raters for the common cases which have the following linear T-scores: (a) 7/2 white, 97 T and 96 T, respectively; (b) 7/2 Black, 89 T and 77 T, respectively; (c) subclinical normal white (Scale 2, 65 T; Scale 9, 58 T); and (d) subclinical normal Black (Scale 7, 66 T; Scale 2, 56 T). The Black and white cases were combined because the Black/white differences were negligible. The data in these tables were pooled across CBTI systems, raters, and race. These data are based on 168 percentages (12 raters × 7 CBTI systems × 2 Black/white cases). Table 4.13 reports all five rating categories and Table 4.14 shows the data grouped according to the relevancy of the ratings to the case. These composite tables provide the base rates for interpreting the results for individual CBTI companies and for evaluating the response tendencies of raters.

These tables show that there are some differences in the relevancy and the accuracy of CBTI narrative statements for the two kinds of profiles. Half of the statements for the subclinical normal profile were Unratable, whereas for the 7/2 code type, the median percentage unratable was only 14 (Table 4.13). The two kinds of profiles show similar medians for the percentages of General/Repetitive statements.

Table 4.14. shows that the median percentage of Inaccurate narrative statements is greater for the 7/2 profile (19) than for the subclinical normal profile (00). (Half of the Inaccurate percentages for the subclinical normal profile were zero.) Otherwise, the medians for the Somewhat Inaccurate and Accurate ratings for the two profiles are similar. The major difference between the ratings of the 7/2 and the subclinical normal cases are in their relevancy to the case histories. The relevancy ratings for the subclinical normal cases are low. This would be expected since the MMPI was designed for use in clinical diagnosis.

Chi-square Results by Subject and Raters for CBTI Systems

The chi-square tables, which may be obtained from the authors, provide frequencies, percentages, and chi-square data. Each table presents data for one rater, for one case, for all seven CBTIs. Half of these tables involve all five rating categories (Chi Square A), the other half collapse the unratable and General/Repetitive ratings into a single "irrelevant" category (Chi Square B).

Chi-square statistics were computed using Tracy L. Gustafson's EPISTAT software (Wise, 1985). Due to the small number of narrative statements for CBTI systems, such as the Morris–Tomlinson Report, the expected cell frequencies were often less than five. No chi-square statistic was reported when such analysis was inappropriate due to empty cells (see Siegel, 1956, p. 110). Cell frequencies reached reasonable levels when percentages were pooled across raters, profile types, or CBTI systems.

In Table 4.15, the vast majority of chi-square statistics are significant beyond the .001 level.

All chi-square values for the 7/2 white and 7/2 Black cases were statistically significant at the .001 level. For the subclinical normal white case, only one chi-square value, for rater 8, was not significant at the .05 level.

The chi-square results for the Black subclinical normal case were less clear-cut. Less than half of the Chi-Square B values, based on data in which the irrelevancy ratings were collapsed into one category for each of the 12 raters, were found to be statistically significant at the 5% level. The difference between raters was greater for the Black subclinical normal case than for the other cases. This will be commented on in a later paper on the Black/white cases.

The results for the unique cases (Table 4.16), each of which was rated by only one rater, parallel the results for the 7/2 cases which were rated by all 12 raters. For the white unique cases, the Chi-Square B values were statistically significant at the 1% level for 11 raters. For the Black unique cases, the Chi-square B values were statistically significant at the 5% level for 10 raters.

The chi-square results for the Black/white pairs for the 13 code types and for the white subclinical normal code type show that raters differentiated among CBTI systems in their ratings of the relevancy and accuracy of CBTI sentences at a statistically significant level. The results, considered in combination with the overall accuracy ratings reported in Tables 4.7 and 4.8, show that raters consistently differentiated among CBTI systems.

Pooled Data for 3 Profile Types

Tables 4.17, 4.18, and 4.19 summarize the relevancy and accuracy ratings for the CBTI systems across raters and subjects for the 7/2, subclinical normal, and unique code types. For the 7/2 code type, the CA and MN systems were evaluated as having the highest percentage of Accurate sentences relevant to the cases (median = 46% and 49%, respectively). For the subclinical normal cases, AI was rated high in the Accurate sentences relevant to the case (median = 50%).

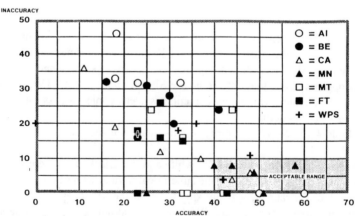

NOTE: 7/2, Subclinical Normal and Unique Cases (1, 2/1, 1/3, 8/1, 2, 2/8, 3, 4/2, 6, 8/6, 9/6, & 8/9) Rated by 12 Raters.

FIG. 4.2. Scatter diagram of median percentages for hit rate of CBTI systems for 3 MMPI profile types for matched Black/White cases.

For the twelve unique cases, WPS and MN were highest in the Accuracy of relevant sentences (median = 40% for both systems). These data show that raters are relatively consistent in their sentence-by-sentence judgments of the accuracy of the different CBTI systems, which differ significantly from each other in the accuracy of clinical and subclinical profile types.

Variation in the rated Accuracy and Inaccuracy of each profile type for Black and white cases is illustrated in Fig. 4.2. The figure presents these data in scatter diagram format, using 42 coordinates for three profile types for matched Black/white pairs for the seven CBTI systems. There are six coordinates for each CBTI system. This provides CBTI users with the comparative Hit Rates for the CBTI systems. The scatter diagram shows the considerable variability in the Hit Rate for the CBTI systems.

The Hit Rate is illustrated in the lower right quadrant using a very stringent set of cut scores: Accuracy median $\geq$ 40% and Inaccuracy median $\leq$ 10%. However, CBTI users may set their own cut scores for the Hit Rate. Using these cut scores, we find that one CBTI system had five profile types that met our criteria and one CBTI system had none.

Pooled Data for Clinical Code Types and Individual Raters

Tables 4.20 to 4.22 provide data on the relevancy and accuracy ratings for each rater for the 7/2, subclinical normal, and unique profile types. Code types 2/8 and 8/9 received the highest ratings in sentence-by-sentence Accuracy (median = 68% and 69%, respectively) and relatively low ratings on the Inaccuracy end of the three-point scale (median = 8% and 12%, respectively). Code types 1 and 1/2 were evaluated relatively low on Accuracy (median = 10% and 8%, respectively) and received relatively high Somewhat Accurate ratings (median = 63% and 72%, respectively). Code types Spike 3 and Spike 6 were rated relatively high in Inaccuracy (median = 39% and 40% respectively).

Table 4.23 reports the rank order of sentence-by-sentence ratings for each rater using the data from the two sets of clinical cases (7/2 and unique code types). The table also reports Kendall's rank-order correlation coefficients for each of the four rating categories (Relevant, Inaccurate, Somewhat Accurate, and Accurate), all of which were statistically significant at the 5% or 1% level. The raters showed significant rank-order agreement in their sentence-by-sentence ratings for the two sets of clinical code types.

From these statistics we may infer that raters showed a response style in making their ratings. We define response style as the clinician's application of his internal criteria in a consistent way. For example, raters who rated the CBTI sentences for the 7/2 code type high in Relevancy were also likely to rate their unique code type relatively high in Relevancy. Information from Table 4.23 may also be used to evaluate the response style of individual raters. For example, rater

2 evaluated the Black and white 2/1 code type. He showed considerable rank-order agreement in evaluating the 7/2 and 2/1 code type (Rank order 10 and 10.5, respectively) for Relevancy. However, his rank-order rating of the Accuracy of the relevant sentences for the 2/1 case was relatively lower (rank = 12), compared with his rank order evaluation of the Accuracy of the 7/2 case (rank = 7). On the other hand, rater 9's rank order of the Relevancy and Accuracy of the 7/2 and 4/2 code type was similar (Relevancy rank order: 2.5 and 1 respectively; Accuracy: 4.5 and 3). These data provide information about individual rater's style and skill in applying clinical criteria in rating common and unique cases.

DISCUSSION

This chapter reports on the development and the application of a methodology for the study of comparative validity of the output of the CBTI systems. Experienced clinical psychologists rated the relevancy, accuracy, and usefulness of the output of CBTI systems. They judged the relevancy and accuracy of the CBTI systems for clinical and subclinical normal cases against an external criterion: case histories or self-report questionnaires. Ratings were made at both sentence-by-sentence and global levels. Sentences were first rated according to their relevancy to each case history, that is, determinations were made as to whether relevant data were available in the criterion, whether a sentence was relevant to the case, or whether sentences were overly general or repetitive. The accuracy of sentences was rated only for those sentences relevant to the case. Global ratings were made of CBTI systems after all sentence-by-sentence ratings for a case were completed and finally after sentence-by-sentence ratings were completed for all cases.

The study controlled for test-taking attitudes and gender, and cases (all males) were selected from a limited age range. Systematic procedures for selecting cases from a large sample of patients and normal personnel from a wide geographical area, using prespecified profile codes and clinical cutoff scores (T $\geq$ 70 on a clinical scale) minimized sample bias. In spite of the fact that only 28 cases were rated and reported, the care with which this sample was selected from 1,500 existing cases, renders the results generalizable to a much larger male sample. Matched cases (Black/white pairs) and CBTI systems were rated in a counterbalanced order. By having each rater judge cases rated by all raters and by also having cases rated by only one rater, it was possible to obtain interrater reliability data and also to rate a large number of different profile types.

The study evaluated the comparative relevancy and accuracy of the output of seven CBTI systems for the MMPI, representing half of the existing commercially available systems in 1985. All but two of the nine CBTI systems invited took part in the project and data from 12 of 13 Army clinical psychologists were received and reported. Data from 28 cases involved 14 matched Black/white male cases and represented subclinical normal and clinical (medical, psychiatric, and neuropsychological) inpatient and out-patient cases. Included were frequently occurring neurotic, psychotic, and characterological code types.

Despite the large amount of empirical evidence available for the MMPI and its potential for actuarial prediction, the output of CBTI systems for the MMPI for individuals were found to vary significantly in their rated relevancy, accuracy, and in their usefulness in case disposition, that is, diagnostic evaluation and disposition planning and accuracy. The quality of a CBTI system apparently depends on how the CBTI developer uses the MMPI's research literature and clinical lore.

The raters showed highly significant agreement in evaluating the overall accuracy of the output of the seven systems in their final global ratings. They also showed agreement in their rating of the overall accuracy of CBTI systems for each of the common cases. Interrater reliability was demonstrated even though raters showed significant response tendencies in their sentence-by-sentence ratings of relevancy and accuracy and despite the differences in the raters' graduate school subspecialties, in their employment experience, and in their experience with CBTI systems. Nine raters were trained in clinical and three in counseling psychology. They had performed different mental health functions in the Army, working in hospitals, community mental health centers, and in organizational settings. Furthermore, they differed in experience with CBTI systems for the MMPI. But experience did not show a linear relationship to ratings of global accuracy. For the three CBTIs with the highest Overall Accuracy ratings, raters reported having prior experience with MN, no experience with CA, and little experience with WPS. All but one rater had reported using Lachar's (1974) manual on which the WPS Test Report is based.

The data support the thesis that the output of CBTI systems show significant differences in their accuracy and relevancy. This conclusion is supported by statistically significant data from the final overall rank order of the CBTI systems (Table 4.7) and the chi-square data (see Tables 4.15 and 4.16) from each rater for each case.

The rater results, at both the sentence-by-sentence and global levels, show consistent, but different results for the subclinical normal and the clinical profiles. These results should be expected, since the MMPI was designed as a tool for psychodiagnosis. Furthermore, the research literature for subclinical cases is more limited than for clinical cases. The subclinical normal cases, rated by all raters, were found to have a high percentage (median 50) of Unratable sentences, whereas the Unratable sentences for the 7/2 common cases was low (median 14). Sentence-by-sentence accuracy ratings for these two cases showed that the judged Accuracy for sentences relevant to the cases was similar (median 33% and 35% for normal and 7/2 cases, respectively; see Table 4.14). Different CBTI systems showed high sentence-by-sentence Accuracy ratings for the subclinical normal and clinical cases. AI showed the highest sentence-by-sentence Accuracy rate (median 50%; Table 4.18) and the most accurate diagnostic evaluations for subclinical normal cases.

The sentence-by-sentence results for the clinical code types, including the 7/2 common cases and the 12 clinical code-type cases, rated by only one rater, were congruent with the final global ratings of the CBTI systems. The three CBTI systems which were assigned the highest rank order for accuracy (MN, CA, & WPS; Table 4.7) showed the highest ratings for sentence-by-sentence accuracy. Their median 7/2 Accuracy rate, pooled across 12 raters, was 49%, 46%, and 33% respectively (Table 4.17). Also their median Accuracy rate, pooled across CBTI systems, for 12 clinical code type cases rated by one rater, was 40%, 34%, and 40% respectively (Table 4.19). On the other hand, AI and BE, respectively receiving final rank-order ratings of 5 and 7, received low sentence-by-sentence ratings. On a three-point scale of Accuracy (Inaccurate, Somewhat Accurate, and Accurate), these two CBTI systems were low in Accuracy for clinical cases (Tables 4.17 and 4.19). These two systems were also evaluated as having less accurate diagnostic evaluations (Table 4.10).

By analyzing the CBTI systems according to their final overall rank order for accuracy and for their Hit Rates for three profile types (7/2, subclinical normal, and unique codes) we find that the output of the higher rated CBTI systems show moderate validity levels.

The results for the 7/2 cases, for which the base rate is constant, parallel those for the unique clinical code types (1, 1/2, 1/3, 8/1, 2, 2/8, 3, 4/2, 6, 8/6, 9/6 and 8/9) for which the base rates may vary. However, the two code types which are the least frequent, spike 3 and 8/1, were rated relatively low in Accuracy (median 16% for spike 3; median 14% for 8/1). But that was also the case for the more frequent 1/2 code type (median 8%).

CBTI systems markedly vary in the length of the narratives. The BE printouts had the most sentences and MT had the fewest. The relationship between length of narratives and the global ratings of accuracy for CBTI systems was not linear: companies with the highest accuracy ratings had relatively short or middle-range length narratives.

CBTI systems also vary in their percentage of relevant sentences for clinical code types. The AI, BE, & CA systems have a relatively high percentage of Unratable sentences for both the 7/2 and the unique cases (Table B–3, and B–5). BE and WPS have the highest percentage of General Repetitive sentences, whereas MN is relatively low in Unratable and in General Repetitive sentences. Because of variations in the length of narratives and in the percentage of sentences relevant to the cases, the data are reported in percentages with a base of 100 and in median percentages for pooled data. By pooling data across raters, profile types or CBTI systems, we were able to base our conclusions on a relatively large number of rater responses.

The study is limited in that it did not focus on evaluating the Barnum effect (O'Dell, 1972) and was limited to the use of existing (file drawer) data available in a hospital setting. Instead of including a bogus case for evaluation, as recommended by Moreland (1985), the authors chose to maximize the number of matched Black/white cases, covering 14 profile types rated. Twelve raters each rated 6 profile type cases, which placed heavy demands on them. For example, each rater had to rate 1,653 sentences for relevancy and accuracy for the four common cases. Therefore, it seemed unreasonable to add a bogus case to the study.

The study used existing hospital data for the clinical cases which vary in content and in detail. However, 23 of the 26 clinical cases were inpatients for whom, in general, there were more detailed case histories than for the outpatients. Unfortunately, the time interval between the administration of the MMPI and the preparation of the case history varied. MMPI scales 2, 8, and 9 (W. G. Dahlstrom, personal communication, October 2, 1987) are most likely to show changes in acute symptoms over time. In spite of this, the two unique code types which were rated highest in sentence-by-sentence Accuracy were two-point codes involving these scales: 8/9 (median Accuracy 69%) and 2/8 (median Accuracy 68%). Time interval data were available for one of these code types. For the 8/9 white case, the interval was 2 months and for the 8/9 Black case it was 7 weeks.

In summary, the study showed that the output of CBTI systems for the MMPI was found to vary in relevancy, accuracy, and usefulness using file drawer histories or self-report data for subclinical normal, neurotic, characterological, and psychotic profile types. The output of CBTI systems was found to differ in the accuracy of both clinical and subclinical normal code types. Raters showed considerable agreement in their global and sentence-by-sentence ratings of accuracy and relevancy. For the most highly rated CBTI systems, moderate validity levels were found for the narrative output.

FURTHER RESEARCH

In additional papers, the authors will address the clinical implications of the results for the matched Black/white cases, for neurological and nonneurological cases, and will analyze the possible reasons for the results found.

The study may be repeated, using a larger number of raters for the clinical code types. The research design may be applied in different mental health settings, civilian and military. And the research methodology may be adapted to evaluate and modify CBTIs developed for other personality inventories. Research of this kind for inventories with a limited research literature cannot be regarded as a substitute for the test validation process (American Educational Research Association, American Psychological Association, and National Council on Measurement in Education, 1985; American Psychological Association Committee on Professional Standards and Committee on Psychological Tests and

Assessment, 1986). Obviously the accuracy of CBTIs is limited by the reliability and validity of the test on which the interpretation is based.

ACKNOWLEDGMENT

This chapter is based in part on a paper presented at the 1986 convention of the American Psychological Association, chaired by A. David Mangelsdorff, for the symposium on "Computer-Based Clinical Assessment for Children, Adults, and Neuropsychological Cases." The authors acknowledge the technical assistance provided by W. Grant Dahlstrom, Kevin L. Moreland, Lois C. Northrop, Dorothea E. Johannsen, Samuel E. Krug, and Mason N. Crook. They thank the computer-based test interpretation (CBTI) companies for donating their CBTIs and greatly appreciate the dedication of the following raters: Phillip Appel, Frank Edwards, Randall C. Epperson, David H. Gillooly, Dennis J. Grill, Gregory Hollis, Lawrence Klusman, James E. McCarroll, John Powell, Robert Rankin, Frank Rath, David Schaefer and Thomas R. Waddell. The authors thank Iris Hepburn and Sandra Stewart for clerical assistance.

The opinions expressed are those of the authors and are not necessarily official policy statements.

REFERENCES

Adair, F. L. (1978a). Review of the Minnesota Multiphasic Personality Inventory. Automated Psychological Assessment. In O. K. Buros (Ed.), *The Eighth Mental Measurements Yearbook*, pp. 945–947.

Adair, F. L. (1978b). Review of the Minnesota Multiphasic Personality Inventory. Behaviordyne Psychodiagnostic Laboratory Service. In O. K. Buros (Ed.). *The Eighth Mental Measurements Yearbook*, pp. 948–949.

Adair, F. L. (1978c). Review of the Minnesota Multiphasic Personality Inventory. Caldwell Report: An MMPI Interpretation. In O. K. Buros (Ed.), *The Eighth Mental Measurements Yearbook*, pp. 952–953.

American Educational Research Association, American Psychological Association, and National Council on Measurement in Education. (1985). *Standards for educational and psychological testing*. Washington, DC: American Psychological Association.

American Psychiatric Association. (1980). *Diagnostic and statistical manual of mental disorders* (3rd ed.). Washington, DC: Author.

American Psychological Association Committee on Professional Standards and Committee on Psychological Tests and Assessment. (1986). *Guidelines for computer-based tests and interpretations*. Washington, DC: Author.

Anastasi, A. (1988). *Psychological testing* (6th ed.). New York: Macmillan.

Black, J. Cited in NCS FASTTEST. (undated). The Minnesota Multiphasic Personality Inventory. Minneapolis: National Computer Systems.

Butcher, J. N. (1978a). Review of the Minnesota Multiphasic Personality Inventory. Automated Psychological Assessment. In O. K. Buros (Ed.), *The Eighth Mental Measurements Yearbook*, pp. 947–948.

Butcher, J. N. (1978b). Review of the Minnesota Multiphasic Personality Inventory. Behaviordyne Psychodiagnostic Laboratory Service. In O. K. Buros (Ed.), *The Eighth Mental Measurements Yearbook*, pp. 951–952.

Butcher, J. N. (1978c). Review of the Minnesota Multiphasic Personality Inventory: Caldwell Report: An MMPI Interpretation. In O. K. Buros (Ed.), *The Eighth Mental Measurements Yearbook*, pp. 953–955.

Butcher, J. N., & Keller, L. S. (1984). Objective personality assessment. In G. Goldstein, & M. Hersen (Eds.), *Handbook of psychological assessment*. New York: Pergamon Press.

Chase, L. L. S. (1974). An evaluation of MMPI interpretation systems. *Dissertation Abstracts International*, 35, 6090B. (University Microfilms No. 75–11, 982).

Colligan, R. C., Osborne, D., Swenson, W. M., & Offord, K. P. (1983). *The MMPI: A contemporary normative study*. New York: Praeger.

Dahlstrom, W. G., Welsh, G. S., & Dahlstrom, L. E. (1972). *An MMPI Handbook: Vol. 1. Clinical interpretation* (rev. ed.). Minneapolis: University of Minnesota Press.

Duthie, B. (1985). *MMPI computerized interpretation manual: Subsection 3.2*. Wakefield, RI: Applied Innovations.

Eyde, L. D. (1985). Review of the Minnesota Multiphasic Personality Inventory. The Minnesota Report: Personnel Selection System. In J. V. Mitchell, Jr. (Ed.), *The Ninth Mental Measurements Yearbook*, pp. 1005–1008.

Eyde, L. D., & Kowal, D. M. (1985). Psychological decision support software for the public: Pros, cons, and guidelines. *Computers in Human Behavior, 1,* 321–336.

Eyde, L. D., Kowal, D. M., & Fishburne, F. J. (1987). *Clinical implications of validity research on computer-based test interpretations of the MMPI*. Paper presented at 1987 Convention of the American Psychological Association, A. D. Mangelsdorff, Chair of Symposium on "Practical Test User Problems Facing Psychologists in Private Practice," New York City.

Eyde, L. D., & Kowal, D. M. (1987). Computerized test interpretation services: Ethical and professional concern regarding U.S.A. producers and users. In L. D. Eyde (Ed.), *Computerised Psychological Testing*. London: Lawrence Erlbaum Associates.

Finney, J. C. (1968). Normative data on some MMPI scales. *Psychological Reports, 23,* 219–229.

Fishburne, F. J., & Parkison, S. C. (1984). Age effects on active duty Army MMPI profiles. *Proceedings, Psychology in the Department of Defense Ninth Symposium* (USAFA–TR–84–2). Colorado Springs, CO: USAF Department of Behavioral Sciences and Leadership, pp. 575–579.

Fishburne, F. J., Eyde, L. D., & Kowal, D. M. (1988). *Computer-based test interpretations of the Minnesota Multiphasic Personality Inventory with neurologically impaired patients*. Paper presented at 1988 convention of the American Psychological Association. A. D. Mangelsdorff, Chair. Atlanta, Georgia.

Fowler, R. D. (1985). Landmarks in computer-assisted psychological assessment. *Journal of Consulting and Clinical Psychology, 53,* 748–759.

Fowler, R. D., & Butcher, J. N. (1986). Critique of Matarazzo's views of computerized testing: All sigma and no meaning. *American Psychologist 41,* 94–96.

Fowler, R. D., & Coyle, F. A., Jr. (1968). Scoring error on the MMPI. *Journal of Clinical Psychology, 24,* 59–69.

Gilberstadt, H., & Duker, J. (1965). *A handbook for clinical and actuarial MMPI interpretation*. Philadelphia: Saunders.

Graham, J. R. (1977). *The MMPI: A practical guide*. New York: Oxford University Press.

Graham, J. R. (1978). The Minnesota Multiphasic Personality Inventory (MMPI). In B. B. Wolman (Ed.), *Clinical diagnosis of mental disorders: A handbook*. New York: Plenum Press.

Graham, J. R. (1987). *The MMPI: A practical guide* (2nd ed.). New York: Oxford Press.

Graham, J. R., & Lilly, R. S. (1984). *Psychological testing*. Englewood, Cliffs, NJ: Prentice–Hall.

Grayson, H. M., & Backer, T. E. (1972). Scoring accuracy of four automated MMPI interpretation report agencies. *Journal of Clinical Psychology, 28*(3), 366–370.

Greene, R. L. (1980). *The MMPI: An interpretive manual*. New York: Grune & Stratton.

Guilford, J. P., & Fruchter, B. (1973). *Fundamental statistics in psychology and education* (5th ed.). New York: McGraw–Hill.

Harris, W. G. (1987). Computer-based test interpretations: Some development and application issues. In L. D. Eyde (Ed.), *Computerised Psychological Testing*. London: Lawrence Erlbaum Associates.

Hathaway, S. R., & Meehl, P. E. (1951). *An atlas for clinical use of the MMPI*. Minneapolis: University of Minnesota Press.

Holden, C. (1986, September 19). Researchers grapple with problems of updating classic psychological test. *Science, 233,* 1249–1251.

Johnson, J. H., Butcher, J. N., Null, C., & Johnson, K. N. (1984). Replicated item level factor analysis of the full MMPI. *Journal of Personality and Social Psychology, 47,* 105–114.

Klett, B., Schaefer, A., & Plemel, D. (1985). Just how accurate are computer-scored tests? *The VA Chief Psychologist, 8,* 7.

Krug, S. (1987). *Psychware Sourcebook 1987–1988: A reference guide to computer-based products for behavioral assessment in psychology, education, and business* (2nd ed.). Kansas City, MO: Test Corporation of America.

Lachar, D. (1974). *The MMPI: Clinical assessment and automated interpretation*. Los Angeles: Western Psychological Services.

Lanyon, R. I. (1984). Personality assessment. In M. R. Rosenzweig & L. W. Porter (Eds.), *Annual Review of Psychology, 35,* 667–701.

Matarazzo, J. D. (1986). Computerized clinical psychological test interpretations: Unvalidated plus all mean and no sigma. *American Psychologist, 41,* 14–24.

Miller, D. A., Johnson, J. H., Klingler, D. E., Williams, T. A., & Giannetti, R. A. (1977). Design for an on-line computerized system for MMPI interpretation. *Behavior Research Methods and Instrumentation, 9,* 117–122.

Mitchell, J. V., Jr. (1984). Computer-based interpretation and the public interest. *CPA Highlights* (Canadian Psychological Association), *6*(4), 4–6, (ERIC, E D 249 286).

Moreland, K. L. (1985). Validation of computer-based test interpretations: Problems and prospects. *Journal of Consulting and Clinical Psychology, 53,* 816–825.

Moreland, K. L. (1987). Computer-based test interpretations: Advice to the consumer. In L. D. Eyde (Ed.), *Computerised Psychological Testing*. London: Lawrence Erlbaum Associates.

National Computer Systems. (1982). *Minnesota Multiphasic Personality Inventory: User's Guide for the Minnesota Report*. Minneapolis: University of Minnesota Press.

NCS FASTTEST. (undated). *The Minnesota Multiphasic Personality Inventory*. Minneapolis: National Computer Systems.

O'Dell, J. W. (1972). P. T. Barnum explores the computer. *Journal of Consulting and Clinical Psychology, 38,* 270–273.

Parkison, S. C., & Fishburne, F. J. (1984). MMPI normative data for a male active duty Army population. *Proceedings, Psychology in the Department of Defense, Ninth Symposium* (USAFA–TR–84–2). Colorado Springs, CO: USAF Department of Behavioral Sciences and Leadership.

Siegel, S. (1956). *Nonparametric statistics for the behavioral sciences*. New York: McGraw–Hill.

Sundberg, N. D. (1985a). Review of the Minnesota Multiphasic Personality Inventory. Behaviordyne Psychodiagnostic Laboratory Service. In J. V. Mitchell, Jr. (Ed.), *The Ninth Mental Measurements Yearbook*. Lincoln, Nebraska: Buros Institute of Mental Measurements. pp. 1003–1005.

Sundberg, N. D. (1985b). Review of the Minnesota Multiphasic Personality Inventory. WPS Test Report. IN J. V. Mitchell, Jr. (Ed.), *The Ninth Mental Measurements Yearbook,* Lincoln, Nebraska: Buros Institute of Mental Measurements. pp. 1009–1011.

Weigel, R. G., & Phillips, M. (1967). An evaluation of MMPI scoring accuracy by two national scoring agencies. *Journal of Clinical Psychology, 23,* 101–103.

Wiggins, J. A. (1973). *Personality and prediction: Principles of personality assessment*. Reading, MA: Addison–Wesley.

Wise, S. L. (1985). Software review of EPISTAT by Tracy L. Gustafson. Round Rock, TX: Author, Undated. *Computers in Human Behavior, 1,* 199–202.

APPENDIX A

Rating Forms and Instructions
General Instructions to Raters

There are now 14 companies that offer CBTIs for the MMPI. Seven of these companies are included in this study, in which you will be evaluating the MMPI interpretations for six cases in terms of their case files. In other words, you are rating the validity of the CBTIs, using case histories as a criterion.

Your data will be reported in summary form only and we will provide you with our resulting paper.

1. Please begin by completing the Background Data Form for Raters.

2. Next study the case file for your first subject. Note that for purposes of this study our consultant, Dr. W. Grant Dahlstrom, has set these raw score criteria for declaring MMPI invalid: (a) Can't say scores of 50 or greater; (b) L or Lie scores of 11 or greater; and (c) F or Frequency scores of 22 or greater.

3. Read over everything in each of the seven CBTI reports for this subject, in the order in which you have been instructed to use them (see individualized instructions).

4. Now you are ready to begin rating the individually numbered narratives for the first CBTI.

5. You are to rate the accuracy of each numbered statement in each CBTI against the data in the subject's case file. Rate each statement's accuracy by using *one* of these *five* rating categories:

0 = Data insufficient to make a rating.

9 = Generally applicable or repetitive statement which does not contribute to the understanding of the particular case.

1 = Narrative statement is inaccurate.

2 = Narrative statement is somewhat accurate.

3 = Narrative statement is accurate.

6. Use the general answer sheet to record your rating (0, 9, 1, 2, or 3) of each narrative statement. On the general answer sheet, the narrative statement numbers appear on the left. Column headings identify each of the seven CBTIs.

7. Begin by rating the first CBTI on your list, rating each numbered narrative statement. Complete all statement ratings before going on to the Special Answer Sheet for this CBTI.

8. Repeat instruction 7 for each of the remaining 6 CBTIs for your first subject.

9. After completing all ratings for your first subject, follow instructions 2 to 8 for each of your remaining five subjects.

10. Now turn to your Final Rating Sheet and complete these overall ratings for all seven CBTIs for all six subjects.

11. When you have completed all ratings for all subjects, mail all the materials, *using the most rapid available mailing procedure,* to:

Dr. Lorraine D. Eyde
2400 S. Arlington Ridge Rd.
Arlington, VA 22202

We thank you for your assistance. You will be hearing more from us at a later date after we finish our papers.

BACKGROUND DATA FORM FOR RATERS

Rater # _____

1. My Ph.D. is in Clinical Psychology: ___yes ___no.
   a. If "no" state specialty area _____.

2. I have completed an APA-approved Clinical Psychology Internship: ___yes ___no.

3. I am licensed to practice psychology: ___yes ___no.

4. I have had the following number of years (full-time or equivalent) of post-doctoral experience in clinical psychology: _____years.

5. I hold a diplomate, issued by the American Board of Professional Psychology: ____yes ____no.
   .
   a. If "yes," state the specialty_____.

6. My race is: _____Caucasian (White) _____Black _____Asian (Oriental) or _____other.

7. My ethnicity is: _____Hispanic _____Nonhispanic.

8. My gender is: _____Male _____Female.

9. Do you currently use the MMPI in your practice? _____yes _____no..

10. What interpretative references or.sources do you presently use in your practice? Please give references:
_____
_____

11. How much experience have you had in using each kind of computer-based test interpretations (CBTIs) of the MMPI?

	No Experience	Some Experience	Extensive Experience
a. Applied innovations			
b. Behaviordyne			
c. Caldwell Report			
d. Minnesota Report: (Adult System)			
e. Morris-Tomlinson Report			
f. Psych Systems			
g. WPS Test Report			

SPECIAL ANSWER SHEET FOR APPLIED INNOVATIONS

Rater #_____

Subject #_____

1.Now that you have rated each narrative statement of the CBTI against the case file for your subject, please list the salient aspects of the case history identified by this particular CBTI.

2. Now list the significant omissions for this case history that this CBTI did not pick up.

3. On the basis of your evaluation of the subject's case file, how would you characterize the mental status of this subject?

___Psychotic   ___Neurotic   ___Personality Disorder   ___Normal

4. Now rate the overall accuracy of the diagnostic evaluation described in the numbered narratives, offered by this CBTI compared with the data in the case history, by placing an X in one of these boxes.

___CBTI does not provide a diagnostic evaluation.
___CBTI's diagnostic evaluation is inaccurate.
___CBTI's diagnostic evaluation is somewhat accurate.
___CBTI's diagnostic evaluation is accurate.

5. Did the CBTI recommend chemotherapy for this subject? ___yes ___no.

If "yes," how appropriate was the recommendation?

___not appropriate   ___somewhat appropriate   ___appropriate.

6. Did the CBTI suggest that the subject may have a neurological/organic problem?
___yes ___no.

If "yes," how accurate was the evaluation?
___inaccurate   ___somewhat accurate   ___accurate

7. How do you evaluate the adequacy of the special scales, reesearch scales, and critical item listings used in this CBTI system?

___not enough listings
___adequate listings
___more listings than needed

8. Rate the overall accuracy of the CBTI System.

___The CBTI System is generally inaccurate.
___The CBTI System is somewhat accurate.
___The CBTI System is generally accurate.

9. Rank the overall helpfulness of the CBTI system in the disposition of the case, i.e., in the diagnostic evaluation and disposition planning.

___The CBTI System is not helpful.
___The CBTI System is somewhat helpful.
___The CBTI System is quite helpful.

10. General comments on this CBTI System.

FINAL RATING SHEET

RATER #_____

Now that you have completed all of your ratings for six subjects, covering seven CBTIs, please make overall ratings across your subjects.

1. First, place the following seven CBTI systems in rank order in terms of the overall accuracy of their CBTIs for all of the subjects you have rated. Place a "1" next to the CBTI system that produced, on the average, the most accurate overall CBTI. Then, place a "2" next to the CBTI system with the second most accurate overall CBTI. Continue doing so, until you have assigned a "7" rating to the system that produced the least accurate overall CBTI.

_____Applied Innovations
_____Behaviordyne
_____Caldwell Report
_____Minnesota Report: Adult System
_____Morris-Tomlinson Reports
_____Psych Systems
_____WPS Test Report

2. Now apply the same overall ranking system to ratings for all subjects in the overall helpfulness of the CBTI system in the disposition of the case, i.e., the diagnostic evaluation and disposition planning. Assign "1" to "7" ratings to these CBTIs.

_____Applied Innovations
_____Behaviordyne
_____Caldwell Report
_____Minnesota Report: Adult System
_____Morris-Tomlinson Reports
_____Psych System
_____WPS Test Report

APPENDIX B

Pooled Data Across All Rating Categories of MMPI CBTI Systems

TABLE B.1
Number of Narrative Statements for Common Cases Rated by All Raters of MMPI CBTI System

Code Type Race	Applied Innovations	Behaviordyne	Caldwell Report	Minn. Report Adult System	Morris-Tomlinson	NCS FAST TEST	WPS Test Report
7/2 White	123	225	45	32	21	54	41
7/2 Black	123	188	41	45	14[a]	52	39
Subclinical Normal White	13[a]	149	51	22	9[a]	32	21
Subclinical Normal Black	23	126	77	16[a]	8[a]	36	27
Range for CBTI system	13-123	126-225	41-77	16-45	8-21	32-54	21-41

[a] Caution should be applied when interpreting percentages based on frequencies < 20.

TABLE B.2
Number of Narrative Statements for Code Types of Unique Cases Rated by One
Rater for MMPI CBTI Systems

Number of Statements for CBTI Systems

Code Type	Rater	AI	BE	CA	MN	MT	FT	WPS
1 W	1	22	198	74	25	10	48	23
1 B	1	16	164	62	28	15	30	25
2/1 W	2	56	124	58	38	16	63	31
2/1 B	2	114	226	57	54	34	72	71
1/3 W	3	106	229	84	38	22	34	27
1/3 B	3	83	139	87	38	28	47	39
8/1 W	4	29	185	73	25	16	35	19
8/1 B	4	119	189	59	33	30	42	27
2 W	6	37	232	65	24	13	9	30
2 B	6	31	151	57	19	12	50	17
2/8 W	7	110	252	49	60	32	51	45
2/8 B	7	115	248	67	56	31	59	62
3 W	8	23	170	53	28	10	36	19
3 B	8	20	183	71	27	14	31	21
4/2 W	9	74	366	53	29	13	62	31
4/2 B	9	104	169	52	30	21	58	34
6 W	10	17	164	70	14	10	30	14
6 B	10	35	166	84	26	9	50	20
8/6 W	11	74	235	48	32	16	42	41
8/6 B	11	107	209	63	37	25	61	63
9/6 W	12	28	192	80	33	15	51	35
9/6 B	12	90	289	83	53	25	52	61
8/9 W	13	66	140	51	31	12	52	49
8/9 B	13	76	176	53	28	17	51	34
Median		70	187	62.5	30.5	16	50	31
Range		16-119	124-366	49-87	14-60	9-34	9-72	14-71

Note. W = White; B = Black

TABLE B.3
Median Percentages for 7/2 Code Type for Ratings of Narrative Statements of
MMPI CBTI Systems Across Raters
(N = 24)

CBTI System	Rating Categories				
	Unratable (1)	General Repetitive (2)	Inaccurate (3)	Somewhat Accurate (4)	Accurate (5)
AI	18	09	24	23	18
BE	20	20	14	24	14
CA	18	07	02	31	26
MN	10	03	05	28	48
MT	14	07	10	19	29
FT	14	06	12	28	22
WPS	10	18	11	30	30

TABLE B.4
Median Percentages for Subclinical Normal Cases for Ratings of Narrative
Statements of MMPI CBTI Systems Across Raters
(N = 24)

CBTI System	*Rating Categories*				
	Unratable (1)	General Repetitive (2)	Inaccurate (3)	Somewhat Accurate (4)	Accurate (5)
AI	54	04	00	12	23
BE	56	16	04	08	06
CA	54	14	06	09	08
MN	55	05	00	13	19
MT	25	17	00	12	12
FT	54	06	00	16	14
WPS	33	25	04	11	14

TABLE B.5
Median Percentages for Unique Cases for Ratings of Narrative Statements of
MMPI CBTI Systems Across Raters
(N = 24)

CBT I Systems	*Rating Categories*				
	Unratable (1)	General Repetative (2)	Inaccurate (3)	Somewhat Accurate (4)	Accurate (5)
AI	30	04	20	24	16
BE	24	20	13	20	11
CA	30	08	04	22	22
MN	10	07	06	20	35
MT	07	12	08	34	29
FT	26	07	10	30	18
WPS	08	20	10	24	30

Note. Covers following code types: 1, 1/2, 1/3, 8/1, 2, 2/8, 3, 4/2, 6, 8/6, 9/6, and8/9..

TABLE B.6
Median Percentage for 7/2 Code Type Ratings of Narrative Statements by
Raters Across MMPI CBTI Systems
(N = 14)

Rater	*Rating Categories*				
	Unratable (1)	General Repetitive (2)	Inaccurate (3)	Somewhat Accurate (4)	Accurate (5)
1	02	22	27	29	10
2	26	04	10	27	26
3	08	04	08	30	46
4	16	16	14	34	12
6	28	10	16	23	17
7	12	14	10	23	35
8	34	19	07	18	16
9	06	11	06	31	37
10	20	05	22	17	28
11	16	02	10	33	28
12	23	06	04	24	28
13	18	11	05	16	36

Note. Rater 5's data lost in the mail.

TABLE B.7
Median Percentages for Subclinical Normal Case Ratings of Narrative
Statements by Raters Across MMPI CBTI Systems
(N = 14)

Rater	Unrated (1)	Rating Categories			
		General Repetitive (2)	Inaccurate (3)	Somewhat Accurate (4)	Accurate (5)
1	06	38	13	32	08
2	44	07	00	28	10
3	24	10	01	18	34
4	46	25	02	21	10
6	54	12	08	08	14
7	08	26	14	14	32
8	55	34	00	00	03
9	60	14	00	08	12
10	74	06	02	00	06
11	25	02	00	38	15
12	82	05	00	04	10
13	68	13	02	00	16

Note. Rater 5's data lost in the mail.

TABLE B.8
Median Percentage for Unique Case Rating of Narrative Statements by Raters
Across CBTI Systems
(N = 14)

Rater	Code Type	Unratable (1)	Rating Categories			
			General Repetitive (2)	Inaccurate (3)	Somewhat Accurate (4)	Accurate (5)
1	1	05	21	10	40	12
2	1/2	39	08	06	32	05
3	1/3	20	08	12	26	27
4	8/1	14	18	14	41	09
6	2	10	04	08	32	35
7	2/8	06	22	05	14	46
8	3	35	23	10	12	12
9	4/2	07	12	14	26	36
10	6	28	03	19	14	22
11	8/6	26	08	16	24	19
12	9/6	50	04	02	19	12
13	8/9	15	06	07	12	43

5 Use of Computer Technology in Behavioral Assessments

Thomas R. Kratochwill
University of Wisconsin–Madison

Elizabeth J. Doll
University of Colorado–Denver

W. Patrick Dickson
Michigan State University

Major developments in the behavioral assessment field have occurred over the past decade (e.g., Barlow, 1981; Ciminero, Calhoun, & Adams, 1986; Haynes & Wilson, 1979; Mash & Terdal, 1988a). The use of computer technology by behavioral assessors has occurred, but this is a relatively recent development (Kratochwill, Doll, & Dickson, 1986; Romanczyk, 1986). Consider, for example, that behavioral assessment texts include little discussion of computer applications and many articles restrict discussion of behavioral assessment to observational measures (see Cone & Hawkins, 1977, for an exception). In psychology and education, issues of journals have been devoted to computer applications in assessment and treatment (e.g., Bennett & Maher, 1984; McCullough & Wenck, 1984a) and these have generally included articles describing applications in the behavioral field.

Developments in computer technology are important in behavioral assessment for a number of reasons. First, although many current applications of computer technology in psychology and education have focused on traditional testing, test scoring, and report generation, there is the potential for application of this technology across a wide range of behavioral measures on various adult and childhood behavior disorders (Reynolds, McNamara, Marion, & Tobin, 1985). Applications (to be reviewed in this chapter) already include interviews, checklists and rating scales, direct observation, self-monitoring, and psychophysiological measures. Thus, the technology available may facilitate behavioral analysis and treatment design, and monitoring across these measures.

Second, computers offer special benefits in practice by reducing the time and cost of assessment. While this might be considered an advantage of computer-assessment applications generally, it is a special feature that should be considered by behavioral assessors. Traditionally, behavioral assessment has been considered very time consuming and costly for use in applied settings. Surveys of practitioners who have engaged in behavioral assessment practices have provided feedback suggesting time and cost limitations (e.g., Anderson, Cancelli, & Kratochwill, 1984), and these dimensions have, in part, explained the reliance on more traditional tests by behavioral assessors (Mash & Terdal, 1988b).

Third, and related, computer technology may help standardize behavioral assessment on procedural and psychometric dimensions. In the past, behavioral assessment has not been highly standardized, even though a movement in this direction could be positive (e.g., Cone & Hawkins, 1977; Kratochwill, 1985; Mash & Terdal, 1988b). Computer programming requires researchers and clinicians to operationalize measures that remained previously at the conceptual level. Thus, this standardization could occur on both psychometric (accuracy, reliability, validity, norming) and procedural dimensions (protocol, instructions, coding) of various behavioral assessment strategies.

Fourth, microcomputer technology, especially accompanying software programs, can facilitate the dissemination of behavioral assessment strategies into diverse areas of practice. The range of applications from least to most influence of the psychologist in therapeutic decision making and client care include the following (Hartman, 1986b): (a) storage and retrieval of clinical records, (b) administration and storage of tests, (c) automated interviewing, (d) automated test interpretation, (e) integrated report writing/evaluations, and (f) treatment programming. Because increasing numbers of practitioners have access to microcomputers, behavioral assessment tools can be disseminated by sharing a disk. Thus, the software provides a portable vehicle for assessment and treatment procedures, encouraging use in diverse settings and with diverse clients.

Fifth, although there is little empirical work in this area, computers in behavioral assessment may strengthen the link between assessment and treatment. Microcomputers have been used for both assessment and treatment of developmentally disabled children (e.g., Romanczyk, 1984, 1986), and may supplement conventional self-help or bibliotherapy formats in psychological treatment (Reynolds et al., 1985). "Expert systems" (discussed subsequently) may also facilitate the assessment treatment link (Kramer, 1985).

In this chapter we discuss the current scope of behavioral assessment and provide an overview of some identifying characteristics. We then review current applications of computer technology across several domains of behavioral assessment. Finally, we present factors bearing on the development and use of computers in behavioral assessment with a specific focus on directions for research.

DIMENSIONS OF BEHAVIORAL ASSESSMENT

Behavioral assessment strategies are associated with contemporary behavior modification or behavior therapy. Within contemporary behavior therapy four major conceptual approaches are represented (Wilson & Franks, 1982). These include neobehavioristic (S–R) theory, applied behavior analysis, cognitive behavior therapy, and social learning theory. The scope of assessment activities and methods vary as a function of the area, but there are some general features that provide unity to the field. Generally, behavioral assessment can be regarded as a hypothesis testing process regarding the nature of problems, causes of problems, and evaluation of intervention programs (Mash & Terdal, 1988b). In this process the assumptions, implications, uses of data, level of inferences, method, timing, and scope of assessment differ from traditional approaches (Hartmann, Roper, & Bradford, 1979).

Table 5.1 provides an overview of the major historical differences between behavioral and traditional assessment. The major differences between behavioral and traditional approaches conveyed in the table vary across the four major areas of behavior therapy. Perhaps the major factor accounting for differences is that the behavioral and traditional approaches to assessment embrace different conceptual systems in explaining behavior (Nelson & Hayes, 1979). Traditional assessors generally consider intraorganismic variables essential in explaining academic and social behavior. Overt behavior, the primary focus in traditional assessment, would be considered symptomatic of some underlying dysfunction or disturbance. For example, in the personality assessment area, computerized testing might be used to reveal unconscious factors or traits potentially related to the client's problem (see Fowler, 1985). Likewise, underlying processes are often said to account for learning problems in reading, math or language and assessment is designed to tap these underlying processes. Traditional assessors generally de-emphasize a situational or environmental functional analysis during the assessment process and in interpretation of assessment data.

In contrast to traditional assessment, behavioral assessors typically place a major focus on sampling *behavior* (overt and covert) in various situations and emphasize the individual–environment interaction (Kazdin, 1978; Mischel, 1968, 1973). Behavior and environmental factors are assessed in multiple settings, and the focus on person and environmental factors is made without heavy reliance on underlying processes or unconscious traits. The methods of behavioral assessment, like those of traditional assessors, include interviews, self-report measures, checklists and rating scales, psychophysiological measures, self-monitoring, and direct observations (see Kratochwill & Sheridan, 1990 for an overview). The utility of computer-based assessment for these measures may vary as a function of the purposes for assessment.

TABLE 5.1
Differences Between Behavioral and Traditional Approaches to Assessment

	Behavioral	Traditional
I. Assumptions		
1. Conception of personality	Personality constructs mainly employed to summarize specific behavior patterns, if at all	Personality as a reflection of enduring underlying states or traits
2. Causes of behavior	Maintaining conditions sought in current environment	Intrapsychic or within the individual
II. Implications		
1. Role of Behavior	Important as a sample of person's repertoire in specific situation	Behavior assumes importance only insofar as it indexes underlying causes
2. Role of history	Relatively unimportant, except, for example, to provide a retrospective baseline	Crucial in that present conditions seen as a product of the past
3. Consistency of behavior	Behavior thought to be specific to the situation	Behavior expected to be consistent across time and settings
III. Uses of data	To describe target behaviors and maintaining conditions	To describe personality functioning and etiology
	To select the appropriate treatment	To diagnose or classify
	To evaluate and revise treatment	To make prognosis; to predict
IV. Other Characteristics		
1. Level of inferences	Low	Medium to high
2. Comparisons	More emphasis on intra-individual or ideographic	More emphasis on inter-individual or nomothetic
3. Methods of assessment	More emphasis on direct methods (e.g., observations or behavior in natural environment)	More emphasis on indirect methods (e.g., interviews and self-report)
4. Timing of assessment	More ongoing; prior, during, and after treatment	Pre- and perhaps post-treatment, or strictly to diagnose
5. Scope of Assessment	Specific measures and of more variabls (e.g., of target behaviors in various situations, of side effects, context, strengths as well as deficiencies)	More global measures (e.g., of cure or improvement) but only of the individual

Note. From "Some relationships between behavioral and traditional assessment," by D. P. Hartmann B. L. Roper, and D. C. Bradford (1979), *Journal of Behavioral Assessment, l,,* 3-21. Reprinted by permission

APPLICATIONS OF MICROCOMPUTERS IN BEHAVIORAL ASSESSMENT

Microcomputers would seem to lend themselves most easily to assessment of intraorganismic traits; traditional strategies for the assessment of traits rely on paper-and-pencil or verbal responses, that allow entry into a computer data base. Indeed, the earliest applications of computer technology to the mental health field have involved scoring programs for traditional tests of personality and intelligence.

Interview

Scope of Assessment. In interview assessment methods, the clinician is concerned with obtaining a verbal report from the client on events and activities related to a problem that usually has occurred at some other time and place. In this regard, interviews represent indirect assessment methods. Interviews have been used relatively often in behavioral assessment, but there still is an inadequate research base in the area (Haynes & Jensen, 1979). While several different formats have been used during conventional behavioral interviews (e.g., Bergan & Kratochwill, 1990; Kanfer & Grimm, 1977; Kanfer & Saslow, 1969), few formal or standardized formats are available for use with computers.

Computer Applications. Computers can potentially be used for the collection of interview data directly from a client, for storage of interview data, and for analysis of the stored data. The interview can proceed according to a standardized format or can direct the client to certain questions contingent upon their answers to other questions, a process called "branching." Specific computer applications in behavioral assessment are relatively rare, even though there are numerous early applications including the interviewing of medical (Logie, Madirazza, & Webster, 1976; Slack & VanCura, 1968) and psychiatric patients (Griest et al., 1973; Griest, Klein, & VanCura, 1973; Gustafson, Griest, Stauss, Erdman, & Laughren, 1977). Sometimes questionnaire formats can be adapted for purposes of an interview. Carr, Ancill, Ghosh, and Margo (1981) administered a self-rating depression questionnaire via microcomputer and found that depressed subjects could be discriminated from normal controls with a very high level of accuracy. Ratings of depression by clinicians correlated .78 with the self-ratings on a microcomputer-administered instrument.

Angle, Ruden–Hay, Hay, and Ellinwood (1977) presented an early application of a computer in behavioral assessment in which they gathered information from up to 16 clients simultaneously in a modified Kanfer and Saslow (1969) interview format.[1] The computer first conducted the Computer Problem Screen, identifying the client's problem behaviors across several life areas (e.g., marriage, child rearing, tension). For problems identified during this initial screen, the client then received a series of more in-depth computer interviews to identify various situational events associated with the behavior. For example, in the sexual area, the computer survey consisted of more than 1,000 questions and took approximately 2 hours. The authors describe their program as quite modest with the major weakness being the omission of a functional analyses of identified problems that would have related directly to treatment. Similar application of computer-based interview assessment is the *Problem Oriented Record* that contains approximately 3,500 multiple-choice questions covering 28 behavioral excesses and deficits (Angle, Ellinwood, Hay, Johnsen, & Hay, 1977; Angle, Johnsen, Grebenkemper, & Ellinwood, 1979).

A more recent application of microcomputer interviewing is the *Behavior Manager* (Tomlinson, Acker, & Mathieu, 1984), a program developed specifically for use by classroom teachers who wish to manage difficult behavior problems of students. The program is designed to help the user develop plans for the following behavior problems: not completing assignments, overactive, attention seeking, work refusal, aggression-anger, shy-withdrawn, social relations, immaturity and self-esteem. The program involves professional consultation through a computer–client interaction. Teachers contribute information about a target child, their personal disciplinary preferences, and the classroom routine. The computer program provides a problem-solving structure bolstered by information about classroom behavior problems and intervention strategies. For example, after choosing a problem area typical of the targeted student (as noted previously), the teacher is asked to review a list of descriptors characteristic of children with the problem and identify those characteristics of the targeted student. The following represents the format used in problem description:

This category includes any of the following characteristics:
- Little participation in class or social activities;
- Little or no group participation;
- Plays or sits by oneself;
- Talks little, soft spoken, few words, passive;
- Doesn't speak at all (elective mute).

---

[1]Kanfer and Saslow (1969) provided a mode of behavioral assessment that included seven components: an analysis of the problem situation, clarification of the problem situation, motivational analysis, developmental analysis, analysis of self-control, analysis of social situations, and an analysis of the social-cultural physical environment. The seven areas have often served as a conceptual framework for the conduct of a behavioral interview.

If any of these statements describe Bob, press space bar to continue. If not, press X to make another choice (p. 9).

The program then branches into a series of forced-choice questions to define the problem behavior further. Similar branching procedures allow for the selection of incentives and responses to common objections and questions of teachers.

After moving through the program, the teacher is provided with an intervention that has incorporated teacher-made observations of the problem student, personal preferences for incentives, and the classroom routine. The plan can be printed out for teacher convenience, and a follow-up routine is available after the plan has been implemented for 2 weeks. The *Behavior Manager* demonstrates the use of microcomputer capability to access systematically large amounts of information while guiding users through a branching decision-making structure. Further, decisions are guided by knowledge derived from a research base in classroom behavior management.

The *Behavior Manager* also provides demonstration of the limitations of computer-managed decision-making structures. First, there is a tradeoff between the complexity of the program structure and the scope of decisions that can be made using it. While the *Behavior Manager* uses a relatively complex decision-making structure, it addresses only a limited number of classroom behavior problems and suggests a limited number of intervention strategies. Second, the program's soundness depends heavily on the adequacy of the knowledge base upon which it draws. Additional work is needed to validate the efficacy of the *Behavior Manager* and the adequacy of the literature review upon which its decisions are based. Third, attention may also need to be paid to the acceptability of the intervention strategies suggested by the program. For example, the program tends to suggest time-out strategies with great frequency, a strategy that may be considered aversive and impractical for use in many classrooms. Finally, the introduction of computer assisted decision-making technology into the behavior management process is new and subject to empirical evaluation. An important question is whether the structure and information provided by the program is sufficient consultation for behavior management planning by novice teachers. Can teachers indeed use such a program successfully without supervision by a mental health professional?

Analogue Assessment Procedures

Scope of Assessment.   A rather wide range of analogue assessment strategies have been adapted to the computer and can be used in behavioral assessment. These measures include academic achievement and intellectual assessment devices. These strategies are conceptualized as analogue measures of behavior because the measurement often occurs under conditions and on measures that are similar to, but no identical with, the environment and/or task in which the client functions.

Computer Applications. A common application of computer technology to psychological assessment is computer-assisted scoring of examiner-administered tests (Butcher, Keller, & Bacon, 1985; Romanczyk, 1986; Skinner & Pakula, 1986). Test-scoring programs usually save the assessor time over manual scoring. In addition, accuracy is usually increased with the assistance of the computer program. There are many test-scoring programs available for standardized intelligence, personality, and achievement scales. Virtually all of these programs can be useful in behavioral assessment, depending on the nature and purpose of assessment. For example, such assessment might be useful during the early phases of assessment when the clinician is trying to identify clearly the treatment focus. Test scoring is termed a *noninteractive* form of computer-assisted assessment, in that the client never interacts with the computer (Romanczyk, 1986).

In the *interactive* form of assessment the instrument itself has been incorporated into the computer program, allowing the computer to implement the complete administration. The interactive type of program has been adapted for assessment in reading and spelling (Hasselbring, 1984). For example, the *Computerized Test of Reading Comprehension* (Hasselbring, 1983a) is a computerized version of the *Test of Reading Comprehension* (Brown, Hammill, & Wiederholt, 1978). The computerized version makes use of the computer's facility for data collection, analysis, and storage. Students are presented the appropriate reading passages via the computer's monitor and key in their responses on the keyboard. The computer scores responses as they are given, discontinues the subtest administration once a ceiling is reached, and stores the response data. Teacher involvement can be limited to introducing the student to the computer initially, and printing out a copy of the results.

The *Computerized Test of Spelling Errors* (Hasselbring, 1983b) coordinates a microcomputer and a cassette tape recording. The prerecorded tape is synchronized to the software to pronounce words and sentences for each of 40 spelling words. Given responses keyed in by students, the computer scores their performance, conducts a diagnostic spelling error analysis for all identified errors, and stores a permanent record of the results.

The *Computerized Cloze Procedure* (Hasselbring, 1983c) creates an individualized reading test from any passage keyed in by an instructor. The program drops every *n*th word, presents the passage with blanks to a student, and scores the responses that students key in from the keyboard. These applications illustrate ways interactive software can incorporate computers into the process of analogue assessment.

The major advantages of interactive systems are similar to those in other assessment domains. There may be savings in time and examiner bias may be reduced. It cannot be assumed, however, that scores from the computer-administered version of a test are equivalent to those of the traditional version. Test equivalence must be established empirically, and until it has been established, a computer-administered measure cannot be substituted for the paper-and-pencil version. Standards now exist for determining when a computer-administered version of a test can be assumed equivalent to the traditional paper-and-pencil version (e.g., American Psychological Association, 1986).

Retrospective Assessment Procedures

Scope of Assessment. A variety of standardized checklists, rating scales, and self-report measures are used in behavioral assessment. These are conceptualized as indirect measures of behavior because the data are gathered in a retrospective fashion and may not be associated with the identified problem target behavior. For example, a general anxiety scale is usually completed on problems that occurred at some time in the past and not on a discrete target behavior that might eventually become the treatment focus.

Microcomputer Applications. Like analogue assessment procedures, retrospective assessment measures can be computer-scored and can also easily be made into interactive forms allowing the checklist or scale to be computer-administered.

The *Dallas Problem Rating Interview* (DPRI) (Fowler, Finkelstein, & Penk, 1986) is an application of an interactive program to the administration of a standardized rating scale. The DPRI is a computer-administered problem checklist developed for use in the Veterans Administration Medical Center of Dallas. It is administered at time of intake, and a follow-up version (DRPI–F) administered at regular intervals throughout hospitalization, to inpatient clients of the mental health facility. To complete it, patients note the presence and rate the severity of up to 245 symptoms, behaviors, or dysfunctions. Computer scoring sorts responses of the DPRI into 20 empirically derived factors, including depression, sleep disturbance, social avoidance, respiratory complaints, among others. In an ongoing research program, Fowler and his colleagues are collecting data to evaluate the validity and psychometric properties of the computer-administered scale. Current data show high correlations between the DPRI and the *Behavior Problem Rating Scale* (BPRS), a widely used measure of drug and treatment effectiveness with psychiatric populations. Further studies are in progress to evaluate the scale's sensitivity to effects of specific treatments in homogeneous groups of patients. The program uses a branching strategy, with the administration of some items conditional upon patient responses to earlier items. As a result of the increased efficiency, even the more severely disturbed clients have been able to complete the scale most of the time (Fowler et al., 1986).

Fowler and his colleagues use the DPRI to provide an ongoing, cost-effective measure of client response to treatment. Individual client reports can be produced that show a single client's response over time to a chosen DPRI factor, along with initial and final ratings on selected items. The resulting DPRI data base illustrates the flexibility of a computer-managed assessment system, and the impact that such flexibility can have on services to clients. Because data can be collected at several points in time, and because collected data are easily sorted and accessed, analyses of change over time in client ratings are possible. Composite reports summarizing change scores across clients can be used for program evaluation.

Fowler (1985) suggested that more accessible computer technology may have a direct impact on the amount of measurement of treatment effect that can occur, whether these effects are assessed as continuous rather than pre-/postmeasures, and the accessibility of that data to predictions of change over time. As a result, the ideal of data-based decision making in clinical practice has become more achievable.

Psychophysiological Assessment

Scope of Assessment.   Physiological responses are generally assessed through some type of special instrumentation that monitors bodily functions (Kallman & Feuerstein, 1977). Among the more common response options in physiological assessment are heart rate, GSR, respiration, and blood pressure. Computers have a long history of use in psychophysiological assessment and especially in biofeedback research (e.g., Rugg, Fletcher, & Lykken, 1980; Russo, 1984). Computers have been used in this way by behavioral assessors for many years.

Computer Applications.   Although it is beyond the scope of the present chapter to review psychophysiological computer assessment in detail (see Romancyzk, 1986; Chapter 10, for a review), a few representative examples will illustrate some exciting applications. Several of the computer applications have focused on assessment as part of treatment of anxiety or anxiety-related problems (Biglan, Villwock, & Wick, 1979; Pope & Gersten, 1977). In the Biglan et al. study, a computer is used to deliver a treatment program for test anxiety. The clients are first presented with a noncomputer program involving audiotaped relaxation. The computer is then used to present a desensitization program. The client is presented with a hierarchy of 20 items related to test anxiety and is instructed to signal comfort level to an item. The program then presents a relaxation period, repeats, or goes on to the next item. The computer stores the assessment information and allows the client to begin the next session at a level appropriate for the client. There is no empirical support for the program, although 9 of 15 subjects showed significant improvement on a self-report measure of test anxiety.

Two issues should be emphasized with this assessment format. First, the amount of data generated through psychophysiological monitoring equipment is extensive, making the computer especially valuable in data storage and organization. The data organization and optional display formats provide a new domain for understanding and interpretation of the data. Second, the quality of information entered into the computer is of primary importance with sophisticated physiological monitoring. Physiological monitoring equipment may fail, habituation and adaptation factors need to be considered, clinician and contextual variables may interact with physiological measures, and physiological measures may not agree with other behavioral assessment procedures (Hersen & Barlow, 1976; Nay, 1979). The computer may not be programmed to discriminate between good and "contaminated" data and the assessor must be alert to the wide range of factors that could lead to error. Nevertheless, the interface of computer and sophisticated physiological monitoring offers promising opportunities in assessment.

Self-monitoring

Scope of Assessment. Self-monitoring involves an individual's discrimination and subsequent recording of his or her own behavior. Self-monitoring is typically used to record various behaviors at the time of occurrence and has been applied to a wide range of target responses (see Ciminero, Nelson, & Lipinski, 1977, for an overview). While self-monitoring is used in assessment, it often is obtrusive and therefore has a reactive effect on the behavior being recorded. As a result of potential recording reactivity, self-monitoring has been used as an active treatment for childhood and adult problems. Self-monitoring is often used as a part of multicomponent self-control programs.

Computer Applications. Microcomputer software for teaching or using self-monitoring are relatively rare. Tombari, Fitzpatrick and Childress (1985) described a computer program to assist in teaching a fifth-grade child, Carl, self-observation and self-recording. The computer was conceptualized as a "program manager" and assisted in goal setting and rehearsal, providing feedback and reinforcement, and maintaining records of behavior change. The target selected was out-of-seat behavior. A Computerized Behavior Management System (CBMS) was executed on an Apple II+. The teacher first provided input into the computer on the average frequency of Carl's out-of-seat behavior, the number of class periods he was expected to take to reach a behavioral goal, a brief description of Carl's behavior problem, and a brief description of his behavioral goal. The computer determined and stored daily goals for Carl.

Carl typed his problem behavior and goal into the computer daily; failure to identify the problem correctly and goal led to a computer shutdown and subsequent discussion with the teacher. When Carl entered his target behavior and goal correctly, he was required to type in the frequency of his out-of-seat behavior for that day. If this frequency met or exceeded the daily goal, he was provided feedback in the form of a graph. Reinforcement was provided in the form of access to video games. Teacher input was also scheduled periodically to check on the accuracy of data and accurate data were reinforced.

Fig. 5.1 shows that the CBMS intervention resulted in a decrease in out-of-seat behavior. What is unclear is what component of the self-control program was responsible for change or whether the computer package was necessary for reduction of the out-of-seat problem.[2] Moreover, the teacher played an active role in the intervention process and it is unclear how much her role in ensuring the integrity of the program was responsible for the observed outcome. This study does demonstrate how self-monitoring computer assessment can be used to document behavior change. The role of self-monitoring in treatment is less clear, however.

Self-monitoring was used as part of a measurement system in a treatment program for obesity in a project reported by Burnett, Taylor, and Agras (1985). The program was implemented using a portable microcomputer system carried by the clients throughout their daily routines. The experimental design in this study provides a more direct test of the impact of computer assistance on a self-monitoring program. Subjects in the experimental treatment group ($n = 6$) made self-reports of consumption of food between meals, at meals, and during exercise. The computer provided immediate feedback on total meal or snack calories for each session, total calories for the day, percentage of daily caloric intake limit eaten, and the remaining caloric intake limit for the day. The computer also provided contingent praise and instructions.

The program also involved a within series design (A/B/A/B). The control group also used self-monitoring, goal setting, and feedback but without the computer assistance. The mean weight loss after the 8 postbaseline weeks was 8.1 lbs. for experimental subjects, compared with 3.3 lbs. for the control subjects.

An important feature of self-monitoring is the feedback and graphic presentation of data. Graphing applications make use of the computer's ability to store large amounts of information and transform it into a variety of formats. Behavioral program data already stored in the computer can be converted readily to graphic form. Progress, or lack of progress, may be easier to recognize, explain, and interpret when accompanied by graphic representations. It is clear that the computer not only has the potential to change the ways in which an intervention might be monitored but can also enhance the power of feedback. The decreasing size and increasing power of microcomputers has made it possible for them to enter natural settings. This has clearly increased their potential and has moved beyond the simple analysis of evaluative data, to include data collection, feed-

---

[2]Although the A/B/A withdrawal design allows some inference for the treatment effect, a replication of the intervention (i.e., A/B/A/B) would have resulted in a stronger inference procedure. "Goal matching" during the intervention phase would also have resulted in stronger inference for the treatment effect.

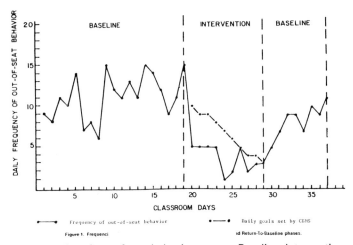

FIG. 5.1.   Frequencies of out-of-seat behaviors across Baseline, Intervention, and Return-to-baseline phases. Source: M. L. Tombari, S. J. Fitzpatrick, & W. Childress, 1985. Using computers as contingency managers in self-monitoring interventions: A case study. *Computers in Human Behavior, 1,* 75–82. Reprinted by permission.

back, and display functions as well. Although this may have a reactive effect and therefore, be therapeutic for the client, self-monitoring effects are usually short-lived and typically need to be supplemented with other treatment components, as was true in the study by Burnett, et al. (1985).

Direct Observational Assessment

Scope of Assessment.   Direct observational measures are the hallmark of the behavioral assessment field (Cone & Foster, 1982; Hartmann, 1982). Direct measures are obtained through development of response definitions, training of observers, and observation of behaviors in the natural environment or under analogue conditions. Observational measures are considered direct in that the target measure is recorded at the time of occurrence, and not retrospectively, thereby hopefully increasing the accuracy and validity of assessment data.

Computer Applications.   Recording complex observational data is often difficult because of the demands placed on the observer. An observer's attention must be divided between accurately observing the behavior and recording the behavior clearly and precisely. Microcomputers have been used to address this and related problems. Using a keyboard, behavior occurrence can be recorded by pushing a button and multiple behaviors can be recorded simultaneously by assigning each behavior to a different key. Current technology allows computers to be fitted with an internal clock allowing for the interval recording of a behavior or for measuring behavior latencies, something that a human observer may

INDEX/BEHAVIOR

	INDEX/BEHAVIOR	CURRNT STATE	CHANGE FROM ENTRY/1 WK
POR NOS	CONCURRENT ACTIVITIES:		
(AP)	WATCHING OTHERS	X.XXX	X.XXX
(AP)	TALKING TO OTHERS	X.XXX	X.XXX
(AP)	LISTENING TO OTHERS	X.XXX	X.XXX
(AP)	PLAYING A GAME	X.XXX	X.XXX
(AP)	GROUP ACTIVITY	X.XXX	X.XXX
(AH)	READING	X.XXX	X.XXX
(AH)	WRITING	X.XXX	X.XXX
(AH)	HOBBY OR HANDICRAFT	X.XXX	X.XXX
(AH)	WORKING	X.XXX	X.XXX
(AH)	EATING	X.XXX	X.XXX
(AH)	DRINKING	X.XXX	X.XXX
(AH)	PERSONAL GROOMING	X.XXX	X.XXX
(AE)	SINGING	X.XXX	X.XXX
(AE)	SMOKING	X.XXX	X.XXX
(AE)	LISTENING TO RADIO.PHONO	X.XXX	X.XXX
(AE)	WATCHING TV	X.XXX	X.XXX
(A)	OTHER	X.XXX	X.XXX
	STEREOTYPE(1)/VARIABLE(17)	X.XXX	X.XXX

FACIAL EXPRESSION:

		CURRNT STATE	CHANGE FROM ENTRY/1 WK
(AP)	SMILING-LAUGHING W/STIM	X.XXX	X.XXX
(AP)	GRIMACING-FROWNING W/STIM	X.XXX	X.XXX
(A)	NEUTRAL NO/STIMULUS	X.XXX	X.XXX
(S)	NEUTRAL W/STIMULUS	X.XXX	X.XXX
(C)	SMILING-LAUGHING NO/STIM	X.XXX	X.XXX
(C)	GRIMACING-FROWNING NO/STIM	X.XXX	X.XXX
	STEREOTYPE(1)/VARIABLE(6)	X.XXX	X.XXX

SOCIAL ORIENTATION:

		CURRNT STATE	CHANGE FROM ENTRY/1 WK
	ALONE	X.XXX	X.XXX
	WITH RESIDENTS (PATIENTS)	X.XXX	X.XXX
	WITH STAFF	X.XXX	X.XXX
	WITH OTHERS	X.XXX	X.XXX
	STEREOTYPE(1)/VARIABLE(4)	X.XXX	X.XXX

PHYSICAL POSITION:

		CURRNT STATE	CHANGE FROM ENTRY/1 WK
(A)	SITTING	X.XXX	X.XXX
(A)	STANDING	X.XXX	X.XXX
(A)	WALKING	X.XXX	X.XXX
(A)	RUNNING	X.XXX	X.XXX
(A)	DANCING	X.XXX	X.XXX
(IS)	LYING DOWN	X.XXX	X.XXX
	STEREOTYPE(1)/VARIABLE(6)	X.XXX	X.XXX

INDEX/BEHAVIOR

	INDEX/BEHAVIOR	CURRNT STATE	CHANGE FROM ENTRY/1 WK
POR NOS	CRAZY BEHAVIORS:		
(IS)	ROCKING	X.XXX	X.XXX
(IS)	REPET-STEREOTYPIC MOVEMENT	X.XXX	X.XXX
(IS)	POSTURING	X.XXX	X.XXX
(IS)	SHAKING-TREMORING	X.XXX	X.XXX
(IS)	PACING	X.XXX	X.XXX
(IS)	BLANK STARING	X.XXX	X.XXX
(IC)	CHATTERING-TALKING TO SELF	X.XXX	X.XXX
(IC)	VERB DEL-HALLUC-S.THRT	X.XXX	X.XXX
(IC)	INCOHERENT SPEECH	X.XXX	X.XXX
(IC)	CRYING	X.XXX	X.XXX
(IC)	SCREAMING	X.XXX	X.XXX
(IH)	SWEARING-CURSING	X.XXX	X.XXX
(IH)	VERBAL INTRUSION	X.XXX	X.XXX
(IH)	DESTROYING PROPERTY	X.XXX	X.XXX
(IH)	INJURING SELF	X.XXX	X.XXX
(I)	PHYSICAL INTRUSION	X.XXX	X.XXX
(I)	OTHER	X.XXX	X.XXX
	STEREOTYPE(1)/VARIABLE(17)	X.XXX	X.XXX

AWAKE-ASLEEP:

		CURRNT STATE	CHANGE FROM ENTRY/1 WK
	EYES OPEN	X.XXX	X.XXX
(IS)	EYES CLOSED	X.XXX	X.XXX

LOCATION:

		CURRNT STATE	CHANGE FROM ENTRY/1 WK
	CLASSROOM-LOUNGE	X.XXX	X.XXX
	TV ROOM	X.XXX	X.XXX
	CORRIDOR-LOUNGE	X.XXX	X.XXX
	OWN BEDROOM	X.XXX	X.XXX
	OTHER-BEDROOM	X.XXX	X.XXX
	ACTIVITY AREA	X.XXX	X.XXX
	LIVING ROOM/DAY ROOM	X.XXX	X.XXX
	OFFICE	X.XXX	X.XXX
	HALLWAY	X.XXX	X.XXX
	DINING AREA	X.XXX	X.XXX
	KITCHEN	X.XXX	X.XXX
	RESTROOM	X.XXX	X.XXX
	BATHING AREA	X.XXX	X.XXX
	LAUNDRY ROOM	X.XXX	X.XXX
	SITTING ROOM	X.XXX	X.XXX
(I)	SECLUSION ROOM	X.XXX	X.XXX
	OFF UNIT	X.XXX	X.XXX
	STEREOTYPE(1)/VARIABLE(20)	X.XXX	X.XXX
(I)	UNAUTH ABS - NO OBSERV	X.XXX	X.XXX
	SICK - NO OBSERVATION	X.XXX	X.XXX
	AUTHORIZED ABS - NO OBSV	X.XXX	X.XXX

SUMMARY INFORMATION & HIGHER-ORDER SCORES

	HIGHER-ORDER SCORES:	CURRNT STATE	CHANGE FROM ENTRY/1 WK
POR NOS			
(A)	TOTAL APPROPRIATE BEHAVIOR	X.XXX	X.XXX
(AP)	INTERPERSONAL INTERACTION	X.XXX	X.XXX
(AH)	INSTRUMENTAL ACTIVITY	X.XXX	X.XXX
(AH)	SELF MAINTENENCE	X.XXX	X.XXX
(AE)	INDIVIDUAL ENTERTAINMENT	X.XXX	X.XXX
(I)	TOTAL INAPPROPRIATE BEHAV.	X.XXX	X.XXX
(IS)	BIZARRE MOTORIC BEHAVIOR	X.XXX	X.XXX
(IC)	BIZARRE FACIAL & VERBALS.	X.XXX	X.XXX
(IH)	HOSTILE-BELLIGERENCE	X.XXX	X.XXX
(X)	ASSAULT FREQUENCY	X.XXX	X.XXX

PROBLEM-ORIENTED RECORDS: BEFORE ENTRY OR REFERENCE, RECORD "T" FOR TEMPORARY PRCSS OR PERMANENT PROB NUMBERS IN "POR" COLUMN AND COMPLETE ID BOX BELOW.

THE "NOS" COLUMN REFERS TO CODES THAT ENTER INTO HIGHER-ORDER SCORES. ALL CODES (A-) OR (I-) ENTER "TOTAL" HIGHER-ORDER SCORES. ALL CODES ENTERING (AP) RECUIR A "WITH" SOCIAL ORIENTATION. "PLAYING A GAME" ALONE ENTERS (AE).

TYPE OF SUMMARY:

NUMBER OF PEOPLE SUMMARIZED W/DATA=   TOTAL=
PROPORTION OF OBSERVATIONS WITH DATA =
NUMBER OF OBSERVATIONS WITH DATA =
NUMBER OF OBSERVATIONS WITHOUT DATA =

DATE ADMITTED TO UNIT: /   /
DATES SUMMARIZED:

FACILITY/UNIT:

_____ TSBC ID NUMBER:

RESIDENTS NAME

RESIDENTS ID (DEPT)

FACILITY NAME

UNIT/SUBUNIT   DATE

STAFF SIGNATURE

138

not be able to detect systematically. The computer also can produce regular audible cues to mark the recording interval, note whether or not a key was depressed during an interval, or measure the time interval between two behaviors or incidents of behavior. When observational data are recorded via computer, the data subsequently may be analyzed by computer without being re-entered. Computer keying systems allow for more automatic reliable observational systems; dual observer systems even allow simultaneous computation of observer agreement scores while both observers collect data.

Microcomputers can record and analyze observational data when the computer can be placed in the environment in which the behavior occurs, or when the behavior is videotaped and the observational data recorded in another site. Portable computers make these recording devices usable in other settings as well. A lap-top portable computer incorporates the processor, display screen, and data storage device into a machine that approximates the size of a large textbook. Even smaller models are now available.

Several existing programs illustrate how computers have been used in observational assessment (Farrell, 1986; Fitzpatrick, 1977; Flowers, 1982; Flowers & Leger, 1982; Romanczyk & Heath, 1985). Romanczyk and Heath marketed a behavior observation software system that can be used for both data collection and analysis. Their system is designed for use on an Epson HX–20 lap-top portable computer that incorporates a small printer in addition to the processor and display screen. Their system offers six options for recording event mode data collection, event mode data analysis, event mode reliability analysis, interval mode data collection, interval mode data analysis, and interval mode reliability analysis. Multiple behaviors can be observed simultaneously, although only one key representing a single behavior can be depressed at any one time. The user is responsible for determining which mode of data collection is most appropriate for the observation being planned and for assigning the keys to the behaviors.

Farrell (1986) described a microcomputer package to facilitate the collection and processing of behavioral assessment data. The program, called Microcomputer Assisted Behavioral Assessment System (MABAS), is a menu-driven package of six computer programs and is available at cost from the author. The program is designed for an Apple II computer equipped with a clock card, modem, and game paddles. The raw data files can be used to calculate total duration and frequency for a single behavior (e.g., gaze while talking, gaze while listening, mutual gaze), to calculate correlations between the two observers, to derive conditional behaviors and sequences of behavior, and to collect data on

FIG. 5.2. Format of Time-sample Behavioral Checklist (TSBC) summary reports. Source: G. L. Paul, 1986 . Rational operations in residential treatment settings through ongoing assessment of client and staff functioning. In D. R. Peterson & D. B. Fishman, (Eds.), *Assessment for decision* (pp. 1–36). New Brunswick, NJ: Rutgers University Press. Reprinted by permission.

PRODUCTION DATE: / /
REQUESTED BY:
SRIC-ID NO.: NO.-1:
             NO.-2:

TYPE OF SUMMARY:

DATES SUMMARIZED: NO.-1: / / - / /
                  NO.-2: (/ / - / /)

FACILITY/UNIT: NO.-1: /
               NO.-2: /

NO. STAFF: NO.-1:
           NO.-2:

NO. OF SRICS SUMMARIZED: NO.-1:
                         NO.-2:

AVG INCIDENCE/HR FOR A SINGLE OCCURRENCE WITH THIS NO. OF SRICS & STAFF IS: NO.-1: X.XX
                                                                            NO.-2:

AVERAGE HOURLY INSTANCES OF STAFF ACTIVITY (MEAN)

CATEGORY OF RESIDENT BEHAVIOR TO WHICH STAFF RESPONDED

CATEGORY OF STAFF BEHAVIOR	APPROPRIATE (AP) NO.-1	NO.-2	INAPPROPRIATE FAILURE (INF) NO.-1	NO.-2	INAPPROPRIATE CRAZY (INC) NO.-1	NO.-2	REQUEST (R) NO.-1	NO.-2	NEUTRAL (N) NO.-1	NO.-2	TOTAL STAFF BEHAVIOR NO.-1	NO.-2	% OF INTERACTION NO.-1	NO.-2	CATEGORY OF STAFF BEHAVIOR
POSITIVE VERBAL	XX.XX	XX.XX	XX.XX	XX.XX	XX.XX	XX.XX	XX.XX	XX.XX	XX.XX	XX.XX	XX.XX	XX.XX	XX.X		(POS VERBAL)
NEGATIVE VERBAL	XX.XX	XX.XX	XX.XX	XX.XX	XX.XX	XX.XX	XX.XX	XX.XX	XX.XX	XX.XX	XX.XX	XX.XX	XX.X		(NEG VERBAL)
POS NONVERBAL	XX.XX	XX.XX	XX.XX	XX.XX	XX.XX	XX.XX	XX.XX	XX.XX	XX.XX	XX.XX	XX.XX	XX.XX	XX.X		(POS NONVERB)
NEG NONVERBAL	XX.XX	XX.XX	XX.XX	XX.XX	XX.XX	XX.XX	XX.XX	XX.XX	XX.XX	XX.XX	XX.XX	XX.XX	XX.X		(NEG NONVERB)
POS NONSOCIAL	XX.XX	XX.XX	XX.XX	XX.XX	XX.XX	XX.XX	XX.XX	XX.XX	XX.XX	XX.XX	XX.XX	XX.XX	XX.X		(POS NONSOC)
NEG NONSOCIAL	XX.XX	XX.XX	XX.XX	XX.XX	XX.XX	XX.XX	XX.XX	XX.XX	XX.XX	XX.XX	XX.XX	XX.XX	XX.X		(NEG NONSOC)
POS STATEMENT	XX.XX	XX.XX	XX.XX	XX.XX	XX.XX	XX.XX	XX.XX	XX.XX	XX.XX	XX.XX	XX.XX	XX.XX	XX.X		(POS STATM)
NEG STATEMENT	XX.XX	XX.XX	XX.XX	XX.XX	XX.XX	XX.XX	XX.XX	XX.XX	XX.XX	XX.XX	XX.XX	XX.XX	XX.X		(NEG STATM)
POSITIVE PROMPT	XX.XX	XX.XX	XX.XX	XX.XX	XX.XX	XX.XX	XX.XX	XX.XX	XX.XX	XX.XX	XX.XX	XX.XX	XX.X		(POS PROMPT)
NEGATIVE PROMPT	XX.XX	XX.XX	XX.XX	XX.XX	XX.XX	XX.XX	XX.XX	XX.XX	XX.XX	XX.XX	XX.XX	XX.XX	XX.X		(NEG PROMPT)
POS GRP REFERENCE	XX.XX	XX.XX	XX.XX	XX.XX	XX.XX	XX.XX	XX.XX	XX.XX	XX.XX	XX.XX	XX.XX	XX.XX	XX.X		(POS GP REF)
NEG GRP REFERENCE	XX.XX	XX.XX	XX.XX	XX.XX	XX.XX	XX.XX	XX.XX	XX.XX	XX.XX	XX.XX	XX.XX	XX.XX	XX.X		(NEG GP REF)
REFLECT/CLARIFY	XX.XX	XX.XX	XX.XX	XX.XX	XX.XX	XX.XX	XX.XX	XX.XX	XX.XX	XX.XX	XX.XX	XX.XX	XX.X		(REFL/CLARIF)
SUGGEST ALTRNATIV	XX.XX	XX.XX	XX.XX	XX.XX	XX.XX	XX.XX	XX.XX	XX.XX	XX.XX	XX.XX	XX.XX	XX.XX	XX.X		(SUGGEST ALT)
INSTRUCT/DEMONSR	XX.XX	XX.XX	XX.XX	XX.XX	XX.XX	XX.XX	XX.XX	XX.XX	XX.XX	XX.XX	XX.XX	XX.XX	XX.X		(INSTRUC/DEM)
DOING WITH	XX.XX	XX.XX	XX.XX	XX.XX	XX.XX	XX.XX	XX.XX	XX.XX	XX.XX	XX.XX	XX.XX	XX.XX	XX.X		(DOING WITH)
DOING FOR	XX.XX	XX.XX	XX.XX	XX.XX	XX.XX	XX.XX	XX.XX	XX.XX	XX.XX	XX.XX	XX.XX	XX.XX	XX.X		(DOING FOR)
PHYSICAL FORCE	XX.XX	XX.XX	XX.XX	XX.XX	XX.XX	XX.XX	XX.XX	XX.XX	XX.XX	XX.XX	XX.XX	XX.XX	XX.X		(PHYS FORCE)
IGNORE/NO RESPONS	XX.XX	XX.XX	XX.XX	XX.XX	XX.XX	XX.XX	XX.XX	XX.XX	XX.XX	XX.XX	XX.XX	XX.XX	XX.X		(IGNORE/NO R)
ANNOUNCE											XX.XX	XX.XX	XX.X		(ANNOUNCE)
ATTEND/RECORD/OBS											XX.XX	XX.XX	XX.X		(A/R/O)
TOTAL INTERACTION	XX.XX	XX.XX	XX.XX	XX.XX	XX.XX	XX.XX	XX.XX	XX.XX	XX.XX	XX.XX	XXX.XX	XXX.XX			TOTAL INTERAC
% OF INTERACTIONS	XX.XX	XX.XX	XX.XX	XX.XX	XX.XX	XX.XX	XX.XX	XX.XX	XX.XX	XX.XX					% OF INTERACT
TOTAL ACTIVITY											XXX.XX				TOTAL ACTIVITY

NOTE: "% OF INTERACTIONS" COLUMN FOR (ANNOUNCE) (A/R/O) AND "TOTAL INTERACTIONS" REFLECT % OF TOTAL ACTIVITY INSTEAD OF INTERACTIONS. "(IGNORE/NO R)-(N)" CODES ARE NOT INCLUDED IN "%" OF INTERACTION FIGURES".

AVG RESIDENTS PRESENT: NO.-1: XX.X CONTACTS/HOUR/RESIDENT: INDIVIDUALLY: NO.-1: X.XX IN A GROUP: NO.-1: X.XX TOTAL: NO.-1: X.XX
                       NO.-2:   NO.-2:   NO.-2:   NO.-2:

AVG INTERACTIONS/CONTACT: NO.-1: X.XX AVG ATTENTION RECVD BY INDIVIDUAL RESIDENT: NO.-1: X.XX
                          NO.-2:   NO.-2:

AVG FUNCT RESPONSIBLE: NO.-1: XX.X CONTACTS/HOUR/RESIDENT: INDIVIDUALLY: NO.-1: X.XX IN A GROUP: NO.-1: X.XX TOTAL: NO.-1: X.XX
                       NO.-2:   NO.-2:   NO.-2:   NO.-2:

AVG INTERACTIONS/CONTACT: NO.-1: X.XX AVG ATTENTION RECVD BY INDIVIDUAL RESIDENT: NO.-1: X.XX
                          NO.-2:   NO.-2:

latencies between two subjects or behaviors such as speech latency. Farrell (1986) identifies the strength of the system as the low level of computer sophistication needed, simplified coding process, ability of the MABAS to record both total frequency and the duration of behavior in real time, and the cost and flexibility of the system.

Computers have also been central to the success of large-scale observational assessment and data management programs such as that described by Paul (1986). Paul and his associates have developed a computer-managed observational information system called the Time-sample Behavioral Checklist (TSBC)/ Staff-Resident Interaction Chronograph (SRIC). The TSBC/SRIC System was "designed to improve the quality, effectiveness, and cost efficiency of residential treatment operations" (p. 16). Computer management is necessary to collect and evaluate efficiently the large amounts of data that result from the large scale observation project.

The TSBC is the primary system for providing data on the nature and amount of client and staff functioning. Data from staff conducted observations are entered into the computer daily. Fig. 5.2 displays the format for computer summaries of the TSBC. The TSBC allows *standard weekly reports* for each individual or group for each treatment unit and *special reports* for individuals and subgroups from a continuous data file, time, behavior setting, or biographical data. Computer-generated reports are used to monitor changes in client behavior and to guide clinical decisions.

The SRIC provides information on the nature and amount of interaction provided by staff to the residents or clients. Like the TSBC, data from observations are entered daily and the system provides *standard weekly reports* and *special reports*. Fig. 5.3 presents the format for the SRIC. While the TSBC involves discrete-momentary hourly time samples of clients and staff, the SRIC involves a continuous-chronographic, 10-minute observation period of a staff member, with an observation of all staff members at the rate of once or twice per hour within a treatment unit. Data from the computer generated SRIC reports are used to provide regular, relevant feedback to staff and to guide staffing decisions.

The TSBC/SRIC System is a sophisticated assessment paradigm that can be used for a wide range of adult populations in residential treatment facilities. A nice feature of the system is that it provides information relevant to any specific theoretical treatment approach.

FIG. 5.3. Format of Staff-resident Interaction Chronograph (SRIC) summary reports. [Source: Paul, G. L. (1986). Rational operations in residential treatment settings through ongoing assessment of client and staff functioning. In D. R. Peterson & D. B. Fishman (Eds.), *Assessment for decision* (pp. 1–36). New Brunswick, NJ: Rutgers University Press. Reprinted by permission.

CONSIDERATIONS IN THE USE OF COMPUTER-BASED BEHAVIORAL ASSESSMENT

Integration of computer technology into behavioral assessment raises numerous conceptual and methodological issues (Kratochwill et al., 1986). These issues include standardization of assessment procedures, integration and application of assessment data, acceptability of computers, and ethical/legal considerations. We will elaborate on each of these issues.

Standardization of Assessment Procedures

Standardized assessment procedures are an important first step toward the development of an applied clinical science (Barlow, Hayes, & Nelson, 1984). Standardization can occur on both procedural (e.g., development of protocols, administration and scoring instructions) and psychometric (e.g., accuracy, reliability, validity) dimensions. Relative to traditional assessment approaches, behavioral assessment has generally reflected an informal and nonstandardized approach to clinical measurement. The application of computer and microcomputer technology can facilitate standardization of behavioral assessment techniques and further capitalize on benefits that standardization brings to assessment efforts generally.

First, a major positive feature of standardization through computer software is that wide-scale dissemination of these procedures may be facilitated in applied settings. The TSBC/SRIC System developed by Paul and his associates (Paul, 1986) provides a good example of how this move toward standardization may facilitate dissemination. Surveys of behavioral practitioners indicate a strong interest in the availability of more standardized assessment techniques (e.g., Anderson et al., 1984). The use of standardized microcomputer formats may well make assessment less costly and more efficient in delivering services in applied settings.

Second, the creation of software programs may further facilitate the investigation of various psychometric features of behavioral assessment. For example, in development of the TSBC, Paul (1986) reports good interobserver interactions replicability coefficients for both one-day and a week's observations. By generating an extensive computer data base of observations of clients and staff, Paul (1986) has been able to converge data into highly reliable composite scores that represent observations across an entire week. Analysis has shown these composite scores to have good psychometric properties: They account for all reliable between-client variance on traditional measures of client change (questionnaires, checklist, rating scales, etc.); they predict client success and level of functioning in the community after discharge; they serve as sensitive measures of treatment effects for a variety of interventions.

Although there continues to be debate over the type of psychometric models to be used in behavioral assessment (see Cone, 1981, for an overview), the use of standardized protocols represents a first step toward an empirical evaluation of different psychometric approaches. The development of formal protocols and adaptation of these to computer data bases does not guarantee development of satisfactory psychometric properties in the protocols. However, the development and adaptation of various standardized measures to the computer data base would appear to make it possible to determine systematically the psychometric properties of the measures.

Third, the development of behavioral assessment software in research may also increase the integrity of the assessment. Careless errors in scoring and administration are less likely to occur when the measures are computer-administered and -scored. This integrity may impact favorably on the decision-making process involved in establishing and monitoring intervention programs. Behavioral assessment may be considered a decision-making hypothesis testing process that requires a great deal of human information processing and clinical judgment (Kanfer, 1985). One of the most promising applications of microcomputers in this regard involves the development of expert systems (Hasselbring, 1985; Schoolman & Bernstein, 1978). As a result of rapid advances in the field of artificial intelligence, diagnostic systems have been developed in medical fields that outperform trained clinicians in making medical diagnoses. For example, a program called MYCIN is designed to diagnose meningitis more accurately than any of a group of experts (see Ham, 1984, for a discussion of MYCIN and other expert systems). Expert systems are developed by analyzing multiple decisions made by experts to determine rules that govern these decisions. The abstracted rules are then applied by the computer to new data. Applications of expert systems to behavioral assessment will need to incorporate all important data used to reach behavioral diagnoses. To the extent that this is possible, expert systems may be able to store and analyze large amounts of clinical information and *assist* in making clinical judgments. We do not believe that such expert systems should or will replace the human clinician. At this time the contribution of expert systems to psychological evaluations is an empirical question (Hartman, 1986b).

Bias in the assessment/treatment link might also be reduced by developing programs that systematically alter their own implementation of treatment or assessment procedures (Reynolds et al., 1985). For example, in the interviewing program presented by Angle et al. (1977), certain types of assessment data are gathered, depending on prior responses from the client. These data, in turn, might lead to the identification of different target behaviors with a unique treatment focus. Human clinicians might be biased toward certain types of questions that might lead to a preferred treatment that has little or no empirical support. As Reynolds et al. (1985) note, computer programs contain the bias of their creators, but modification of software may be easier than changing clinicians' theoretical persuasions. Clearly, this issue also needs to be addressed at the empirical level.

Integration/Application of Assessment Data for Treatment Planning

Microcomputer applications in behavioral assessment have been summarized in separate areas in this chapter. Behavioral assessment is more than a series of separate measurement domains, however. Behavioral assessment is guided by a conceptual framework and various models for organizing the data from separate assessment areas have been developed (e.g., Kanfer & Saslow, 1969). Behavioral assessment also involves multiple uses of data, including diagnosis, design of a treatment program, and monitoring the program. Our thesis is that computers offer more than a duplicate of services performed previously by the clinician; they offer new options for the nature of services. This option appears most evident in some recent developments in behavioral assessment where computer feedback has been used to enhance treatment of obesity (Burnett et al., 1985) and where computers have been used for data management and treatment planning in residential settings (Paul, 1986). Unfortunately, computer applications in behavioral assessment have not developed to the level of multiple data use and integration.

One potentially useful application of computers to data integration in behavioral assessment is the "free form data base" (Romanczyk, 1986). Many computer-filing systems search files only for perfect matches between the entered data and the value guiding the search. For example, if asked to find all bills owed by "John Doe," the computer might not select bills owed by "J. Doe" or by "John T. Doe, Jr." Data-filing systems are now available that can be searched "free form," and would select all of the examples that have been given. If client notes were kept on a computer, free-form searching would allow a practitioner to select from clinical case notes the dates of all instances where specific clinical information emerged during the course of an assessment process, such as all instances where a client reported anxiety. Research on this process should be a high priority.

There should also be a rapid increase in the use of graphic displays of data in software for behavioral assessment, both for analyzing the assessment data and for communicating the results of the analysis to clients. Visual displays can make quantitative data easier to understand and communicate. On the negative side, visual displays have the potential to distort the meaning of data unless accompanied by instructions from a clinician. Stimulated by developments in computer graphics, substantial research is being conducted on the issue of how the characteristics of graphic displays affect their interpretation (see Kosslyn, 1985, for a review of recent works). Given the potential importance of graphic displays in behavioral assessment, software developers and practitioners should scrutinize carefully the types of displays being generated. Researchers in this area should bring the research on graphic displays in other fields to bear upon the special needs of behavioral assessment.

Traditionally, behavioral assessors have conceptualized assessment as a process where the focus is unique to individual environments in which the client functions. The practical (and empirical) issue that emerges is whether computer assessment can facilitate treatment efficacy. Recently, a conceptual approach for the investigation of the treatment utility of assessment has been proposed (Hayes, Nelson, & Jarrett, 1986, 1987). The treatment utility of assessment refers to the "degree to which assessment is shown to contribute to beneficial treatment outcome" (Hayes et al., 1987, p. 963). Treatment utility research can span a wide range of questions on the assessment–treatment link. Within the present context, the treatment utility of computerized assessment strategies can be evaluated. For example, the treatment utility of a computer assessment of a client's problems can be examined by comparing treatment outcome of clients exposed to the computer program with those individuals receiving noncomputerized assessment for some target problem. Questions related to the efficacy of the computer in assessment should be framed within the context of treatment utility.

Acceptability of Microcomputers

In the past few years there has been increasing concern on the part of behavior therapists with the acceptability of the various procedures used (see Elliott, 1988; Reimers, Wacker, & Koeppl, 1987; Witt & Elliott, 1985, for a review). With the proliferation of microcomputers in assessment, important questions regarding acceptability have also been raised (Hartman, 1986b; Romanczyk, 1986; Skinner & Pakula, 1986).

Acceptability of the computer may affect the use of the computer as well as the data obtained during assessment. Romanczyk (1986) reviewed research examining client reactions to computerized assessment and raised some methodological issues. For example, the groups to whom questions are posed may yield important differences in reports of acceptability. Griest et al. (1973) assessed the reactions of suicidal and nonsuicidal clients on six dimensions. On one dimension, 52% of the suicidal clients indicated they would rather provide personal information to the computer than to the physician. In contrast, only 27% of the nonsuicidal group indicated they would prefer the computer. As part of a study designed to assess the reliability of computer-controlled administration of the *Peabody Picture Vocabulary Test* (PPVT), children (4–13 years) were asked their reactions to the computer-administered test (Elwood & Clark, 1978). They tended to evaluate it favorably as being easy and more like play than work.

Acceptability of computers by clients has been documented and should increase as they are exposed to this form of assessment (see Skinner & Pakula, 1986). However, as Skinner and Pakula note, acceptability of computers by mental health staff has been problematical. These authors advance three factors that may influence acceptance of computerized assessment; structure, process, and function. Structural factors refer to the interaction between the human and computer, such as the manner of inputting and outputting data. Process factors refer to involvement of the user in the design of the system. Presumably, client and/or staff involvement in design of a system would promote greater acceptability of computers. Function factors relate to the role computers play in professional job roles. These factors are likely to revolve around such questions as, "What is the role of the computer in client decision making?" and "What job functions will the computer replace?"

Studies of the acceptability or satisfaction with computerized assessment need to be more methodologically sound before any firm conclusion can be drawn (Romanczyk, 1986). Studies focusing primarily on the three acceptability dimensions outlined by Skinner and Pakula (1986) are needed. To assess these issues properly, studies need to be designed that involve acceptability as the primary dimension of the analysis. In research and practice, measures of acceptability also need to be more systematic, reliable, and valid (see Witt & Elliott, 1985). In existing studies, measures tend to be quite informal and lack the psychometric characteristics necessary to draw valid conclusions. For example, it would be useful if standardized measures of "computer satisfaction" were developed and used to study acceptability as aspects of the situation and the computer application were varied. Although many studies have typically assessed "client" responses to computer use, there is no reason why responses of clinicians-assessors should not be evaluated as well. Information is needed on the acceptability of computer assessment from the individuals who draw conclusions, make inferences, and develop treatment programs.

As we attempt to understand how clients and clinicians react to computer assessment, we should be alert to the likelihood of large individual differences on dimensions of computer satisfaction. Wagman (1983) reports a factor-analytical study of attitudes toward the computer across 10 areas of application. Interestingly, the respondents had the least favorable attitude toward the use of computers in counseling. Further, men had more favorable attitudes toward computers than women. Analysis further revealed several different aspects of the use of computers that loaded on different factors. Rather than seeking answers to the question of whether computers should be used in assessment, perhaps we should attempt to identify types of individuals who may be especially uncomfortable with computerized assessment and attempt to design environments that make use of computers more acceptable to these groups. As a practical application, the introductory part of any computer-generated assessment might include assessment of the user's comfort with the process and, if discomfort is indicated, the program might terminate with a suggestion that concerns should be discussed with a human clinician before proceeding.

Legal and Ethical Issues

There is a rapidly growing body of literature being published on legal and ethical issues in application of computer-based assessment. These papers may serve as a blueprint for issues that must be addressed in computer-based behavioral assessment (e.g., Hartman, 1986a; Hofer, 1985, Reynolds et al., 1985; Skinner & Pakula, 1986; Thomas, 1984; Walker & Myrick, 1985).

Legal liability issues have been raised over the use of software in psychological diagnosis, assessment, and treatment. The issue relates to legal *responsibility* in the event of inadequate or harmful psychological care (Hartman, 1986a). It is not completely clear if the software manufacturer or licensed (or unlicensed) psychologist is responsible if harmful decisions are made. Responsibility may fall on the manufacturer if the software is considered a *product;* whereas if it is considered a *service,* a reasonable standard of care doctrine is applied and the psychologist is legally accountable. Hartman notes:

> Current practice of clinical psychology suggests that diagnosis or treatment determined solely via software output might violate this doctrine, in which case the psychologist might be held legally accountable. However, as psychologists increasingly adopt the computer, it may soon become the norm for software to determine diagnosis or treatment. This could have the paradoxical effect of lessening rather than increasing the liability of the psychologist. (1986a, pp. 463–464)

In the ethical domain, a number of issues can be raised. One issue that must be the focus of attention relates to the development of guidelines. Past discussions of ethical and legal considerations in the behavioral literature (e.g., Martin, 1975; Stolz & Associates, 1978) have not included computer issues, and ethical guidelines from the Association for Advancement of Behavior Therapy (1977) contain no statements for computer use. Some professional psychological organizations have recently developed guidelines. For example, the revised version of the *Principles for Professional Ethics* of the National Association of School Psychologists (1984) includes three items that relate to computerized or technological services.

The most current discussion of the ethical implications of computer-based assessment can be found in the *Guidelines for Computer-Based Tests and Interpretations* (American Psychological Association, 1986). Included are 31 guidelines addressing ethical responsibilities of both users and developers of computer-based assessment programs, based on the *Ethical Principles of Psychologists* (APA, 1981), the *Standards for Providers of Psychological Services* (APA, 1977), and the *Standards for Educational and Psychological Testing* (American Educational Research Association, 1985). Although these were written clearly with traditional psychological testing in mind, their applicability to behavioral assessment is great. Some of the most relevant issues will be discussed here. For a more complete description of the issues, readers are referred to the original documents.

First, the psychologist providing services retains ethical responsibility for ensuring that services are appropriate. Users of computer-based assessment procedures cannot abdicate responsibility for clinical decisions to the software developers, but must actively continue to review and edit decisions made for clients using the computer-based data. Similar cautions have been made by Walker and Myrick (1985) when they note that computer packages should be used for developing tentative hypotheses, but computer interpretations should not be considered sufficient to make program recommendations. Clearly, clinicians cannot monitor unfamiliar clinical procedures properly, and so psychologists are admonished in the *Guidelines* not to use the microcomputer to extend their clinical competence. Rather, use of the computer should be confined to procedures the psychologist would be competent to perform without computer assistance.

Second, clinicians utilizing computer-based assessment strategies assume additional responsibility to ensure that the integrity of the equipment used is monitored carefully. Minor differences in the computer system used could inadvertently alter the functioning of or decisions made by the program. Where clinicians interact with the computer, the primary concern must be with the continuing accuracy of the program. Whenever the client interacts directly with the computer, additional concerns with the legibility of the monitor screen and comfortable placement of the machine also need be addressed. Clients should be trained on the equipment prior to using it in order to limit any impact of the program due to the lack of familiarity or comfort with the equipment. Finally, accommodations should be offered to any clients who are unable or unwilling to adapt to the machine.

The clinician utilizing computers in behavioral assessment must establish that the computer-based procedures used are both reliable and validated for the purposes for which they serve. Equivalence with similar assessment procedures implemented without the use of the computer cannot be assumed, but the *Guidelines* offer some useful suggestions for the kinds of evidence needed to support such equivalence.

The clinical utility of large data bases of client information has been discussed earlier. Where large amounts of client information are maintained in computer recorded data banks, psychologists are ethically responsible for seeing that special steps are taken to ensure the confidentiality of the records. In the same way that the computer permits rapid analysis of data in its memory banks, rapid access to that data is also permitted unless special protections are implemented to control access (Doll, 1985). Similarly, steps must be taken to ensure that the data are not lost due to mishandling of the storage or memory crashes.

Integration of computers into behavioral assessment and intervention training seems like a useful focus for a significant impact on responsible computer use. Competency-based approaches to training could be useful since the focus would be on training clinicians in specific assessment and treatment techniques. For example, Alpert (1986) demonstrated that a microcomputer could be used to increase the reflective response skills of novice counselors. In view of the rapid expansion of computer programs, trainers can provide education only for a few exemplary programs.

We see no easy way to address the potential abuse of computers by unqualified individuals (Reynolds et al., 1985). Realistically, nothing seems likely to prevent companies from marketing "psychological software" such as Mind Prober with the advertising slogan, "We'll get you into her mind—the rest is up to you" (Doll, 1986; Lima, 1984). The marketplace is being flooded with the software equivalent of patent medicine for every human ill. Hartman (1986a) has suggested, as have others (e.g., Langyon, 1984), that federal regulation may be necessary to protect the public.

Another ethical concern in computerized assessment relates to the importance of human relationships in the assessment process (Matarazzo, 1983; Reynolds, et al., 1985). Reynolds et al. argued that:

> Until research proves otherwise, it is proposed that the use of computers in psychology be restricted to health and mental health services for which relationship variables are not hypothesized to be essential to positive outcomes. When relationship variables are deemed important, the computer can provide services (e.g., MMPI administration and interpretation) to supplement human clinical activity (e.g., psychotherapy). (1985, p. 349)

In behavior therapy there is evidence that the relationship between therapist and client plays a role in treatment effectiveness (e.g., Goldfried & Davison, 1976; Wilson & Evans, 1977), but there is no research in the area of computer-based behavioral assessment. Researchers need to examine both client and therapist factors (Morris & Magrath, 1983). Such factors as expectancy (i.e., the client's expectation for beneficial effects of therapy), imitation (i.e., structuring the assessment relationship so as to make the client act like an assessor), and general characteristics and style (e.g., personality characteristics, history of treatment, and interactional style) should be examined. Therapist variables that may have a bearing on the assessment process include the presence of the therapist during assessment, physical proximity, and therapist "warmth."

CONCLUSIONS

In this chapter we provided an overview of behavioral assessment and recent adaptations, modifications, and innovations of computer technology in the field. Behaviorally oriented practitioners can learn much from the rapidly growing literature on computer-based psychological assessment and, hopefully, avoid some of the pitfalls that have become apparent in applications of computers in traditional assessment.

There is one area that will hopefully guide applications of the computer in behavioral assessment activities. One of the most salient and fundamental characteristics of behavioral assessment is its relation to design, implementation, and monitoring of treatment program. Basically, this issue translates into one of utility of assessment, but this *treatment utility* concept is not yet well recognized in current measurement standards, despite its importance in clinical treatment.

ACKNOWLEDGMENT

The authors express appreciation to Ms. Karen Kraemer for her assistance in word-processing the manuscript.

This chapter is an expansion and update of a manuscript by the authors entitled "Microcomputers in behavioral assessment: Recent advances and remaining issues," in *Computers in Human Behavior*, 1986, *1*, 277–291. Parts of the chapter were also presented at the Buros–Nebraska Symposium on Testing and Measurement entitled in 1986.

REFERENCES

Acker, N. E., & Tomlinson, J. R. (1986). *Contract writer for secondary students.* Minneapolis: ATM.

Alpert, D. (1986). A preliminary investigation of computer-enhanced counselor training. *Computers in Human Behavior, 2*, 63–70.

American Educational Research Association, American Psychological Association, & National Council on Measurement in Education. (1985). *Standards for educational and psychological testing.* Washington, DC: American Psychological Association.

American Psychological Association. (1977). *Standards for Providers of Psychological Services.* Washington, DC: Author.

American Psychological Association. (1981). Ethical principles of psychologists. *American Psychologist, 36*, 633–651.

American Psychological Association. (1986). *Guidelines for computer-based tests and interpretations.* Committee on Professional Standards, and Committee on Psychological Tests and Assessment. Washington, DC: Author.

Anderson, T., Cancelli, A. A., & Kratochwill, T. R. (1984). Self-reported assessment practices of school psychologists: Implications for training and practice. *Journal of School Psychology, 22*, 17–29.

Angle, H. V., Ellinwood, E. H., Hay, W. M., Johnsen, T., & Hay, L. R. (1977). Computer-aided interviewing in comprehensive behavioral assessment. *Behavior Therapy, 8*, 747–754.

Angle, H. V., Johnsen, T., Grebenkemper, N. S., & Ellinwood, E. H. (1979). Computer interview support for clinicians. *Professional Psychology, 10*, 49–57.

Angle, H. V., Ruden–Hay, L., Hay, W. M., & Ellinwood, E. H. (1977). Computer assisted behavioral assessment. In J. D. Cone & R. P. Hawkins (Eds.), *Behavioral assessment: New directions in clinical psychology* (pp. 369–380). New York: Brunner/Mazel.

Association for Advancement of Behavior Therapy. (1977). Ethical issues for human services. *Behavior Therapy, 8*, v–vi.

Barlow, D. H. (Ed.). (1981). *Behavioral assessment of adult disorders.* New York: Guilford Press.

Barlow, D. H., Hayes, S. N., & Nelson, R. O. (1984). *The scientist practitioner: Research and accountability in clinical and educational settings.* New York: Pergamon.

Bennett, R. E., & Maher, C. A. (Eds.). (1984). Microcomputers and exceptional children: An overview. *Special Services in the Schools, 1*, 3–5.

Bergan, J. R., & Kratochwill, T. R. (1990). *Behavioral consultation and therapy.* New York: Plenum.

Biglan, A., Villwock, C., & Wick, S. (1979). The feasibility of a computer controlled program for the treatment of test anxiety. *Journal of Behavior Therapy and Experimental Psychiatry, 10*, 47–49.

Brown, V., Hammill, D., & Wiederholt, T. J. (1978). *The test of reading comprehension.* Austin, TX: Pro-Ed.

Burnett, K. F., Taylor, C. B., & Agras, W. S. (1985). Ambulatory computer-assisted therapy for obesity: A new frontier for behavior therapy. *Journal of Consulting and Clinical Psychology, 53*, 698–703.

Butcher, J. N., Keller, L. S., & Bacon, S. F. (1985). Current development and future directions in computerized personality assessment. *Journal of Consulting and Clinical Psychology, 53*, 801–815.

Carr, A. C., Ancill, R. J., Ghosh, A., & Margo, A. (1981). Direct assessment of depression by microcomputer. *Acta Psychiatrica Scandinavia, 61*, 415–422.

Ciminero, A. R., Calhoun, K. S., & Adams, H. E. (Eds.). (1986). *Handbook of behavioral assessment* (2nd ed.). New York: Wiley.

Ciminero, A. R., Nelson, R. O., & Lipinski, D. P. (1977). Self-monitoring procedures. In A. R. Ciminero, K. S. Calhoun, & H. E. Adams (Eds.), *Handbook of behavioral assessment* (pp. 195–232). New York: Wiley.

Cone, J. D. (1981). Psychometric considerations. In M. Hersen & A. S. Bellack (Eds.), *Behavioral assessment: A practical handbook* (pp. 38–68). New York: Pergamon.

Cone, J. D., & Foster, S. L. (1982). Direct observation in clinical psychology. In P. C. Kendall & J. M. Butcher (Eds.), *Handbook of research methods in clinical psychology* (pp. 311–354). New York: Wiley.

Cone, J. D., & Hawkins, R. P. (Eds.). (1977). *Behavioral assessment.* New York: Brunner/Mazel.

Doll, E. J. (1985). Use of computerized data files in professional practice. *Newsletter of the NASP Committee on Computer and Technological Applications in school psychology,* Spring, 2–3.

Doll, E. J. (1986). Review of mind prober. *Computers in Human Behavior, 2*, 87–88.

Elliott, S. N. (1988). Acceptability of behavioral treatments in educational settings. In J. C. Witt, S. N. Elliott, & F. M. Gresham (Eds.), *The handbook of behavior therapy in education* (pp. 121–150). New York: Plenum.

Elwood, D. L., & Clark, C. L. (1978). Computer administration of the Peabody Picture Vocabulary Test to young children. *Behavior Research Methods and Instrumentation, 10*, 43–46.

Farrell, A. D. (1986). The microcomputer as a tool for behavioral assessment. *The Behavior Therapist, 1*, 16–17.

Fitzpatrick, L. J. (1977). Automated data collection for observed events. *Behavior Research Methods and Instrumentation, 9*, 447–451.

Flowers, J. H. (1982). Some single Apple II software for the collection and analysis of observational data. *Behavior Research Methods and Instrumentation, 14*, 241–249.

Flowers, J. H., & Leger, D. W. (1982). Personal computers and behavior observation: An introduction. *Behavior Research Methods and Instrumentation, 14,* 227–230.

Fowler, R. D. (1985). Hallmarks in computer-assisted psychological assessment. *Journal of Consulting and Clinical Psychology, 53,* 748–759.

Fowler, D. R., Finkelstein, A., & Penk, W. (1986). *Measuring treatment responses by computer interview.* A paper presented at the 94th annual convention of the American Psychological Association, Washington, DC, August 24.

Goldfried, M. R., & Davison, G. C. (1976). *Clinical behavior therapy.* New York: Holt, Rinehart, & Winston.

Griest, J. H., Gustafson, D. H., Stauss, F. F., Rowse, G. L., Laughren, T. P., & Chiles, J. A. (1973). A computer interview for suicide-risk prediction. *American Journal of Psychiatry, 12,* 1327–1332.

Griest, J. H., Klein, M. H., & VanCura, L. J. (1973). A computer interview for psychiatric patient target symptoms. *Archives of General Psychiatry, 29,* 247–254.

Gustafson, D. H., Griest, J. H., Stauss, F. F., Erdman, J., & Laughren, T. (1977). A probabilistic system for identifying suicide attemptors. *Computers in Biomedical Research, 10,* 1–7.

Ham, M. (1984). Playing by the rules. *Byte,* January, 35–41.

Hartman, D. E. (1986a). On the use of clinical psychology software: Practical, legal, and ethical concerns. *Professional Psychology: Research and Practice, 17,* 462–465.

Hartman, D. E. (1986b). Artificial intelligence or artificial psychologist? Conceptual issues in clinical microcomputer use. *Professional Psychology: Research and Practice, 17,* 528–534.

Hartmann, D. P. (Ed.). (1982). *Using observers to study behavior: New directions for methodology of social and behavioral science.* San Francisco: Jossey–Bass.

Hartmann, D. P., Roper, B. L., & Bradford, D. C. (1979). Some relationships between behavioral and traditional assessment. *Journal of Behavioral Assessment, 1,* 3–21.

Hasselbring, T. S. (1983a). *Computerized test of reading comprehension* [Computer program]. Nashville, TN: Expert Systems Software.

Hasselbring, T. S. (1983b). *Computerized test of spelling errors* [Computer program]. Nashville, TN: Expert Systems Software.

Hasselbring, T. S. (1983c). *Computerized cloze procedure* [Computer program]. Nashville, TN: Expert Systems Software.

Hasselbring, T. S. (1984). Computer-based assessment of special needs students. *Special Services in the Schools, 1,* 7–19.

Hasselbring, T. S. (1985). *Computer-based assessment in the schools: Expert systems applications.* Paper presented at the 93rd annual convention of the American Psychological Association, Los Angeles, August 27.

Hayes, S. C., Nelson, R. O., & Jarrett, R. B. (1986). Evaluating the quality of behavioral assessment. In R. O. Nelson & S. C. Hayes (Eds.), *Conceptual foundations of behavioral assessment* (pp. 463–503). New York: Guilford Press.

Hayes, S. C., Nelson, R. O., & Jarrett, R. B. (1987). The treatment utility of assessment: A functional approach to evaluating assessment quality. *American Psychologist, 42,* 963–974.

Haynes, S. N., & Jensen, B. J. (1979). The interview as a behavioral assessment instrument. *Behavioral Assessment, 1,* 97–106.

Haynes, S. N., & Wilson, C. C. (1979). *Behavioral assessment.* San Francisco: Jossey–Bass.

Hersen, M., & Barlow, D. H. (1976). *Single-case experimental designs: Strategies for studying behavior changes.* New York: Pergamon.

Hofer, P. J. (1985). Developing standards for computerized psychological testing. *Computers in Human Behavior, 1,* 301–315.

Kallman, W. M., & Feuerstein, M. (1977). Psychophysiological procedures. In A. R. Ciminero, K. S. Calhoun, & H. E. Adams (Eds.), *Handbook of behavioral assessment* (pp. 329–364). New York: Wiley.

Kanfer, F. H. (1985). Target selection for clinical change programs. *Behavioral Assessment, 7,* 7–20.

Kanfer, F. H., & Grimm, L. G. (1977). Behavior analysis: Selecting target behaviors in the interview. *Behavior Modification, 1,* 7–28.

Kanfer, F. H., & Saslow, G. (1969). Behavioral diagnosis. In C. M. Franks (Ed.), *Behavior therapy: Appraisal and status* (pp. 417–444). New York: McGraw–Hill.

Kazdin, A. E. (1978). *History of behavior modification: Experimental foundations of contemporary research.* Baltimore: University Park Press.

Kosslyn, S. M. (1985). Graphics and human information processing. *Journal of the American Statistical Association, 80,* 499–512.

Kramer, J. J. (1985). *Computer-based test interpretation in psychoeducational assessment.* Paper presented at the 93rd annual convention of the American Psychological Association, Los Angeles, August 27.

Kratochwill, T. R. & Sheridan, S. M. (1990). Advances in behavioral assessment. In C. R. Reynolds & T. B. Gutkin (Eds.), *Handbook of school psychology* (2nd ed.) (pp. 364). New York: Wiley.

Kratochwill, T. R., Doll, E. J., & Dickson, W. P. (1986). Microcomputers in behavioral assessment: Recent advances and remaining issues. *Computers in Human Behavior, 1,* 277–291.

Langyon, R. I. (1984). Personality assessment. *Annual Review of Psychology, 35,* 667–701.

Lima, T. (1984). Review of Mind Prober. *InfoWorld,* December 17, pp. 48–49.

Logie, A. R., Madirazza, J. A., & Webster, W. (1976). Patient evaluation of a computerized questionnaire. *Computers and Biomedical Research, 9,* 169–176.

Martin, R. (1975). *Legal challenges to behavior modification.* Champaign, IL: Research Press.

Mash, E. J., & Terdal, L. G. (Eds.). (1988a). *Behavioral assessment of childhood disorders* (2nd Ed.). New York: Guilford Press.

Mash, E. J., & Terdal, L. G. (1988b). Behavioral assessment of child and family disturbance. In E. J. Mash & L. G. Terdal (Eds.), *Behavioral assessment of childhood disorders* (2nd Ed.). (pp. 3–76). New York: Guilford Press.

Matarazzo, J. D. (1983). Computerized psychological testing. *Science, 221,* 1.

Mischel, W. (1968). *Personality and assessment.* New York: Wiley.

Mischel, W. (1973). Toward a cognitive social learning reconceptualization of personality. *Psychological Review, 80,* 252–283.

Morris, R. J., & Magrath, K. H. (1983). The therapeutic relationship in behavior therapy. In M. J. Laniter (Ed.), *Psychotherapy and patient relationships* (p. 154–189). Homewood, IL: Dorsey–Jones–Irwin.

National Association of School Psychologists. (1984). *Principles for professional ethics.* Washington, DC: Author.

Nay, W. R. (1979). *Multimethod clinical assessment.* New York: Gardner Press.

Nelson, R. O., & Hayes, S. C. (1979). Some current dimensions of behavioral assessment. *Behavioral Assessment, 1,* 1–16.

Paul, G. L. (1986). Rational operations in residential treatment settings through ongoing assessment of client and staff functioning. In D. R. Peterson & D. B. Fishman (Eds.), *Assessment for decision.* New Brunswick, NJ: Rutgers University.

Pope, T. T., & Gersten, C. D. (1977). Computer automation of bio-feedback training. *Behavior Research Methods and Instrumentation, 9,* 164–168.

Reimers, T. M., Wacker, D. P., & Koeppl, G. (1987). Acceptability of behavioral treatments: A review of the literature. *School Psychology Review, 16,* 212–227.

Reynolds, R. V. C., McNamara, J. R., Marion, R. J., & Tobin, D. L. (1985). Computerized service delivery in clinical psychology. *Professional Psychology: Research and practice, 16,* 339–353.

Romanczyk, R. G. (1984). Micro-computers and behavior therapy: A powerful alliance. *Behavior Therapist, 7,* 59–64.

Romanczyk, R. G. (1986). *Clinical utilization of microcomputer technology.* New York: Pergamon.

Romanczyk, R. G., & Heath, J. (1985). *Behavior observation software system.* Available from Clinical Behavior Therapy Associates, 1819 Gary Drive, Vestal, NY, 13850.

Rugg, M. D., Fletcher, R. P., & Lykken, D. T. (1980). Computers in psychophysiological research. In I. Martin & P. H. Venables (Eds.), *Techniques in psychophysiology* (pp. 583–595). New York: Wiley.

Russo, D. C. (1984). Computers as an adjunct to therapy and research in behavioral medicine. *Behavior Therapist, 7,* 99–102.

Schoolman, H. M., & Bernstein, L. M. (1978). Computer use in diagnosis, prognosis, and therapy. *Science, 200,* 926–931.

Skinner, H. A., & Pakula, A. (1986). Challenge of computers in psychological assessment. *Professional psychology: Research and practice, 17,* 44–50.

Slack, W. V., & Van Cura, L. J. (1968). Patient reaction to computer-based medical interviewing. *Computers and Biomedical Research, 1,* 527–531.

Stolz, S. B., & Associates. (1978). *Ethical issues in behavior modification.* San Francisco: Jossey–Bass.

Thomas, A. (1984). Issues and concerns for microcomputer uses in school psychology. *School Psychology Review, 13,* 469–472.

Tombari, M. L., Fitzpatrick, S. J., & Childress, W. (1985). Using computers as contingency managers in self-monitoring interventions: A case study. *Computers in Human Behavior, 1,* 75–82.

Tomlinson, J. R., Acker, N. E., & Mathieu, P. J. (1984). *The behavior manager* [computer program]. Minneapolis: ATM.

Wagman, M. (1983). A factor analytic study of the psychological implications of the computer for the individual and society. *Behavior Research Methods and Instrumentation, 15,* 413–419.

Walker, N. W., & Myrick, C. C. (1985). Ethical considerations in the use of computers in psychological testing and assessment. *Journal of School Psychology, 23,* 51–57.

Wilson, G. T., & Evans, I. M. (1977). The therapist-client relationship in behavior therapy. In A. S. Gurman & A. M. Razin (Eds.), *Effective psychotherapy: A handbook of research* (pp. 544–565). New York: Pergamon.

Wilson, G. T., & Franks, C. M. (Eds.). (1982). *Contemporary behavior therapy: Conceptual and empirical foundations.* New York: Guilford Press.

Witt, J. C., & Elliott, S. N. (1985). Acceptability of classroom management strategies. In T. R. Kratochwill (Ed.), *Advances in school psychology* (Vol. 4, pp. 251–288). Hillsdale, NJ: Lawrence Erlbaum Associates.

6

The Use of the Computer in the Practice of Industrial/ Organizational Psychology

Lyle F. Schoenfeldt
Jorge L. Mendoza
Texas A and M University

The rapid proliferation of computer technology, in the form of mainframe computers, networks of interconnected machines, and stand-alone personal computers, is having a profound effect on many areas of life. As a result of the spread of computer equipment to offices, homes, and educational institutions, the variety of software applications has grown at an unprecedented rate. With this as background, it should be no surprise that computers have assumed an increasing role in professional practice, including applications in providing services in the area of industrial and organizational psychology.

Industrial-organizational psychologists function in a variety of settings, but primarily provide human resource management expertise to organizations. As such, typical industrial-organizational psychologists are either employed by larger organizations or provide services to smaller organizations as consultants. The organizations in which industrial-organizational psychologists work have long had computer capability; in fact most such organizations are of sufficient size to be among those at the cutting edge of this new technology.

In addition, many of the activities undertaken by industrial-organizational psychologists lend themselves to possible computerization. Included among the major services are the selection of employees, placement of employees on jobs within the organization, training of employees, the design and management of performance evaluation systems, the development of systems to manage career progression, and planning of organizational interventions. Most of these areas involve dealing with large groups or manipulation of substantial data bases in ways that lend themselves to computer application.

Thus it is somewhat surprising that despite the availability of computer resources, industrial-organizational psychologists have been slow to develop innovative applications of this new technology. Computers have played a role in the practice of industrial-organizational psychology, but most often as a means of using sophisticated statistical procedures rather than as an adjunct to practice (Denton, 1987). For example, the *Handbook of Industrial and Organizational Psychology* (Dunnette, 1976), one of the most respected compendiums of information on industrial-organizational psychology, mentions computers only in conjunction with computer-assisted instruction, an application that has been in place for more than two decades. The more recent compilation on *Human Performance and Productivity* (Alluisi & Fleishman, 1982; Dunnette & Fleishman, 1982; Howell & Fleishman, 1982) also failed to address the topic of computer applications, except for computer-assisted instruction. The popular texts in the areas of industrial-organizational psychology, personnel selection, and human resource management also uniformly sidestep the topic of applications of computers to human resource management. One exception is the Schuler text (1987), *Personnel and Human Resource Management,* which touches on topics of computer applications in compensation, job analysis, performance appraisal, recruitment, selection, training, and related areas.

The purpose of the present review is to examine some of the computer applications for the practice of industrial-organizational psychology. Areas covered will be those that are the traditional service provider activities of industrial-organizational psychologists, and include human resource planning, job analysis, selection, placement, performance evaluation, training, career progression, and organizational facilitation. As will be seen, in most of these areas of practice, progress has been slow, but the prospects for the future are bright. Innovative computer applications are possible, and progress is being made in adapting the new technology to the delivery of industrial-organizational psychological services.

HUMAN RESOURCE PLANNING

For small organizations with limited human resource needs, the planning process is not an important concern. For large organizations the planning process is essential to meet the personnel needs that result when complex and multiple demands are pitted against the changing forces of a dynamic environment. The planning process consists of developing and implementing programs to ensure that the right numbers and types of individuals are available at the right time and place to fulfill organizational needs. Organizations depend on "what if" scenarios that look at future needs in the context of demographics, economic projections, anticipated technological changes, eligibility standards (i.e., current and future selection standards), recruitment success, and retention goals. In addition, more sophisticated techniques factor into the planning process job preferences among current and future employees, values toward work, and values toward geographical mobility (Dyer, 1982).

It should be no surprise that recruitment-planning models have been developed to take into consideration the many factors involved in developing human resource forecasts. As with several other human resource applications, the military, as one of the largest and most complex organizations, has led the way in developing and using models to forecast future needs. Traditionally, such analyses have been either on the basis of econometric or demographic analyses. However, more recent approaches have brought divergent methodological techniques together to allow more unified forecasts of needs and supply.

In 1987, Borack outlined a model to incorporate what he termed the three distinct approaches to investigating supply issues, demographic analysis, attitudes toward military service, and economic models. One innovation of the Borack model was the inclusion of interest and intention, as well as the usual aptitude and physical variables that tend to determine qualification, as a barometer of the size of the available supply of individuals. By following a panel of respondents over time, Borack found it possible to measure the relative intent to enlist as a function of demographic and geographical factors.

Another way in which psychological variables can figure into the planning process are through determination of factors that influence staying versus leaving. Recent studies (Clay–Mendez, 1985; Hosek, Fernandez, & Grissmer, 1985) have looked at plans to enter the service, or to remain, as a function of demographic factors and economic considerations. As might be expected, predictions of continuation were heavily influenced by the other opportunities available, and the attractiveness of these alternatives. At the same time, both researchers found that predictions based on single trends or overly simple models did not measure up as a result of failure to take into consideration the interactions between psychological and economic factors.

The planning process is an important one, not only for the military, but also for other large organizations. It is critical to look at the change trajectory within the organization, including such factors as growth areas, skills, and talents that will be needed, as well as factors that will lead to attrition. Set against such internal projections are external considerations, including among others, demographic estimates, competitive factors, and attitudinal considerations of potential recruits. It is then possible to use computer models, as suggested by Borack (1987), to project supply as a dynamic interplay of many factors and forces rather than a specific result of a discrete survey or analysis.

The unique contribution of the industrial-organizational psychologist is in the measurement and incorporation of attitudinal and value trends in human resource projections. The computer plays an integral role in the process in modeling the human resource environment at future times (Dyer, 1982). These models include the many measurements involved and use sophisticated regression, time series, stochastic, and Markov chain procedures to project labor force characteristics.

JOB ANALYSIS

Job analysis is the process for obtaining information about a particular job. Researchers throughout the years have utilized a variety of procedures to collect data from jobs, methods which were recently reviewed by Feild and Gatewood (1987). Besides using the computer for the data analysis part of the job analysis, a number of investigators have used the computer to assist in the job analysis.

Christal (1974) at the Air Force Human Resources Laboratory has developed a series of programs (Comprehensive Occupational Data Analysis Programs) to evaluate task inventories. This system contains more than 40 programs performing a variety of features. One program generates job descriptions which include the average percentage of incumbents in each group performing a task, and the average amount of time spent on the task. A second program identifies and describes jobs within an occupational area. Another classifies jobs by their similarities on the percentage of time spent per task. According to Fleishman and Quaintance (1984), the occupational data supplied by these programs are useful in classification and training.

McCormick and his associates have also done extensive work on developing methods of job analysis (McCormick, 1979). The primary products of these efforts have been the Position Analysis Questionnaire (PAQ) and the Professional and Managerial Position Questionnaire (PMPQ). Both of these questionnaires utilize the computer to score and generate the work dimensions that characterize the job.

Recently, Coovert (1986) discussed how artificial intelligence (AI) can be used to generate task statements for a job. Computer software could be developed to interact with job incumbents to generate task statements describing the job. Another procedure that can be adapted to generate task statements for a job analysis is that of Computerized Adaptive Testing (CAT). The CAT procedure tailors the test to the applicant's ability, resulting in a shorter test with higher validity and reliability. The same principles could be applied to job analysis questionnaires, presenting only those tasks that are relevant for the job. The process could be similar to the decision tree procedure utilized by Mallamad, Levine, and Fleishman (1980) in estimating ability requirements for a job task. The procedure requires that the observer make a number of binary decisions about a task statement, resulting in assessing the presence or absence of an ability. (Software for the Mallamad, et al., procedure is being written for the Apple II computer.) The decision tree, of course, would have to be reversed to flow from an ability to tasks.

Fine's (1977) functional job analysis scales could also be used to implement a computer-based tailored job analysis. Fine claims that what workers do, they do in relation to people, things, and data. Each category is subdivided into smaller subcategories ranging from simple to complex. For example, in relation to people, the following are nine functions in ascending order of complexity: (a) taking instructions, helping, (b) serving, (c) speaking-signaling, (d) persuading, (e) diverting, (f) supervising, (g) instructing, (h) negotiating, and (i) mentoring. Since the worker functions are hierarchical and ordinal, it would be possible to utilize them in the construction of some sort of computerized adaptive job analysis. A number of other classificatory systems could also be used.

In summary, through the Comprehensive Occupational Data Analysis Programs and the PAQ, the computer has proved a valuable adjunct to job analysis. Further advances are possible through use of computerized adaptive testing in job analysis.

SELECTION

Computers can be used to improve personnel selection in a number of ways. The objective in personnel selection is to determine whether applicants meet the qualifications for a specific job, and then to select those applicants who are most qualified for the job. The computer can assist in testing the qualifications of applicants though adaptive testing or other computer-based cognitive or personality procedures discussed in other chapters of this volume. In addition, a more recent development has been that of computer-aided interviewing.

Rodgers (1987) discusses the role of the interview in selection, and the advantages of a computer-based approach. Research has shown that the best interviews, in terms of both reliability and validity, are structured or patterned. The advantage of using a computer to undertake an interview is in the standardization achieved and the ability to strip out those aspects of the interview that tend to reduce validity, such as overweighting of first impressions or applicant style.

Computer-aided interviewing uses a computer to present a structured interview directly to an applicant without the presence of an interviewer. The interview typically probes the applicant's background, experience, education, skills, knowledge, and work attitudes as these topics relate to the specific position or positions involved. Branching to follow-up questions allows specific areas to be pursued during the interview, much as would be done with the presence of an interviewer. The results are scored and followed with a more traditional interview to answer applicant questions, clarify responses, and obtain further information. According to Rodgers (1987), computer-aided interviewing has been validated in a variety of settings.

Selection can be enhanced in an organization with the implementation of an integrated personnel data system (PDS), also termed a human resource information system (HRIS). A personnel data system can be designed to store test scores, attendance records, performance appraisal information, job analysis data, assessment center evaluations and promotion records. A number of corporations have such, or similar, systems. In fact, such information systems have represented the single most dramatic application of the computer to human resources and, in turn, industrial and organizational psychology (DeSanctis, 1986; Harris, 1986; Hyde & Shafritz, 1977; Murdick & Schuster, 1983; Schuster, 1985; Walker, 1981).

The popularity of the human resource or personnel data system is related to the pivotal nature of the information captured and the opportunity to interconnect the data from several domains in working toward problem solutions in all areas of concern to the industrial-organizational psychologist. Beyond the utility of the information in addressing issues that comprise the separate areas of industrial-organization services is the possibility of creating enhanced human resource programs using data previously unavailable.

For selection, the HRIS can be utilized to identify candidates within the organization who have the appropriate background and qualifications for a job vacancy. (The system can also be used to design training courses for the candidates.) A decision can then be made whether to recruit within the organization or from outside of it. A PDS can also be designed to have a bidirectional flow of information between performance appraisals and job analysis data (Harvey, 1986). As changes are made in the performance evaluations to incorporate new job dimensions, the information is incorporated into the job analysis data, thus keeping track of job changes and eliminating the need for large, periodic job analysis (Johnson, Moorhead, & Griffin, 1983).

Organizations with HRIS can upgrade their selection weights periodically at little expense. As performance data become available for each employee, the computer can be set to upgrade the selection weights automatically. The computer can also be utilized to implement complicated selection models which balance recruiting cost against misclassification cost. Once the statistical relationship among selection cost, training cost, external labor market and the probabilities of success and failure are established, a computerized selection model can be used to evaluate the cost of alternative selection strategies.

The federal government is responsible for a number of selection programs. For instance, the Navy has developed the Cost of Attaining Personnel Requirement (CAPER) model (Sands, 1973). The CAPER model contains 20 equations, which are simultaneously solved by the computer to determine an optimal selection strategy for minimizing the estimated cost of selecting, recruiting, inducting, and training personnel. The program estimates the actual and the potential cost of selection. Actual cost consists of expenses incurred in obtaining the personnel; potential cost includes the cost of making erroneous decisions. The computer is also used by employment agencies to identify applicant–employer matches. Applicant data are stored in the computer along with employers' requirements. A computer search is made to print a list of possible successful

matches. Some matching programs give a relative ranking of potential candidate–employer pairs.

In summary, it is hard to look at computer applications to selection as a stand-
alone component of the human resource management process. Computers can
administer and score both tests and interviews. At the same time, the real advances are through the use of the computer to connect selection to other human
resource and strategical concerns.

PLACEMENT

Successful performance is a function of selecting the right employees and maximizing the utilization of those hired through effective placement. In its simplest
form, a position exists within an organization and applicants are screened until a
suitable candidate is found. In other words, the job requirements guide a specific
selection effort for the position. Placement is not an issue in this case.

A more general view of the placement function would consist of the following
sequence: (a) the assessment of individual characteristics, (b) the identification
of the psychological requirements of jobs, and (c) the matching of those con-
stituting the labor supply with available opportunities. This approach would be
the procedure of choice by the military, for example, where there is a steady flow
of recruits that need to be placed in assignments or jobs. Selection is accomplished by "hiring" all those in the range of acceptability with subsequent
emphasis on placement as being the function that is one of the critical linchpins
to a successful organization.

Some private-sector organizations might find placement to be more important
than selection. This would be true in organizations with a large number of lines
of progression in a bounded geographical area. For example, an auto manufacturer may have several distinct operations in and around Detroit with a central
screening and placement function. Each line would have an entry position, and
the challenge would be placing qualified applicants in the progression that represented the best utilization of their talents.

To the extent the computer has been applied to the selection-placement problem of human resource management, the emphasis has been on the selection part
of the equation. Schoenfeldt (1974) introduced an assessment-classification
model aimed at joining selection and placement into a systems approach to
matching people with employment opportunities. The assessment-classification
model, included as Fig. 6.1, follows from other statistical approaches, (Campbell, Dunnette, Lawler, & Weick, 1970; Dunnette, 1963) and involves the assessment of individuals, measurement of jobs, and the prediction of job success.

The assessment of individuals or the inventory of the psychological capabilities the individual brings to the job market has two aspects. The first
involves using standard predictors found to be valid for the jobs in question, the

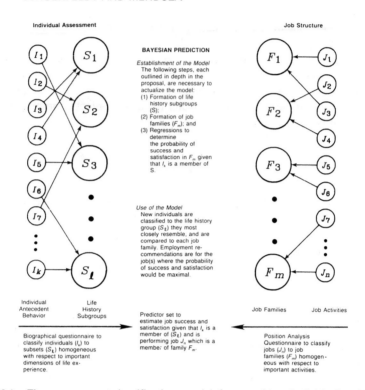

FIG. 6.1. The assessment-classification model for matching individuals with job families.

individual differences variables of the Campbell et al. (1970) model. The second aspect involves implementation of the approach described by Owens (1968, 1971), suggesting the formation of subgroups with respect to the major dimensions of antecedent behavior and relating the subgroups to relevant criteria. This would involve administering a biographical questionnaire to assess the antecedent behaviors. Individuals would then be classified on the basis of their responses to the life history items to form subgroups homogeneous with respect to important dimensions of life behavior.

The job structure segment of the model would consist of an occupational taxonomy, forming job families on the basis of suitable descriptors. Thus, in the same way individuals are placed in subgroups homogeneous with respect to past behavior, jobs can be classified into families homogeneous with respect to task elements, worker elements, or required attributes. The assessment-classification model is then developed by the use of a maximization procedure, such as discriminant analysis or canonical correlation, to determine the probability of success and satisfaction in a particular job family given that the individual is a member of a particular life history subgroup. The goal of the model is the prediction and understanding or person–job relationships.

Schoenfeldt (1974) examined the validity of the model with a large sample of students ($N = 1934$) working toward college degrees. Subgroups, formed on the basis of previous behavioral data collected during the freshman year, differed with respect to criterion (major, grade-point average, and so forth) measurements taken 4 years later. More important, the subgroups differed with respect to the curricular paths taken during college. The results indicated that it was possible to differentiate people in meaningful ways, to identify "job families," and to match people with jobs.

Two industrial studies have been reported using the assessment-classification model. In the first, Morrison (1977) tested the model's efficacy in making placement decisions in an industrial setting with hourly employees. Eight developmental-interest dimensions describing life choices, values, and interests of 438 blue-collar workers were formulated. Job analysis identified two clusters of positions that were homogeneous within, and differentiated between, each other on relevant job attributes. One cluster consisted of process operator positions and had 102 incumbents with more than 6 months' service. The other cluster was composed of heavy equipment operator positions that had 148 incumbents. A discriminant function was calculated on a validation group of incumbents in an effort to develop a linear combination of the life history factors that maximally differentiated the two job families. Cross–validation demonstrated that three psychologically meaningful dimensions discriminated among the groups at both statistical and practical levels. The process operators were more likely to be raised in an urban environment, to have a more favorable self-image, and to prefer standardized work schedules.

The second study was by Brush and Owens (1979) and covered a total of 1,987 hourly employees of a major oil company. Each employee completed an extensive biographical inventory. Hierarchical clustering of the resulting biographical profiles produced 18 subgroups of employees, such that within any one subgroup, background experiences and interests were similar, and among subgroups, they were different. A similar methodology was applied to job analysis data in creating a structure of 19 job families for 939 office and clerical jobs. Significant relationships were found between biodata subgroups and criteria, such as sex, educational level, termination rate, job classification and, most important, performance rating.

The value of the assessment-classification model is in the potential to place applicants in jobs for which the probability of success and satisfaction is maximal. Other purely statistical approaches exist, but do not incorporate dimensions psychologists would suggest are important to the match of individuals to jobs.

In a more recent study, Granrose and Portwood (1987) looked at placement in the context of career management. Programs that attempt to match individual career plans with overall trends and needs within the organization are simply matching individual characteristics, psychological requirements of jobs, and available opportunities on a continuous basis. The core of the Granrose and Portwood research was the development of a path-analytical model of organizational influences on individual career beliefs and attitudes. Their data suggested that the extent of perceived matching between individual and organizational career plans is related to individuals' attitudes concerning their careers. To quote Granrose and Portwood:

> [M]atches [between individual and organizational career plans] seem to have an influence on satisfaction and desires to leave or remain with an organization. . .[B]oth perceptions of organizational planning activity and the perceived availability of career information increase[d] participation in company-sponsored career assistance programs, and perceptions of organizational planning activity also increase[d] employees' awareness of organizational plans for their careers. (1987, p. 714)

In these examples, placement and career management is the function of complex, computer-based models, either the assessment-classification model or a path-analytical model designed to predict the match between individual and organizational career alternatives. What has been at best ad hoc processes in most organizations, placement and career management, are greatly facilitated by the adaptation of computer models to the complexities of the task. The result is an orderly process that incorporates the important individual and organizational elements in maximizing overall utility and satisfaction.

PERFORMANCE EVALUATION

The process of appraising employee performance, along with the feedback of results, is typically thought of as a singular evaluation process whereby a supervisor considers information collected over a period of time with respect to subordinate performance, and makes judgments. As such, it is not seen as a process amenable to computer technology. However, the computer can be used in two important ways.

First, performance evaluation inevitably involves subjective judgments, even when objective information is available. Employee characteristics, such as initiative, dependability, relationships with coworkers, and so forth, are incorporated into evaluations. The problem in depending on such judgments is that of bias, either intentional or inadvertent. Intentional bias is very difficult, if not impossible, to detect, especially if undertaken selectively. However, the general feeling among industrial-organizational psychologists is that it is not a widespread problem (Gatewood & Feild, 1987). However, the frequent sources of inadvertent bias, halo (rating the subordinate equally on different performance scales because of a general impression), leniency or severity (disproportionately high or low ratings), and central tendency (large number of subordinates receive ratings in the middle of the scale) can be detected by comparing the separate ratings of a superior and by comparing the ratings of one supervisor with those of other supervisors. The computer can be valuable in facilitating the process of error detection, and thus is important as a quality control mechanism in performance evaluation.

A second role of the computer is as an important link between the results of the performance evaluation process and other aspects of human resource management activities (Verdin, 1987). For example, performance evaluation results are indicative of training needed, of further challenge the individual is capable of undertaking (i.e., career progression), and of salary progression. Computer technology can facilitate the link between performance appraisal and other human resource management functions.

Brush and Schoenfeldt (1982) outlined computer-based performance appraisal applications that facilitate the achievement of wider personnel and human resource goals of the organization. The system they described was developed by a major energy corporation for appraisal of all salaried personnel. In addition to providing performance feedback to employees, the system was used for enhancing human resource procedures throughout the organization. The system included the following core performance dimensions: (1) Past accomplishments, (2) Administration, (3) Job knowledge, (4) Forecasting and planning, (5) Innovation, (6) Communication, (7) Initiative and responsibility, (8) Work relationships, (9) Salesmanship, (10) Decision making, (11) Leadership, (12) Selection and development (of subordinates).

In one application, organizational strengths and weaknesses were determined by comparing job families constructed on the basis of job analysis data collected to establish the core dimensions. The major groups were comprised of corporate officers, manufacturing managers, distribution managers, and sales staff. Each functional group was further stratified into four organizational levels. This characterization was done on the basis of the number of job evaluation points (based on the Hay system of evaluating salaried positions) assigned to the job. The result was a functional area by organizational-level matrix where performance factors could be studied free from the potentially confounding influences of function and/or level.

Average performance ratings within each of the functional areas were obtained. The question became one of factors which are ranked consistently low or consistently high, regardless of organizational level, within a functional group. The results for the four groups are illustrated in Fig. 6.2. For example, at least three of four levels of corporate officers ranked communication skills and work relationships in the bottom quartile of performance ratings. Decision making and responsibility, on the other hand, consistently ranked high as performance factors. Thus, within each group, performance deficiencies that were consistent

Performance Factor	Functional group			
	Corporation officers Officers of subsidiaries	Manufacturing management	Sales/distribution management	Saleswork chemicals & drugs
Forecasting & planning		L	L	L
Communication skills	L	L	L	
Selection & development		L	L	
Work relationships	L			H
Salesmanship		L	H	H
Decision-making	H	H		L
Job knowledge		H	H	
Initiative & responsibility	H	H	H	

Note: L = Factor ranked in the lowest quartile in at least 3 or 4 organizational levels.
H = Factor ranked in the highest quartile in at least 3 of 4 organizational levels.
All other factors received mixed or moderate rankings.

FIG. 6.2   Performance factors rated consistently high or low by area.

throughout a functional group could be identified. In addition, deficiencies across groups could also be identified. For example, three of the four groups consistently rated forecasting and planning as a low factor, suggesting this to be a problem throughout the organization.

The result is an illustration of a computer-based system for transforming the separate performance evaluations of hundreds of salaried employees into information of strategical value to the organization. It should be pointed out that a first step after entering the performance ratings into the computer would be to check for the common errors mentioned previously. This would be done by comparing the several ratings from each manager and by contrasting the average ratings submitted by each manager to comparable managers from the same unit or from similar units. Problems detected should be reviewed with the appropriate managers, and needed corrections incorporated into the data set. The data set can then be used to diagnose and solve organizational issues.

COMPUTER-BASED TRAINING

According to Kearsley (1983) the main advantage of computer-based training (CBT) is its interactive nature, which transforms passive learning into active learning. Other advantages are increased control over the material that is being taught (increasing standardization), and individualization of training which allows the student to learn at his or her own pace. Also, CBT increases the availability of training by making the training virtually always accessible to the students. Orlansky and String (1979) claimed that CBT saves 30% of the time required for training while increasing learning and satisfaction. An important feature of CBT is that it can be used in conjunction with a video disk for instantaneous access to a multimedia data base (e.g., photos, audio, scenarios).

As the microcomputer becomes more technologically advanced with multi-user capacity, hard-disk-on-board, faster chips, and more memory, interactive video disk becomes a reality for training. The key hardware component in realizing interactive video is the newly developed optical disk. Similar in nature to the popular compact disk, the optical video disk can store large amounts of information. (You can store an entire encyclopedia on one side of a $5\frac{1}{2}$-inch optical disk.) Optical storage provides users instant access to large data bases by storing blocks of text or visual images in frames. The laser-read system can access each frame quickly and precisely. With appropriate software and hardware, the laser system can be coupled with a microcomputer for interactive video.

Currently most interactive video is found in the corporate training centers and in the military. McDonnell Douglas uses interactive video for training and production. For example, in a training system developed for the F–15 fighter plane, pilots can experience simulations of engine failure utilizing a video disk. Maintenance personnel, on the other hand, can learn to repair the plane with the system evaluating the results of their work. The company claims that interactive video disk training is safer and less expensive than field training. McDonnell Douglas is also experimenting with interactive video for visual storage of technical drawing and reference materials for on-board-display ("Computer-Based Training," 1987) to assist pilots and technical personnel in flight. Another company that utilized video disk for training is the Wilson Learning Corporation. This group is using the video disk to teach strategies, concepts, and management principles. As the software becomes more flexible and the hardware becomes less expensive, we should experience an increase in video disk use for training.

Computer-based training can take many forms. One popular form of CBT is that of Computer-managed Instruction (CMI). In CMI the computer is used to manage the instructional resources (media, simulators, classrooms) and the student's progress. The CMI system coordinates all teaching and testing activities while keeping track of student records. The system monitors the student's progress to make adjustments, identifying students who may be in danger of failing and, similarly, those who are likely to succeed.

A number of industries presently make use of CBT to train their employees. American Airlines uses a CBT to train its flight crews. American Airlines claims to have reduced training time by 50% with savings of approximately $30 million per year in fuel costs (Kearsley, 1983). Other airlines also utilize CBT to train crews. The IBM corporation uses CBT to train field engineering staff (Branscomb, 1983). Banks and insurance companies also use CBT. Aetna Life and Casualty uses CBT to train personnel in mathematics (Lowe, 1979). The largest users of CBT, however, are the armed services. The Navy, for example, uses CBT to manage the daily instruction of thousands of students, in a number of courses, at nine schools (Davis, 1978).

Computer simulations can play an important role in training and selection. The computer can be used to simulate a particular piece of equipment or situation. A simulator is such a device. Generally computer-controlled, the simulator is used to train employees to operate a particular piece of equipment (e.g., an airplane, radar scope, or letter sorter). The computer simulates the critical aspects of equipment operation responding to the student's commands or instructions. It also records the student's action for assessment and training purposes. Simulators range from those which are very expensive, flight simulators, to those which are not, such as "Resusci-Annie" used to teach cardiopulmonary resuscitation (Kearsley, 1984). Simulators are generally less expensive than the actual equipment and in some cases much safer.

Simulators are used by a variety of organizations to train and assess personnel. The Navy and Air Force use simulators to train flight crews and maintenance personnel. Farrow (1982) reports 10 different types of simulators in military air training. NASA also uses simulators for training. Shelly and Groom (1970) describe one of the simulators used to train Apollo II personnel. Another organization which utilizes the simulator is the Postal Service. The Postal Service has developed a simulator to train employees on mail sorter machines (Kearsley, 1984). The simulator is similar in size to the sorter machine, but it does not use real mail. Instead, letters are simulated by the computer, at the terminal display. The rate which these electronic letters are generated can be varied. Thus, new employees can be trained at lower speeds.

The future for CBT appears bright as more companies move to automate their training programs. In a recent special issue of *Training* ("Computer-Based Training," 1987), a number of experts concurred on the growth of CBT, but cautioned that this growth will be moderate, since good CBT development is still very expensive. This high cost is countered, however, by pressures within many organizations for accountability in their training programs. This has created an environment that favors CBT. Additionally, as the cost of hardware and software decreases and jobs become more knowledge-intensive in the workplace, conventional forms of training will be less adequate, increasing the need for good CBT.

CAREER PROGRESSION

Hall and Goodale distinguish between career planning, an individual-level approach, and career management, an organizationally focused process.

> Career planning is a deliberate process of becoming aware of self, opportunities, constraints, choices, and consequences, identifying career-related goals, and programming work, education, and related developmental experiences to provide the direction, timing, and sequence of steps to attain a specific career goal. Career management is an ongoing process of preparing, implementing, and monitoring

career plans undertaken by the individual alone or in concert with the organization's career systems. (1986, pp. 391–392)

Yet another perspective was that articulated by Glinow, Driver, Brousseau, and Prince (1983) in their design of a "career-sensitive" human resource system. Their concern was the propensity to view career management as a separate, add-on, component in the overall utilization of human resources. Career information is available on a continuous basis from multiple sources. Viewed in this manner, the problem is one of having the data in usable form at points when career decisions need to be considered and implemented.

The computer can play a valuable role in bringing together the information needed into an integrated framework. The application of the computer in this way was undertaken by Brush and Schoenfeldt (1982) in the research described previously. Analyses were performed to examine factors differentiating effective from ineffective managers by level within each functional group. For example, Fig. 6.3 illustrates five performance factors that are important for top corporate officers in this particular corporation. They were found to be important for two

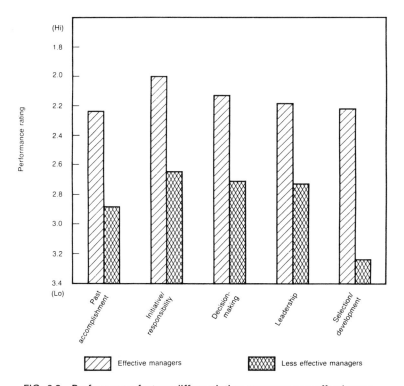

FIG. 6.3   Performance factors differentiating management effectiveness.

reasons. First, they are factors for which were found statistically significant differences between effective and less effective managers. Secondly, they were rated by the managers themselves as being either extremely important to their job or performed frequently, or both. It would appear that in considering career management positions, particular attention should be paid to these critical factors which may mean the difference between success or failure.

An incident at the time of this study illustrates the point well. The situation involved a top-ranking manufacturing manager who was under consideration for a position within the corporate group. Fig. 6.4 illustrates his performance profile compared with that of the average profiles of the effective corporate officer. Several points are of interest. First, the manufacturing manager appears to be a higher performer in both communication skills and work relationships than the corporate group. This is particularly noteworthy, since corporate officers at all levels were consistently ranked low in these areas. On the other hand, the candidate is ranked lower in decision making and selection and development. This is equally important because these two factors represent two of the four factors significantly differentiating effective from less effective managers within this group (Fig. 6.3). Perhaps these data raise more questions than they answer. However, it does give management a way of pinpointing and evaluating strengths and weaknesses relative to a particular target group. In this case, a decision had to be made whether to train in those weak areas, provide more developmental

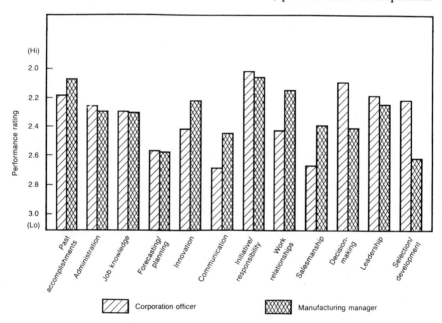

FIG. 6.4 Comparison of a manufacturing manager with the corporation officer performance profile.

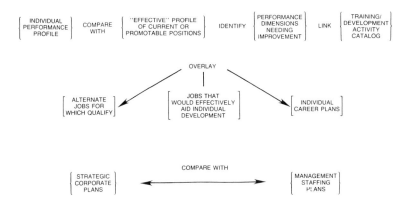

FIG. 6.5   Management career progression.

experiences or pass over for promotion. An evaluation of the company's training and development resources and an understanding of those areas which the company felt it could effectively develop led management to the decision that this manager was most suited to his or her current position.

It should be noted that this is not a static system. Although performance profiles of effective managers are useful in establishing a framework from which to evaluate future candidates, management is not necessarily wedded to a design that continues to manage careers on the basis of what has been effective in the past. Indeed, the whole notion of management is likely to change dramatically over the next several decades. New attributes and skills anticipated as important for the future can be built into models with which to compare, select, or suggest training and development for future employees.

Software, along the lines of that shown in Fig. 6.5, was developed to manage the career progression process. Using the system, individual performance appraisal data, along with individual career plans generated in conjunction with the performance evaluation and feedback process, are compared with average values for salaried employees in different functional areas and at different organizational levels. Areas found to be needing improvement can be linked with training alternatives. Promotional opportunities can be evaluated in relation to strengths and weaknesses as well as individual career plans. All other things being equal, the goal would be job changes which capitalize on some individual strengths while developing some of the areas that need improvement.

The result is a system that allows the identification of organization-wide strengths and weaknesses. It also has been shown that a meaningful structure involving both functional area and organizational level can be used to determine performance factors that are important in differentiating effective from less effective managers and to allow managers to evaluate alternative career possibilities.

ORGANIZATIONAL ISSUES

The computer has created organizational issues and, in turn, is involved in addressing organizational problems. The former has been addressed by Fleischer and Morell (1985) in an examination of the organizational consequences of computer technology. Specifically, Fleischer and Morell surveyed managers with respect to the impact of computers on their ability to obtain, analyze, and transmit information. They found important changes occurred in three areas: (1) information used for decision making; (2) beliefs concerning what kinds of problems can be solved; and (3) locus of decision-making authority and managerial job characteristics. In other words, in the sample they surveyed, the ready availability of information through personal computers and computer networks changed the organizations and the nature of the managerial role within those organizations.

In a related study, Gardner, Souza, Scabbia, and Breuer (1986) examined the impact of the microcomputer on the delivery of services in an nonprofit agency. The study was unique in that it involved the application of the computer in multiple aspects of organizational life over a 5-year period. The computer was used in direct care (production), research, and administration. Within the direct-care function there were multiple applications, including assessment, evaluation, intervention, quality assurance, and management information. The result was the finding that computers can be enormously beneficial in terms of productivity and quality of service delivery, but not without organizational cost. To quote the authors, "For every promise there are a dozen corresponding pitfalls, each one waiting to engulf individuals and systems and to create as many new problems as the innovations solve" (p. 155).

Organizational issues emerge as a result of the introduction of the computer into organizational activities. In addition, the computer can be applied to addressing organizational issues. To quote Heneman, Schwab, Fossum, and Dyer (1980),

> Organizational development consists of processes and techniques designed to attain such goals as improved communications between groups, restructured authority relationships to base decision-making power more on expertise than hierarchical position, and organizational flexibility in the face of rapid environmental changes. (p. 349)

A first step to any intervention is the diagnosis of the problem. A popular method is by way of an organizational survey. An organizational survey measures the quality of the organization's internal environment in an effort to develop necessary changes. Also, it helps in evaluating the effectiveness of any interventions.

As indicated by Schuler (1987), an organizational survey might solicit

[E]mployee perceptions of organizational characteristics, including the consequences of job performance, organizational policies, frequency of feedback, job
design qualities, task interference characteristics, aspects of goal setting, role conflict and awareness, and supervisor behaviors. Equally necessary is gathering data
on the employee's reactions to the organizational conditions, the quality of work
life, and reactions such as satisfaction and job involvement. (p. 674)

Many other aspects of work, perceptions of job activities, and reactions to
policies can also be measured.

An example of a fairly sophisticated application of the computer to this type of
organizational diagnosis is provided by M. A. Lewis (personal communication,
February 1, 1988), and is based on efforts to develop a useful base of organizational information in a major corporation. More specifically, information is
sought on such elements of organizational life as management practices, communication patterns, and possible areas of conflict. Traditionally this type of information has been gathered by interview and/or paper-pencil questionnaire. The
development of questionnaires, the actual collection of information, analysis,
and reporting of results were all extremely time consuming. In fact, the process
is generally regarded as so cumbersome as to preclude anything but a long-range
approach to addressing organizational issues.

In the case of the system developed by M. A. Lewis, the microcomputer
replaces the questionnaire in the gathering, analysis, interpretation, and feedback
of organizational information. Employees respond to questions about various
organizational issues presented on the computer screen and can also enter comments. Results are organized in terms or each item, and also by area. Interpretation is by comparison of results with the team at previous times and to other units
of the organization. In this way, group leaders can track management issues and
communications within their groups over a period of time and compare their
progress with that of other teams.

In the system reported by M. A. Lewis, as well as similar approaches,
organizational information can be used to guide interventions. The questionnaire
information, along with the rich data provided by comments, becomes a practical
basis for improving both individual and organizational performance.

SUMMARY

Industrial-organizational psychologists have been slow to embrace the computer
as a tool for the delivery of personnel and human resource services. Despite this,
models and procedures exist for innovative computer applications to all major
phases of industrial-organizational psychology.

An even more encouraging note has to do with the trend to use the computer to
bridge areas of human resource and organizational behavior that have been tradi-

tionally considered as distinct entities. For example, in the present review, we observed instances where selection systems incorporated input from other segments of the organization. Job analysis information is combined with planning data as an indication of current job activities/requirements and future activities/skills that will be needed. Thus selection can be more dynamic, and individuals brought into the organization have the capabilities needed immediately and skills anticipated as valuable for future organizational changes.

Another example of potential integration would be the combining of selection and placement functions. Performance appraisal information can be used to refine both, that is to suggest adjustments needed in the identification of skills and knowledge required as a part of the selection-placement system. Performance appraisal issues might also suggest organizational and training issues needing attention, that is deficiencies in current performance that could be addressed on a programmatic basis. Finally, performance information can be extremely valuable in terms of career progression decisions of either an individual or organizational nature. In this way, performance appraisal becomes the quality control element of the entire personnel-human resource framework.

Computers have proved to be a valuable adjunct to the delivery of services in a variety of areas, and are now finding increasing use in the management of personnel and human resources. Look for large organizations and the military to lead the way with respect to innovative computer applications, and for research-oriented professionals to provide the necessary theory and models to facilitate this new direction. The trend will be one of increasing use of computers to bring together human resource and organizational issues into an integrated system.

ACKNOWLEDGEMENT

The authors acknowledge the helpful comments and suggestions provided by Jon W. Beard of Texas A&M University.

REFERENCES

Alluisi, E. A., & Fleishman, E. A. (Eds.). (1982). *Human performance and productivity: Stress and performance effectiveness*. Hillsdale, NJ: Lawrence Erlbaum Associates.

Borack, J. I. (1987). A framework for investigating military manpower supply. *Defense Management Journal, 23*(1), 11–17.

Branscomb, L. M. (1983). Future technology and its applications. *Computers and People, 32*, Nos. 7–8, 7–11.

Brush, D. H., & Owens, W. A. (1979). Implementation and evaluation of an assessment classification model for manpower utilization. *Personnel Psychology, 32*, 369–383.

Brush, D. H., & Schoenfeldt, L. F. (1982). Performance appraisal for the '80's: Problems of validity and utility. *Personnel Administrator, 27*(12), 76–83.

Campbell, J. P., Dunnette, M. D., Lawler, E. E., III, & Weick, K. E., Jr. (1970). *Managerial behavior, performance, and effectiveness*. New York: McGraw–Hill.

Christal, R. E. (1974). The United States Air Force occupational research project (AFHRL–TR–73–75) Lackland Air Force Base, TX: USAF, AFHRL, Occupational Research Division.

Clay–Mendez, D. (1985). A total-force approach to manpower planning. *Defense Management Journal, 21*(2), 10–17.

Computer-based training. (1987, October). *Training, 24*(9).

Coovert, M. D. (1986, April). Altering artificial intelligence heuristics to provide data for specific applications. In S. Goel (chair), *Advances in tailoring job analysis methods for specific applications*. Symposium conducted at the annual conference of the Society for Industrial and Organizational Psychology, Chicago.

Davis, J. D. (1978). The Navy CMI system: A brief overview. *Journal of Educational Technology System, 6,* 143–150.

Denton, L. (1987, November). Computers: Partners in practice. *APA Monitor*, p. 7.

DeSanctis, G. (1986). Human resource information systems: A current assessment. *MIS Quarterly, 10,* 15–27.

Dunnette, M. D. (1963). A modified model for test validation and selection research. *Journal of Applied Psychology, 17, 317–323*.

Dunnette, M. D. (Ed.). (1976). Handbook of industrial and organizational psychology. Chicago: Rand McNally.

Dunnette, M. D., & Fleishman, E. A. (Eds.). (1982). *Human performance and productivity: Human capability assessment*. Hillsdale, NJ: Lawrence Erlbaum Associates.

Dyer, L. (1982). Human resource planning. In K. Rowland & G. Ferris (Eds), *Personnel management*. Boston: Allyn & Bacon.

Farrow, D. R. (1982). Reducing the Risks of Military Aircrew Training through Simulation Technology. *NSPI Journal*, 13–18.

Feild, H. S., & Gatewood, R. D. (1987). Matching talent with the task. *Personnel Administrator, 32*(4), 113–126.

Fine, S. A. (1977). *Job analysis for heavy equipment operators*. Washington, DC: International Union of Operating Engineers.

Fleischer, M., & Morell, J. A. (1985). The organizational and managerial consequences of computer technology. *Computers in Human Behavior, 1,* 83–93.

Fleishman, E. A., & Quaintance, M. K. (1984). *Taxonomies of human performance: The description of human tasks*. Orlando, FL: Academic Press.

Gardner, J. M., Souza, A., Scabbia, A., Breuer, A. (1986). Microcare—promises and pitfalls in implementing microcomputer programs in human service agencies. *Computers in Human Behavior, 2,* 147–156.

Gatewood, R. D., & Feild, H. S. (1987). *Human resource selection*. Chicago: Dryden Press.

Glinow, M. A. V., Driver, M. J., Brousseau, K., & Prince, J. B. (1983). The design of a career oriented human resource system. *Academy of Management Review, 8,* 23–32.

Granrose, C. S., & Portwood, J. D. (1987). Matching individual career plans and organizational career management. *Academy of Management Journal, 30,* 699–720.

Hall, D. T., & Goodale, J. G. (1986). *Human resource management: Strategy, design, and implementation*. Glenview, IL: Scott, Foresman.

Harris, D. (1986). Beyond the basics: New HRIS developments. *Personnel, 63*(1), 49–56.

Harvey, R. J. (1986). Computerized dedication and mapping of job analysis data for managerial level positions. In S. Goel (chair), *Advances in tailoring job analysis methods for specific applications*. Symposium of the Society for Industrial and Organizational Psychology, Chicago.

Heneman, H. G. III, Schwab, D. P., Fossam, J. A., & Dyer, L. D. (1980). *Personnel/human resource management*. Homewood, IL: Irwin.

Hosek, J. R., Fernandez, R. L., & Grissmer, D. W. (1985). Enlisted strength in the '80s: A midterm reassessment. *Defense Management Journal, 21*(2), 3–9.

Howell, W. C., & Fleishman, E. A. (Eds.). (1982). *Human performance and productivity: Information processing and decision making.* Hillsdale, NJ: Lawrence Erlbaum Associates.

Hyde, A. C., & Shafritz, J. M. (1977). HRIS: Introduction to tomorrow's system for managing human resources. *Public Personnel Management, 6,* 70–77.

Johnson, B. H., Moorhead, G., & Griffin, R. W. (1983). Human resource information systems and job design. *Human Resource Planning, 6,* 35–40.

Kearsley, G. (1983). *Computer-based training: A guide to selection and implementation.* Reading, MA: Addison–Wesley.

Kearsley, G. (1984). *Training and technology: A handbook for HRD professionals.* Reading, MA: Addison–Wesley.

Lowe, N. (1979). A commitment to education: Basic math and CAI at the Aetna Life and Casualty. *ADCIS Proceedings.* San Diego.

Mallamad, S. M., Levine, J. M., & Fleishman, E. A. (1980). Identifying ability requirements by decision flow diagrams. *Human Factors, 22*(1), 57–68.

McCormick, E. J. (1979). *Job analysis: Methods and applications.* New York: American Management Association, AMACOM.

Morrison, R. F. (1977). A multivariate model for the occupational placement decision. *Journal of Applied Psychology, 62,* 271–277.

Murdick, R. G., & Schuster, F. (1983). Computerized information support for the human resource function. *Human Resource Planning, 6*(1), 25–33.

Orlansky, J., & String, J. (1979). Cost-effectiveness of computer-based instruction in military training. IDA P–1375. Arlington, VA.

Owens, W. A. (1968). Toward one discipline of scientific psychology. *American Psychologist, 23,* 782–785.

Owens, W. A. (1971). A quasi actuarial prospect for individual assessment. *American Psychologist, 23,* 992–999.

Rodgers, D. D. (1987). Personnel computing: Computer-aided interviewing overcomes first impressions. *Personnel Journal, 66,* 148–150.

Sands, W. A. (1973). A method for evaluating alternative recruiting-selection strategies: The CAPER model. *Journal of Applied Psychology, 57,* 222–227.

Schoenfeldt, L. F. (1974). Utilization of manpower: Development and evaluation of an assessment-classification model for matching individuals with jobs. *Journal of Applied Psychology, 59,* 583–595.

Schuler, R. S. (1987). *Personnel and human resource management.* St. Paul, MN: West Publishing Co.

Schuster, F. E. (1985). Human resource information systems. In F. E. Schuster (Ed.), *Human resource management: Concepts, cases, and readings* (2nd ed.). Reston, VA: Reston Publishing Co.

Shelly, C. B., & Groom, V. (1970). The Apollo Flight Controller Training System Concept and Its Education Implications. In W. Holtzman (Ed.). *Computer Assisted Instruction, Testing and Guidance.* New York: Harper & Row.

Verdin, J. A. (1987). The HRIS and managerial performance. *Personnel Administrator, 32*(1), 24–28.

Walker, A. J. (1981). Management selection systems that meet the challenges of the '80s. *Personnel Journal, 60,* 775–780.

7 Implementation Decisions in Designing Computer-Based Instructional Testing Programs

John V. Noonan
Applied Learning International, Naperville, IL

Paul D. Sarvela
Department of Health Education, Southern Illinois University, Carbondale, IL

INTRODUCTION

From preschool to graduate school, computer-based instruction (CBI) has become an increasingly common event in today's education and training community. The interactive characteristics of CBI and its ability to simulate advanced concepts and operations, such as patient management simulations for medical students (Whiteside & Whiteside, 1987/88) or the maneuvering of a jet airplane (Conkright, 1982), make CBI an attractive new instructional delivery system for educators working in many different fields.

Because of these qualities, the computer has tremendous potential in educational and psychological measurement. For example, Millman & Arter (1984) describe how the computer aids in maintaining test-item banks. Item forms can be used by test specialists to develop computer-generated items from a set of well-defined item characteristics (Hambleton, 1984), which saves valuable time in item construction. Millman and Outlaw (1978) suggest that an additional advantage of item forms is that more items can be produced than those stored on a computer. Computers can also be used to administer tests. The advantages of using computer-administered tests range from the ability to individualize testing to increasing the efficiency and economy of analyzing testing information (Ward, 1984). Finally, computers can be used to score tests, report results, and conduct statistical analyses on the scores (Noonan & Dugliss, 1985).

Although the computer has a wide variety of instructional applications, computer technology is not a panacea for solving all educational problems. For instance, although there are a number of ways in which the computer could possibly improve the quality of instruction in our schools, there is currently a

177

paucity of high-quality courseware available for educational purposes. Some educational software evaluation specialists suggest that up to 90% of the educational software available today is not worth purchasing (Olds, 1983). Measurement and evaluation specialists face similar problems. The costs associated with the design and development of good computer-based testing (CBT) programs are often prohibitively expensive. For this reason, when the computer is chosen as the testing delivery system, careful analysis of implementation questions and issues must take place.

The purpose of this chapter is to identify a number of practical implementation decisions that must be made when designing and developing criterion-referenced tests (CRTs) as a part of a larger system of computer-based instruction. Many of the concepts discussed generalize beyond large-scale courseware development efforts and apply to areas such as CBT in professional certification or licensing examinations, minimal competency testing at the local or state level, and norm-referenced testing. This chapter extends earlier guidelines that addressed microcomputer-based testing (Mizokawa & Hamlin, 1984) and computer use for various stages of the testing process (Noonan & Dugliss, 1985).

We have clustered CBT development decision areas into four categories: test construction, test security, item presentation, and response capturing and scoring. Many of the decisions are interrelated, since the actions resulting from one decision limit choices at another decision point (i.e., a decision to allow a student to preview items at the start of a test generally precludes the option of adaptive testing when deciding item sequencing, since item presentation strategies in adaptive testing are dependent on the student's history of responses to previous items). The chapter concludes by introducing a checklist (Appendix A) designed to aid courseware developers and measurement specialists in making appropriate CBT implementation decisions.

Test Construction

A number of issues must be considered when constructing tests to be used for computer-based testing and instruction systems. This section will discuss areas related to the following test construction decisions: the decision to use either diagnostic or mastery tests; routing; how and which objectives are to be tested; item type; the use of embedded or block tests; size of item pools; test-taking policy; and item tryout and analysis.

Diagnostic Versus Mastery Tests. The test designer must determine whether tests to be developed are to be used to diagnose areas of difficulty or simply provide more global measures of mastery. Because diagnostic and mastery tests are used for different purposes, the methods used to construct these types of tests are also different. For example, a diagnostic test (sometimes called or used as a placement test) implemented on a CBI system would usually use an elaborate set of routing decisions, where the testing sequence is directly related to performance on earlier subsets of items. If incorrect answers are given, the student could be routed to a set of items structured to identify or classify the types of errors the student has made. The diagnostic information could then be used to tailor the CBI to the student's needs. In a mastery test, the student might simply proceed through the test, and either pass or fail the examination; no branching decisions take place until the student completes the test.

In addition to these differences, discontinue criteria can also be applied differently for mastery and diagnostic tests. Discontinue criteria are those standards which determine when students leave the test; students may meet the discontinue criteria by either passing the test or receiving too many errors on the test. (Discontinue criteria will be discussed in detail in a later section.) In a mastery test, once the student passes the minimal number of items or objectives required to establish mastery, or once the student fails a certain amount of the material, the testing could be stopped and the student would be returned to instructional material. In diagnostic tests, failure at a certain test level might move the student to new and less difficult material. Given the elaborate possibilities for branching students based on their responses, the decision to use either mastery or diagnostic type tests is a major concern in test construction.

Other problems related to the differences between mastery and diagnostic tests are the ways in which test items and test objectives are matched. In a mastery test, subscoring of objectives might not be needed; however, in a diagnostic testing scenario, test items and their associated objectives must be carefully matched so that decisions can be made concerning the branching of students to appropriate sections of the test. This impacts the complexity with which the tests are programmed.

Finally, the way in which response analysis is to be used must be considered. Sophisticated analyses of student errors, particularly when using diagnostic testing procedures, are indeed desirable. However, valuable computer-programming time is needed to produce the complicated scoring routines. Therefore, one must be certain that the benefits derived from an elaborate response analysis program outweigh the costs associated with constructing such a system.

Routing Decisions.   The CBT test designer needs to consider routing (also known as branching) decisions that have to be made. The designer needs to determine if the student will be remediated when incorrect answers are given, as well as determine where remediation takes place. If poor performance is indicated, it should be decided if the student will be prevented from entering future lessons. Finally, one must determine if students who perform well on pretests (if there is a pretest) may bypass the lesson.

Objectives Tested.   CBI programs are usually linked to well-defined instructional objectives, and it is the responsibility of the test designer to decide how mastery of the objectives will be tested. One might simply conclude that each objective should be tested at the end of the unit or lesson in which the content is covered. However, there are situations in which this strategy is not advisable. Testing numbers of objectives can consume too much time, both for the student and the programmer. In many cases, the designer may want to replace some of the testing with lesson practice items that have some sort of mastery criteria. In addition, the designer should analyze the hierarchy of learning objectives to see if any of the objectives can be subsumed by testing higher-level objectives. In other settings, when critical or important information is to be learned, retesting two or three times is necessary to determine if mastery has been retained over the course of instruction.

The type of learning objective to be tested should also be considered, since traditional instructional theory (e.g., Gagné & Briggs, 1974) suggests that the learning objective determines, in part, the method of testing. For example, the Instructional Quality Inventory (IQI), an instructional systems quality assurance model currently used by the Department of Defense in the design and development of their training programs (Wulfeck, Ellis, Richards, Wood, & Merrill, 1978), carefully considers the learning objectives when designing and developing curriculum materials, instructional methods, and tests. Using the IQI system, one can classify learning objectives on the basis of the task to be performed and the type of information that must be learned. Any given objective can be classified as a fact, category, procedure, rule, or principle. An objective can further be classified as one which must be either recalled (from memory) or recognized, or, performed either with a job aid ("use-aided" IQI classification) or without a job aid ("use-unaided" IQI classification). If one uses IQI in the design and development of tests, recall-fact type of objectives would be tested in a manner quite different from recognize-fact type of objectives. For instance, if the objectives are recall-fact type of objectives, *theoretically,* only constructed-response items (short answer, essay, fill-ins) can be used. If the objectives are recognize-fact, selected-response items (such as multiple-choice, true–false, or matching) can be used. These issues not only have an impact on the method in which the test is programmed into the computer, but also affect the types and numbers of items which need to be constructed for each test.

Item Type.   Most CBT software programs and authoring systems are well equipped to handle selected-response items. The programming for these item types is relatively easy, and the response analysis for correct and incorrect items is also fairly easy to construct and implement. On the other hand, constructed-response items are extremely difficult to design, put "on-line," and score on the computer. Since most CBT delivery systems do not have natural language processing (artificial intelligence), it becomes extremely difficult to specify and program all possible correct student-constructed answers. Therefore, the testing system is at risk of unfairly penalizing students who actually provide a correct answer (false negative). At the same time, the system might mistakenly interpret an incorrect answer as a correct one, and unfairly give a student credit (false positive).

Embedded Versus Block Tests.   It is sometimes desirable to test the student while he or she is working through the instruction, through a series of items which are administered throughout the lesson (embedded tests). Embedded testing might occur where there is a large amount of information which needs to be learned, or when formal postinstruction testing (block tests) is not feasible. It may also be useful in the beginning stages of learning, where frequent checks on student understanding of fundamental concepts is necessary.

If embedded tests are to be used, the test designer should determine if the students will be told that they are being tested. There are advantages and disadvantages of informing (or not informing) an individual that he or she is being tested. For example, if a student believes the embedded test is actually just a series of practice items, he or she might bypass them or answer them carelessly. Conversely, embedded tests can be used to reduce test anxiety. In this case it could be inappropriate to tell an individual that he or she is being tested. Also, one must consider the type of learning that is taking place. An objective that synthesizes prior objectives would be tested at the end of instruction. One would not use an embedded test strategy in this situation.

Finally, the decision to use embedded or block tests can be influenced by requirements for parallel or equivalent forms of tests. If strict psychometric specifications are put into place, it may be better to use block rather than embedded tests, because psychometric analyses of tests (e.g., reliability, discrimination, and difficulty) are based on assumptions related to tests that are delivered in "block" form. If tests are administered in an "embedded" manner, it may be difficult to compute parallelism between measures. (This problem is eliminated if item analysis and reliability assessment is conducted before the tests are incorporated into the courseware.)

Item Pools.   Several factors influence the size of the item pools for computer-based tests. Requirements for parallel and equivalent forms of the test must be considered. If students who fail a test are to be retested, it may be appropriate to offer a second form of the test. In this case, a larger pool of items will need to be developed.

Larger item pools will probably be needed if the test is diagnostic in nature. For example, a test designer will need to develop more items if he or she is testing six objectives with five items per objective than if the test designer only samples one or two items across the six objectives.

The method of presenting test items also impacts the size of the item pool. For example, if test specifications call for three forms of a test with no item overlap, then a larger item pool is needed than would be required if items can be randomly selected from a pool and some overlap among tests is considered acceptable.

Test-taking Policy.   When determining testing requirements and test specifications, the test-taking policy must also be carefully considered. Will a student be allowed to retake a test once he or she has failed it? If retesting occurs, is it to be the same test, or a parallel or equivalent form? It should also be determined how many times the student will be allowed to take the test before remediation or administrative action outside the CBI environment takes place. These issues impact not only the number of items which need to be developed (see item pool discussion) but also influence the manner in which the test is programmed onto the computer.

Another issue related to test-taking policy is the method in which it is decided that a student will take a test. It may be determined that students should have the option to take a test whenever they feel ready to be tested. Or, tests could be made available only after completion of each unit of instruction, with all students being required to take the same test at that time. These issues not only have an impact on the test-taking policy, but also have a large effect on the evaluation of the courseware. Tests administered throughout the course of instruction, or administered at student request, will create situations where gain scores and item statistics will be difficult to compute and analyze (Sarvela & Noonan, 1988).

Item Tryout and Analysis.   There are several problems associated with the use of CBT when attempting to analyze the quality of the tests. Because of the unique nature of testing in CBT scenarios (e.g., random selection of items from a pool), it is possible that all students will not be tested on the same items (therefore, the students will not have taken the "same" test) and that the students did not experience the same instructional treatment (because of branching variations). In this situation, meaningful item analysis, reliability and validity measures, and pre–post gain scores are difficult to compute and interpret (Sarvela & Noonan, 1988).

Test Security

Test security is most often concerned with the *access* students have to a test. For a variety of reasons (e.g., evaluation of pre- and posttest gain scores, reducing student cheating), it is desirable to limit student access to tests. The following issues are discussed in this section: student access to tests, test preview, and test review.

Access Limitations.   The most important consideration in test security is deciding when students can access tests. One possibility, though perhaps the least likely, is to allow the student to take any test at anytime, with no mastery criteria and no special access controls. A more typical procedure is to: (1) Allow the student to take pretests only before entering a lesson or unit of instruction and (2) Limit access to posttests to students who have completed the lesson or unit. In other words, pretests can only be taken before any instruction and posttests taken only after all components of the lesson or unit have been completed. There are variations on this strategy, but implementation of the variations could be difficult to achieve because the programming would become more complicated and expensive. In addition, different approaches jeopardize evaluation efforts; for example, if students can take pretests or posttests at any time, an evaluation strategy that uses gain or change scores is thwarted by the inequality of the pre- and posttest groups. The evaluator cannot reasonably assume that students within a posttest group have had the same treatment or that students in a pretest group have had equal exposure to the instructional material.

Once decisions have been reached on *when* the student can access a test, specific coding procedures for limiting access have to be implemented. There are generally two options: (1) internal coding flags or (2) passwords. With internal coding flags, the code is usually written such that access to a test is dependent upon a flag being "ON" (set to 1) or "OFF" (set to 0). The password option requires the student or proctor to enter a password once a test point has been reached. Passwords require greater involvement and monitoring by a proctor or tutor, and, hence, are usually only feasible in large-scale CBI.

Test Preview.   Some curriculum specialists argue that it may be instructionally beneficial to allow students to preview a test before starting a lesson, or, having completed a lesson, before taking the test for credit (i.e., Gebhardt & Munn, 1985). With the former, students can see exactly what will be expected of them; the test preview functions somewhat like a presentation of the lesson objectives. With the latter, students can self-assess their readiness for the test and, if needed, re-enter the lesson for extra study. A disadvantage of test preview lies in the potential compromise of the test items. If the items are written as a representative (perhaps random) sample of a domain of knowledge, then access to the items can bias the test results. If the student only studies to answer specific questions, then there is no assurance that whatever learning occurred will generalize to the broader domain of knowledge.

In addition, programming issues arise. Extra programming will be needed to keep track of when the students are in the "test" mode and when they are in "preview" mode. This extra programming would have to disable student-input, scoring, and feedback functions. Also, if the number of test attempts is controlled, then extra programming might be needed to bypass or disable the counter for test attempts.

Test Review.   After a student has completed a test, he or she should be presented with the test results. This could be as simple as notification of pass or failure, or it could include a listing of the number of items attempted, number correct, and mastery criteria. Still another option is to allow the student to review the actual items, with notation of which ones were answered correctly and incorrectly. The review might also include the correct answer and remediation for incorrect responses. Such a review can be beneficial to students in helping them pinpoint specific problem areas. The danger is, again, in item contamination. If the identical items are used in a second attempt at the test, then the student may learn how to answer specific items without having mastered the entire domain of knowledge. Allowing test review with item-level feedback is more defensible if parallel forms of a posttest are available.

The particular review options that one provides will influence the complexity with which the test is programmed. For example, if one allows students to review actual items with corresponding correct/incorrect item feedback, then it might be necessary to create and track extra scoring variables to redisplay the students' answers, the item scores, and the corresponding feedback. In addition, extra programming might be needed to disable student-input, scoring, and counters for test attempts—so that the review does not inadvertently end up as another fully scored test attempt.

Item Presentation

The manner in which items are presented to students in CBT situations is an important implementation decision. This section identifies and discusses the following CBT item presentation issues: access to test directions; item skipping; random, sequential, and adaptive item selection; screen display conventions; time-out; feedback; student discontinue criteria; and log-off procedures.

Access to Directions. Test directions and sample items are standard elements in paper-pencil tests. Students are presented with the directions and sample items at the start of the test, and they can review them at anytime during the test. Special actions must be taken by test designers to afford this same option to students when using computer-based testing. Directions and sample items can still be presented at the start of a test, but special keys or functions might have to be programmed in order to enable access to the directions and sample items one the student has begun to see test items. An icon or line of text could be displayed on the screen (perhaps on a bottom menu line) throughout item presentation to remind the student of the keystrokes needed to access the directions and sample items. Sample items become especially important in CBT because students must be told how to answer each item type. For example, a multiple-choice item could require students to enter the letter of the option they choose and then press "ENTER" or "RETURN." Or, students may have to TAB among the options until the cursor is beside their answer and then press "ENTER" or "RETURN" to register their response. Coding must be written so that once students access directions, they go back to the same item upon returning to item presentation. Test designers have to plan for cases where students are being presented items and need assistance in remembering how to respond to a particular item type. Nothing could be more frustrating to a student than to know an answer to an item but be unable to register the response in the computer.

Item Skipping. Test designers must decide whether or not students will be able to preview or skip items once they are taking the test. A common student test-taking strategy for paper-pencil tests is to: (1) Preview the items to gain an idea of the scope and content of the test, (2) Go back and answer the "easy" items, (3) Allot the remaining time among the items which require greater thought and study, and (4) Review the answers at the completion of the test. Designing CBT to accommodate this strategy can be a programming nightmare. If skipping is allowed, then test designers must decide when responses are scored. If the items are scored immediately (before presentation of the next item), then precautions will have to be taken about coding "null" responses (when a student elects to skip an item). The test designer must determine when such a null response will be scored as incorrect. Also, the designer has to decide upon a key or key function that students use to skip an item. This again must be included as an icon or line of text to remind the students how they can skip items.

Another consideration relates to how skipped items are recycled. If a student gets to the end of an initial item cycling, and has skipped items during the test, the student should receive a prompt concerning the unanswered items and instructions on how to move to and answer the skipped items. Also, the designer has to decide if all items or only the skipped items will be seen again. If all items are seen again, the designer must decide if students can change answers.

Options of allowing item preview or skipping also relate to item selection strategies. If items are selected randomly from a pool, then all of the random selection must occur before item presentation begins. A decision to use item preview or skipping impacts on other presentation decisions. For instance, one could not utilize computer-adaptive testing (CAT) if item preview is used. With CAT, items are selected on the basis of the student's responses to previous items; the computer is programmed to select the item that will provide the most information about the student's level of performance. CAT relies upon a response to each item as it is presented, therefore item preview cannot be used with CAT.

Item Selection. Decisions must be made regarding the procedures for item selection. Several options are open to the test designer. Items could be selected randomly from a pool. They could be presented sequentially, as in a paper-pencil or individually administered test. Or, one could use adaptive testing, where the item selection depends on the student's success or failure on previous items. Each strategy has its own advantages and disadvantages, and a decision to use one strategy impacts other design decisions.

If items are selected randomly from a pool, then complications arise if the test designer wants to allow item preview or skipping. To accomplish this, all of the items would have to be randomly preselected at the start of the test. One could not randomly select items as they are administered. And, if test review is allowed, the courseware must be coded to store in memory the particular items chosen for each student. If different items are to be seen on a retest, then code must be written to "lockout" those items seen on the first administration.

Aside from these coding complications, there are two serious conceptual problems with random item selection. The first problem is the implicit assumption that the items administered to one student will be equal in difficulty to items that are presented to another student. Imagine that a pool of items has an average p-value (difficulty index) of .80 and a standard deviation of p-values of .12. For most courseware environments the item pool is relatively small, so also assume that there are 15 items in the pool and 5 will be selected for administration. If the test is going to be fair to students, the items that one student sees should be comparable in difficulty with the items on which another student is tested. In the long term, random selection will produce comparable tests, but one certainly would expect that at times one student would receive all of the easier items and another would receive the harder items. The frequency with which this occurs will depend on the degree of variance in item difficulty. It is clear that with a random selection of items, problems occasionally will arise concerning test difficulty. One possible control for this undesirable effect is to randomly select items within strata of difficulty. For example, 1 item could be randomly selected from the p-value range of .90–1.00, three items from the range of .80–.89, and 1 item from the range .00–.79.

The second conceptual difficulty with random item selection relates to compromises on program and test evaluation. If students see different items it becomes extremely difficult to compute item and test statistics (e.g., total score, point biserial, KR–20). The major problem is that there is no sensible total score. With random item selection, a total test score only becomes defensible for item analysis if every item is of equal difficulty and equal discrimination (otherwise, the students have not seen the "same test"). And, pretest and posttest comparisons presume parallel forms of a test (equal means, standard deviations, reliabilities, and validity coefficients). With random item selection, parallel test criteria can only be met if each item in the test domain pool is of equal difficulty and discrimination, a highly improbable condition (Sarvela & Noonan, 1988).

Many of the problems mentioned disappear if items are presented in sequence. Usually, a sequential item delivery is used with a fixed-length test; a set number of items are presented in a particular order. This format is most closely analogous to a paper-pencil test. Total test scores fit well into the logic of test theory and less concern can be given to establishing equal item difficulty and discrimination. Also, fewer items are needed and the test designer is not forced to choose a particular option on other decision points (e.g., item preview, back-up, answer changing, when scoring occurs, etc.).

Parallel advances in computer technology and item response theory (IRT) (Green, Bock, Humphreys, Linn, & Reckase, 1984; Jaeger, 1987; Lord, 1980) have generated a considerable degree of interest in CAT. In CAT, an ability estimate is computed after each item is presented and answered by the student (Weiss & Kingsbury, 1984). This ability estimate is used to select the item that will produce the most information for the next ability estimate (technically, an item that the estimate predicts the student will have a 50% probability of answering correctly). Items are presented and ability estimates are computed until a discontinue criterion is reached (usually an error limit associated with the ability estimate). The primary advantage of CAT has been in a reduction in testing time (Ward, 1984). Interestingly, CAT has not been implemented in CBT–CBI environments. The primary hindrance to its use is that the item parameters that are needed require extensive item tryout and analyses on very large samples. This kind of test development effort is normally not supported in traditional courseware development environments. IRT also assumes that items are unidimensional (the items all measure a single underlying attribute). For many CBI environments, training is aimed at multiple objectives; the resulting tests are, by design, *not* unidimensional.

Also, a decision to use CAT forces, by default, the test designer to choose particular options at other decision points. One cannot allow test preview, item preview or skipping, or back-up and changing of answers. Items must be scored immediately and a CAT discontinue criterion must be used.

Screen Display Conventions.   Screen design is an important consideration in all aspects of CBI courseware development (Sweeters, 1985) and should be carefully considered when developing CBT programs because presentation of items in traditional (paper-pencil) formats differ significantly from CBT item presentation. For instance, a "matching" test item can usually be placed on one page of a paper-pencil test. It may be difficult to fit the same matching item on one computer screen due to display constraints. Because of the "terseness" that is required in CBT development, the test designer could be limited in the types of items that can be developed.

Time Out.   One of the often-cited advantages of CBI is that the computer is infinitely patient. The computer will wait for an input without generating the social pressure to respond that often occurs in a traditional classroom setting. In certain test settings, however, it is often desirable to set time limits for responding to individual items. If a time limit is set for the test as a whole, then time limits on individual items help the student move through the test. This would be especially important if item preview or skipping is now allowed. Also, time limits provide a safeguard against students' simply leaving the terminal and having the item(s) open for viewing by other students. The difficulty is in deciding when it is reasonable to conclude that the student has left the terminal. One alternative is to select an amount of time, say 180 seconds, and then prompt the student to respond if no response has been made in the allotted time. The prompt could be "Please answer now!"; the student could then have additional time to answer, say 30 seconds, before the test is discontinued. If no time limits are set, the test designer risks having a student sit for extended periods of time without answering.

Item Feedback.   One of the primary advantages of CBI is the potential for immediate feedback during a lesson. As students answer practice questions, they can receive immediate information on their answers. Given the instructional advantages to immediate feedback, there is a great temptation to provide item feedback during a test. From an instructional perspective, it makes perfect sense to correct an error during a test. (For purposes of scoring, an incorrect item could still be counted wrong.) However, there is a danger of contaminating future items if all items are not totally independent. That is, the student could use the feedback as an aid in answering future items. The reply from the instructional perspective is that it really does not matter *where* the students learned the material, the lesson or the test, as long as the students show that they have mastered the material.

The research of Wise and his associates suggest caution in using item feedback. In a study with elementary schoolchildren (Wise & Wise, 1987), they found that item feedback on a computer-administered test increased state anxiety among high-achieving math students. In another study they found item feedback to interact with item arrangement (Wise, Plake, Eastman, Boettcher, & Lukin, 1986); item feedback did not affect anxiety or performance level when items were presented in an easy-to-hard order, but anxiety increased and performance decreased with random presentation of items. Other research on item feedback is mixed; some have found positive effects (Morris & Fulmer, 1976; Rocklin & Thompson, 1985), while others have found debilitating effects (Strang & Rust, 1973). In summarizing the research, Wise and Wise (1987) go so far as to say that "the use of such feedback in computer-administered tests is not recommended until its effects are better understood" (p. 19).

Another factor to consider is student motivation. If a student is consistently answering items incorrectly, the negative feedback can be detrimental to motivation on future items. Likewise, a series of correct-answer feedbacks can promote greater motivation in future items. The danger here is the differential effects of item feedback across high and low achieving students. Most, if not all, individually administered tests do *not* include item feedback in their instructions. Moreover, test directions often caution about the motivational dangers of giving subtle cues about the correctness of the student's responses (Wechsler, 1974).

Discontinue Criteria.   In a fixed-length test, the student is presented with all of the items on a form of a test (i.e., all students see all of the 40 items on a test).

The computer can allow the test designer to stop testing once the student has passed or failed the test. If a test has 40 items and 30 has been set as the passing score, the computer could be programmed to discontinue the test once the student passes (provides a 30th correct answer) or fails (provides an 11th incorrect answer). Discontinue rules could be set up according to a fixed number of correct or incorrect responses, a percentage correct, or consecutive right or wrong. For CAT, the discontinue criteria are normally some limit or error associated with an ability estimate. If the test is to be discontinued early, the test designer must specify and program the decision rules.

Discontinue rules are often contraindicated if the testing is diagnostic in nature. There might be cases where entire sets of items must be presented in order to assess mastery of subskills. For example, suppose a 30-item test covers 6 objectives (5 items per objective), and the designer has specified mastery scores of 4 out of 5 items for each objective. If the test is stopped before information is collected on the last set of five items, the system might not have the information to route the student past or into the corresponding segment of instruction.

If discontinue rules are used in conjunction with backing up and changing answers, the student would have to be cautioned about casual answer changing. It would be possible for a student to back up, change an answer, and then suddenly satisfy a discontinue rule for early failure. In other words, a student could change a correct response into an incorrect answer and then receive notice about failing a test.

If discontinue rules are used, the designer must be wary of the possible compromises to program evaluation, mentioned earlier under item selection. One needs a comparable or sensible total score in order to compute item statistics or use gain scores in program evaluation and discontinue criteria may make these calculations difficult.

Finally, the designer will have to decide whether or not the students will be informed of the discontinue criteria. Normally, students would be told up front. However, if complicated discontinue rules are used, the designer might opt to withhold an explanation of the criteria.

Student Log-off.   The test designer will have to address the difficult issues related to student log-off in the middle of a test. If a student leaves in the middle of a test, will the test be failed? Will only the last item seen be counted wrong? Will items seen but not answered be counted wrong? What sort of warning will the student receive? Which items will the student see when he or she returns to the test? Will the counter for correct answers be reset to 0 when the student logs back on to the test? Will a parallel form of the test be provided on the next attempt? Will the student be allowed to change answers given prior to the early log-off?

The simplest procedure would appear to be counting the test as failed and providing a parallel form upon returning to the test. When a student tries to log off during a test, he or she could be told that the test will be failed and then asked if they want to return to the test. In this case, programming is complicated because the normal log-off has to be intercepted and a procedure for returning to the test, without penalty, must be coded. If there are negative consequences to logging off, then students should be given some idea of time estimates for the test before they enter the test.

Response Capturing and Scoring

The final cluster of issues to be discussed concerning CBT implementation decisions are response capturing and scoring considerations. The CBT designer must decide when answers are to be registered, if backing up and changing of answers will be allowed, how error trapping will occur, how response latency analysis will occur, and finally, the types of response analysis and scoring that will be used.

Answer Registration. For almost all interactions with a computer, the student must somehow signal the end of an input to the computer. Normally, ENTER or RETURN keys are used for this purpose. Regarding answers to test questions, there must be a procedure for the students to mark the end of their answers. For single character responses (e.g., true–false or multiple-choice items) the system could be set up to accept the single character input and then proceed to the next item. Alternately, and perhaps preferably, the student would make a double keystroke; press a letter for the answer, and then press RETURN or ENTER to register the response and trigger the next item. The advantage to the double keystroke response is that accidental or stray keystrokes are not counted as inputs. A designer could conceivably even offer greater student control by presenting "Are you sure? y/n" after the "answer and ENTER" input. These additional safeguards could become more of a nuisance than they are worth, but they might have application if more than one item is shown on a page (e.g., a matching exercise).

Backing up and Changing Answers. In paper-pencil tests, students often go back to items they have already answered and change their responses. A recent review of research (Benjamin, 1984) suggests that, more often than not, the answer changing is from an incorrect answer to a correct answer. If these features are going to be afforded to students in a CBT environment, then complications will arise in coding. The designer has to provide for the student returning to the appropriate item after the back-up has been completed. Also, procedures for determining exactly how the back-up is accomplished need to be developed and coded. Will a designated key back-up items one-at-a-time? Or, will a request for back-up produce a menu in which the student is prompted to enter the number of the item to which they want to return?

There are some arguments for disallowing this feature on CBTs. If there is extensive routing within the test, as in CAT or diagnostic testing, then items must be scored as they are answered. What happens if a student has been routed to a particular subtest because of failure on some routing test and then the student opts to back up and change an answer on the routing test? With CAT, answer changing seriously complicates the algorithm for generating ability estimates between item presentation: a test-wise student could notice that the items are getting easier and decide to go back and change earlier answers. Also, students could try to look back at items continually in order to get clues that help them answer other items (e.g., help eliminate distractors on a multiple-choice item).

Finally, it is conceivable that the test designer could permit students to back up and see earlier items but *not* allow them to change the answer. These two features can be kept distinct. However, it could be overly frustrating (perhaps unfair as well) for a student to back up and find an error, and then *not* be allowed to change the answer.

Error Trapping.   Computers are usually programmed to expect particular types of inputs. The most simple cases would be inputs of numerical and string variables. If the system is awaiting an input of a numerical variable and the student types a letter, the program could crash. Programmers usually include error trapping routines to avoid these problems. If the system is awaiting a numerical input, the system is programmed to determine if the real input is numerical before it tries to assign the input to the predesignated variable label. Similarly, test designers need to include error traps to make sure that the response is of an appropriate type or within a particular limit. For instance, if a multiple-choice item has the options of "a," "b," "c," or "d," then the program should ask for a reanswer if any other input is made. Likewise, true–false items could be programmed to only accept inputs of "t" (true) or "f" (false). If a number is expected, then letter inputs should not be accepted. Error traps also guard against accidental keystrokes if answer registration uses a single keystroke. If the CBT system does not already provide these error traps, then the test designer or programmer must code for them.

Response Latency Analysis.   Response latency is the time between presentation of a test item and the student's response. The test designer should decide if response times are going to be collected and, if so, how the data will be analyzed. Latency analysis has been proposed as a promising area for computer-based testing (Space, 1981). One would expect that longer response times are associated with "uncertainty" in achievement and ability testing; for personality testing, longer response times might be expected for items that are more "ego-involved" and, hence, generate emotional blocking. Dunn, Lushene, and O'Neil (1972) conducted early research on the feasibility of latency analysis in personality assessment. They administered the MMPI via computers to 165 college students. Response times were averaged across students and entered as the dependent variable in stepwise multiple regression analysis. Predictor variables included a number of item characteristics, such as item length, social desirability, ambiguity, tense, and voice. They found that item length accounted for 47% to 58% of the variance, while three other variables—ambiguity, social desirability, and social desirability dispersion—accounted for only an additional 3% to 8% of the variance. One difficulty in interpreting the research of Dunn and his associates is that they did not look at intraindividual differences. One wonders what results would have been found if response times were analyzed for individual examinees—where psychological blocking on particular items would not be lost in aggregated data.

Using response latency analyses in computer-based instructional testing poses additional problems. If latency analyses are going to be conducted, then the following cautions are in order. First, latency analyses presumes a rather high degree of vigilance on the part of the students. This might not be as much of a problem for stand-alone ability and personality tests, where testing times can be rather short. But, for large-scale computer-based training, students could be at a terminal for several hours at a time. Variations in attention during longer sessions at a computer could produce highly variable response times, and the test designer should be cautious about overinterpreting response latencies. What if a student sneezes or helps out another student at a nearby station?

Secondly, latency analysis requires a very simple response format, such as a single-letter input. It would be very difficult to interpret response times for constructed response items, because additional time must be allowed for typing in an answer. Students could arrive at answers quickly and then have their latencies misinterpreted because of slowness in typing in the answers.

Finally, response time can be easily confounded with reading speed, reading comprehension, and item length. The test designer has to be cautious about decisions or judgments that are made on the basis of a short or long response time to a particular item.

Latency analysis might be appropriate for learning objectives that focus on teaching students how to perform already learned skills more quickly (e.g., drill-and-practice exercises). If students have learned a skill to the point of being "correct, but hesitant" (Rosenshine & Stevens, 1986), latency analyses would be entirely appropriate for measuring learning objectives that are designed to bring the students to full automatization of the skill.

Response Analysis and Scoring. Once a student has registered an answer and the input has passed the error traps, the system must analyze the input for correctness and score the item accordingly. Response analysis can be the most complicated coding aspect of CBT. Response analysis is least difficult in a selected-response mode and most difficult in a constructed-response mode. Checking the input for a match to "a," "b," "c," or "d" (even upper- or lowercase) on a multiple-choice item, or "t" or "f" (again upper- or lowercase) in a true–false item is relatively straightforward.

Constructed responses require considerably more complex analyses. Decisions must be made about handling such things as upper- and lowercase, spelling errors, punctuation errors, and extra spaces in the input. Once the designer decides upon how these elements are scored/analyzed, the code must be written for the actual analysis. The first major difficulty arises in trying to detail *all* possible correct answers. As an example, consider the following constructed-response item: "What are the two steps in preparing the XYZ radio tuner?" Suppose that the two steps are: (1) turning the power on and (2) turning the mode selector dial to "tune." Further suppose that the order of these steps is not important. The following are some correct answers:

- Turn it on and turn the mode dial to tune.
- Set mode switch to tune and then turn on the power.
- First you press the power switch, then you rotate the other dial to "tune."
- I think you flip the power switch and turn the dial selector to tune.

The list could obviously go on ad infinitum. The second major problem is in programming time. Imagine, without some kind of artificial intelligence, how much programming is involved for even a partial subset of all possible correct answers. If diagnostic tests are used, then extra code is needed for error analyses.

A second issue in response analysis and scoring is deciding when scoring will occur. In cases of diagnostic or adaptive testing, scoring must be done before the next item is presented because the student's history of successes and failures is used to route the student to particular subtests or items. If discontinue criteria are utilized, the system must keep a running count of correct and incorrect answers. If early student log-off is allowed, it might be advisable to score items immediately so that response data are not lost with the log-off. If item feedback is provided immediately, then the item must be scored immediately.

There are also times when it would be advisable to delay scoring until the test is completed. The interests of test security might dictate that scoring be delayed to the end of the test. This is more likely to occur in microcomputer configurations involving floppy diskettes; enterprising students might figure out a way to retrieve correct answers from the diskette. In a response to this potential problem, test designers at Psychological Corporation created an item presentation diskette and a scoring diskette on a microcomputer version of the Ohio Vocational Interest Survey (OVIS, 1984). The product is configured in such a way that the student never handles the scoring diskette. The presentation diskette (called the Survey diskette) presents the items and stores responses in a file. The Scoring diskette, which is used exclusively by the test administrator, reads the file, scores the instrument, and writes the scores onto a student file.

It might also be advisable to score items at the end of a test if the student will be allowed to back up and change answers. If there is going to be answer changing, scoring immediately could result in a lot of extra or wasted processing.

Finally, the test designer has to assign points to items. Usually, one point is given for each correct item; however differential weighting is possible and sometimes desirable since research suggests that it increases the reliability of tests (Haladyna, 1984). If weights are used, the programming usually involves another variable (a weighting variable) that is applied to the items.

SUMMARY

Although the computer has a number of potential applications in the testing environment, the costs associated with the design and development of computer-based tests are quite high. When the computer is selected as the testing delivery system, careful analysis of the implementation issues and questions must take place. This chapter has identified four decision areas which need to be addressed when designing CBT programs as a part of computer-based instruction courseware development efforts: test construction, test security, item presentation, and response capturing and scoring. A checklist which can be used during the CBT development effort, covering these major decision areas, appears in Appendix A.

ACKNOWLEDGMENT

The authors would like to thank William Sweeters, of Ford Aerospace and Communications Corporation, for his helpful comments on an earlier draft of this chapter.

REFERENCES

Benjamin, L. T. (1984). Staying with initial answers on objective tests: Is it a myth? *Teaching of Psychology, 11,* 133–141.

Brzezinski, E. J. (1984), Microcomputers and testing: Where are we and how did we get there? *Educational Measurement: Issues and Practice, 3,* 7–10.

Conkright, T. D. (1982). PLATO applications in the airline industry. *Journal of Computer-Based Instruction, 8,* 49–52.

Dunn, T. G., Lushene, R. E., & O'Neil, H. F. (1972). Complete automation of the MMPI and a study of its response latencies. *Journal of Consulting and Clinical Psychology, 39,* 381–387.

Gagné, R. M., & Briggs, L. J. (1974). *Principles of Instructional Design.* New York: Holt, Rinehart, & Winston.

Gebhardt, R. F., & Munn, J. (1985). Tests that teach. *Educational Technology, 25,* 27–29.

Green, B. F., Bock, R. D., Humphreys, L. G., Linn, R. L., & Reckase, M. D. (1984). Technical guidelines for assessing computerized-adaptive tests. *Journal of Educational Measurement, 21,* 347–360.

Haladyna, T. M. (1984). *Increasing Information from Multiple-Choice Tests*. Paper presented at the annual meeting of the National Council for Measurement in Education, New Orleans.

Hambleton, R. K. (1984). Using microcomputers to develop tests. *Educational Measurement: Issues and Practices, 3,* 10–14.

Jaeger, R. M. (1987). Two decades of revolution in educational measurement!? *Educational Measurement: Issues and Practice, 6,* 6–14.

Lord, F. M. (1980). *Applications of Item Response Theory to Practical Testing Problems*. Hillsdale, NJ: Lawrence Erlbaum Associates.

Millman, J. C., & Arter, J. A. (1984). Issues in item banking. *Journal of Educational Measurement, 21,* 315–330.

Millman, J. C., & Outlaw, W. S. (1978). Testing by computer. *AEDS Journal, 11,* 57–72.

Mizokawa, O. T., & Hamlin, M. D. (1984). Guidelines for computer-managed tests. *Educational Technology, 24,* 12–17.

Morris, L. W., & Fulmer, R. S. (1976). Test anxiety (worry and emotionality) changes during academic testing as a function of feedback and test importance. *Journal of Educational Psychology, 68,* 817–824.

Noonan, J. V., & Dugliss, P. (1985). *Computer-Assisted Assessment: Technological Fit and Illusion*. Paper presented at the annual meeting of the American Psychological Association, Los Angeles.

Olds, H. F. (1983). Evaluating the evaluation schemes. In N. B. Jones & L. Vaughan (Ed.), *Evaluation of Educational Software: A Guide to the Guides*. Chelmsford, MA: Northwest Regional Exchange, Inc.

OVIS II Microcomputer Version. (1984). San Antonio, TX: Psychological Corporation.

Rocklin, T., & Thompson, J. M. (1985). Interactive effects of test anxiety, test difficulty, and feedback. *Journal of Educational Psychology, 77,* 368–372.

Rosenshine, B., & Stevens, R. (1986). Teaching functions. In M. C. Wittrock (Ed.), *Handbook on Research and Teaching* (3rd ed.), New York: Macmillan.

Sarvela, P. D., & Noonan, J. V. (1988). Testing and computer-based instruction: Psychometric considerations. *Educational Technology, 28*(5), 17–20.

Space, L. G. (1981). The computer as psychometrician. *Behavior Research Methods and Instrumentation, 13,* 596–606.

Strang, H. R., & Rust, J. O. (1973). The effects of immediate knowledge of results and task definitions on multiple-choice answering. *Journal of Experimental Education, 42,* 77–80.

Sweeters, W. (1985). *Screen Design Guidelines*. Paper presented at the annual meeting of the Association for the Development of Computer-based Instructional Systems, Philadelphia.

Ward, W. C. (1984). Using microcomputers to administer tests. *Educational Measurement: Issues and Practice, 3,* 16–20.

Wechsler, D. (1974). *Manual for the Wechsler Intelligence Scale for Children—Revised*. San Antonio, TX: Psychological Corporation.

Weiss, D. J., & Kingsbury, G. G. (1984). Application of computerized adaptive testing to educational problems. *Journal of Educational Measurement, 21,* 361–365.

Whiteside, M. F., & Whiteside, J. A. (1987/1988). Microcomputer authoring systems: Valuable tools for health educators. *Health Education, 18,* 4–6.

Wise, S. L., Plake, B. S., Eastman, L. A., Boettcher, L. L., & Lukin, M. E. (1986). The effects of item feedback and examinee control on test performance and anxiety in a computer-administered test. *Computers in Human Behavior, 2,* 21–29.

Wise, S. L., & Wise, L. A. (1987). Comparison of computer-administered and paper-administered achievement tests with elementary school children. *Computers in Human Behavior, 3,* 15–20.

Wulfeck, W. H., Ellis, J. A., Richards, R. E., Wood, N. D., & Merrill, M. D. (1978). *The Instructional Quality Inventory*. (NPRDC SR 79–3). San Diego: Navy Personnel Research and Development Center.

Decision Points in Developing Computer-Based
Testing Programs

A. TEST CONSTRUCTION
   Diagnostic or mastery tests
   Routing
       within the test
       within the courseware
   Types of learning objectives
   Item types
       selected-response
       constructed-response
   Embedded or block tests
   Size of item pools
   Test-taking policy
   Item tryout and analyses

B. TEST SECURITY
   Access limitations
   Test preview
   Test review

C. ITEM PRESENTATION
   Access to directions
   Item skipping (preview)
   Item selection
       random
       sequential
       adaptive
   Display conventions
       format
       color
       headings, titles
       highlighting
       menus and icons
   Time out
   Item feedback
   Discontinue criteria
   Student log-off

D. RESPONSE CAPTURING AND SCORING
   Answer registration
   Backing up and changing answers
   Error trapping

Response latency analysis
Response analysis and scoring
    selected-constructed response
    when scoring occurs
    points per item

8

Issues in Intelligent Computer-Assisted Instruction: Evaluation and Measurement

Harold F. O'Neil, Jr.
University of Southern California

Eva L. Baker
Center for Research on Evaluation, Standards, and Student Testing
University of California, Los Angeles

In this chapter we plan to explore two issues in the field of intelligent computer-assisted instruction (ICAI) that we feel offer opportunities to advance the state of the art. These issues are evaluation of ICAI systems and the use of the underlying technology in ICAI systems to develop tests. For each issue we will provide a theoretical context, discuss key constructs, provide a brief window to the appropriate literature, suggest methodological solutions and conclude with a concrete example of the feasibility of the solution from our own research.

INTELLIGENT COMPUTER-ASSISTED INSTRUCTION (ICAI)

ICAI is the application of artificial intelligence to computer-assisted instruction. Artificial intelligence, a branch of computer science, is making computers "smart" in order to (a) make them more useful and (b) understand intelligence (Winston, 1977). Topic areas in artificial intelligence have included natural language processing (Schank, 1980), vision (Winston, 1975), knowledge representation (Woods, 1983), spoken language (Lea, 1980), planning (Hayes–Roth, 1980), and expert systems (Buchanan, 1981). The field of Artificial Intelligence (AI) has matured in both hardware and software. The most commonly used language in the field is LISP (List Processing). A major development in the hardware area is that personal LISP machines are now available at a relatively low cost (20–50K) with the power of prior mainframes. In the software area two advances stand out: (a) programming support environments such as LOOPS (Bobrow & Stefik, 1983) and (b) expert system tools. These latter tools are now running on powerful micros. The application of "expert systems" technology to a host of real-world problems has demonstrated the utility of artificial intelligence techniques in a very dramatic style. Expert system technology is the branch of artificial intelligence at this point most relevant to ICAI.

Expert Systems

Knowledge-based systems or expert systems are a collection of problem-solving computer programs containing both factual and experiential knowledge and data in a particular domain. When the knowledge embodied in the program is a result of a human expert elicitation, these systems are called expert systems. A typical expert system consists of a knowledge base, a reasoning mechanism popularly called an "inference engine" and a "friendly" user interface. The knowledge base consists of facts, concepts, and numerical data (declarative knowledge), procedures based on experience or rules of thumb (heuristics), and causal or conditional relationships (procedural knowledge). The inference engine searches or reasons with or about the knowledge base to arrive at intermediate conclusions or final results during the course of problem solving. It effectively decides when and what knowledge should be applied, applies the knowledge and determines when an acceptable solution has been found. The inference engine employs several problem-solving strategies in arriving at conclusions. Two of the popular schemes involve starting with a good description or desired solution and working backwards to the known facts or current situation (backward chaining), and starting with the current situation or known facts and working toward a goal or desired solution (forward chaining). The user interface may give the user choices (typically menu-driven) or allow the user to participate in the control of the process (mixed initiative). The interface allows the user: to describe a problem, input knowledge or data, browse through the knowledge base, pose question, review the reasoning process of the system, intervene as necessary, and control overall system operation. Successful expert systems have been developed in fields as diverse as mineral exploration (Duda & Gaschnig, 1981) and medical diagnosis (Clancy, 1981).

ICAI Systems

ICAI systems use approaches artificial intelligence and cognitive science to teach a range of subject matters. Representative types of subjects include: (a) collection of facts, for example, South American geography in SCHOLAR (Carbonell & Collins, 1973); (b) complete system models, for example, a ship propulsion system in STEAMER (Stevens & Steinberg, 1981) and a power supply in SOPHIE (Brown, Burton, & de Kleer, 1982); (c) completely described procedural rules, for example, strategy learning, WEST (Brown, Burton, & de Kleer, 1982), or arithmetic in BUGGY (Brown & Burton, 1978); (d) partly described procedural rules, for example, computer programming in PROUST (Johnson & Soloway, 1983); LISP Tutor (Anderson, Boyle, & Reiser, 1985); rules in ALGEBRA (McArthur, Stasz, & Hotta, 1987); diagnosis of infectious diseases in GUIDON (Clancey, 1979); and an imperfectly understood complex domain, causes of rainfall in WHY (Stevens, Collins, & Goldin, 1978). Excellent reviews by Barr and Feigenbaum (1982) and Wenger (1987) document many of these ICAI systems. Representative research in ICAI is described by O'Neil, Anderson, and Freeman (1986) and Wenger (1987).

Although suggestive evidence has been provided by Anderson et al. (1985), few of these ICAI projects have been evaluated in any rigorous fashion. In a sense they have all been toy systems for research and demonstration. Yet, they have raised a good deal of excitement and enthusiasm about their likelihood of being effective instructional environments.

With respect to cognitive science, progress has been made in the following areas: identification and analysis of misconceptions or "bugs" (Clement, Lockhead, & Soloway, 1980), the use of learning strategies (O'Neil & Spielberger, 1979; Weinstein & Mayer, 1986), expert versus novice distinction (Chi, Glaser, & Rees, 1982), the role of mental models in learning (Kieras & Bovair, 1983), and the role of self-explanations in problem solving (Chi, Bassok, Lewis, Reimann, & Glaser, 1987).

The key components of an ICAI system consist of a knowledge base: that is, (a) what the student is to learn; (b) a student model, either where the student is now with respect to subject matter or how student characteristics interact with subject matters, and (c) a tutor, that is, instructional techniques for teaching the declarative or procedural knowledge. These components are described in more detail by Fletcher (1985).

Knowledge Base. This is the "expert" part of the system. Ideally, this component would represent the relevant knowledge domain. In effect, it must contain the knowledge and understanding of a subject matter expert. It must be able to generate problem solutions from situations never before encountered and not anticipated by the training system designers. It must be able to infer the true state of the system from incomplete and/or inaccurate measurements. It must be able to solve problems based on this knowledge.

Student Model. This component represents the learner. Just as the knowledge base must "understand" the subject matter, so the student model must understand and be able to model the learner. The function of the student model is to assess the student's knowledge state and to make hypotheses about his or her conceptions and reasoning strategies. There are two main approaches to student modeling: (1) The overlay model, in which a model is constructed by comparing the student's performance with the computer-based expert's behavior on the same task. Thus, the student's knowledge state is a subset of an expert's knowledge

(Carr & Goldstein, 1977); and (2) The buggy model, which represents student's mislearned subskills as variants of the expert's knowledge. Thus, misconceptions are modeled as incorrect procedures (Brown & Burton, 1978). Some systems emphasize a student's knowledge/gaps in his or her knowledge base. Others emphasize students' misconceptions. Few do both of these very well; however, none of the current ICAI systems represents the role of traditional individual differences (i.e., smart students learn faster than not-so-smart students [Sternberg, 1982]).

Tutor.   This component represents the teacher and must be able to apply the appropriate instructional tactics at the appropriate times. This capability implies the presence of both a large repertoire of instructional tactics and a strategical understanding of how best to use them. It should model the desirable properties of a human tutor. Fig. 8.1 presents some of these properties. In general, the tutor must know what to say to the learner and when to say it. In addition, it must know how to take the learner from one stage of skill to another and how to help the learner, given his or her current state of knowledge.

However, little of instructional design considerations (e.g., Ellis, Wulfeck, & Fredericks, 1979; Markle, 1967; Merrill & Tennyson, 1977; O'Neil, 1979; Park, Perez, & Seidel, 1987; or Reigeluth, 1987) are reflected in ICAI tutors. Instructional design is concerned with "prescribing optimal methods of instruction to bring about desired changes in student knowledge and skills" or alternatively is viewed as a "linking science . . . a body of knowledge that prescribes instructional actions to optimize designed instructional outcomes, such as achievement and affect" (Reigeluth, 1983). More recently, there have been several systematic attempts to provide instructional information in the design of ICAI systems. Such

```
* The tutor causes the problem solving heuristics of the
  student to converge to those of the tutor.

* The tutor chooses appropriate examples and problems
  for the student.

* The tutor can work arbitrary examples chosen by the
  student.

* The tutor is able to adjust to different student
  backgrounds.

* The tutor is able to measure the student's progress.

* The tutor can review previously learned material
  with the student as the need arises.
```

FIG. 8.1.   Desirable properties of a human tutor (adapted from Gamble and Page, 1980).

attempts include the design of a new ICAI tutor (O'Neil, Slawson, & Baker, 1987) and the design of instructional strategies to improve existing ICAI programs (Baker, Bradley, Aschbacher, & Feifer, 1985). However, neither of these efforts systematically evaluated the resulting "improved" ICAI programs. Research in progress by McArthur of the Rand Corporation is addressing this issue in the domain of algebra.

Evaluation

Evaluation is an activity purported to provide an improved basis for decision making. Among its key elements are the identification of goals, the assessment of process, the collection of information, analysis, and the interpretation of findings. A critical issue in any sort of evaluation is the meaning ascribed to the findings. Meaning derives from the use of measures that are valid for the intervention, from the adequacy of the inferencing processes used to interpret results, and from the utility of the findings for the intended users. These facets of meaning require that the designer/developer as well as funding sources articulate their goals, processes, and potential decision needs so that the evaluation team can provide results that have meaning for interested parties.

Summative Evaluation.   The most common model for evaluation is the summative (Scriven, 1967), which focuses on overall choices among systems or programs based on performance levels, time, and cost. In this mode, evaluation is essentially comparative and contrasts the innovation to other options. These comparisons may be against explicit choices or may be implicit in terms of current practice or ways resources might be spent in the future (opportunity costs).

Summative evaluation asks the question, "Does the intervention work?" In a military or industrial training environment, a common question is "Has training using X approach been effective?" Implicit in that question is comparison, for the intervention must be judged in comparison with other alternatives, either current practice, or hypothetically, in terms of other ways the resources could be used. A second part of the summative evaluation question is "How much does it cost?" Again, comparisons may be implicit or explicit. Third, summative evaluation develops information related to a third, critical question, "Should we buy it?" Here, the issue is the confidence we have in our data, and the validity of the inferences we draw from such data. We judge the credibility of our cost information case against the validity and credibility of quality data and cost of competing alternatives.

Where summative evaluation is weak is in identifying what to do if a system or intervention is not an immediate, unqualified success. Given that this state is most common for most interventions in early stages of development, comparative, summative-type evaluations are usually mistimed and may create an unduly negative environment for productivity. Furthermore, because summative evaluation is typically not designed to pinpoint weaknesses and to explore potential remedies, it provides almost no help in the development/improvement cycle which characterizes the systematic creation of training interventions.

Formative Evaluation.   Evaluation efforts that are instituted at the outset or in the process of an innovation's development typically have different purposes. Formative evaluation (Baker, 1974) seeks to provide information that focuses on the improvement of the innovation and is designed to assist the developer.

Formative evaluation also addresses, from a metaevaluation perspective, the effectiveness of the development procedures used, in order to predict whether the application of similar approaches will likely have effective and efficient results. In that function, formative evaluation seeks to improve the technology at large, rather than the specific instances addressed one at a time. The approach, formative evaluation, is designed so that its principal outputs are identification of success and failure of segments, components, and details of programs, rather than a simple overall estimate of project success. The approach requires that data be developed to permit the isolation of elements for improvement and, ideally, the generation of remedial options to assure that subsequent revisions have a higher probability of success. Formative evaluation is a method that developed to assist in the development of instructional (training) programs. While the evaluation team maintains "third-party" objectivity, they typically interact with and understand program goals, processes, and constraints at a deeper level than evaluation teams focused exclusively on bottom-line assessments of success or failure. Their intent is to assist their client (either funding agency or project staff) to use systematic data collection to promote the improvement of the effort.

Basic literature in formative evaluation was developed by Scriven (1967), Baker and Alkin (1973), Baker (1974), and Baker and Saloutos (1974). Formative evaluation now represents the major focus of evaluation efforts in the public education sector (Baker & Herman, 1985) in the guise of instructional management systems. Multiple models and procedures are common within formative evaluation. An example of one approach to formative evaluation for ICAI is depicted in Fig. 8.2. As is shown, formative evaluation begins with checking whether the design is congruent with specifications and ends with revision, which includes new data collection on Steps 3–5. An attempt to use this approach was conducted by Baker et al. (1985).

Tensions in Evaluation.   A persistent fact of evaluation is that those evaluated rarely see the value of the process. It is something done to them, a necessary evil, a new chance for failure, often seen as largely irrelevant to their major purpose. This view generally holds whether it is a person who is evaluated (for selection or credentialing purposes), such as students and teachers at universities

1. Check ICAI design against its specifications.
2. Check validity of instructional strategies in tutor with research literature.
3. Conduct feasibility review with instructor.
4. Assess instructional effectiveness.   *cognitive   *Affective
5. Assess unanticipated outcomes.
6. Conduct revision.

FIG. 8.2.   Formative evaluation activity.

or in the public schools, a program evaluated (either as small as a segment or as large as a federal initiative), or a technological innovation. Those who get evaluated are almost always reluctant players.

A persistent fact, however, is that those in authority have come to believe that evaluation is a useful process. Their belief is fostered in part by actual research studies showing that evaluation findings, when used, improve the state of affairs. But a more likely reason that evaluation has been fastened upon as a useful endeavor resides in the belief that it provides a mechanism for management, or for the appearance of management, by those in charge of resources. Objectivity, accountability, and efficiency are themes underlying this commitment to evaluation.

The tension is obvious between those who must participate and those who push the evaluation process from positions of authority. Evaluation experts have to mediate among these two sets of views, a challenging, if not always pleasant task.

The Evaluability of ICAI Applications.   Evaluating an emerging technology presents serious technical as well as practical problems, and the ICAI field incorporates most known or imaginable difficulties. First, much has been claimed by proponents of Artificial Intelligence (AI). The claims have led many sponsors to support projects that they believe intend to produce a fully developed instructional innovation (such as a tutor). In fact, the intention of the designers may not be to create a working, effective tutor, but to work toward this goal and thereby to explore the limits of the computer science field. In this case, the tutor becomes a context for R&D, a constraint under which the designer really seeks to conduct research, that is, produce new knowledge about AI processes. Such a process makes sense in an emerging field but requires great patience from sponsors.

Because ICAI efforts develop largely in a research rather than in a development context, certain facts characterize them. First, research goals contributing to knowledge and theory building appear to be paramount. Focusing on academically respectable efforts frequently characterizes emerging, synthetic fields. (See, for instance, the spate of theory building in educational evaluation in the late 1960s.) Second, efforts are selectively addressed based on the research predilections (rather than the project development requirements) of any particular set of investigators. Third, there are no real off-the-shelf-item components available for easy substitution into the project. Thus, if the researcher invests effort in knowledge representation, his final product may not work because of the lagged emphasis in another important component, for example, a tutor. The fore-knowledge of uncertain success to the researcher need not impair the ICAI enthusiasm. Again, rhetoric of the goal of a complete ICAI system is useful. In an emerging field, breakthroughs are anticipated. Secondly, keeping the idea, even as an idea, of a complete future ICAI in the mind of the researcher suggests fruitful paths of exploration.

Thus, the lines between research and application in ICAI are murky and undercut neat categories of R&D processes, such as those identified by Glennan (1968) and Bright (1968) and used as program elements in DoD work[1] (Basic Research [6.1], Exploratory Development [6.2], Advanced Development [6.3], and Engineering Development [6.4]). This reality presents problems for evaluation. Compared with other innovations, the ICAI *what* to be evaluated is less concrete and identifiable, and more like the probabilistic view of where a photon is at any point in time. In addition, the field of ICAI uses multiple metaphors to describe its activity. Fig. 8.3 depicts these multiple metaphors. We believe that each setting requires a different role for the student and, thus, a different evaluation focus.

Secondly, ICAI has evaluability problems, partly because of its visibility; the public persona of AI (see national magazines, films, television, trade books) is high profile. In startling contrast, the accessibility to AI processes is limited. To the uninitiated, it is embedded in the recesses of special language (e.g., LISP, PROLOG) and in arcane jargon (modified petri net, overlay models). Coupled with the fact that AI work is conducted in a relatively few centers by a relatively small number of people, understanding an AI implementation well enough to create sensible options for its assessment is a difficult proposition. These states are compounded by the strongly capitalistic environment in which AI research is conducted. The proprietary nature of much work, either that conducted by large private corporations or by small entrepreneurial enterprises also works to obscure the conceptual and procedural features of the work. Perhaps AI experts can assist in evaluation, but, understandably, they are more interested in creating some-

---

[1]The numbers (e.g., 6.1) refer to budget lines in the DoD budget. Thus Basic Research is a 6.1 program.

SETTING	STUDENT ROLE	EVALUATION FOCUS
Laboratory	Applied scientist	Problem-solving ability increased
Classroom	Learner	Learning increased
Arcade	Game player	Enjoyment and learning increased
Workbench	Troubleshooter	Ability to fix faults increased
Expert system or automated job performance aid	Human system component	System goal achieved

FIG. 8.3. ICAI metaphors.

thing new of their own. All of this is asserted with full knowledge that at least some of these problems characterize any rapidly developing new technology.

The utility of evaluation processes also needs to be judged in terms of what techniques and options are useful, where there is differential confidence in our ability to measure and infer, and which procedures have been used credibly in the last 10 years. In addition, we must consider what requirements ICAI evaluation creates and explore new methodology to meet these needs. We have begun to develop such a methodology. Table 8.1 presents questions we believe that an ICAI evaluation should answer and thus increase the evaluability of ICAI.

Distance Between the Evaluator and the Evaluated. One way to think about either formative or summative evaluation techniques is in terms of the distance among those who are conducting the evaluation work, those responsible for the actual day-to-day design and development of the project, and those who are responsible for providing resources to the project. These distances are often represented as the "party" of the evaluation.

First-party evaluation is evaluation conducted by the project staff itself. Common examples would be pilot test data conducted for input into the design of a final project. It has the benefit of intimate connection and understanding of the project. Its problem is lack of distance and detachment. In AI applications, this evaluation work is informal, and relatively infrequently addressed to the issue of overall effectiveness of the intervention. Further, many ICAI projects are conceptualized to advance the state of the art in computer science (a view of the developer). This perspective may conflict with the view of the funder of a project to create an ICAI system with of an instructionally sound tutor.

Second-party evaluation involves the assessment of progress or outcomes by the supervising funding agency. IPRs and site visits are examples of second-party evaluation. Arbitrary timing, limited agency attention spans, and objectivity are

TABLE 8.1
Evaluation Questions

I. Are the measures and procedures planned and used for formative and summative evaluation providing a fair test of the ICAI system?

II. Does the ICAI system meet its multiple goals?

   a. Generalization

      1. Does the prototype provide the desired level of education/training?

      2. Is this level maintained or improved as the prototype addresses more complex education/training missions; greater numbers of students; distributed sites?

      3. Will the prototype easily generalize (or adapt) to other content areas (e.g., algebra to English)?

   b.Technology Push

      1. Does the development of the existing hardware/software components for the system (e.g., knowledge representation, graphics) contribute to the capability for future education/training?

      2. Have other technological approaches to education/training (e.g., metacognitive skill training) been considered and integrated into planned future prototype?

   c. Unplanned Outcomes (Side-effects analysis)

      1. Does the system create requirement to train teachers for new role (e.g., expert remediator)?

      2. Will intensive data collection systems permit answers to "old" questions, e.g., relative value of discovery learning, estimation of transfer both near and far?

      3. Is the prototype a good environment to validate analytical techniques to predice the education/ training effectiveness?

      4. Will intensive data collection permit answers to "new" questions from cognitive science (e.g., analysis of misconceptions or bugs; differences between experts and novices; role of models in proficiency)?

---

problems here. Further, a real intellectual give and take is difficult when agency personnel control funds.

Third-party evaluation is evaluation conducted by an independent group. GAO performs many third-party summative evaluations. Independent contractors reporting to state legislatures, school boards, or school districts also conduct such evaluation. The benefit of such an approach is the disinterested nature of the investigation, contributing to the credibility of the findings. However, the validity of external evaluation presents some difficulty, and requires that the third party get up to speed in technical issues so that the evaluation methodologies applied are appropriate. The learning required by the evaluation staff represents an additional "overhead" to the project staff and may be perceived as a distraction from their primary effort. This sort of evaluation costs more than the other two.

All types of evaluation described thus far can be done using formative or summative techniques. Third-party formative evaluations are rare in general and to our knowledge have only been applied once in ICAI (Baker et al., 1985).

Evaluation Technology.   Contrary to popular practice, there is no inherent reason for totally separating formative and summative evaluation efforts. We have mentioned that the approaches differ in purpose and client. They also differ in the types of data appropriate (cost for summative, componential analysis for formative). However, in the area of performance, they should share some common procedures and criterion measures. In addition, since ICAI shares some common attributes with CAI, evaluation technology appropriate to CAI could be used in ICAI (e.g., Merrill et al., 1986; Alessi & Trollip, 1985). The CAI lesson evaluation techniques in Table 8.2 present some formative (quality review and pilot testing methods) and some summative techniques (i.e., validation). These activities were adapted from Alessi and Trollip (1985). Information of this sort is a necessary but not sufficient set for ICAI evaluation. What is missing in Table 8.2 and needs to be developed for ICAI are specific procedures that focus on the unique attributes of ICAI. Table 8.3 provides a first cut of such attributes. To our knowledge, there are no known techniques to evaluate systematically and instructionally the features in Table 8.3. However, an interesting approach for the analysis of rapid prototyping is provided by Carroll and Rosson (1984), and Richer (1985) discusses knowledge acquisition techniques.

It is not likely that evaluation as it is currently practiced can be transferred directly to an application field such as ICAI. One approach to exploring the merging of existing technologies (ICAI applications with evaluation technology) is to shift points of view in order to determine where reasonable matches exist.

TABLE 8.2
CAI LESSON EVALUATION TECHNIQUES

QUALITY REVIEW
    Check the language and grammar (e.g., appropriate reading level.)
    Check the surface features (e.g., uncluttered displays).
    Check questions and menus (e.g., making a choice is clear).
    Check all invisible functions (e.g., appropriate student records kept).
    Check all subject matter content (e.g., information is accurate).
    Check the off-line material (e.g., direction in operator manual are clear).
    Revise the lesson.
    Apply the same quality-review procedure to all revisions.

PILOT TESTING
    Enlist about three helpers (i.e., representative of potential students).
    Explain pilot-testing procedures (e.g., encourage note-taking).
    Find out how much they know about the subject matter.
    Observe them go through the lesson.
    Interview them afterwards.
    Revise the lesson.
    Pilot-test all revised lessons.

VALIDATION
    Use the lesson in the setting for which it was designed.
    Use the lesson with students for which it was designed.
    Evaluate how the students perform in the setting for which you are preparing them.
    Obtain as much performance data as you can from different sources.
    Obtain data on student achievement attribution to the lesson.
    Obtain data on student attitudes toward the lesson.

Adapted from Alessi and Trollip (1985, p. 393).

TABLE 8.3
AI Features in ICAI Systems

Topic	Examples
Knowledge representation techniques	Production rules, frames, networks
Reasoning mechanisms	Backward and Forward chaining, inheritance
Development environment	User-interface, editors and debuggers, documentation and on-line help systems
Rapid prototypes	Rapidly developed simulation, exhibit functionality, convey requirements; not meant to be operational systems
Student modeling methods	Overlay, buggy, individual differences
Knowledge acquisition techniques	"Shells," knowledge-base elicitors
Validation tools	Check integrity of knowledge base to identify conflicting rules or syntactical errors
Cost Factors	Price of software, support, training, required hardware, skilled personnel
Expert tutor	Domain-independent instructional strategies
Cognitive or process model	Model of how system accomplishes its tasks, may be based on models of human reasoning (e.g., schema)
Languages	LISP, PROLOGUE

Looking first from the evaluation perspective, let us explore where evaluation has some strengths and could make a substantial contribution to ICAI development.

Evaluation's Contribution to ICAI

Research and development in measurement is one of the major productive areas in psychology. Sophisticated models for estimating performance have been developed and come in and out of vogue. Many of these were created to assist in the selection process, to sort those individuals who were better or worse with regard to a particular competency or academic domain. However, these approaches, while venerable, have little to contribute to the evaluation of programs, either those completed or under continuing development. Most standardized achievement tests were based on this model, and their use to evaluate innovation is not recommended for a variety of technical reasons. These reasons can be summed up on a simple phrase: Standardized tests are not sensitive enough to particular curriculum focuses; thus, they are unlikely to detect effects present (the false negative problem) and will underestimate effects that exist.

Measurement of Student Achievement Outcomes.   However, there are newer approaches to the measurement of human performance which do have implications for the assessment of ICAI interventions designed to improve learner performance. Specifically, the use of domain-referenced achievement testing seems to provide a good match with ICAI approaches. In domain-referenced testing (Baker & Herman, 1983; Baker & O'Neil, 1987; Hively, Patterson, & Page, 1968) one attempts to estimate student performance in a well-specified content domain. The approach is essentially top–down, with parameters for content selection and criteria for judging adequacy of student output specified (albeit successively revised) in advance. Test items are conceived as samples from a universe constrained by the specific parameters. For example, in the area of reading comprehension, parameters would need to be explicated regarding the genre and content to be read, the characteristics of the semantics and syntax, including variety, ambiguity, complexity of sentence patterns, and the presupposed knowledge that the learner would bring into the instructional/testing setting. In addition, the characteristics of the items would be identified, in terms of gross format, that is, short answer, essay, multiple-choice, and in terms of subtler features, such as the rules for the construction of wrong answer alternatives, or for the assessment of free responses. Theoretically, such rules permit the generation of a universe of test items which can be matrix resampled to provide progress and end-of-instruction testing.

The use of such approaches have the added benefit of utility to small numbers of students. They do not depend, as does the selection approach described, on normal (and large) distributions of respondents to derive score meaning. On the other hand, such tests are more demanding to develop, and they depend on close interaction with the innovation designer to assure that the specifications are adequate. They contrast to the common approach of "tacking on" existing measures (such as commercially available standardized tests), an easy enough process but one unlikely to provide information useful for the fair assessment of improvement of a product. Domain-referenced tests derive their power from the goodness of their specifications. Their weakness is their idiosyncrasy; however, the matching of testing procedures to designer's intentions is also their strength.

Because of the attention that ICAI applications devote to representing properly the knowledge domain and determining student understanding in process, the application of improved assessment techniques, particularly those based on domain-referenced testing, seems like a good fit.

Measurement of Individual Differences.   A second area in measurement that could contribute to the efficient design and assessment of ICAI applications is the measurement of individual differences. Psychology has long invested resources in determining how best to assess constructs along which individuals show persisting differences. For these areas to be useful, such constructs should interact (statistically) with instructional options and desired outcomes of the system under study (Corno & Snow, 1986). Common constructs such as ability and intelligence undoubtedly have relevance for the analysis and implementation of alternative student models and tutoring strategies. Other constructs related to cognitive style preferences, for example, the need for structure, the need for reflection, the attribution of success and failure, could illuminate design options and results analyses for ICAI applications. Similarly, constructs related to affective states, that is, state anxiety (Hedl & O'Neil, 1977), could also provide explanations of findings otherwise obscure.

Process Measurement and Analysis.   In formative evaluation, much is made of the role of process evaluation, that is, tracking what occurs when, to assure that inferences about system effectiveness are well placed. Central to this function, however, is deciding, to the extent possible, what data should be collected and which inferences should be drawn from the findings. Technology-based innovations often make two seemingly conflicting classes of errors. One error is collecting everything possible that can be tracked. Student response times, system operation, errors, student requests, and so on, can be accumulated ad nauseam. The facts seem to be that rarely do developers attend to this glut of information. They have no strategies for determining how such data should be arranged in priority, nor ways to draw systematic conclusions from findings. By the time the data base is assembled, developers are often on to new ideas and prospects; old data, particularly painfully analyzed and interpreted old (to the developer) data, remain only old and often unused. The other error in technology process measurement is when relevant information which could be painlessly accumulated and tabulated on-line is ignored.

The challenge for the evaluator is to help decide what data are likely to be most relevant. Relevance will presuppose a clear overall goal, such as teaching a target group a set of skills. In fact, in the entire gamut of measurement options available, the most significant contributions evaluators may make is clarifying the goals that the designer possesses but has not articulated. Because of the mixture of research and development goals inherent in much ICAI work in education, this is a nontrivial problem. The designers may feel they have all the goals they can tolerate.

Generation of Instructional Options.   Formative evaluators can assist ICAI designers to explore different ways in which they can successfully meet their goals. Of particular interest, for example, is the extent to which evaluation can highlight alternatives for the instructional strategies used in the application. In all instructional development, not the least in ICAI-based approaches, the designer fastens early upon a particular strategy. Research findings have suggested that teachers and developers are most reluctant to change the approach they have taken. They will play at the edges rather than rethink their overall method

(Baker, 1976). Furthermore, they could easily adapt their basic approach by adding particular instructional options to their basic plan, assuming that they make their choice informed by prior research. A recent study (Baker, et al., 1985) adopted such an approach and experimentally modified WEST to strengthen its teaching capability. Although largely unsuccessful due to implementation issues, it demonstrated the feasibility of the concept.

Formative Evaluation of ICAI: A Case Study

This section will focus on the Baker et al. (1985) formative evaluation of PROUST as an example of a formative evaluation of ICAI. PROUST (Johnson & Soloway, 1983, 1987) was selected by Baker et al. as one of the projects to evaluate formatively because its designers communicated serious interest in whether PROUST was instructionally effective with students.

Evaluation Focus.   A three-phase evaluation template was designed for use in the project evaluation. The first phase of the evaluation included an attempt to understand the "product" development cycle employed, the ideological orientations of the designers, and their stated intentions. A second phase of analysis involved reviewing the internal characteristics of the ICAI systems from two perspectives: first, the quality of the instructional strategies employed; and second, the quality of the content addressed. A third and major phase of the study was empirical testing of the programs. Here, the intention was to document effects of the program with regard to individual difference variables among learners and with regard to a broadly conceived set of outcome measures, including achievement and attitude instruments. An explicit intent was to modify the instructional conditions under which the ICAI system operated and make it more effective. Planned experimental comparisons were one option by which these instructional conditions could be contrasted. Based on these three major phases (theoretical, instructional, and empirical analyses), recommendations for the improvement of this particular project and for the ICAI design and development process in general were to be developed. A wide range of evaluation techniques were to be included, for instance, both quantitative and qualitative data collection and analyses. This process is a variant of Fig. 8.2.

Evaluation Questions.   The evaluation questions guiding the study are presented below. These questions are a variant of Tables 8.1, 8.2, and 8.3. In each of these, information related to the adequacy of the AI components (i.e., knowledge representation, instructional strategy, and student model) are treated as appropriate.

1. What is the underlying theoretical orientation of the system under evaluation? To what extent does the program serve as a model for ICAI?

2. What instructional strategies and principles are incorporated into the program? To what extent does the project exhibit instructional content and features potentially useful to future Army applications?
3. What are the learning outcomes for students? To what extent do learners achieve project goals? Do students with different background characteristics profit differentially from exposure to the project? To what extent does the program create unanticipated outcomes, either positive or negative?

Each of these questions was applied to the PROUST ICAI project.

PROUST: Program Description. PROUST was designed by Johnson and Soloway at Yale University. The system title is a literary allusion: *Remembrances of Bugs Past,* with apologies to the original author.

PROUST is designed to assist novice programmers to use the PASCAL language in their own writing of computer programs. The approach taken is to provide intelligent feedback to beginning students about the quality of their efforts in an attempt to approximate the feedback that a human tutor might provide. In the words of its designers, PROUST is: "a tutoring system which helps novice programmers to learn to program" and "a system which can be said to truly understand (buggy) novice programs" (Johnson & Soloway, 1983).

Thus, PROUST is not a trivial effort. The designers have had to map the cognitive domain of computer programming, with PASCAL as the specific instance. The evaluated implementation (circa 1985) of PROUST permitted students to submit their programs in response to two specific (but intended to be prototypical) programming problems. PROUST takes as its input programs which have passed through the PASCAL compiler and are syntactically correct. In analyzing these programs, PROUST attempts to infer students' intentions and to identify any mistakes (bugs in their software) that occurred in the code (Johnson & Soloway, 1983).

As an example of a functioning ICAI system, PROUST represents only a partial solution for the need to evaluate formatively a complete ICAI system. It contains the knowledge representation in software for the problem space of the specific PASCAL programming problems. It also contains the diagnostic part of a tutoring component, which analyzes the student program to determine both student intentions and bugs. PROUST then provides feedback about its inferences about students' intentions and how well the student program implements the assumed plans. However, it does not have a robust tutor. Currently (circa 1987) under development is the pedagogical expert, which knows how to interact with and instruct (tutor) students effectively, and contains a student model to monitor student progress cumulatively. Although it has been anticipated that these components would be available for a full test of the ICAI system, schedule constraints restricted our activities to the completed components. The Yale project staff attempted to include an additional level of feedback in the analyzer as a precursor to the full development of the tutor.

Evaluation Approach.   As was discussed previously, for the evaluation of PROUST, three sets of questions guided our efforts. The evaluation questions, dimensions of inquiry, measurement method, and data sources guiding the study are presented in Table 8.4

Because the questions clearly call for a variety of data collection an analysis, ranging from review of documentation, inspection of the program, close observa-

TABLE 8.4
Instrumentation and Data Collection Strategy

Evaluation Question	Dimensions of Inquiry	Measurement Method	Data Source
1. What is the underlying theoretical orientation of PROUST? To what extent does the project serve as a model of development for ICAI?	Theory of programming	Content review	Primary documents
	Cognitive underpinnings of programming	Interviews	Project developers
	Theoretical view of learning and instruction		
	ICAI development process		
2. What instructional strategies and principles are incorporated into the program? To what extent does the project exhibit instructional content and features potentially useful to future Army applications?	Instructional strategies and principles	Program review	Subject matter experts (instruction and PASCAL programming)
	Subject matter content		
	Army needs		
3. What are the learning outcomes for students? To what extent do learners achieve project goals? Do students with different background characteristics profit differentially from exposure to the project?	Programming Skills (bug identification and bug articulation)	Paper-and-pencil test	Novice PASCAL programmers (college students)
	Background characteristics (academic history, computer-related experience)	Questionnaire	Novice PASCAL programmers (college students)
	Intellectual self-confidence	Rating scale	Novice PASCAL programmers (college students)
	Reactions to PROUST	Questionnaire	Novice PASCAL programmers (college students)
	Opinions toward computers, PASCAL programming	Opinion survey	Novice PASCAL programmers (college students)
	Transportability of technology	Observation interviews	Technology transfer process

tion of outputs from the programs, and student performance and self-report information, the procedures in the study were complex. Thus, Table 8.4 summarizes the instrumentation, data collection, and respondents required for aspects of the program under review.

Formative Evaluation Results.   The report by Baker et al. (1985) presents the complete description and evaluation of PROUST. There are three major sections of their document: a theoretical analysis of the program, a formative review, and a report of two effectiveness studies conducted with PROUST. As was discussed, the purpose of their evaluation was to provide information relevant to the potential improved effectiveness of the system. For the purposes of this chapter, we will provide a concise summary of their findings. We suggest that their methodological approach and measuring procedures are appropriate for a formative evaluation of ICAI systems in general.

The theoretical orientation of PROUST is a top–down approach based on intentions and plans. Rather than compare the student program with an ideal implementation, PROUST compares it to the plan it believes the student was attempting. PROUST inspects a student's program and attempts to classify the inferred intentions against a set of possibilities based on prior student approaches. The program's greatest strength is perhaps its ability to deal with alternative goal decompositions. Its weakness is that it does not explicitly ask the student to confirm the plan that the program "thinks" the student is pursuing.

Because PROUST was only a partial ICAI system, recommendations for improvement focused on two instructional features: type of feedback provided to students and bug analysis. Suggestions for improving feedback were made, especially the content, tone, and learner-control of feedback. Additional recommendations were made for increasing the interactive aspects of PROUST's implementation through verification of student plans, input/output analysis, and student control of timing. In general, Baker et al.'s (1985) study showed few significant findings of use of PROUST related to learning outcomes. However, the students were generally positive about using the program. The designers continue their own evaluation efforts, and Soloway has recently presented workshops (circa 1987) on the topic.

How Can Evaluation Assist ICAI Applications?: Some Suggestions

The history of evaluation of ICAI implementations is light reading. For evaluation to work to the mutual benefit of application designers and their resource providers, we suggest the following:

1. The expectation of evaluation should be developed in the minds of the ICAI developers. The description of the instructional effectiveness of applica-

tions needs to become part of the socialized ethic, as in science, the expectation of repeatability, verifiability and public reporting is commonplace.

2. Rewards for designers' participation in evaluation are necessary. These must be over and above the intrinsic value of the evaluation information for the designer. Because evaluation is not a common expectation, special benefits must be developed to create cooperation.

3. The credibility of the evaluation team must be seriously addressed. AI experts need to participate in AI and ICAI evaluations. Their participation needs to depend less on frantic persuasion and more on a developed sense of professional responsibility (such as reviewing for a journal). If the approach taken is formative, then the designer can receive "help" from friendly reviewers. The goal of evaluation of this sort is to aid in revision rather than to render a judgment.

4. Approaches to evaluation must take account of specific features of ICAI development. Rather than waiting for the completed development, the evaluation team can assist in some decision making related to instruction or utilization. While this sounds easy, it depends on the view that "outsiders" know psychology or performance measurement in ways that may be useful to ICAI experts. We need to overcome the "not invented here" syndrome.

5. Evaluation needs to be componential and focus on the utility of the piece of software under development. Records of rapid prototyping and redesign need to be integrated into the formative evaluation. It is as useful to record the blind alleys as the successes.

6. Evaluation needs to be responsible and responsive. Objectivity must be preserved, but at the same time, those evaluated must not feel victimized. A reasonably positive example occurred in the formative evaluation of PROUST (Baker et al., 1985). Among the most interesting phases of that activity was the dialogue following the submission of the draft of the report to Soloway. Through an interactive process, the evaluation report was strengthened, fuller understanding of the intentions and accomplishments of the project staff were developed, and points of legitimate disagreement were identified. In all cases, the AI expert was able to present (directly quoted) his point of view. The overall outcome was that the fairness of the report was not questioned.

ARTIFICIAL INTELLIGENCE AND TEST DEVELOPMENT

Although AI has a number of branches that may have educational implications (e.g., work in vision to assist the handicapped student), our interest in this section of our chapter will focus on the processes related to the design of expert systems and intelligent computer-assisted instruction (ICAI) as they may help to improve test design. We believe that this technology has enormous implications for the creation of rigorous test materials in the future. Expert systems provide an opportunity for specific knowledge domains to be identified, structured, and incorporated into computer software, while efforts in cognitive science have focused on alternative forms of representing such knowledge accurately and completely.

The expertise of "expert" systems sometimes comes from comparing the problem-solving approaches of skilled people and attempting to represent them within the computer, thus allowing the computer to perform tasks with equivalent expertise (although often with greater speed and reliability). The techniques to represent knowledge developed for AI expert systems could potentially be used in the vexing problems of assuring full content representation on tests. Because content of tests (especially those commercially produced) varies enormously in depth, comprehensiveness, and accuracy (Baker & Quellmalz, 1980; Burstein, Baker, Aschbacher, & Keesling, 1985; Floden, Freeman, Porter, & Schmidt, 1980; Herman & Cabello, 1983), using a knowledge representation approach may in itself be a contribution for test development, even without incorporating it as part of a complex, computer-delivered system. Content sampling, and theory in support of it, is an area of continuing weakness in many test development activities, particularly those which are locally based.

Knowledge representation is the core of any ICAI system. It focuses on what is the principal data base of interest, which is a knowledge base. Since expert systems combine the idea of knowledge base and representation with the expert's "wisdom," pertinent issues to this area in the testing field are: (1) who are the experts (subject matter specialists, teachers, test developers) and (2) what options are available for eliciting and representing knowledge in a field. To the first issue, two different approaches have been reported. One has the expert create a unique knowledge base relevant to a particular subject matter domain. These domains are usually quite narrow (such as particular microcircuitry) rather than similar to school subject matter (English literature). Thus, the question of extension of this approach to real school-based learning is at issue. Another possibility is the use of so-called expert tools. EMYCIN, (Heuristic Programming Project, Stanford), ROSIE (Rand Corporation), ART (Inference Corporation) and KEE (Intellicorp) are examples of systems designed to aid the efficient development of the knowledge base without specifying subject matter (Richer, 1985). More recently, tools have been created for personal computer environments, for example, M-1 (Teknowledge) and NEXPERT. These options may permit development of content for test and item generation. UCLA is currently exploring the feasibility of using tools of this sort to represent school subject matter.

A second concern in AI related to assessment is representing the range of errors for diagnostic and instructional improvement purposes. Here, the work on Intelligent Computer-assisted Instruction comes into play. ICAI depends on the creation of a student model, a representation of the pattern of responses individual students make and a comparison of either their performance with expert problem-solving strategies or a bug catalog. The latter is a collection of incorrect procedures or "bugs," particularly as they apply to identifying micro errors or larger misconceptions (Johnson & Soloway, 1987). We believe this technology may be useful for the generation of wrong-answer alternatives. Also relevant to this area is how test formats and psychometric quality get into such a system. Researchers at the Educational Testing Service (Freedle, 1985) have done some exploratory work on item generation, using AI-based environments, presumed to be an improvement over non-AI assisted computer generation of test item formats.

We believe that the next 5 years will result in research which addresses overall how developments in ICAI can support the creation of test development systems. Such research will need to synthesize the science and application base, estimate the feasibility of building all or pieces of such a system, and to create small prototypes.

The AI Test Developer: A Developmental History

At UCLA, work began in 1985 on exploring the feasibility of an AI Test Developer. The original goal for the AI Developer was fairly grandiose. We were looking for a technology to decentralize testing—to pull some (but not all) of the responsibility of test design and publishing away from large, commercial entities and place sufficient testing expertise in the hands of the local educator. The benefits of such a system would be large. First, at least some fraction of school-administered tests would be consistent with local views of curriculum and responsive to instructional experiences of students. Second, earlier research at UCLA (See, for example, Herman & Dorr–Bremme, 1983; Baker, 1976) suggests that standardized test information is a relatively unused commodity in teachers' decision-making practices. However, teachers report that their own tests provide the basis for data-driven instructional decisions. An AI Test Developer could provide the needed expertise and efficiency for teachers in the design of their own measures. Such a system would obviate the high cost of training teachers in test development (see Baker, 1978, Baker, Polin, & Barry, 1980; Rudman et al. 1980), and should allow local teachers, district administrators and curriculum personnel, state managers, and private test developers to create tests that meet local curriculum needs. Such a global "expert" would fill in deficient competencies of personnel, whether in item generation, quantitative analyses, or test interpretation. Of most interest are the two ICAI features mentioned earlier: the content domain issue ad the assessment of student errors.

Critical Components in the Test Developer.   At the outset, the AI Developer was conceived as a complex, interacting system. However, a set of practical decisions modified the view. First, we decided to use commercially available expert system tools for the implementation of the developer. Secondly, we decided to constrain development hardware to likely user hardware in the short term (3 to 5 years) and limit ourselves to software compatible with personal computers in school districts and schools. Third, with a relatively scant set of resources, we decided to explore what expertise (other than the main test design function) was needed. Interviews with school district evaluation managers, personnel in private test development, and academic experts in achievement measurement provided an extensive list of discrete topics. Our focus then shifted from developing an integrated, memory-eating monster to a set of test expert associates: the Test Expert Associate System (TEAS). During 1987, the first prototype of TEAS was undertaken with the expertise represented of Ronald Hambleton of the University of Massachusetts. Using the M–1 expert tool, Hambleton dealt with the problem of the reliability of criterion-referenced tests. Following the complete encoding of the rules gleaned from Hambleton, the system will be presented a set of problems to solve and its answers will be validated by independent trials by Hambleton and two other psychometric experts. Then the system will be tested by school district personnel in order to document the utility of the format, the comprehensiveness of the advice, and their reaction to the system itself. At the same time, we carefully tracked time and cost of the design of the TEAS prototype to determine the feasibility of subsequent effort.

With a short lag, a second TEAS module is under development. Here it is the intent to attempt to represent a part of school subject matter in order to determine whether it can be used as a generation context for test items. We have selected speeches from American History, particularly the Lincoln–Douglas debates. We are interested in whether the original idea of the test developer (as an item generator) can be implemented in a low-cost environment. We are also interested in seeing whether we can find a way to use the TEAS component to help us generate criteria for adequate student essay responses, another critical measurement problem. The TEAS work is in process and will undoubtedly be affected by advances in software, predisposition to technology use, and research in cognitive science. An area of intense interest for us will be the future developments in natural language interfaces and understanding. To the extent that the natural language field matures, testing may become less circumscribed, constrained, and formal and its development more distributed. We still feel we have the right goal (although, like ICAI designers, we view it as a context rather than a product to be engineered), the development of a system that uses school subject matter knowledge bases, a system that could be standardized and shared. Assessment devices would grow from these knowledge bases and might differ in symbolic representation presented or elicited from the learner and capitalize on student individual differences.

Conclusion

We have attempted to take a Janus view—of the ICAI field on the one hand and measurement and evaluation on the other. We have described how evaluation and measurement might be useful to the improvement of ICAI design and function and have provided the few examples from our own work. We have also discussed new work in progress on the application of AI technology (TEAS) for the intermediate good of educational quality, as a resource to improve the measurement of achievement. Neither of these areas, either ICAI- or AI-based measurement has a secure future. They may merely be side-trips on a longer, more important educational journey. Of importance, however, is to analyze the processes involved in their development, and keep the good ideas. By taking both critical and empirical perspectives, we may be able to find productive, perhaps technological ways to our diverse educational goals.

ACKNOWLEDGEMENT

The research reported herein was supported in part by Air Force Human Resources Laboratory, Army Research Institute for the Behavioral and Social Sciences, NASA Jet Propulsion Laboratory, Navy Training Systems Center, Office of Technology Assessment, Advance Design Information and The U. S. Department of Education/Office of Educational Research and Improvement. However, the views, opinions and/or findings contained in this report are the authors' and should not be construed as an official department position, policy or decision, unless so designated by other official documentation. Critical assistance in the use of the M–1 expert tool was provided by Dean Slawson and Zhonmin Li.

REFERENCES

Alessi, S. M., & Trollip, S. R. (1985). *Computer-based instruction: Methods and development.* Englewood Cliffs, NJ: Prentice–Hall.

Anderson, R. J., Boyle, C. F., & Reiser, B. J. (1985). Intelligent tutoring systems. *Science, 228,* 456–462.

Baker, E. L. (1974). Formative evaluation in instruction. In J. Popham (Ed.), *Evaluation in education.* Berkeley, CA: McCutchan.

Baker, E. L. (1976). *The evaluation of the California Early Childhood Education Program* (Vol. 1). Los Angeles: UCLA Center for the Study of Evaluation.

Baker, E. L. (1978). The evaluation and research of multi-project programs: Program component analysis. *Studies in Educational Evaluation.* Tel Aviv University, Israel.

Baker, E. L., & Alkin, M. C. (1973). Formative evaluation in instructional development. *AV Communication Review, 21*(4).

Baker, E. L., Bradley, C., Aschbacher, P., & Feifer, R. (1985). *Intelligent computer-assisted instruction (ICAI) study.* Final Report to Jet Propulsion Laboratory. Los Angeles: UCLA Center for the Study of Evaluation.

Baker, E. L., & Herman, J. L. (1983). Task structure design: Beyond linkage. *Journal of Educational measurement, 20*(2), 149–164.

Baker, E. L., & Herman, J. L. (1985). Educational evaluation: Emergent needs for research. *Evaluation Comment, 7*(2).

Baker, E. L., & Linn, R. L. (1986, April). *New testing technologies.* Sherman Oaks, CA: Advance Design Information, Inc.

Baker, E. L., & O'Neil, H. F., Jr. (1987). Assessing instructional outcomes. In R. M. Gagné (Ed.), *Instructional Technology: Foundations*. Hillsdale, NJ: Lawrence Erlbaum Associates.

Baker, E. L., Polin, L., & Burry, J. (1980). *Making, choosing, and using tests: A practicuum on domain-referenced tests*. Report to the National Institute of Education. Los Angeles: UCLA Center for the Study of Evaluation.

Baker, E. L., & Quellmalz, E. (1980). *Educational testing and evaluation: Design, analysis and policy*. Beverly Hills, CA: Sage.

Baker, E. L., & Saloutos, W. A. (1974). *Formative evaluation of instruction*. Los Angeles: UCLA Center for the Study of Evaluation.

Barr, A., & Feigenbaum, E. A. (Eds.). (1982). *The handbook of artificial intelligence* (Vol. 2). Los Altos, CA: William Kaufmann.

Bloom, B. S. (1984 June/July). The 2 Sigma problem: The search for methods of group instruction as effective as one-to-one tutoring. *Educational Researcher, 13*(6).

Bobrow, D. G., & Stefik, M. (1983). *The LOOPS manual*. Palo Alto, CA: Xerox.

Bright, J. R. (1968). *Research, development, and technical innovation—An introduction*. Homewood, IL: Richard D. Irwin.

Brown, J. S., & Burton, R. R. (1978). Diagnostic models for procedural bugs in basic mathematical skills. *Cognitive Science, 2*, 155–192.

Brown, J. S., Burton, R. R., & de Kleer, J. (1982). Knowledge engineering and pedagogical techniques in Sophie I, II, and III. In D. Sleeman & J. S. Brown (Eds.), *Intelligent tutoring systems*. New York: Academic Press.

Buchanan, B. G. (1981). *Research on expert systems*. Report number CS–81–837, Computer Science Department, Stanford University, Stanford, CA.

Burstein, L., Baker, E. L., Aschbacher, P., & Keesling, J. K. (1985). *Using state test data for national indicators of educational quality: A feasibility study*. Los Angeles: UCLA Center for the Study of Evaluation.

Burton, R. R., & Brown, J. S. (1982). An investigation of computer coaching for informal learning activities. In D. Sleeman & J. S. Brown (Eds.), *Intelligent tutoring systems*. New York: Academic Press.

Carbonell, J. R., & Collins, A. (1973). Natural semantics in artificial intelligence. *International Journal of Computer Aided Instruction, 3*, 344–352.

Carr, B., & Goldstein, I. P. (1977). *Overlays: A theory of modeling for computer aided instruction*. (Artificial Intelligence Memo 406). Cambridge, MA: MIT.

Carroll, J. M., & Rosson, M. B. (1984). *Usability specifications as a tool in interactive development* (Research Report RC 10437, No. 46642, 4/3/84). Yorktown Heights, NY: IBM Watson Research Center, Computer Science Department.

Chi, M. T. H., Bassok, M., Lewis, M. W., Reimann, P., & Glaser, R. (1987, November). *Self-explanations: How students study and use examples in learning to solve problems* (Tech. Rep. No. 9). University of Pittsburgh, Learning Research and Development Center.

Chi, M. T. H., Glaser, R., & Rees, E. (1982). Expertise in problem solving. In R. J. Sternberg (Ed.), *Advances in the psychology of human intelligence* (Vol. 1, pp. 7–76). Hillsdale, NJ: Lawrence Erlbaum Associates.

Clancey, W. J. (1979). Tutorial rules for guiding a case method dialogue. *International journal of Man-Machine Studies, 11*, 25–50.

Clancy, W. J. (1981). *The epistemology of a rule-based expert system: A framework for explanation* (Report No. CA 81–896). Computer Science Department, Stanford University, Stanford, CA.

Clancy, W. J. (1982). Tutoring rules for guiding a case method dialogue. In D. Sleeman & J. S. Brown (Eds.), *Intelligence tutoring systems*. London: Academic Press.

Clement, J., Lockhead, J., & Soloway, E. (1980). *Positive effects of computer programming on students' understanding of variables and equations*. Proceedings of the National Association for Computing Machinery, Nashville, TN.

Corno, L., & Snow, R. E. (1986). Adapting teaching to individual differences among learners. In M. C. Wittrock (Ed.), *Handbook of research on teaching* (3rd ed.). New York: Macmillan.

Duda, R. O., & Gaschnig, J. G. (1981). Knowledge-based expert systems come of age. *BYTE, 6,* 238–281.

Ellis, J., Wulfeck, W. H., & Fredericks, P. S. (1979). *The instructional quality inventory: II. User's manual.* (NPRDC SR 79–24). San Diego: Navy Personnel Research and Development Center. (AD–A083–678).

Fletcher, J. D. (1985). Intelligent instructional systems in training. In S. A. Andriole (Ed.), *Applications in artificial intelligence.* Princeton, NJ: Petrocelli.

Floden, R. E., Freeman, D. J., Porter, A. C., & Schmidt, W. H. (1980). Don't they all measure the same thing? Consequences of selecting standardized tests. In E. L. Baker & E. Quellmalz (Eds.), *Design analysis and policy in testing and evaluation.* Beverly Hills, CA: Sage.

Freedle, R. (1985). *Implications of language programs in artificial intelligence for testing issues.* (Final Report, Project 599–63). Princeton, NJ: Educational Testing Service.

Gaschnig, J., Klahr, P., Pople, H., Shortliffe, E., & Terry, A. (1983). Evaluation of expert systems: Issues and case studies. In F. Hayes–Roth, D. A. Waterman, & D. B. Lenat (Eds.), *Building expert systems.* Reading, MA: Addison–Wesley.

Gamble, A., & Page, C. V. (1980). *IJ Man-Machine Studies, 12,* 259–282.

Glennan, T. K., Jr. (1967). Issues in the choice of development policies. In T. Manschak, T. K. Glennan, Jr., & R. Summers (Eds.), *Strategies for research and development.* New York: Springer–Verlag.

Hayes–Roth, B. (1980). *Human planning processes* (Report No. R–2670). Rand Corp., Santa Monica, CA.

Hedl, J. J., Jr., & O'Neil, H. F., Jr. (1977). Reduction of state anxiety via instructional design in computer-based learning environments. In J. Seiber, H. F. O'Neil, Jr., & S. Tobias, (Eds.), *Anxiety, learning and instruction.* New York: Lea/Wiley.

Herman, J., & Cabello, B. (1983). *An analysis of the match between the California Assessment Program and commonly used standardized tests.* Los Angeles: UCLA Center for the Study of Evaluation.

Herman, J., & Dorr–Bremme, D. (1983). Uses of testing in the schools: A national profile. *New Directions for Testing and Measurement.* (No. 19). San Francisco: Jossey–Bass.

Hively, W., Patterson, J., & Page, S. (1968). A "universe defined" system of arithmetic achievement testing. *Journal of Educational measurement, 5*(4), 275–290.

Hollan, J. D., Hutchins, E. L., & Weitzman, L. (1984). STEAMER: An interactive inspectable simulation-based training system. *Artificial Intelligence magazine, 5,* 15–27.

Johnson, W. L., & Soloway, E. (1983). *PROUST: Knowledge-based program understanding.* (Report No. 285). Computer Science Department, Yale University, New Haven, CT.

Johnson, W. L., & Soloway, E. (1987). PROUST: An automatic debugger for PASCAL programs. In G. P. Kearsley (Ed.), *Artificial intelligence: Applications and methodology.* Reading, MA: Addison–Wesley.

Kieras, D. E., & Bovair, S. (1983). *The role of a mental model in learning to operate a device* (Technical Rep. No. 13 RZ/DP/TR–83/ONR–13). University of Arizona, Tucson, Department of Psychology.

Lea, W. (Ed.). (1980). *Trends in speech recognition.* Englewood Cliffs, NJ: Prentice–Hall.

Markle, S. M. (1967). Empirical testing of programs. In P. C. Lange (Ed.), *Programmed instruction.* Sixty-sixth yearbook of the National Society for the Study of Education, Part II. University of Chicago Press.

McArthur, D., Stasz, C., Hotta, J. (1987). Learning problem-solving skills in algebra. *Journal of Educational Technology Systems, 15*(3), 303–324.

Merrill, M. D., & Tennyson, R. D. (1977). *Teaching concepts: An instructional design guide.* Englewood Cliffs, NJ: Educational Technology Publications.

Merrill, P. F., Tolman, M. N., Christensen, L., Hammons, K., Vincent, B. R., & Reynolds, P. L. (1986). *Computers in educatino.* Englewood Cliffs, NJ: Prentice–Hall.

O'Neil, H. F., Jr. (Ed.). (1979). *Procedures for instructional systems development.* New York: Academic Press.

O'Neil, H. F., Jr., Anderson, C. L., & Freeman, J. A. (1986). Research in teaching in the Armed Forces. In M. C. Wittrock (Ed.), *Handbook of research on teaching* (3rd ed.). New York: Macmillan.

O'Neil, H. F., Jr., & Paris, J. (1981). Introduction and overview of computer-based instruction. In H. F. O'Neil, Jr. (Ed.), *Computer-based instruction.* New York: Academic Press.

O'Neil, H. F., Jr., Slawson, D. A., & Baker, E. L. (1987). *First application's domain-independent and domain-specific instructional strategies for knowledge bases,* August 31. Sherman Oaks, CA: Advance Design Information, Inc.

O'Neil, H. F., Jr., & Spielberger, C. D. (Eds.). (1979). *Cognitive and affective learning strategies.* New York: Academic Press.

Park, P., Perez, R. S., & Seidel, R. J. (1987). Intelligent CAI: Old wine in new bottles or a new vintage? In G. P. Kearsley (Ed.), *Artificial intelligence: Applications and methodology.* Reading, MA: Addison–Wesley.

Reigeluth, C. M. (1983). Instructional design: What is it and why is it? In C. M. Reigeluth, (Ed.), *Instructional-design theories and models: An overview of their current status.* Hillsdale, NJ: Lawrence Erlbaum Associates.

Reigeluth, C. M. (Ed.). (1987). *Instructional theories in action: Lessons illustrating selected theories and models.* Hillsdale, NJ: Lawrence Erlbaum Associates.

Richer, M. H. (1985). *Evaluating the existing tools for developing knowledge-based systems* (Knowledge Systems Laboratory Report No. KSL 85–19). Stanford, CA: Stanford University, Stanford Knowledge Systems Laboratory.

Rudman et al. (1980). *Integrating assessment with instruction: A review 1922–1980* (Research Series, No. 75). East Lansing, MI: Institute for Research on Teaching.

Schank, R. C. (1980). Language and memory. *Cognitive Science, 4,* 243–284.

Scriven, M. (1967). The methodology of evaluation. In R. W. Tyler, R. M. Gagné, & M. Scriven (Eds.), *Perspectives of curriculum evaluation. AERA Monograph Series on Curriculum Evaluation, No. 1.* Chicago: Rand McNally.

Sternberg, R. (Ed.). (1982). *Advances in the psychology of human intelligence.* Hillsdale, NJ: Lawrence Erlbaum Associates.

Stevens, A. L., Collins, A., & Goldin, S. (1978). *Diagnosing students' misconceptions in causal models* (Report No. 3786). Cambridge, MA, Bolt, Beranek, & Newman.

Stevens, A., & Steinberg, C. (1981). *Project STEAMER,* NPRDC Technical Note No. 82–21. San Diego, CA: Navy Personnel Research and Development Center.

Weinstein, C. F., & Mayer, R. F. (1986). The teaching of learning strategies. In M. C. Wittrock (Ed.), *Handbook of research on teaching* (3rd ed.). New York: Macmillan.

Wenger, E. (1987). *Artificial intelligence and tutoring systems.* Los Altos, CA: Morgan.

Winston, P. H. (Ed.). (1975). *The psychology of computer vision.* New York: McGraw–Hill.

Winston, P. H. (1977). *Artificial intelligence.* Reading, MA: Addison–Wesley.

Woods, W. A. (1983). What's important about knowledge representation? *Computer, 16,* 22–29.

9 Legal Issues in Computerized Psychological Testing

Donald N. Bersoff
Hahnemann University and Villanova University School of Law

Paul J. Hofer
Federal Judicial Center, Washington, DC

A decade ago a scholar writing in a legal journal asked the question, "Can/ Should Computers Replace Judges?" (D'Amato, 1977). The article explored problems involved in developing computer systems capable of making the difficult assessments and judgments required in judicial decision making. In discussing these problems, the author quoted extensively from Joseph Weizenbaum, who in a well-known critique of computerized psychotherapy, sagely asserted, "Since we do not now have any ways of making computers wise, we ought not now to give computers tasks that demand wisdom" (Weizenbaum, 1976). Nevertheless, the legal scholar concluded that any humanistic misgivings about computerized decision making are, at least for many kinds of functions performed by judges, outweighed by the considerable savings in time and money the new expert systems can provide.

If this volume had been published a decade earlier, we might have raised a comparable question: Can/should computers replace psychologists in the administration and interpretation of psychological tests? But that question is now moot. Computers already have replaced psychologists in many routine aspects of assessment. Computerized psychological testing (CPT) is making significant inroads in educational evaluation, personnel selection, occupational counseling, and mental health diagnosis. There is little doubt that computers will generate new methods of assessment in the foreseeable future.

Yet the question of whether CPT *should* replace psychologists has only recently received the attention given the question of *how* CPT might do so. Coincidental with the rise of computer-testing technology is the countervailing trend toward greater scrutiny of test use, particularly in employment and educational settings (Bersoff, 1983). We must carefully examine CPT to ensure that it does not unnecessarily create any new legal problems for testing, and in fact contributes to a high level of scientific and ethical merit in psychological testing practice.

As we have indicated elsewhere (Hofer & Bersoff, 1983), computerized tests may be vulnerable to many of the same legal attacks as conventional tests. Claims of cultural bias and other forms of unfairness are the predominant source of litigation involving tests, and such claims are likely to continue with any test showing disproportionate adverse impact on minorities or women, regardless of method of administration or interpretation. Although some types of litigation may become less likely by the switch to computers, especially challenges to the standardization and procedural regularity of the administration of the test itself, CPT could conceivably lead to new legal problems for developers and practitioners. A leading editorial in *Science* predicted a "flood of litigation involving unqualified users" of computerized tests (Matarazzo, 1983, p. 323).

THE LEGAL PROFESSION'S RESPONSE TO CPT

To this point, it is not so much a flood as a trickle. There is, to date, only one reported case even tangentially involving unqualified use of CPT that we have discovered (*United States v. Curtis,* 1974) and that case, while having its own intrinsic interest, is irrelevant to our concerns. The defendant advertised a "Computer Matching Institute" dating service, where couples were to be paired through testing by qualified psychologists and prompt computer processing. In fact, the defendant did not have the intent or capacity to match applications by computer or expert psychological testing, and simply hired clerks to match applications by hand. The court found a clear basis for a criminal indictment for fraud.

There is now one reported case directly concerned with CPT which is germane to those mental health professionals who purchase software for scoring and interpreting psychological tests. We discuss that case at some length in the section on intellectual property, which appears later in this chapter. Aside from that, the most interesting treatment of some of the legal issues raised by CPT is found in two advisory opinions written by state attorneys general.

The attorney general of Georgia (Unofficial Opinion, 1983) was asked by a judge of a county juvenile court if the interpretation of psychological tests administered to juveniles might be computerized. Apparently the judge was sufficiently concerned and unsure of the implications of CPT that an outside legal opinion was sought. The attorney general found no legal barriers to computerizing the testing process, so long as adequate steps were taken to protect the confidentiality of juvenile records, in this instance, by disguising the names of examinees so that no identifying information appeared in the computerized records. The replacement of names with identification codes before entry into electronic memory is common practice among testing companies and, along with safeguards required for all clinical material, should protect the confidentiality rights of clients. The opinion, however, does raise the concern that CPT might infringe unduly on the fundamental right to be protected against governmental "disclosure of personal matters" (*Whalen v. Roe,* 1977, p. 599).

In Kansas, the state board charged with licensing and regulating psychologists requested an opinion on several issues raised by CPT. One question is of great interest to many clinicians—whether CPT may be used by professions other than psychology. The Kansas attorney general (Attorney General Opinion, 1983), interpreting that state's laws, found nothing to prevent use of CPT by others if such use was consistent with their training and with their profession's code of ethics, and if they did not hold themselves or their work out to the public as "psychology" or "psychological." This issue is likely to be a continuing source of concern, and resolution may vary from state to state. For the most part, test developers and marketers have refrained voluntarily from providing clinical tests to nonpsychologists, but some CPT services have been less circumspect. A thoughtful analysis by state legislatures and professional organizations, such as the American Psychological Association (which has been studying the general problem of test user qualifications), of the responsibilities of CPT developers and users is required to protect the interests of the public.

Another issue raised in the Kansas attorney general's opinion is whether the signing, by a psychologist, of a report actually generated by a computer could be construed as "taking credit for work not personally performed." Such a finding is evidence, under Kansas law, of "lack of good moral character," and could lead to revocation or suspension of the psychologist's certification. The attorney general concluded that the mere signing of the report does not, ipso facto, violate the provision, but that the entire report and surrounding circumstances would have to be examined to see if it would appear, to the average person, that the psychologist was representing the report as his or her own work product. It seems unlikely that a psychologist who reviews and endorses a report without any attempt to deceive others into believing the report was personally written would be found lacking in good moral character. But practices such as retyping reports as part of an effort to appear to have written the report personally may be looked upon unfavorably by regulatory boards. The new APA guidelines on computer testing (APA, 1986), which we will discuss more fully, make clear that there is a considerable role for the clinician using CPT services without pretending that the cookbook interpretations generated by the computer represent the user's personal insights.

As with any other system where important interests of the examinee are at stake, CPT developers, marketers, and users must assure that tests are responsibly administered, scientifically sound and sensitive to ethical issues of fairness, privacy, and professional responsibility. Though most litigation involving tests has been in the context of employment or education, clinical tests may not escape judicial scrutiny. There are many cases concerning medical diagnostic tests, such as blood tests, which were negligently conducted and led to treatment decisions detrimental to clients. The analogy between these and psychological tests may be even more compelling for computerized tests, since CPT appears more technical and scientific than the traditional subjective interpretation of clinical tests. Therefore, the same rules of negligence as are applied to laboratory tests could be applied to CPT.

PSYCHOLOGY'S RESPONSE TO CPT

The threat of litigation is one of the reasons it is important to build a consensus about the requirements of good practice for developing and using CPT. This work involves not only analyzing the scientific and ethical issues, but also formalizing this consensus into written standards, into contracts among practitioners and testing services, and into state laws and regulations. Some of the issues are not strictly scientific or ethical but represent the profession's pragmatic judgment about the best way to allocate the burdens and risks of CPT among the different professionals engaged in developing, marketing, and using computerized tests.

Though professional standards do not have the force of law, they do play an important role in actions for professional negligence. In these malpractice actions, one of several points a plaintiff must prove is that the practitioner violated the prevailing "standard of care." The standard of care is usually placed in evidence through the testimony of expert witnesses who rely on their own opinion, current research, scholarly publications, and documents developed by relevant professional and scientific associations. If the plaintiff can show that the test user, developer, or publisher violated the standard of care (plus the other components of a malpractice claim), the plaintiff prevails. Violations may occur, for example, through negligent entry of data, the selection of a system that the psychologist should know is inappropriate for the client, creating unreasonable risks as a result, or through unreasonable reliance and interpretation of the information gleaned from CPT (Nimmer, 1985). Conversely, if the defendant can show that he or she conformed with the standard of care there is a greatly increased probability that no liability will be found.

In addition to their use in legal actions, professional standards can serve as rules of conduct binding on members of the professional organization adopting the standards. Failure to conform to them subjects members to censure by professional ethics committees and, perhaps, delicensure by the state. Alternatively, standards can be adopted as purely aspirational guidelines. APA/AERA/NCME Test Standards (1985) distinguish between those that are primary and should be followed in the absence of sound professional reasons not to do so and those that are secondary and more advisory and aspirational. Any CPT-specific guidelines must have a clearly stated purpose, and the obligations they create for APA members must be explicit.

There are several sources of ethical guidelines relevant to CPT. The APA first adopted interim standards of "Automated Test Scoring and Interpretation Practices" more than 20 years ago (APA, 1966). In addition, the 1974 Standards for Educational and Psychological Tests (APA, AERA, NCME, 1974), the revised 1985 Standards (APA, 1985), the 1977 *Standards for Providers of Psychological Services* (APA, 1977) and its recently adopted revision, the General Guidelines for Providers of Psychological Services (APA, 1987), as well as the 1981 *Specialty Guidelines for the Delivery of Services,* (APA, 1981) all contain references to computerized assessment. However, in these latter documents, many CPT issues are subsumed under general standards applicable to all types of testing or psychological practices and the specific implications for CPT may not be clear.

Several state associations and private groups have tackled the problem of CPT-specific standards. For example, the Colorado Psychological Association has adopted recommended "Guidelines for the Use of Computerized Testing Services" (Colorado Psychological Association, 1982) and the Kansas Psychological Association has apparently done so as well (Petterson, 1983). A group of respected psychometricians working on the implementation of an adaptive version of the Armed Services Vocational Aptitude Battery, produced some "Technical Guidelines for Assessing Computerized Adaptive Tests," (Green, Bock, Humphreys, Linn, & Reckase, 1984). A book (Schwartz, 1984) on the use of computers in clinical practice contains several chapters (e.g., Zachary & Pope, 1984) addressing ethical issues. Many articles addressing the need for standards are appearing in the psychological literature (e.g., Skinner & Pakula, 1986; Matarazzo, 1986, in press; Burke & Normand, 1985; Hofer & Green, 1985). The present authors prepared a document (Hofer & Bersoff, 1983), "Standards for the Administration and Interpretation of Computerized Psychological Testing," for a testing service concerned about the void left by the absence of adequate guidelines.

Given all these sources, many observers have seen the need for organizing the issues unique to CPT under more specific, official, and national standards. The American Psychological Association's Board of Directors in January, 1984, instructed the Committee on Professional Standards and the Committee on Psychological Tests and Assessment to develop guidelines specific to CPT. These guidelines, having gone through several revisions and review by the APA governance, were adopted by the APA Council of Representatives in February, 1986. Importantly, at this point, the guidelines are considered advisory. After they have been tested in the real world, the APA may wish to revise them once again and make them binding standards. For now these guidelines are the clearest statement of the requirements of good practice, and professionals should familiarize themselves with them. Hofer (1985) and Hofer and Green (1985) provide an overview and discussion.

RIGHTS AND RESPONSIBILITIES OF PROFESSIONALS

Should there be any legal challenge to the administration, interpretation, and decisions related to computer-based tests, both the testing service and the test user are likely to be named as defendants. Both may be ultimately liable, either as joint wrongdoers or as individuals each responsible for their own negligence. In such cases, it might appear that clinicians could rely on a defense that they were ignorant of the underlying bases for the interpretations they accepted and passed along to their clients. But, such a defense would be an admission that the clinician violated the APA Ethical Principles and engaged in professional negligence. The *Ethical Principles of Psychologists,* Principle 8(e) (APA, 1981, p. 637) states: "Psychologists offering scoring and interpretation services are able to produce appropriate evidence for the validity of the programs and procedures used in arriving at interpretations."

Conversely, testing services will probably not be able to place the entire blame on the user for injurious decisions resulting from negligent interpretations, and they could be held liable under a number of legal theories. Placing the responsibility for the validity of reports entirely on the user might erode the usefulness of CPT as reviewing the validity of each interpretive statement could be comparable with writing the entire report oneself, and most people use CPT to save time and effort. Actuarial interpretations and statistical predictions of behavior are best made using the power of the computer to summarize empirical relations. Interpretations that can be validated empirically should be. Predictive validation is often legally required when selecting applicants for jobs, and it should be encouraged for other important interpretations, such as treatment recommendations and prognoses. In cases where interpretations are based on empirical findings rather than clinical judgment, and where the clinician has no additional reason to believe the finding is invalid for that test taker, it may be better for practitioners to accept the computerized interpretation without alteration.

These considerations suggest that some division of labor and responsibility between developer and user must be found. The gist of the APA guidelines is: The validity and reliability of the computerized version of a test should be established by the developer, but CPT interpretations should be used only in conjunction with professional review. This rather general principle might be elaborated into a more specific assignment of responsibilities. The developer seems in the best position to assure that the scales and research on which the report is based are not obsolete or otherwise inadequate. Actuarially based interpretations should use the best research and statistical equations. Developers can stay abreast of relevant research, incorporate new findings into the system, and direct practitioners to research that may assist them in properly using the report. Users can then concentrate on overseeing the context of the testing and evaluating the appropriateness of the norms and validation studies used by the system for interpreting any particular client's scores. They can concentrate on gathering clinical information not used by the CPT system but relevant to clinical decision making. By specializing and working together, developers and users can assure the full advantages of CPT are realized.

For users to meet their responsibilities to review the validity of a CPT report for each test taker, they must have information about the interpretation system. They need to know how interpretations are derived from original item responses. Some of this information is best suited for inclusion in each report, and some can be included in a manual outlining general features of the interpretation system. A major potential conflict in CPT is the tension between users' needs for sufficient information to review reports, and developers' proprietary interest in their algorithms, software, and other business assets.

This conflict is real, but a satisfactory compromise may be available. The APA guidelines call for disclosure of "how interpretations are derived" and information on "the nature of the relationship" between scores and interpretations. Users need not know all the decision rules and algorithms used by the testing service, but they must know enough to review any report they actually use. For this type of review it would be helpful to know the examinee's score on relevant tests or scales, or the entire matrix of responses. The clinician must be informed of the research or clinical evidence used to make the interpretations. Ideally, the link between scores and interpretations would be made explicit by indicating which statements are derived from which scales. Users can then review the validity of the inference from test score to interpretation, based on their own knowledge of the test, validation research, and the examinee. In cases where interpretations are clinically based, users must have information needed to weigh the credibility of the expert. The names and credentials of these experts could be provided, along with their theoretical rationale.

In addition to the demands for disclosure created by the user's need for information to select a system and review reports, the traditions of science and scholarship require that some of the CPT enterprise be open to critical scrutiny. Independent critical review has been a special tradition in psychological testing, including CPT (Buros, 1978), and has helped maintain links between research and practice. The Buros–Nebraska Institute is mentioned specifically in the guidelines, and the APA has expressed a strong preference that the tradition of open and critical review of tests be maintained.

The guidelines stop short of requiring full access, however, calling instead for "adequate" disclosure and describing several methods reviewers might use to test a system without infringing on the developer's proprietary rights. For example, the guidelines call for free communication between reviewers and technically qualified and knowledgeable professional developers. They suggest that reviewers be given access to the system for "exercising" its components. The "general structure of the algorithms and the basis for transforming test responses into interpretive reports" should be made known (APA, 1986, p. 23). But the guidelines specifically exclude a requirement of access to the full library of interpretive statements or the specific values of cutting scores or configurations. The guidelines express the opinion that algorithms can usually be explained in enough detail without disclosing trade secrets. But if access to trade secrets is needed for adequate review, the testing service's rights should be protected through contracts between the service and scholar. Even though secrecy is crucial to maintaining one's usual rights under trade secret protection, properly drafted agreements can protect the information against disclosure by reviewers or employees.

INTELLECTUAL PROPERTY

The issue of disclosure of information about interpretive systems to practitioners and scholars is but one of many issues surrounding the ownership of intellectual property—copyrights, trade secrets, and patents. *Copyright* protects against the unauthorized reproduction of literary or other works. The printed questions in a test booklet or, in most cases, the object code of a CPT program are two examples. *Trade secrets* are generally defined as formulas, patterns, devices, or compilations of information used in one's business, giving the owner a competitive advantage over others who do not know or use them. The formula for a soft drink or a source code, kept in secret, by a CPT developer are two examples. *Patent law* protects novel processes, machines, and manufactured items and gives the owner of the patent a 17-year monopoly. Patents have been granted to some computerized processes, but the law in this area is so unsettled that most computer-law experts advise against using patent law to protect computer programs, at least for the foreseeable future (Remer, 1982).

There are several complex and unresolved legal problems related to copyright as well. Indeed, any litigation arising from the growth of CPT could create important legal precedents. As a precursor to these brief remarks, let us say—as a means of protecting ourselves—that we are offering a personal opinion on these matters and not legal advice on which readers should rely.

The debate about the copyright protection accorded computer-testing systems is, in important respects, a debate about software protection. What causes difficulties in the analysis of software protection is that software is both mechanical and symbolic. That is, a program installed on a computer is used to mechanically operate the machine, but the program itself only symbolically represents the hard-wiring of the machine. Software engineers do not build software, they write it. Because of this and because literary works are copyrightable, software has been argued to be suitable for copyright protection. Copyright law protects the computer program itself—the specific language of the program that can be expressed in human-readable symbols. How far the law goes or will go to protect other forms of the program—the object code, the appearance of the output display, or a flow chart of the logic, for example—is not completely settled (Mandel, 1984).

Object codes are created from source codes. Source codes are the program that the programmer writes—the computer instructions in a specific computer language. The object code is created from the source code and is usually printed as ones or zeros, the machine-readable instructions for the computer. As a practical matter, it is generally only the object code of a program that becomes available to the public and thus requires copyright protection. Flow charts and source codes can be held as trade secrets. The output and visual display of a program often reveals significant aspects of the underlying logic and information contained in a program. "Reverse engineering" can give competitors a head start in developing similar programs. It is unclear what protection, if any, copyright might offer against this. And, unlike patent law, copyright does not protect against independent discovery of the information or process.

Various forms of the computer program are but a part of the intellectual property needed to create and interpret tests. Other types of potential intellectual property involved in CPT are: (1) test questions and interpretive statements used to construct reports; (2) answer sheets and scoring keys; (3) norms or other data used for interpretation, and (4) classification systems, i.e., the algorithms used to assign interpretations to scale values or configurations of scale values. Each category of subject matter raises interesting and complex questions of ownership.

The actual statements contained in a test or the library of statements used to generate reports are clearly copyrightable subject matter. They are the expression of ideas, rather than the ideas themselves. They are "original works of authorship" as to which copyright protection subsists under the Federal Copyright Act of 1976 (17 U.S.C. § 102(a)), i.e., Volume 17 of The United States Code, the federal copyright laws. Accordingly, assuming the other requirements for copyright protection have been met, the copyright holder undoubtedly enjoys protection for the actual language used in the test statements and reports. Any copying of those statements, including the entering of the statements into a computer memory in digital form, could subject the copier to liability for copyright infringement. Copyright infringement consists of copying or substantial copying of copyright materials to which one has had access.

A thornier problem arises if paraphrases of statements are used. Whether copyright protection would extend to these paraphrases depends on the degree of similarity between the paraphrase and the original statement. It is impossible to assess in the abstract whether entering paraphrases would or would not violate any copyrights held by the publisher. As a general matter, the closer the relationship between the paraphrase and the original statement, the more likely it is that the paraphrase will be held to infringe the copyright in the original. An even more interesting question arises if a user simply puts in the number of the item on a program while the test taker has a copy of the test in front of him or her. There is no actual copying but we would imagine that test publishers would complain about this. If we were acting as a prudent counselor to a client, we would advise that there are significant risks in this regard in the absence of reasonable compensation to the publishers.

The particular form of answer sheet or scoring key is also subject to copyright protection. It would violate the law to make a photocopy or otherwise duplicate a copyrighted answer sheet and use it as one's own. However, a copyright in a particular answer sheet does not give the copyright holder an absolute right to control all possible forms of answer sheets for a test. Courts are likely to rule that one could develop one's own answer sheet for use in grading tests, unless the test was explicitly and exclusively designed in consumable format. There are several ways in which test publishers may be compensated for multiple administration of their tests. One way may be through licensing agreements. In those cases, use of the questions without compensation to the copyright holder of the test could be prohibited regardless of what form of answer sheet or scoring keys were used.

As a practical matter, answer sheets are needed only if one has access to the test. The computerization of testing may eventually preclude concerns raised by the present splitting of the components of testing into questions, answer sheets, and other separately copyrighted pieces. But for now, the information and processes required for testing and interpretation are accessible to the public in various forms and subject to varying protections under existing law. As a result, there are many difficult questions of ownership. For example, in the purely physical sense, the scoring key is the mechanical means of identifying significant responses on a test. But, in a fuller symbolic sense, it also represents a major part of the theoretical bases for interpretation of test responses, and thus is crucial to the usefulness of the test. Here the legal issues become murkier, and we need to draw distinctions between what the law says, what the legal system will probably do, and what we think the law should be.

The legal question is whether scoring keys are an "original work of authorship" within the meaning of 17 U.S.C. § 102(a), or whether it better falls under the terms of 17 U.S.C. § 102(b), which provides that:

> In no case does copyright protection for an original work of authorship extend to any idea, procedure, process, system, method of operation, concept, principle, or discovery, regardless of the form in which it is described, explained, illustrated, or embodied in such work (Copyright Act of 1976).

This provision seems to suggest the information contained in the scoring key is not copyrightable, although the format and design of the scoring key would be. That seems to us a good prediction of how courts will apply the law. But there may be reasoned disagreement about whether this is what the law should be.

Norms, reliability and validation research, and the cookbook classification schemes underlying many interpretive systems, raise similar problems as scoring keys. Whenever the work of *expressing* an idea or information, such as the percentile ranks of test scores in a population, is but a small part of the work of *discovering* or *establishing* that information, there is a tension between the protection, or lack of it, offered by current copyright law and the protection we may desire under some moral theory that would reward hard work and expenditure of time. Lawyers and psychologists have yet to sort out the rights of test authors in the theoretical rationale represented by a scoring or classification scheme, beyond its expression in a particular key or cookbook (which is clearly copyrightable), as well as the rights of researchers in the information contained in their findings, beyond its expression in a particular table or graph.

On the one hand, the language of § 102(b) and a literal interpretation of § 103(b) of the Copyright Act, which offers no exclusive protection for pre-existing material collected in a compilation of facts, suggest that the data expressed in tables of norms are not copyrightable subject matter. Norms are numerical figures that reflect the results of relevant calculations derived from standardization groups. They are, it could be argued, experimentally derived, discovered and pre-existing information, not original works of authorship. Under this interpretation, one could use norms published by a test publisher or researcher to score a computer-administered version of a test and to develop an original interpretive system and subsequent report without a copyright infringement. This approach seems consistent with academic traditions of wide and open dissemination of scientific knowledge without any proprietary constraints on use of the information.

On the other hand, one of the purposes of copyright law may be to encourage the discovery of useful information by offering protection to those who undertake the work, especially if they expend a great deal of time and energy in producing the work, the so-called "sweat of the brow" test. If such protection is not offered, people may be discouraged from doing the work, or do so only in secret. This would seriously inhibit scientific progress.

A recent case illustrates the uncertainty in this area of the law. In 1984, a federal district court in Illinois rendered a decision in *Rand McNally & Co. v. Fleet Management Systems, Inc.* (1984), holding that rearrangement of protected printed data, in this case mileage from one city to another, in computer form was not sufficient to circumvent allegations of infringement because of the great cost and energy expended in obtaining the original data. However, a year later, a court of appeals having jurisdiction over federal cases in Illinois ruled in another case, *Rockford Map Pub., Inc. v. Directory Service of Colorado, Inc.* (1985), that, "The copyright laws protect the work, not the amount of effort expended," that, "the input of time is irrelevant," and that copyright does not cover "the underlying information" (p. 148). In light of that decision, the defendant in *Rand McNally* successfully petitioned the Illinois federal district court to reconsider its 1984 decision. After reconsideration, in February, 1986, the court conceded that the reasoning of its 1984 decision would have been different if had been decided after *Rockford Map*.

However, the court ruled for the plaintiff on other grounds. The court acknowledged that facts, as opposed to their means of expression, are not copyrightable. However, the court asserted that the Rand McNally atlas was a copyrightable compilation of facts that was copied in its entirety into the data base by the defendant and the fact that the information had to be formatted to be useful for a particular computer or program was irrelevant. As a consequence, it was reasonable to find a copyright infringement (*Rand McNally & Co. v. Fleet Management Systems, Inc.*, 1986). Yet the court freely acknowledged that "The copyrightability of factual compilations . . . presents intellectual difficulties in determining where protectible copying of facts ends and unlawful copying of the compilation begins." It went on to say, "Case law and scholarly authority . . . only confirm the degree to which the courts are divided on the scope of copyright protection in this area" (p. 9). For confirmation of this assertion compare Patry (1985) with Denicola (1981).

In conventional testing, the publisher's time and expense in producing test materials and whatever other work they undertake to develop, such as norms and other data, are recaptured when the test user pays for the test materials and test booklets themselves. Researchers have been compensated, if at all, by working with or for publishers, or by other rewards of academic status and the like. But the economic conditions of academic life are changing (see, e.g., Shank, 1984), as is the competitive environment for test publishers. We should expect difficulties surrounding the ownership of intellectual property to continue until a new consensus concerning the rights of all the players has been established by science and the law.

There is now one judicial opinion concerning CPT which exemplifies the issues and the conflicts we have been discussing. The opinion is by no means definitive as it represents a single decision rendered by one federal court of appeals. However, it should be taken seriously, especially by small computer software vendors.

The case involves the University of Minnesota and National Computer Systems (NCS) as plaintiffs and Applied Innovations (AI), a software entrepreneur, as defendant. AI sold two software programs for scoring the Minnesota Multiphasic Personality Inventory (MMPI), the test at issue in this case. One contained 38 test statements gleaned from the MMPI, commonly known as the "Grayson Critical Items." The other program did not contain any test items but provided directions to the software user on how to copy the user's self-chosen MMPI test statements into the software program. Once the user typed in the statements, the copied statements that were answered by the client in the critical direction were printed, along with the report of the client's score.

The University of Minnesota and NCS, a private for-profit company licensed by the university to distribute MMPI test products and services, sued AI for copyright infringement, along with several other intellectual property and unfair competition claims. Among other issues were the copyrightability of the test statements, scoring data, and correlation tables.

With regard to the test statements, AI argued that because the test statements are short phrases, copied from prior works, and were only a small part of the 550 items, they were not due copyright protection. However, the trial court held that the MMPI test statements used by AI were copyrightable. The court said that the MMPI's authors "used sufficient creative intellectual labor" and significant independent intellectual effort" to create the test statements, thus satisfying the copyright law's originality requirement, even though the authors had relied on prior scales for the MMPI items (*Regents of the University of Minnesota v. Applied Innovations, Inc.*, 1987, p. 707).

More importantly, the court also held that the scoring direction, scale membership, and T-score conversion data for the various scales were protected by copyright as well. AI had argued that these scoring data were merely discovered facts (such as mileage between cities) and not copyrightable. The court said that "methods used to assess human characteristics or traits are not within the meaning of discovered facts. . . " (p. 708). The court further stated that the T-Score conversion data were not simply an accidental marriage between the raw score and an arbitrary value. Rather, it said, "the authors exercised significant judgment and creative intellectual effort in deciding which norming device to use" (p. 708) and should be accorded copyright protection as well.

Finally, the plaintiffs prevailed on their claim that its correlation tables were copyrightable. Compilations (the arranging, organizing, and selecting of previously existing material) can be copyrighted. However, the copyright protection is granted to the form of the compilation, not necessarily to the data themselves. The court agreed with the plaintiffs that the hard work associated with bringing together the data in tabular form was "sufficient to satisfy the originality requirement and justify copyright protection as a compilation." However, the court did not find that AI had infringed on the plaintiffs' tables as there was no proof supporting the allegation that AI has reproduced the information in the tables in the same arrangement as the plaintiffs.

Notwithstanding the court's finding concerning the correlation tables, AI lost on all other copyright issues. "AI copied everything of commercial significance with regard to scoring and interpreting the MMPI test" (p. 711), the court held. As a result, the court ordered AI to pay NCS more than $225,000 in damages. In a later hearing in early 1988, the court enjoined AI from reproducing or distributing software containing MMPI test statements, scale definitions and correction factors, and normative statements or *T*-score conversion data pending appeal of its decision by the defendant. The court also awarded an additional $162,000 in damages to the university. However, all monetary awards were suspended pending resolution of the appeal.

The Court of Appeals for the Eighth Circuit rendered its decision in May 1989, affirming virtually all of the trial court's ruling. The appellate tribunal agreed that the MMPI test statements were copyrightable, including the revisions of questions in preexisting tests, which the court called copyrightable "distinguishable variations" (p. 635), and that the normative test data were copyrightable as well as "expressions of facts or processes," although the court called it a "close question" (p. 636):

> We think the MMPI testing data are copyrightable expressions of factors or processes. Our conclusion is expressly based upon the district court's findings of fact about the methods the authors used to develop the MMPI testing data. The district court found that although the authors began with certain discovered facts, statistical models and mathematical principles, which cannot be copyrighted, they then made certain adjustments on the basis of their expertise and clinical experience. In other words, the MMPI testing data, at least for purposes of analysis under the copyright law, do not represent pure statements of fact or psychological theory; they are instead original expressions of those facts or processes as applied and as such are copyrightable (p. 636).

With regard to damages, the court of appeals upheld the entire damage award. It did affirm the district court's decision to deny plaintiffs the attorney's fees they had expended in litigating the case, indicating that "the litigation involved numerous complex or novel questions which defendant had litigated vigorously and in good faith" (p. 638).

By far, the most controversial aspect of MMPI case is the court's decision concerning the normative data. As we have indicated, test items are copyrightable (although AI did have a credible argument that the precise MMPI items used were not copyrighted as original expressions, given the fact that they were gleaned from prior texts). Scoring tables, as tables, are copyrightable as well as compilations of pre-existing material (although the material in the tables itself may not be copyrightable). We find less persuasive the court's holding that scoring tables are not merely discovered facts (which are not copyrightable) but protected under the copyright law because of the judgment and hard work that went into developing the scoring system. As we have seen, another court of appeals in the *Rockford Map* case held that the copyright laws do not protect the amount of effort expended or the underlying information that is placed in the computer. But in ruling for the university and NCS, the district court in the MMPI case adopted the "sweat of the brow" test and the court appeals did not challenge that reasoning. Finally, in holding that the scoring data were copyrightable, both courts relied on *Rubin v. Boston Magazine Co.* (1981) to support their position. However, in that case, a magazine had copied a psychologist's test items, not his scoring system. Thus, *Rubin* is inapposite in supporting the courts' holding. In any event, the university and NCS have prevailed and AI is prevented from selling its MMPI software programs and has suffered a tremendous, if not business-killing monetary loss.

Thus, we will reiterate our original caveat. The copyrightability of scoring systems is a highly controversial area and the law in this area is very unsettled. At an APA-sponsored forum on computerized testing issues a few years ago, it was very clear from the comments made by traditional test publishers that they are ready and willing to litigate the issue of copyright of norms. The MMPI case illustrates their genuine determination to do so. So, if readers are contemplating developing scoring and interpretive systems based on published norms, they should consult their own legal counsel.

Interestingly, concealing and protecting the information contained in scoring keys, classification systems, and research useful for interpretation is easier in CPT than in conventional paper-and-pencil tests, where the human-readable paper key or published cookbook is available to test users who can easily recast the information in a different form and, perhaps, avoid copyright infringement. CPT offers the possibility of embedding much of this information in a secret program. Only if required to divulge the information to users does the CPT developer creating a new fully computerized test place this data in the public arena. It should be obvious that how the professions of law and psychology resolve these issues will greatly determine the future of research and development in psychological assessment.

THE RIGHTS OF TEST TAKERS

The final issue we discuss concerns the major legal challenge to psychological tests in recent years. Critics have charged that testing denies minorities, women, and the handicapped a fair evaluation due to bias in the test. A new concern is that because the advantages of computer technology are distributed unevenly, a modern version of cultural bias may result. Some may argue that groups lacking in computer experience will be disadvantaged if forced to take tests on computers. This concern is genuine; people familiar with computers could well have an advantage taking a CPT over a novice whose normal test anxiety is compounded when they are confronted with an unfamiliar machine.

Unfamiliarity with computers could be correlated with ethnicity, gender, age, and socioeconomic status, so any effect due to unfamiliarity might appear statistically as poorer performance by some groups, even though the more direct explanation of any performance difference would be the unfamiliarity, not group membership. (We are here discussing only those group differences that arise from the mode of test administration, not all group differences though the analysis may apply to some of them as well. In analysis of variance terms, we are discussing the group × mode interaction, not any main effect for group.) Currently, there is no evidence suggesting any particular group is disadvantaged when tested by computer instead of conventionally, but the research is scanty. Investigators have noted that many elderly persons are uncomfortable with CPT (Carr, Wilson, Ghosh, Ancil, & Woods, 1982; Volans & Levy, 1982). One early study found that Blacks did better on a computerized version of an intelligence test than on a pencil-and-paper version, though whites' scores were unchanged (Johnson &

Mihal, 1973), prompting the authors to hypothesize that CPT may eliminate some sources of examiner–examinee bias allegedly present in conventional testing. This study had only 10 subjects in each group, and there were other methodological flaws (Jensen, 1980), so any conclusions are highly speculative.

In fact, a "group differences" approach to the study of test performance is often misguided. The legal system has encouraged this kind of study since judicial recognition of unfairness in a test has been largely limited to cases where the unfairness is cast in terms of ethnic or gender group differences. But the unfairness of a test, if any, probably will not divide cleanly along these lines. Averaging across individual group members to determine Black/white or male/female differences obscures the most important information. Not every group member will be uniformly affected by taking a test on a computer. What we need is a refined list of test taker characteristics that could alert us to potential problems with computer administration and, if possible, allow us to remedy the source of the problem. Mere group membership is likely to be a very imprecise predictor of problems as it sheds no light on the cause of a problem and it offers no prescription for remediation. Characteristics that may be direct sources of diminished performance, such as unfamiliarity, are a better focus of study than are weak and indirect predictors such as gender.

All test takers should be familiar with the equipment and procedures so that they can devote their full attention to the substance of the test items. Training and practice should be provided to those who need it for as long as they like. For example, Johnson and White (1980) found that elderly people who received 1 hour of training in the use of a terminal prior to testing scored significantly higher on the Wonderlic Personnel Inventory than did those who received no training. Current evidence suggests any initial anxiety caused by the computer is short-lived for most people if they are given adequate practice (Lushene, O'Neil, & Dunn, 1974), and may be more a result of poorly designed procedures than of anything intrinsic to the computer (Hedl, O'Neil, & Hansen, 1973). However, the advent of such novel complaints as "cyberphobia," and the development of potential cures (e.g., user-friendly terminals and computer tutorials) suggest that the psychologist must be aware of the effect of computerized administration on the test taker, and not assume everyone is comfortable with the machine.

A major concern about computer-generated reports is that they may not be as individualized as those generated in the conventional manner. Some information, such as demographic characteristics of the examinee, can be included in interpretation programs so that the computer will use more appropriate norms or base rates if they exist and qualify interpretations to take into account the particular test taker's characteristics. But no program can consider all the unique attributes of each individual and in most cases the same programmed decision rules will be applied to all test scores.

The revised *Standards for Educational and Psychological Testing* (APA et al., 1985), clearly indicates that test users are ultimately responsible for their test interpretations, no matter from what format the data are derived. Assessing the validity of interpretations requires that a human being observe the testing situation and decide if conditions are present that could invalidate test results. It is imperative that the final act of decision making be that of a qualified practitioner, consistent with state law, ethical principles, and professional standards, who takes responsibility for overseeing both the process of testing and judging the applicability of the interpretive report for individual examinees.

There must be an interposition of human judgment between the CPT report and decision making to ensure that decisions are made with full sensitivity to all the nuances of test administration and interpretation, and the unique constellation of attributes in each person is evaluated. Relying solely on test developers' computerized conception of the test taker's responses isolated from a clinician's trained observation of the test taker's behavior during the administration of the test, may tend to create bland, impersonal, and nonspecific assessments that fail to capture the test taker's cognitive, affective, and behavioral functioning across a variety of situations.

CONCLUSION

Anyone who doubts the importance of remaining sensitive to the individuality of each test taker might benefit from reflecting on what could happen if our friend, the legal scholar, gets his way and computers replace judges in courts of law. The laws relevant to CPT would be expressed as a set of preprogrammed rules: If certain conditions are met, then a certain consequence would follow. Deciding a case of malpractice, for example, would then be a simple matter of plugging in the facts and letting the machine generate the verdict.

There would be a tendency to use rules that have clearly discernible conditions, instead of rules that require difficult determinations of sincerity or good faith. Only if the rules were continuously updated could they take into account relevant new developments in CPT, and only if *every* relevant factual condition were a part of the system could we be sure that the verdict was a correct one. In those cases where factual issues were in dispute, the legal system's traditional rule of relying on the discretion of judges and juries to determine the credibility of witnesses or assign the proper weight to be given admissible evidence would be severely attenuated, if not eliminated. In all cases, even where the facts were agreed upon and only the application of the law to the facts was at issue, there would be less room for creativity in decision making, and more centralized control. We might even fear that widespread computerized justice would lead to an abdication of responsibility among lawyers, who would blindly accept machine verdicts without knowing how they were made or without questioning if the verdict was a good one.

We cannot treat our clients with any less respect than we would want from someone empowered to make decisions affecting *our* vital interests. If we bear in mind both the potential and the limits of CPT, the future of psychological testing should be bright. And there should be no need to develop a computer judge to decide if CPT is being practiced in an ethical and legal manner.

REFERENCES

American Psychological Association. (1966). Minutes of the annual meeting of the Council of Representatives. *American Psychologist, 21,* 1141.

American Psychological Association. (1977). *Standards for providers of psychological services.* Washington, DC: Author.

American Psychological Association. (1981). Specialty guidelines for the delivery of services. *American Psychologist, 36,* 640–681.

American Psychological Association. (1985). *Standards for educational and psychological tests.* Washington, DC: Author.

American Psychological Association. (1986). *Guidelines for computerized-based tests and interpretations.* Washington, DC: Author.

American Psychological Association. (1987). *General guidelines for providers of psychological services.* Washington, DC: Author.

American Psychological Association, American Educational Research Association, & National Council of Measurement in Education. (1974). *Standards for educational and psychological tests.* Washington, DC: Author.

Attorney General Opinion No. 83–130. Office of the Attorney General of the State of Kansas, Sept. 3, 1983.

Bersoff, D. (1983). Social and legal influences on test development and usage. In B. Plake & S. Elliot (Eds.), *Buros–Nebraska Symposium on Measurement and Testing.* Lincoln, NE: University of Nebraska Press.

Burke, M., & Normand, J. (1985). *Computerized psychological testing: An overview and critique.* Manuscript submitted for publication.

Buros, O. (1978). *Mental measurements yearbook.* Highland Park, NJ: Gryphon Press.

Carr, A., Wilson, S., Ghosh, A., Ancil, R., & Woods, R. (1982). Automated testing of geriatric patients using a microcomputer-based system. *International Journal of Man-Machine Studies, 28,* 297–300.

Colorado Psychological Association. (1982). *Guidelines for use of computerized testing services.* (Available from Colorado Psychological Association, 245 Columbine, Denver, CO 80206)

Copyright Act of 1976, 17 U.S.C. §§ 101 et seq. (1976).

D'Amato, D. (1977). Can/should computers replace judges? *Georgia Law Review, 11,* 1277–1301.

Denicola, R. (1981). Copyright in collections of facts: A theory for the protection of nonfiction literary works. *Columbia Law Review, 81,* 516–542.

Green, B., Bock, R., Humphreys, L., Linn, R., & Reckase, M. (1984). Technical guidelines for assessing computerized adaptive tests. *Journal of Educational Measurement, 21,* 347–360.

Hedl, J., O'Neil, H., & Hansen, D. (1973). Affective reactions toward computer-based intelligence testing. *Journal of Consulting and Clinical Psychology, 40,* 217–222.

Hofer, P. (1985). Developing standards for computerized psychological testing. *Computers in Human Behavior, 1,* 301–315.

Hofer, P., & Bersoff, D. (1983). *Standards for the administration and interpretation of computerized psychological testing.*

Hofer, P., & Green, B. (1985). The challenge of competence and creativity in computerized psychological testing. *Journal of Consulting and Clinical Psychology, 53,* 826–838.

Jensen, A. (1980). *Bias in mental testing.* New York: Free Press.

Johnson, D., & Mihal, W. (1973). The performance of blacks and whites in computerized versus manual testing environments. *American Psychologist, 28,* 694–699.

Johnson, D., & White, C. (1980). Effects of training on computerized test performance in the elderly. *Journal of Applied Psychology, 65,* 357–358.

Lushene, R., O'Neil, H., & Dunn, T. (1974). Equivalent validity of a completely computerized MMPI. *Journal of Personality Assessment, 38,* 353–361.

Mandel, S. (1984). *Computers, data processing, and the law.* St. Paul, MN: West Publishing Co.

Matarazzo, J. (1983). Computerized psychological testing. *Science, 221,* 323.

Matarazzo, J. (1986). Computerized clinical psychological test interpretations: Unvalidated plus all mean and no sigma. *American Psychologist, 41,* 14–24.

Matarazzo, J. (in press). Clinical psychological test interpretation by computer: Hardware outpaces software. *Computers in Human Behavior.*

Nimmer, R. (1985). *The law of computer technology.* Boston: Warren, Gorham & Lamont.

Patry, W. (1984). Copyright in collection of facts: A reply. *Communications and the Law, 6,* 11–42.

Petterson, J. (1983, November). Computer testing spurs writing of ethics codes. *Kansas City Times.*

Rand McNally & Co. v. Fleet Management Systems, Inc., 600 F. Supp. 933 (E.D. Ill. 1984), *reaffirmed on other grounds,* 634 F. Supp. 604 (N.D. Ill. 1986).

Regents of the University of Minnesota v. Applied Innovations, 685 F. Supp. 698 (D. Minn. 1987), *aff'd,* 876 F.2d 626 (8th Cir. 1989).

Remer, D. (1982). *Legal care for your software.* Berkeley, CA: Nolo Press.

Rockford Map Pub. v. Directory Service Co. of Colorado, 768 F.2d 145 (7th Cir. 1985), *cert. denied,* 106 S. Ct. 806 (1986).

Rubin v. Boston Magazine Co., 645 F.2d 80 (1st Cir. 1981).

Schwartz, M. (1984). (Ed.). *Using Computers in Clinical Practice.* New York: Haworth Press.

Shank, R. (1984). *The cognitive computer.* Reading, MA: Addison–Wesley.

Skinner, H., & Pakula, A. (1986). Challenge of computers in psychological assessment. *Professional Psychology, 17,* 44–50.

Unofficial Opinion U83-25. Office of the Attorney General of the State of Georgia. May 31, 1983. 1983 Op. Atty. Gen. Ga. 238.

United States v. Curtis, 506 F.2d 985 (10th Cir. 1974).

Volans, P., & Levy, R. (1982). A re-evaluation of an automated tailored test of concept learning with elderly psychiatric patients. *British Journal of Clinical Psychology, 21,* 93–101.

Weizenbaum, J. (1976). *Computer power and human reason: From judgment to calculation.* San Francisco: Freeman.

Whalen v. Roe, 429 U.S. 589 (1977).

Zachary, R., & Pope, K. (1984). Legal and ethical issues in the clinical use of computerized testing. In M. D. Schwartz, (Ed.), *Using computers in clinical practice.* New York: Haworth Press.

10 Guidelines for Computer Testing

Bert F. Green
Johns Hopkins University

Testing by computer is big business. Many companies are offering software enabling a psychologist to test a client by seating him or her at a computer terminal and pressing Return. The software presents the instructions on the screen, guides the test taker through some sample items to see if the instructions are understood, and then presents the test, automatically recording the responses. After one or more tests have been completed, the equipment scores the responses, and delivers test scores. But it doesn't stop there. It then continues by printing out a complete test interpretation in fairly well-constructed narrative prose. The prose often shows a few signs of having been pasted together out of standard phrases, sentences, and paragraphs, but then so do many reports written by real psychologists.

The proliferation of testing systems and automated test interpreters has generated consternation among some clinical psychologists. Matarazzo (1983) cried "Wolf" in an editorial in *Science,* and went a little far, seeming to condemn all computerized testing. I replied (Green, 1983b) that there is much less concern about the computer *giving* the test than about the computer *interpreting* the test. In fact, a group at the Navy Personnel Research and Development Center in San Diego (McBride & Martin, 1983; Moreno, Wetzel, McBride, & Weiss, 1984) had just successfully transferred the Armed Services Vocational Aptitude Battery to the computer, with no major difficulties.

The Navy group used Computerized Adaptive Testing (CAT), the most important advance in cognitive testing (Green, 1983a; Weiss, 1985). In a CAT, the computer chooses the next item to be administered on the basis of the responses to the previous items. This procedure requires a new kind of test theory—classical test theory is not adequate. The new theory is called item response theory (IRT), and is now quite well developed, although it is still new and cumbersome. Using IRT, a computer can readily tailor the test to each test taker. The Navy group has successfully used the technique to administer the Armed Services Vocational Aptitude Battery (ASVAB). It has been found that a conventional test can be replaced by an adaptive test with about half the items, at no loss of reliability or validity. For many test takers, a conventional test has a lot of wasted items—items that are too easy for the good students, items that are too hard for the poor students. If the items are chosen to be most informative about the individual test taker, a lot of time can be saved. Of course, this means developing an estimate of the test taker's ability as the test progresses, and it implies many intermediate calculations, but the computer is good at that. An interesting by-product of CAT is that nearly everybody who takes it likes it. Such a test provides more success experiences than the lower half of the ability spectrum is used to, and does not seem to disconcert the high scorers. Also, the computer is responsive. As soon as an answer is input, another item appears on the screen; The computer is attending to the test taker in an active way that an answer sheet cannot emulate. Hardwicke and Yoes (1984) report that one recruit said, of the CAT version of the ASVAB, "It's faster, it's funner, and it's more easier."

Although computerized administration seemed to be working well in the cognitive area, there was more concern about personality tests. The American Psychological Association began getting several calls each week from its members asking about, or complaining about computerized testing. Apparently, some guidelines were needed for the users and the developers of computer-based tests and assessments. We hoped to stimulate orderly, controlled growth in an important and volatile field. The *Guidelines* (APA, 1986; see Appendix) address the development, use, and technical evaluation of computerized tests and test interpretations. They emphasize personality tests and personality assessments, but are relevant to all computer testing.

Why develop guidelines when we have just finished congratulating ourselves about the new joint Testing Standards (APA, AERA, & NCME, 1985)? Because the Testing Standards cover this situation only in a generic sort of way, and deserve amplification in particular details; especially computer-based assessments, that is, narrative interpretations. The new *Guidelines* are viewed as a special application of the new *Testing Standards* and as subordinate to them in case of any perceived conflict.

Some credits are in order here. Although the *Guidelines* can be viewed as a derivative of the *Testing Standards* they didn't really grow out of the *Standards*, except generically. Another precursor was a set of guidelines for computerized adaptive cognitive tests, prepared for the Navy by Green, Bock, Humphreys, Linn, and Reckase (1984). However, the document that eventually evolved into the *Guidelines* was first prepared by Paul Hofer and Don Bersoff for a computer-testing company (Bersoff & Hofer, 1986; Hofer, 1985). These authors drew on the *Standards,* the adaptive tests guidelines, and many earlier guidelines adopted by state psychological associations. Much work was also done by Barbara Wand, a member of the APA's Committee on Professional Standards. The final revision, taking into account hundreds of useful comments from many interested APA members was a task assigned to Lyle Schoenfeldt and myself, with the able assistance of Debra Boltas of the APA staff.

The general purpose of these *Guidelines* is to interpret the *Testing Standards* as they relate to computer-based testing and test interpretation. When the circumstances of computer testing are essentially equivalent to those of conventional tests, it was presumed that the issue was covered in the *Testing Standards.* For example, test security is essential to the integrity and meaning of scores on any test, whether the test is administered conventionally or by computer. Users should guard computer software for a test as diligently as they would guard booklets of a conventional test, so no special mention was deemed necessary.

As a matter of fact, guarding software probably *does* deserve special mention, because of the peculiar standards of morality that have arisen in copying software. Many people who own personal computers have pirated some software, and don't even feel very badly about it. We only start worrying when piracy threatens us. We are in the awkward position of saying that copying someone's word processor is naughty but copying someone's test is profoundly unethical. The concern is not so much the copying, but the chance that the copy won't be guarded as diligently as the original.

An aspect of security that the *Guidelines* do mention is privacy and confidentiality (Guideline 15). The scores must be kept in a way that only people with a legitimate need to know may have access to them. That is one of the problems in academic record automation at universities. Once the student's transcript is in a computer, there is the lurking fear that it can be altered by students, coaches, or others. Severe competition for grades has caused many colleges and universities to abandon the honor system, and we must beware of the possibility that an unscrupulous person might get access to the grade files, or in our case today, files of test scores, and cause real trouble.

If the *Guidelines* are tacit on test security, they do treat many other issues. This chapter discusses four main areas of concern: equivalence, administration, interpretation, and review.

ESTABLISHING THE EQUIVALENCE OF SCORES

When a conventional test is transferred to a computer, the computer scores can be interpreted using norms from the conventional test only if the conventional and computer forms are equivalent, that is to say, essentially parallel. The *Guidelines* say

> Scores from conventional and computer administrations may be considered equivalent when (a) the rank orders of scores of individuals tested in alternative modes closely approximate each other, and (b) the means, dispersions, and shapes of the score distributions are approximately the same, or have been made approximately the same by rescaling the scores from the computer mode.

Roughly speaking, the two aspects of equivalence are first, correlations and second, score distributions (see Hofer & Green, 1985, for more detail). If the cross-mode correlation is low, there is no point in going further, because the test is measuring different things in the two modes. If the cross-mode correlation is high, there is still the matter of test score distribution. If the means, standard deviations, and shapes of the score distributions are different, the computer scores will have to be rescaled, or calibrated to the conventional scale before using the conventional scale norms.

An excellent example of establishing correlational equivalence was reported by Vicino and Hardwicke (1984). They described the Navy's validity study comparing computer and conventional versions of the Armed Services Vocational Aptitude Battery (ASVAB). With 10 tests in each mode, a 20×20 correlation matrix was obtained. Four correlated factors emerged, as they usually do with the ASVAB. The factor patterns were remarkably similar for the two modes. There are a few minor subtleties, but plainly the modes are giving essentially the same information.

Not many differences should be expected in cognitive tests due to mode of administration, but there are some. Two different studies (Lee, Moreno, & Sympson, 1984; Sachar & Fletcher, 1978), done several years apart at NPRDC, show a mean shift in a test of math knowledge, but no mean difference in verbal comprehension; the correlations were very high in both cases. The mean shift was slight, amounting to about one raw score point, or about 0.25 standard deviations, in favor of the conventional test. Careful work showed that the results were attributable to not permitting review of earlier items on the test. If the math test is given in a paper version of the computer, one item per sheet, with no looking at earlier sheets, the difference disappears.

Although software could be modified to permit review, it would be awkward, and psychometrically it is better to keep items independent. However, if the computer is not to permit review, the score scale may need adjustment before using conventional norms, because the conventional format permits review.

Paragraph comprehension tests of reading can also be a problem. Some paragraphs won't fit on the screen along with several associated questions. One can think of shifting back and forth between the paragraph screen and the query screen, which could be awkward, or the paragraph could be shortened, with only one question about it. However, with short paragraphs there is a chance that the test might become more of a vocabulary test. Of course it would be fun to prohibit rereading the paragraph once the query is encountered, but that is clearly a different task.

Time limits are critical to equivalence. The computer is a one-on-one test administration, and in that mode, much more liberal time constraints would be possible. Tests are timed mainly as a matter of administrative convenience. But changing the timing will change the score distributions.

Highly speeded tests pose an especially severe problem. Two tests on the ASVAB, numerical operations and coding speed, are simple clerical tests. Very few errors are made. The issue is how fast the examinee can do the task. Since pressing a computer key takes much less time than marking an answer sheet, scores on computer versions of clerical tests tend to hit the ceiling. Greaud and Green (1986) compared several different computer scoring schemes, and got best results by recording the time taken by an examinee to finish a fixed number of items, and then calculating a rate measure, the mean number of correct items per minute. With this score the conventional and computer forms of the test could be made equivalent by rescaling.

In the personality domain, Allred (1986) found a big difference in conventional and computer administrations of the Adjective Check List (ACL) (Gough & Heilbrun, 1980). This instrument asks respondents to examine 300 adjectives and check those that apply to them. People tend to select many more adjectives in the computer mode. The conventional ACL is a checklist; on a checklist, nonresponse can mean either. "This doesn't apply to me," or "I didn't read the item." The computer forces the respondent to step through all the adjectives, so pressing the key marked NO can only mean, "No, this doesn't apply to me." The effect can be reduced simply by changing the labels on the keys from YES–NO to CHECK–NEXT ITEM, but there is still a tendency to check more adjectives on the computer. Worse, most of the additional adjectives are favorable. When forced to say more about themselves, people tend to say more nice things. Partly for this reason, the cross-mode correlations are not as high as one would like, and, of course, the score distributions are very different. Forcing a response is not likely to be a problem on tests of skills and knowledge, but it could well be a problem in interest inventories, or attitude surveys.

The MMPI has a similar problem. The conventional form asks for a response of yes or no, but instructs test takers that if in a few cases they cannot say, they may leave the item blank. A test protocol with more than a few blanks is considered suspect. Again the computer cannot permit an item to be left blank passively. If a category called "cannot say" is added as a third possible response, it creates a response demand. That is, people use the cannot-say response too much. White, Clements, and Fowler (1985) claim that the effect can be minimized by not using the "cannot say" option on the computer. Very little difference was observed in their studies. The mean differences are nonzero but slight. Individual correlations are not given, but are reported as a group to be between .5 and .7. The high scale index, greatly admired by MMPI interpreters of both electronic and human types, are not very stable in either medium. This casts uncertainty on all MMPI interpretations.

TEST ADMINISTRATION

In test administration, the computer can often be much more helpful than a test supervisor in an ordinary group testing situation, or a clinician in an office. Many people feel uncomfortable about asking for help in taking the test. For one thing, the computer can monitor the test taker's readiness for the test (Guideline 6; see also Guidelines 3–5). By demanding active responses to the instructions and the practice problems, the computer can determine whether the test taker understands the task. The computer can refuse to move on to the main test until the demonstration and practice items have been successfully negotiated. This is a great advantage over the conventional test, where one can only hope that the test takers have read and worked through the preparatory material.

Many people are concerned that some students will be unfamiliar with computers and will therefore be at an unfair disadvantage. Guideline 7 says,

> Test takers should be trained on proper use of the computer equipment, and procedures should be established to eliminate any possible effect on test scores due to the test taker's lack of familiarity with the equipment.

This concern seems to be exaggerated. Remember that the test taker is not being asked to program the computer or even to use some special software. He or she has only to press one of a few buttons—indeed it may be wise to replace the full keyboard by a special response box. Remember also that computers are no more novel to young people today than are VCRs and phonographs. The computer is part of their world and they accept it—indeed they welcome it.

It is not the young we must worry about, it is their elders. The computer is not a part of their world, especially the older ones. The elderly need careful training—with detailed explanation of the equipment, and demonstration of what to do if some trouble occurs.

The computer is a boon when testing the handicapped (Guideline 8). Pressing keys can be made easy. The computer is especially good for the deaf. Whether it is as good as large print for the near-blind remains to be determined. Letters can be made any size, but at the expense of reduced screen capacity. Creativity is still needed here.

Adaptive testing is a major contribution of computation. In a CAT, the system's facility in matching the item difficulty to the examinee's ability leads to important efficiency. Whether content should also be balanced in these customized tests is still a matter of technical debate (Yen, Green, & Burket, 1986).

Many have argued that tests should do more than provide a score, and do more than adapt to the overall ability level of the candidate. Tests should diagnose specific difficulties. If Johnny can't read, where is his trouble? If Suzy can't subtract, what is she doing wrong? In arithmetic, that can be done today. In other areas it will not be as easy but it can be done. Diagnosis is easier when assessment is built into computer-based instruction, or computer drill.

However, when new tests are to be devised, the *Guidelines* bow to the *Testing Standards*. Apart from some special opportunities in test administration, a computer-administered test is still a test, and ordinary methods apply. The sooner we start devising new tests that take advantage of the computer's power, rather than transporting our tired old paper-and-pencil tests to the computer, the sooner some of these *Guidelines* can fade away.

TEST INTERPRETATIONS

Equivalence of test scores, and computer administration of tests are psychometric challenges, which are not particularly exciting to clinical psychologists. What gets the clinicians so exercised is not automated test scores, but the subsequent step of automated interpretation. If the clinician merely signs the printout and hands it over to the patient or to some third party, professional care has not been maintained. Matarazzo tells of a man who indicated, in response to some test questions, that he stayed home most of the time, and didn't get out much. The computer diagnosed him as reclusive and withdrawn, when in fact the fellow was bedridden with a broken hip. Guideline 9 points out that any automated report should be adjusted by the clinician to take into account the context of the particular examinee.

On the other hand, the *Guidelines* also comment,

A long history of research on statistical and clinical prediction has established that a well-designed statistical treatment of test results and ancillary information will yield more valid assessments than will an individual professional using the same information. Only when the professional uses more information than the statistical system will the professional be in a position to improve the system's results. Therefore, if the system has a statistical, actuarial base, the professional should be wary of altering the system's interpretation. Likewise, if the system represents the judgments and conclusions of one or more skilled clinicians, the professional must recognize that changing the computerized interpretation means substituting his or her judgment for that of the expert.

The *Guidelines* then come down firmly on both sides of the issue. "The final decision must be that of a qualified provider with sensitivity for nuances of test administration and interpretation. Altering the interpretation should not be done routinely, but only for good and compelling reasons. "

When judging the appropriateness of an individual test interpretation, users need general information about the validity of the interpretive system. If the system has an actuarial base, the user needs to know the empirical facts. If validity is based on clinical judgment, as in an expert system, then the qualifications of the experts should be reported. The most useful information would come from empirical studies of the validity of interpretations produced by the system.

Test interpretation is branching out to other areas than personality assessment. Vale and Keller (1984) report developing an interpretive system for executive personnel evaluation that combines personality and ability measures. The Psychological Corporation is now marketing a system to prepare automatic assessments of a child's need for special education, the McDermott Multidimensional Assessment of Children (McDermott & Watkins, 1985). The system is well designed, and provides a lot of diagnostic information. Career guidance is also highly computerized, and the evaluation of ordinary educational progress is likely to follow.

We must consider the field as evolving its methods and standards. For the user to evaluate a test interpretation system, the user must have some idea of the basis for the various statements. A good, extensive manual is essential. In fact, there should be both a standard users manual and also a technical manual describing the technical basis for the interpretation (Guidelines 25–29).

Interpretations are often triggered by score profiles, and even response patterns. The reliability with which persons can be classed into categories becomes an issue. Consequently, discussing the reliability and validity of the narratives requires new methods. This area cries out for more technical work.

Review

The *Guidelines* do not suggest that all aspects of the algorithms and statement files of computer-based test interpretation systems be available to reviewers. Instead, Guideline 31 says,

> Adequate information about the system and reasonable access to the system for evaluating responses should be provided to qualified professionals engaged in a scholarly review of the interpretive service.

An early version of this guideline did suggest that reviewers be permitted access to the entire system, but it quickly became clear that system publishers would not accept such guidance. Their counterproposals led to the present language.

Actually, reviewers probably could not make good use of the source code and file listings. Deciphering programs is usually difficult, and examining the code to determine what the system will do in a variety of circumstances is virtually impossible. There are too many interactive contingencies. Moreover, most programs are not adequately annotated.

A much better reviewing strategy, it would seem, would be to use the system. The reviewer could enter sets of responses and examine the resulting interpretations. Some shortcuts could be provided. The reviewer may want to enter one response pattern, and then to alter a few of the responses to see what difference it makes. Also, for comparative purposes, it would be useful to see how each of several systems react to the same response patterns. Systems should probably be reviewed together in batches, as is now commonly done with introductory texts.

Another relevant question is the vulnerability of the system to inadvertent or malevolent responding, which can best be determined by exercising the system.

With review, as with many other areas of the *Guidelines,* the profession will learn as it proceeds. The *Guidelines* should be viewed as a living document, which will require regular attention and frequent revision. Today, they provide an important start.

REFERENCES

Allred, L. J. (1986). *Sources of Non-equivalence between Computerized and Conventional Psychological Tests.* Unpublished doctoral dissertation, Johns Hopkins University, Baltimore.

American Psychological Association. (1986). *Guidelines for Computer-based Tests and Interpretations.* Washington, DC: Author.

American Psychological Association, American Educational Research Association, & National Council on Measurement in Education. (1985). *Standards for educational and psychological tests.* Washington, DC: Author.

Bersoff, D., & Hofer, P. (1986). *Legal issues in computerized psychological testing.* Paper presented at the Buros–Nebraska Symposium on Measurement and Testing, Lincoln, NE, April.

Gough, H. G., & Heilbrun, Jr., A. B. (1980). *The adjective check list manual.* Palo Alto, CA: Consulting Psychologists Press.

Greaud, V., & Green, B. F. (1986). Equivalence of conventional and computer presentation of speed tests. *Applied Psychological Measurement, 10,* 23–34.

Green, B. F. (1983a). Adaptive Testing by Computer. In R. B. Ekstrom (Ed.), *Measurement, Technology, and Individuality in Education. New Directions for Testing and Measurement, No. 17.* San Francisco: Jossey–Bass.

Green, B. F. (1983b, December 16). Computer testing. *Science, 222,* 1181.

Green, B. F., Bock, R. D., Humphreys, L. G., Linn, R. L., & Reckase, M. D. (1984). Technical guidelines for assessing computerized adaptive tests. *Journal of Educational Measurement, 21,* 347–360.

Hardwicke, S. B., & Yoes, M. E. (1984). *Attitudes and performance on computerized vs. paper-and-pencil tests.* Rehab Group, Inc., 1360 Rosecrans St., San Diego, CA 92106.

Hofer, P. J. (1985). Developing standards for computerized psychological testing. *Computers in human behavior, 1,* 1–15.

Hofer, P. J., & Green, B. F. (1985). The challenge of competence and creativity in computerized psychological testing. *Journal of Counseling and Clinical Psychology, 53,* 826–838.

Lee, J. A., Moreno, K. E., & Sympson, J. B. (1984). *The effects of mode of test administration on test performance.* Paper presented at the annual meeting of the Eastern Psychological Association, Baltimore, April.

Matarazzo, J. P. (1983, July 22). Computerized psychological testing. *Science, 221,* 323.

McBride, J. R., & Martin, J. T. (1983). Reliability and validity of adaptive ability tests in a military setting. In D. J. Weiss (Ed.), *New Horizons in Testing.* New York: Academic Press.

McDermott, P. A., & Watkins, M. W. (1985). *Microcomputer systems manual for McDermott Multidimensional Assessment of Children* (Apple version). New York: Psychological Corporation.

McDermott, P. A., & Watkins, M. W. (1987). *Microcomputer systems manual for McDermott Multidimensional Assessment of Children* (IBM version). New York: Psychological Corporation.

Moreno, K. E., Wetzel, C. D., McBride, J. R., & Weiss, D. J. (1984). Relationship between corresponding Armed Services Vocational Aptitude Battery and computerized adaptive testing subtests. *Applied Psychological Measurement, 8,* 155–163.

Sachar, J., & Fletcher, J. D. (1978). Administering paper-and-pencil tests by computer, or the medium is not always the message. In D. J. Weiss, *Proceedings of the 1977 Computerized Adaptive Testing Conference.* Department of Psychology, University of Minnesota, Minneapolis, July.

Vale, C. D., & Keller, L. S. (1984). *Development and validation of a computerized narrative interpretation system for the Sears Executive Screening Battery.* St. Paul, MN: Assessment Systems Corporations.

Vicino, F. L., & Hardwicke, S. B. (1984). *An evaluation of the utility of large scale computerized adaptive testing.* Paper presented at the AERA convention, March.

Weiss, D. (1985). Adaptive testing by computer. *Journal of consulting and clinical psychology, 53,* 774–789.

White, D. M., Clements, C. B., & Fowler, R. (1985). A comparison of computer administration with standard administration of the MMPI. *Computers in Human Behavior, 1,* 153–162.

Yen, W. M., Green, D. R., & Burket, G. R. (1986). *Valid normative information from customized tests.* Paper presented at the NCME convention, April.

APPENDIX

Guidelines for Computer-based Tests and Interpretations

Committee on Professional Standards and Committee on Psychological Tests and Assessment

Guidelines.   The use of computers in psychological testing and assessment is not a recent development. With the introduction of user-friendly microcomputers and software within the economic grasp of the individual practitioner, however, the variety of such uses has increased at a hitherto unequalled rate. These uses include computer administration of psychological tests, computerized test scoring, and computer-generated interpretations of test results and related information. The rapid increase in the availability and use of these applications of computer technology has served as the impetus for the writing of this document.

In addition, the market is swiftly expanding for automated test scoring services, computerized test interpretations, computer-administered tests, and software to perform these functions. It is essential that the users, developers, and distributors of computer-based tests, scoring services, and interpretation services apply to these technological innovations the same ethical, professional, and technical standards that govern the development and use of traditional means of performing these functions.

The American Psychological Association (APA) first adopted interim standards on "Automated Test Scoring and Interpretation Practices" many years ago (Newman, 1966, p. 1141). The 1974 *Standards for Educational and Psychological Tests* (APA) included several references to computerized assessment. The 1985 *Standards for Educational and Psychological Testing* (APA) contains even more. The guidelines that follow are a special application of the revised *Testing Standards* and relate specifically to the use of computer administration, scoring, and interpretation of psychological tests.

Purpose

In January 1984 the APA Board of Directors instructed the Committee on Professional Standards (a committee of the Board of Professional Affairs) and the Committee on Psychological Tests and Assessment (a committee of the Board of Scientific Affairs) to develop guidelines for computer-based test administration, scoring, and interpretation. During the development of these Guidelines the Committee on Professional Standards has consisted of Susan R. Berger, William Chestnut, LaMaurice H. Gardner, Jo–Ida Hansen, Carrie Miller, Marlene Muse, Lyle F. Schoenfeldt, William Schofield (chair), and Barbara Wand. The Committee on Psychological Tests and Assessment has consisted of Wayne F. Cascio, Fritz Drasgow, Richard Duran, Bert F. Green (chair, 1984), Lenore Harmon, Asa Hilliard, Douglas N. Jackson (chair, 1985), Trevor Sewell, and Hilda Wing. Central Office staff assistance was provided by Debra Boltas and Rizalina Mendiola.

These Guidelines were written to assist professionals in applying computer-based assessments competently and in the best interests of their clients. The Guidelines were designed also to guide test developers in establishing and maintaining the quality of new products.

Specific reference is made to existing APA standards of particular relevance to computerized testing, which are abbreviated as follows: the *Ethical Principles of Psychologists* (*Ethical Principles;* APA, 1981); the *Standards for Educational and Psychological Testing* (*Testing Standards;* APA, 1985); and the *Standards for Providers of Psychological Services* (*Provider Standards;* APA, 1977). In addition, use has been made of selected sections of *Standards for the Administration and Interpretation of Computerized Psychological Testing* (Hofer & Bersoff, 1983).

The general purpose of these Guidelines is to interpret the *Testing Standards* as they relate to computer-based testing and test interpretation. They are intended to indicate the nature of the professional's responsibilities rather than to provide extensive technical advice, although some technical material of particular relevance to computer-based assessment has been included. The *Testing Standards* provide complete technical standards for testing. Technical guidance in computerized adaptive cognitive testing can be found in Green, Bock, Humphreys, Linn, and Reckase (1982, 1984).

When the circumstances of computer testing are essentially equivalent to those of conventional tests, it is presumed here that the issue is covered in the *Testing Standards*. For example, test security is essential to the integrity and meaning of scores on any test, whether the test is administered conventionally or by computer. Users should guard computer software for a test as diligently as they would booklets of a conventional test, so no special mention was deemed necessary.

The Guidelines are deliberately slanted toward personality assessment and the migration of conventional tests to the computer form of presentation. Many new tests are now being developed specifically for computer presentation, including many tests requiring novel responses. In general, the *Testing Standards* provides pertinent guidance for the development of such tests and should be considered to take precedence over these Guidelines.

In preparing these Guidelines, the Committee on Professional Standards (COPS) and the Committee on Psychological Tests and Assessment (CPTA) were aware that the sale and use of computerized test scoring and interpretive services extends beyond the membership of APA and that the guidelines may be of some relevance to others. Nevertheless, as an APA document, it has been appropriate to refer to APA documents throughout, even though they are binding only on APA members.

The Committees were further aware that APA standards refer to the obligations of individual members, whereas computerized testing services are usually the products of incorporated companies. The purpose of these Guidelines is to alert APA members to their personal obligations as professional psychologists when they use, develop, or participate in the promotion or sale of computerized test scoring or interpretive services, either alone or as an agent or director of a company. Furthermore, the Guidelines apply to the administration and use of tests for individual decision making. When the test results are to be used only in research or in general group evaluation, the Guidelines should be treated as advisory and in no way restrictive.

Participants in the Testing Process

Test Developer. The *Testing Standards* identifies the test developer as an individual or agency who develops, publishes, and markets a test. For purposes of this document it is useful to distinguish among the following: (a) the *test author,* who originally develops a test; (b) the *software author,* who develops the algorithm that administers the test, scores the test and, in some cases, provides interpretive statements; and (c) the *test or software publisher,* who markets the computer software and accompanying documentation for the test.

Test User.   The professional who requires the test results for some decision-making purpose. In some cases the test user provides the scores or an interpretation of the results to some separate decision maker, such as a probation officer or a director of college admissions. In that case, both parties bear responsibility for proper test use.

Test Taker.   The individual who takes the test. In some cases, such as in a self-directed guidance system, the test taker may be the ultimate consumer and is in this sense both test taker and test user. When the test taker is the ultimate consumer, special care is needed in providing an appropriate context for understanding the test results.

Test Administrator.   The individual who actually supervises and has professional responsibility for administering the test. In cases where the test administrator delegates the proctoring of test administration to another person, the administrator retains responsibility for adherence to sound professional practice.

Responsible actions of these various parties all contribute to the effective delivery of services to clients. Many of these responsibilities have been set forth in the *Ethical Principles* and *Provider Standards.* Reference is made here to these documents even though it is recognized that the parties might not be psychologists in all cases. Although binding only on psychologists, these documents provide sound advice for any person responsible for developing and offering computer-based administration, scoring, and interpretation of psychological tests.

THE USER'S RESPONSIBILITIES

Some aspects of testing can be carried out advantageously by a computer. Conditions of administration of some tests can be better standardized and more accurately timed and controlled when the test is administered by a computer. Test scoring can be done more efficiently and accurately by a computer than it can by hand. Test score interpretation based on complex decision rules can be generated quickly and accurately by a computer. However, none of these applications of computer technology is any better than the decision rules or algorithm upon which they are based. The judgment required to make appropriate decisions based on information provided by a computer is the responsibility of the user.

The test user should be a qualified professional with (a) knowledge of psychological measurement; (b) background in the history of the tests or inventories being used; (c) experience in the use and familiarity with the research on the tests or inventories, including cultural differences if applicable; and (d) knowledge of the area of intended application. For example, in the case of personality inventories, the user should have knowledge of psychopathology or personality theory.

The responsibilities of users are expressed by the following clauses from the *Ethical Principles*.

Principle 1: Responsibility

> In providing services, psychologists maintain the highest standards of their profession. They accept responsibility for the consequences of their acts and make every effort to ensure that their services are used appropriately.

Interpretation: Professionals accept personal responsibility for any use they make of a computer-administered test or a computer-generated test interpretation. It follows that they should be aware of the method used in generating the scores and interpretation and be sufficiently familiar with the test in order to be able to evaluate its applicability to the purpose for which it will be used.

Principle 2: Competence

> Psychologists recognize the boundaries of their competence and the limitations of their techniques. They only provide services and only use techniques for which they are qualified by training and experience. They maintain knowledge of current scientific and professional information related to the services they render.

2e. Psychologists responsible for decisions involving individuals or policies based on test results have an understanding of psychological or educational measurement, validation problems, and test research. *Provider Standards* 1.5 and 1.6 further underscore the nature of the professional's responsibility:

> 1.5 Psychologists shall maintain current knowledge of scientific and professional developments that are directly related to the services they render.
>
> 1.6 Psychologists shall limit their practice to their demonstrated areas of professional competence.

Interpretation: Professionals will limit their use of computerized testing to techniques with which they are familiar and competent to use.

Principle 6: Welfare of the Consumer

Psychologists fully inform consumers as to the purpose and nature of an evaluative . . . procedure.

Principle 8: Assessment Techniques

8a. In using assessment techniques, psychologists respect the right of clients to have full explanations of the nature and purpose of the techniques in language the clients can understand, unless an explicit exception to this right has been agreed upon in advance. When the explanations are to be provided by others, psychologists establish procedures for ensuring the adequacy of these explanations.

8c. In reporting assessment results, psychologists indicate any reservations that exist regarding validity or reliability because of the circumstances of the assessment or the inappropriateness of the norms for the person tested. Psychologists strive to ensure that the results of assessments and their interpretations are not misused by others.

Interpretation: The direct implication of Principles 8a and 8c for the user of computer-based tests and interpretations is that the user is responsible for communicating the test findings in a fashion understandable to the test taker. The user must outline to the test taker any shortcoming or lack of relevance the report may have in the given context.

GUIDELINES FOR USERS OF COMPUTER-BASED TESTS AND INTERPRETATIONS

The previous references to the *Ethical Principles, Provider Standards,* and *Testing Standards* provide the foundation for the following specific guidelines for computer-based tests and interpretations.

Administration

Standardized conditions are basic to psychological testing. Administrative procedures for tests are discussed in Chapters 15 and 16 of the 1985 *Testing Standards.* The main technical concern is standardization of procedures so that everyone takes the test under essentially similar conditions. Test administrators bear the responsibility for providing conditions equivalent to those in which normative, reliability, and validity data were obtained. The following guidelines are of particular relevance to the computerized environment.

1. Influences on test scores due to computer administration that are irrelevant to the purposes of assessment should be eliminated or taken into account in the interpretation of scores.
2. Any departure from the standard equipment, conditions, or procedures, as described in the test manual or administrative instructions, should be

demonstrated not to affect test scores appreciably. Otherwise, appropriate calibration should be undertaken and documented (see Guideline 16)

COMMENT: A special problem with computerized administration may arise with the use of different equipment by different professionals or use of equipment different from that for which the system originally was intended. Where equipment differences are minor, it may be determined on the basis of professional judgment that test scores are unlikely to be affected. In other cases, users . . . should demonstrate empirically that the use of different equipment has no appreciable effects on test scores.

3. The environment in which the testing terminal is located should be quiet, comfortable, and free from distractions

COMMENT: The overall aim is to make the environment conducive to optimal test performance for all test takers. Ideally, a separate cubicle for each terminal is recommended. If this is not possible, at a minimum, terminals should be located in a comfortable, quiet room that minimizes distractions. Users should be prepared to show that differences in testing environments have no appreciable effect on performance.

The test administrator should be careful to ensure that the test taker is free from distraction while taking the test and has adequate privacy, especially for tests or inventories involving personal or confidential issues. The environment should be quiet, free of extraneous conversation, and only the test administrator and test taker should be in a position to see either the test items or the responses. In addition to maintaining consistency in the testing environment, this helps to prevent inadvertent item disclosure.

4. Test items presented on the display screen should be legible and free from noticeable glare.

COMMENT: (See *Testing Standards,* 1985, 15.2) The placement of the equipment can introduce irrelevant factors that may influence test performance. Proper design and position of the display screen will avoid reduction in the legibility of the test materials by reflections from windows, ceiling lights, or table lamps.

5. Equipment should be checked routinely and should be maintained in proper working condition. No test should be administered on faulty equipment. All or part of the test may have to be readministered if the equipment fails while the test is being administered.

COMMENT: Proper equipment design and optimum conditions do not ensure against malfunctioning equipment. To prevent disruptions such as sticky keys or dirty screens that may adversely affect test performance, there should be a schedule of regular and frequent maintenance, and the equipment should be checked for each test taker prior to its use.

6. Test performance should be monitored, and assistance to the test taker should be provided, as is needed and appropriate. If technically feasible, the proctor should be signalled automatically when irregularities occur.

COMMENT: Monitoring test performance is essential so that the user can remedy any problem that might affect the psychometric soundness of the eventual score or interpretation. For users who test a few individuals, this can be done by simply looking in on the test taker; users who regularly test large numbers of people may wish to monitor automatically. This can be done by using computer programs that notify the test proctor if a test taker is responding too quickly or slowly or outside the range of response options. Peculiar responses might generate a warning to the proctor that the test taker does not understand the test directions, is not cooperating, or that the terminal is malfunctioning. In most cases, help should be immediately available to the test taker. In the case of self-administered tests for guidance and instruction, help may not be urgently needed, but some provision should always be made for assisting the test taker.

7. Test takers should be trained on proper use of the computer equipment, and procedures should be established to eliminate any possible effect on test scores due to the test taker's lack of familiarity with the equipment.

COMMENT: It is important to ensure that test takers are so familiar with the equipment and procedures that they can devote their full attention to the substance of the test items. Adequate training should be given to those who need it. This may require an ample store of sample items. It is very likely that such practice will reduce anxiety, increase confidence, and improve the reliability and validity of test results.

8. Reasonable accommodations must be made for individuals who may be at an unfair disadvantage in a computer testing situation. In cases where a disadvantage cannot be fully accommodated, scores obtained must be interpreted with appropriate caution.

COMMENT: Computerized testing may facilitate testing persons with some physical disabilities by providing especially large type or especially simple response mechanisms. In other cases, the computer may place persons who have certain handicapping conditions at a disadvantage. Chapter 14 of the 1985 *Testing Standards* addresses the testing of persons who have handicapping conditions.

Although tests have been successfully administered by computer to large numbers of both younger and older adults, some older people may need special reassurance and extended practice with the equipment and can be expected to respond more slowly than younger test takers. Of course, no accommodation is appropriate when the disadvantage is what is being tested. A person with poor eyesight is at a disadvantage in a test of visual acuity; it is precisely that disadvantage that is being assessed.

Interpretation

9. Computer-generated interpretive reports should be used only in conjunction with professional judgment. The user should judge for each test taker the validity of the computerized test report based on the user's professional knowledge of the total context of testing and the test taker's performance and characteristics.

COMMENT: A major concern about computer-generated reports is that they may not be as individualized as those generated in the conventional manner. Some information, such as demographic characteristics of the test taker, can be included in interpretation programs so that the computer will use more appropriate norms or base rates, if they exist, and qualify interpretations to take into account the particular test taker's characteristics. But no assessment system, whether computer based or conventional, can, at this time, consider all the unique relevant attributes of each individual.

A test user should consider the total context of testing in interpreting an obtained score before making any decision (including the decision to accept the score). Furthermore, a test user should examine the differences between characteristics of the person tested and those of the population for whom the test was developed and normed. This responsibility includes deciding whether the differences are so great that the test should not be used for the person (*Testing Standards*, 1985, 7.6). These, as well as other judgments (e.g., whether conditions are present that could invalidate test results), may be ones that only a professional observing the testing situation can make. Thus, it is imperative that the final decision be made by a qualified professional who takes responsibility for overseeing both the process of testing and judging the applicability of the interpretive report for individual test takers, consistent with legal, ethical, and professional requirements. In some circumstances, professional providers may need to edit or amend the computer report to take into account their own observations and judgments and to ensure that the report is comprehensible, free of jargon, and true to the person evaluated.

A long history of research on statistical and clinical prediction has established that a well-designed statistical treatment of test results and ancillary information will yield more valid assessments than will an individual professional using the same information. Only when the professional uses more information than the statistical system will the professional be in a position to improve the systems results. Therefore, if the system has a statistical, actuarial base, the professional should be wary of altering the system's interpretation. Likewise, if the system represents the judgments and conclusions of one or more skilled clinicians, the professional must recognize that changing the computerized interpretation means substituting his or her judgment for that of the expert. The final decision must be that of a qualified provider with sensitivity for nuances of test administration and interpretation. Altering the interpretation should not be done routinely, but only for good and compelling reasons.

THE DEVELOPER'S RESPONSIBILITIES

Developers of computerized test administration, scoring, and interpretation services are referred to the *Testing Standards* (1985), which provides standards for test development. The following general principles from the *Ethical Principles* and the *Provider Standards* also are relevant.

From *Ethical Principles:*

8b. Psychologists responsible for the development and standardization of psychological tests and other assessment techniques utilize established scientific procedures and observe the relevant APA standards.

8d. Psychologists recognize that assessment results may become obsolete. They make every effort to avoid and prevent the misuse of obsolete measures.

8e. Psychologists offering scoring and interpretation services are able to produce appropriate evidence for the validity of the programs and procedures used in arriving at interpretations. The pubic offering of an automated interpretation service is considered a professional-to-professional consultation. Psychologists make every effort to avoid misuse of assessment reports.

8f. Psychologists do not encourage or promote the use of psychological assessment techniques by inappropriately trained or otherwise unqualified persons.

From the *Provider Standards:*

1.5 Psychologists shall maintain current knowledge of scientific and professional development that are directly related to the services they render.

3.4 Psychologists are accountable for all aspects of the services they provide and shall be responsible to those concerned with these services.

When advertising and selling computer-based testing services, the following from the *Ethical Principles* are relevant.

Principle 4: Public Statements

Public statements, announcements of services, advertising, and promotional activities of psychologists serve the purpose of helping the public make informed judgments and choices. Psychologists represent accurately and objectively their professional qualifications, affiliations, and functions, as well as those of the institutions or organizations with which they or the statements may be associated. In public statements providing psychological information or professional opinions or providing information about the availability of psychological products, publications, and services, psychologists base their statements on scientifically acceptable psychological findings and techniques with full recognition of the limits and uncertainties of such evidence.

4b. Public statements include, but are not limited to, communication by means of periodical, book list, directory, television, radio, or motion picture. They do not contain (i) a false, fraudulent, misleading, deceptive, or unfair statement; (ii) a misinterpretation of fact or a statement likely to mislead or deceive because in context it makes only a partial disclosure of relevant facts; (iii) a testimonial from a patient regarding the quality of a psychologist's services or products; (iv) a statement intended or likely to create false or unjustified expectations of favorable results; (v) a statement implying unusual, unique, or one-of-a-kind abilities; (vi) a statement intended or likely to appeal to a client's fears, anxieties, or emotions concerning the possible results of failure to obtain the offered services; (vii) a statement concerning the comparative desirability of offered services; (viii) a statement of direct solicitation of individual clients.

4e. Psychologists associated with the development or promotion of psychological devices, books, or other products offered for commercial sale make reasonable efforts to ensure that announcements and advertisements are presented in a professional, scientifically acceptable, and factually informative manner.

4g. Psychologists present the science of psychology and offer their services, products, and publications fairly and accurately, avoiding misrepresentation through sensationalism, exaggeration, or superficiality. Psychologists are guided by the primary obligation to aid the public in developing informed judgments, opinions, and choices.

4j. A psychologist accepts the obligation to correct others who represent the psychologist's professional qualifications, or associations with products or services, in a manner incompatible with these guidelines.

4k. Individual diagnostic and therapeutic services are provided only in the context of a professional psychological relationship. When personal advice is given by means of public lectures or demonstrations, newspaper or magazine articles, radio or television programs, mail, or similar media, the psychologist utilizes the most current relevant data and exercises the highest level of professional judgment.

And from the *Provider Standards:*

2.3.1 Where appropriate, each psychological service unit shall be guided by a set of procedural guidelines for the delivery of psychological services. If appropriate to the setting, these guidelines shall be in written form.

GUIDELINES FOR THE DEVELOPERS OF COMPUTER-BASED TEST SERVICES

The *Testing Standards* (1985) and the previous cited sections of the *Ethical Principles* and *Provider Standards* provide the foundation for the following specific guidelines for the developers of computer-based test services.

Human Factors

10. Computerized administration normally should provide test takers with at least the same degree of feedback and editorial control regarding their responses that they would experience in traditional testing formats.

COMMENT: For tests that involve a discrete set of response alternatives, test takers should be able to verify the answer they have selected and should normally be given the opportunity to change it if they wish. Tests that require constructed responses (e.g., sentence completion tasks) typically require more extensive editing facilities to permit test takers to enter and modify their answers comfortably. Tests that involve continuous recording of responses (e.g., tracking tasks) can make use of a variety of visual, auditory, or tactile feedback sources to maximize performance and minimize examinee frustration.

11. Test takers should be clearly informed of all performance factors that are relevant to the test result.

COMMENT: Instructions should provide clear guidance regarding how the test taker is to respond and the relative importance of such factors as speed and accuracy. If changes are permitted, directions should explain how and when this is to be done. Before the actual test begins, the testing system itself or the proctor should check that these instructions are understood and that the examinee is comfortable with the response device.

The availability of screen prompts, an on-line help facility, or a clock display (in the case of timed performances) may be used advantageously to guide the examinee through the test instructions, test practice, and possibly the test itself. If used during the test, such devices become a part of the test itself, and cannot be changed without recalibrating the test.

12. The computer testing system should present the test and record responses without causing unnecessary frustration or handicapping the performance of test takers.

COMMENT: Advances in hardware and software design have provided a wide range of ways to transmit information to the computer. Computer test design should explore ways that are most comfortable for test takers and allow them to perform at their best. For example, a touch-sensitive screen, light pen, and mouse may all be perceived as being significantly less confusing than a standard computer keyboard. When a standard keyboard is used, it may be appropriate to mask (physically or through software control) all irrelevant keys to reduce the potential for error.

The type of test and test item may create special design problems. Speed tests must have especially quick and uniform time delays between items to minimize frustration. Tests that require reading of long passages or that have complicated directions to which test takers may want to refer occasionally require procedures that allow display changes and recall. Diagrams with fine detail require displays with greater resolution capacity than normal. If such modifications are not possible, the test takers should be provided with the diagrams or instructions in booklet form.

13. The computer testing system should be designed for easy maintenance and system verification.

COMMENT: When teleprocessing is involved, reasonable efforts should be made to eliminate transmission errors that could affect test scores. Software design should permit ways of checking that scoring and interpretive parameters recorded on a disk, for example, remain intact and accurate.

14. The equipment, procedure, and conditions under which the normative, reliability, and validity data were obtained for the computer test should be described clearly enough to permit replication of these conditions.

15. Appropriate procedures must be established by computerized testing services to ensure the confidentiality of the information and the privacy of the test taker.

COMMENT: Several services that provide computerized administration of clinical instruments maintain confidentiality by avoiding any use of test takers' names. (See Chapter 16 of the 1985 *Testing Standards*.)

Psychometric Properties

16. When interpreting scores from the computerized versions of conventional tests, the equivalence of scores from computerized versions should

be established and documented before using norms or cutting scores obtained from conventional tests. Scores from conventional and computer administrations may be considered equivalent when (a) the rank orders of scores of individuals tested in alternative modes closely approximate each other, and (b) the means, dispersions, and shapes of the score distributions are approximately the same, or have been made approximately the same by rescaling the scores from the computer mode.

COMMENT: If individuals obtain equivalent scores from both conventional and computer administration, computer-specific factors will have been shown to have no appreciable effect, and the computer version may legitimately be used in place of the conventional test. If condition (a) is not met, the tests cannot be claimed to be measuring the same construct and should not be used interchangeably. If (a) is met but (b) is not, then one set of scores can be rescaled to be comparable with scores from the other test. If conventional norms are being used, then the computer test scores must be rescaled. If condition (b) is met but (a) is not, then scaling will produce similar distributions, but test equivalence has not been demonstrated. If the tests are not equivalent, new norms must be established. Chapter 4 of the *Testing Standards* (1985) concerns norming and score comparability. Testing Standard 4.6 states that data on form equivalence should be made available, together with detailed information on the method of achieving equivalence (see also the comment on Standard 2.11, pp. 22–23).

A number of research designs can be used to study equivalence. Differences in the means, dispersions, or shapes of computer and conventionally obtained test score distributions all indicate a lack of strict equivalence when equivalent groups are tested. Although perfect equivalence may be unattainable (and unnecessary), the following condition should be satisfied if one wishes to use norms from a conventionally developed test to interpret scores from a computerized test. Computer-obtained test scores should preserve, within the acceptable limits of reliability, the ranking of test takers. If ranking is maintained, then scale values can be transformed through such procedures as linear or equipercentile equating so that test takers receive the same score as they would have obtained through conventional administration. In this way, cutting scores, validity estimates, norms, and other data generated from the conventional scale can be applied to the computer-obtained scores. The same considerations would apply (with the obvious changes) to a test developed entirely in the computer medium that was later printed in paper-and-pencil format. The equivalence of the forms should be established before norms developed for the computer version are used in interpreting the derivative paper-and-pencil format.

The present Guidelines are conservative in suggesting empirical information about equivalence for each test that is rendered in a different presentation mode. At present some tests in some situations show differences; others do not. As the literature expands, generalizations presumably will permit accurate expectations of the effect of presentation mode.

17. The validity of the computer version of a test should be established by those developing the test.

COMMENT: Procedures for determining validity are the same for tests administered conventionally and by computer (see Chapter 1 of the 1985 *Testing Standards*). A new computer test should be validated in the same way as any other test. If equivalence has been established between the conventional and computer-administered forms of a test, then the validity of the computer version can be generalized from the validity of the conventional version. If equivalence has not been established, the validity and meaning of the computer version should be established afresh. At present, there is no extensive evidence about the validities of computerized versions of conventional tests. Until such evidence accumulates, it will be better to obtain new evidence of predictive and construct validity.

18. Test services must alert test users to the potential problems of nonequivalence when scores on one version of a test are not equivalent to the scores on the version for which norms are provided.

COMMENT: This will most often be a problem when comparing a computer version of a test with a conventional paper-and-pencil version, but it can also be a problem when comparing tests presented on two different computer systems. Screens of very different size, or special responding devices such as a light pen, could in some circumstances affect test norms. This is especially an issue with timed responses, which are known to vary in speed for different types of required responses. Until enough information accumulates to permit generalization about the relevance of equipment variation, caution is prudent. When a test is offered on different equipment the offerer should provide assurance of comparability of results, and the accompanying manual should reflect the different equipment.

19. The test developer should report comparison studies of computerized and conventional testing to establish the relative reliability of computerized administration.
20. The accuracy of computerized scoring and interpretation cannot be assumed. Providers of computerized test services should actively check and control the quality of the hardware and software, including the scoring, algorithms, and other procedures described in the manual.
21. Computer testing services should provide a manual reporting the rationale and evidence in support of computer-based interpretation of test scores.

COMMENT: The developer is responsible for providing sufficient information in the manual so that users may judge whether the interpretive or classification systems are suited to their needs. Chapter 5 of the 1985 *Testing Standards* summarizes the information that should be presented in the manual.

Classification

Certain classification systems depend on the determination of optimal cutting scores. The determination of the cutting score is, in turn, dependent on a number of statistical and practical variables including (a) the base rate of the characteristic to be inferred, (b) the error of measurement at various points along the test score scales, (c) the validity of the tests for the inference to be made, and (d) the costs of errors of classification. Balancing all these considerations is as difficult in making computerized test interpretations as it is in making clinical interpretations.

22. The classification system used to develop interpretive reports must be sufficiently consistent for its intended purpose (see Chapter 2 of the 1985 *Testing Standards*). For example, in some cases it is important that most test takers would be placed in the same groups if retested (assuming the behavior in question did not change).

COMMENT: There is a tradeoff between consistency and precision. The more classification decisions the test is asked to make, the less consistent will such assignments be. Making too few classifications may lead test users to ignore meaningful differences among test takers; too many may lead test users to overestimate the precision of the test.

Classification systems should be sufficiently consistent so that most test takers would be placed in the same groups and given the same interpretations if retested, and sufficiently precise to identify relevant differences among test takers. Consistency depends both upon the reliability of the test and the size of the score intervals in each class. Precision requires that the test be capable of discriminating meaningfully among test takers. Cutting scores and decision rules should take into account the discriminability of the test at different points of the measurement scale and the purposes for which the interpretations will be used. At a minimum, classification categories must represent rational decisions made in the light of the goals users have in mind. The more important the consequences for the test taker, the more assurance there should be that the interpretation and ultimate decisions are fair and accurate. Developers of interpretive systems must exercise discretion in deciding how many and what kinds of classifications will be useful.

23. Information should be provided to the users of computerized interpretation services concerning the consistency of classifications, including, for example, the number of classifications and the interpretive significance of changes from one classification to adjacent ones.

Validity of Computer Interpretations

24. The original scores used in developing interpretive statements should be given to test users. The matrix of original responses should be provided or should be available to test users on request, with appropriate consideration for test security and the privacy of test takers.

25. The manual or, in some cases, interpretive report, should describe how the interpretive statements are derived from the original scores.

COMMENT: Professionals who provide assessment services bear the ultimate responsibility for providing accurate judgments about the clients they evaluate. It should be possible to fulfill these ethical demands without infringing on the testing service's proprietary rights. To evaluate a computer-based interpretation, the test user must know at least two facts: (a) the nature of the relationship of the interpretations to the test responses and related data, and (b) the test taker's score or scores on the relevant measures. (In addition, raw data or item responses often will be very useful.) For example, the test developer could describe the organization of interpretive statements according to the scale on which they are based, otherwise provide references for statements in the report, or provide in the manual all the interpretive statements in the program library and the scales and research on which they are based. Each test taker's test and scale profile can be printed along with the narrative interpretations, together with the original set of responses where appropriate.

26. Interpretive reports should include information about the consistency of interpretations and warnings related to common errors of interpretation.

COMMENT: Test developers must provide information that users need to make correct judgments. Interpretive reports should contain warning statements to preclude overreliance on computerized interpretations. Unusual patterns of item responses can lead to seemingly inconsistent statements within a single report ("the respondent shows normal affect;" "the respondent may have suicidal tendencies"). Either the manual or the introductory comments on the interpretation might indicate that inconsistent statements result from inconsistent test responses, which may indicate that the result is not valid.

27. The extent to which statements is an interpretive report are based on quantitative research versus expert clinical opinion should be delineated.

28. When statements in an interpretive report are based on expert clinical opinion, users should be provided with information that will allow them to weigh the credibility of such opinion.

COMMENT: Some interpretations describe or predict objective behavior, whereas others describe states of mind or internal conflicts. Some interpretations are quite specific. Others are very general. Some make statements about the test taker's present condition; others make predictions about the future. Some make use of well-established, consensually understood constructs, others use terms drawn from ordinary language. The type of interpretation determines the nature of the evidence that should be provided to the user.

29. When predictions of particular outcomes or specific recommendations are based on quantitative research, information should be provided showing the empirical relationship between the classification and the probability of criterion behavior in the validation group.

COMMENT: Computerized interpretation systems usually divide test takers into classes. It is desirable to present the relationship among classes and the probability of a particular outcome (e.g., through an expectancy table) as well as validity coefficients between test scores and criteria.

30. Computer testing services should ensure that reports for either users or test takers are comprehensible and properly delimit the bounds within which accurate conclusions can be drawn by considering variables such as age or sex that moderate interpretations.

COMMENT: Some reports, especially in the area of school and vocational counseling, are meant to be given to the test taker. In many cases, this may be done with limited professional review of the appropriateness of the report. In such cases, developers bear a special burden to ensure that the report is comprehensible. The reports should contain sufficient information to aid the test taker to understand properly the results and sufficient warnings about possible misinterpretations. Supplemental material may be necessary.

Review

31. Adequate information about the system and reasonable access to the system for evaluating responses should be provided to qualified professionals engaged in a scholarly review of the interpretive service. When it is deemed necessary to provide copyrighted information or trade secrets, a written agreement of nondisclosure should be made.

COMMENT: Arrangements must be made for the professional review of computer-based test interpretation systems by persons designated as reviewers by scholarly journals and by other test review organizations, including the Buros–Nebraska Institute of Mental Measurement. Such reviewers need more information than a regular consumer could absorb, but generally will not need access to the computer code or the entire array of statements from which interpretations are fashioned. At present, there is no established style for reviewing a CBTI system, and different reviewers may want different information. At a minimum, a reviewer should be able to communicate freely with technically qualified, knowledgeable persons associated with the test developer, who can answer questions about the system. Access to the system should be provided for trying actual or simulated test responses and for exercising the offered components of the system.

In some cases it may be necessary to impart trade secrets to the reviewer, in which case a written agreement should state the nature of the secret information and the procedures to be used to protect the proprietary interests of the test author, the software author, and the test publisher. As a rule, however, it is advisable to make readily available enough information for a reviewer to evaluate the system. This would certainly include the general structure of the algorithms and the basis for transforming test responses into interpretive reports, but it might not extend to the entire library of interpretive statements or to the specific numerical values of the cutting point and other configural definitions. The general size of the statement library or equivalent process of generating interpretations should be provided, along with information about its source. The algorithms can usually be explained in reasonable detail without disclosing trade secrets.

ACKNOWLEDGEMENT

This material is reprinted from the APA *Guidelines for Computer-Based Tests and Interpretations* (1986). Copyright 1986 by the American Psychological Association. Permissions fee paid. Further reproduction of this material without the expressed written permission of the American Psychological Association is prohibited. Copies of the Guidelines may be ordered by writing the APA Order Department, P.O. Box 2710, Hyattsville, MD 20784.

REFERENCES

American Psychological Association. (1981). Ethical principles of psychologists. *American Psychologist, 36*(6), 633–638.

American Psychological Association. (1977). *Standards for providers of psychological services.* Washington, DC: Author.

American Educational Research Association, American Psychological Association, & National Council on Measurement in Education. (1985). *Standards for educational and psychological testing.* Washington, DC: American Psychological Association.

American Psychological Association, American Educational Research Association, & National Council on Measurement in Education. (1974). *Standards for educational and psychological tests.* Washington, DC: Author.

Green, B. F., Bock, R. D., Humphreys, L. G., Linn, R. B., & Reckase, M. D. (1982). *Evaluation plan for the computerized Adaptive Vocational Aptitude Battery.* Baltimore: Johns Hopkins University, Department of Psychology.

Green, B. F., Bock, R. D., Humphreys, L. G., Linn, R. B., & Reckase, M. D. (1984). Technical guidelines for assessing computerized adaptive tests. *Journal of Educational Measurement, 21,* 347–360.

Hofer, P. J., & Bersoff, D. N. (1983). *Standards for the administration and interpretation of computerized psychological testing.* (Available from D. N. Bersoff, APA, Suite 511, 1200 Seventeenth St., N.W., Washington, DC 20036).

Newman, E. B. (1966). Proceedings of the American Psychological Association, Incorporated, for the year 1966. *American Psychologist, 21*(12), 1125–1153.

Author Index

Subject Index